Exploring
Web Marketing &
Project Management

ISBN 0-13-016396-1

90000

9 780130 163967

THE FOUNDATIONS OF WEB SITE ARCHITECTURE SERIES

AVAILABLE DECEMBER 1999

UNDERSTANDING WEB DEVELOPMENT
Arlyn Hubbell, *Merrimack College*

ADMINISTRATING WEB SERVERS, SECURITY & MAINTENANCE
Eric Larson, *Sun Microsystems & Merrimack College*
Brian Stephens, *Sun Microsystems & Merrimack College*

EXPLORING WEB MARKETING & PROJECT MANAGEMENT
Donald Emerick, *Merrimack College & WOW*
Kimberlee Round, *Merrimack College & Surf's Up Web Development*
Susan Joyce

COMING SPRING 2000

CREATING WEB GRAPHICS, AUDIO & VIDEO
Mike Mosher

COMING SPRING 2000
THE ADVANCED WEB SITE ARCHITECTURE SERIES

DESIGNING WEB INTERFACES, HYPERTEXT & MULTIMEDIA
Michael Rees, *Bond University*
Andrew White, *FirstTech Computer*
Bebo White, *Stanford Linear Accelerator Center, Stanford University*

SUPPORTING WEB SERVERS, NETWORKING, PROGRAMMING, & EMERGING TECHNOLOGIES
Joseph Silverman, *UCSF Stanford Health Care*
Michael Wendling, *@Home Network*
Bebo White, *Stanford Linear Accelerator Center, Stanford University*

EXPLORING ELECTRONIC COMMERCE, SITE MANAGEMENT, & INTERNET LAW
Dianne Brinson, *Ladera Press*
Benay Dara-Abrams, *Dara-Abrams Ventures*
Kathryn Henniss, *HighWire Press, Stanford University*
Jennifer Masek, *Stanford Linear Accelerator Center, Stanford University*
Ruth McDunn, *Stanford Linear Accelerator Center, Stanford University*
Bebo White, *Stanford Linear Accelerator Center, Stanford University*

Exploring
Web Marketing &
Project Management

Donald Emerick
Webmaster Program Director, Merrimack College

Kimberlee Round
with Susan Joyce

Prentice Hall PTR
Upper Saddle River, NJ 07458
www.phptr.com

Editorial/production supervision: *Kerry Reardon*
Project coordination: *Anne Trowbridge*
Acquisitions editor: *Karen McLean*
Editorial assistant: *Michael Fredette*
Manufacturing manager: *Alexis R. Heydt*
Marketing manager: *Kate Hargett*
Cover design director: *Jerry Votta*
Interior designer: *Meryl Poweski*

 © 2000 Prentice Hall PTR
Prentice-Hall, Inc.
Upper Saddle River, NJ 07458

Prentice Hall books are widely used by corporations and government agencies for training, marketing, and resale.

The publisher offers discounts on this book when ordered in bulk quantities. For more information, contact: Corporate Sales Department, Phone: 800-382-3419; Fax: 201-236-7141; E-mail: corpsales@prenhall.com; or write: Prentice Hall PTR, Corp. Sales Dept., One Lake Street, Upper Saddle River, NJ 07458.

Printed in the United States of America
10 9 8 7 6 5 4 3

ISBN   0-13-016396-1

Prentice-Hall International (UK) Limited, *London*
Prentice-Hall of Australia Pty. Limited, *Sydney*
Prentice-Hall Canada Inc., *Toronto*
Prentice-Hall Hispanoamericana, S.A., *Mexico*
Prentice-Hall of India Private Limited, *New Delhi*
Prentice-Hall of Japan, Inc., *Tokyo*
Pearson Education Asia Pte. Ltd.
Editora Prentice-Hall do Brasil, Ltda., *Rio de Janeiro*

DEDICATIONS

My chapters in this book are dedicated to my father, Frank E. Morse, Sr.

I grew up in a generation that revered science fiction and Western television heroes. However, I have always been very lucky not to have to look far at all for real-life heroes. I only had to look as far as my own family.

Through my dad's direction in my youth and friendship in my adulthood, he has shown me what heroism, good character, and practicality truly mean. These acts are not high profile. Rather, they are often as quiet as well-timed encouragement to another, optimism in the face of difficult circumstances, and the courage to not only follow through with responsibilities but to excel. My father never advertised that he has done all these things and more. Everyone has just always known.

Thanks, dad, for being my hero when I was a kid—now and always.

Kim Round

This book is dedicated to my father, Tracy Emerick.
Thank you for creating your trade and sharing it with me so completely.

Donny Emerick

CONTENTS

CHAPTER 3 Developing and Integrating Internet Communication Strategy   61

CHAPTER 9 The Project Team   343

CHAPTER 10 Project Bids, Contracts, and Specifications   373

FROM THE EDITOR

As the Internet rapidly becomes the primary commerce and communications medium for virtually every company and organization operating today, a growing need exists for trained individuals to manage this medium. Aptly named Webmasters, these individuals will play leading roles in driving their organizations into the next millennium.

Working with the World Organization of Webmasters (WOW), Prentice Hall PTR has developed two book series that are designed to train Webmasters to meet this challenge. These are *The Foundations of Website Architecture Series* and *The Advanced Website Architecture Series*.

The goal of *The Foundations of Website Architecture Series* is to provide a complete, entry-level Webmaster training curriculum. This series is designed to introduce and explain the technical, business, and content management skills that are necessary to effectively train the new Webmaster.

Books in *The Foundations of Website Architecture Series* include:

- *Understanding Web Development*
- *Administrating Web Servers, Security & Maintenance*
- *Exploring Web Marketing & Project Management*
- *Creating Web Graphics, Audio & Video*

The Webmaster who masters the materials in these books will be able to build and maintain static Web sites with limited database-enabled and interactive functionality; have a working knowledge of server administration, multi-media technologies, and security issues; and be able to interface with IT and content development professionals on these topics. The Webmaster will understand the basics of Web marketing and effective communication and know how to manage the creation and construction of Web sites and manage teams of professionals responsible for Web communication and have a firm understanding of the various Web technologies.

The Advanced Website Architecture Series offers more in-depth coverage of the content, business, and technical issues that challenge Webmasters. Books in this series are:

- *Designing Web Interfaces, Hypertext & Multimedia*
- *Supporting Web Servers, Networking, Programming, & Emerging Technologies*
- *Exploring Electronic Commerce, Site Management, & Internet Law*

Thank you for your interest in *The Foundations of Website Architecture Series,* and good luck in your career as a Webmaster!

Karen McLean
Senior Editor
Pearson PTR Interactive

EXECUTIVE FOREWORD

Within the next few years, you will think about the Internet in the same way you think about electricity today. Just as you don't ask your companion to "use electricity to turn on a light," you will assume the omnipresence of the Web and the capabilities that it delivers. The Web is transforming the way we live, work, and play, just as electricity changed everything for previous generations.

Every indication suggests that the explosive growth of the Web will continue. The question we need to address is, "how can we deliver the most value with this ubiquitous resource?" Today, most of the world's Web sites were created and are maintained by self-taught Webmasters. Why? Because there were limited opportunities to receive formal standards-based education. Quality accessible and affordable education will help provide the broad range of knowledge, skills, and abilities to meet the demands of the marketplace.

Over the last three years, the World Organization of Webmasters has worked with colleges and universities, business and industry, and its own membership of aspiring and practicing Web professionals to develop the Certified Professional Webmaster (CPW) program. Our three-part goal is to provide:

- Educational institutions with guidelines around which to develop curricula.
- Students with an organized way to master technical skills, content development proficiency, and personal workplace ability.
- Employers with a standard of achievement to assess Webmaster candidates.

The Foundations of Web Site Architecture Series and *The Advanced Web Site Architecture Series* grew organically from the communities they will serve. Written by working professionals and academics currently teaching the material, and reviewed by leading faculty at major universities and the WOW Review Board of industry professionals, and published by Prentice

Hall PTR, these books are designed to meet the increasingly urgent need for Webmasters with expertise in three areas: technical development, design and content development, and business.

Projections indicate greater than 25 million Web sites online worldwide by 2002. Think of these books as state-of-the-art field guides for those who will shape our online future.

William B. Cullifer
Executive Director-Founder
World Organization of Webmasters
Bill@joinwow.org

INTRODUCTION

Welcome to the wild, wild West of both personal and professional communications. It's an exciting time out in the business world and the institutional, nonprofit, and governmental world as well. Many new interactive communication technologies are being developed and utilized every day by every type of person and audience who has access to a networked computer. Students, grandparents, executives, assistants, officers, technicians, and every other type of person are finding reasons to access the worldwide network of computer networks called the Interent using its latest "super-application," the World Wide Web.

If you are reading this book, you probably have some desire to use the Web to communicate something. If you don't, you should. While it is very easy to get involved in the technology, business, and hype surrounding the Internet and the Web, I'd like to introduce a very important point that will be repeated in many ways throughout this publication: The Internet and World Wide Web are communications vehicles.

Networked computers and supporting database technologies utilize the client-server model of computing to provide a worldwide communications network. But a significant premise for the first half of this publication is that the Internet and World Wide Web are a means to an end. And that end is better, more effective, and less expensive communication.

So the marketing and communication part of this book is about using the Internet and Web for marketing and communication. The majority of concepts and discussions center on traditional communications methods (mail, phone, TV, radio etc.) and how their communication qualities and functions can be adopted and improved using Internet technologies.

This book should be considered an introduction to marketing concepts that can be used on the Web. It is written for beginning Webmasters without a lot of marketing or communications experience.

It is presented to introduce nonmarketing people to marketing techniques used in Web communications. It is not designed to be a reference book for experienced marketing professional, though it can serve as a primer for marketing or communications folks who are looking for an introduction to Web-based communication.

You'll notice that the terms *Internet* and *World Wide Web* are being used simultaneously in these paragraphs. The same is true throughout this section of the publication. Though most of the discussion in this book and series centers on the World Wide Web application, other Internet applications can and will be employed by Webmasters to communicate over the Internet. The options available to Web communicators involve more than just the Web itself, so the Internet is regularly mentioned as a communications vehicle. The Web can also serve as a gateway to the other applications available.

Some exercises may seem quite simple but are designed to inspire thinking. We see or hear marketing and communication efforts every day but rarely understand or even pay attention to their motives or know about their development and delivery. Due to expense involved with communication, almost everything we do experience in this media-rich culture was probably designed and paid for by somebody to reach us for some reason. We will use a number of seemingly rudimentary exercises to examine other media examples and experiences. Such dissection will lead to discussion on the best ways to communicate using the Web.

In Part II, *Exploring Web Marketing and Project Management,* you will learn how to manage the project and not let the project manage you. The Web is a new medium, bringing with it a platform for entrepreneurs to stage initiatives, both profitable and unprofitable. The project manager, who helps bring the entrepreneur's vision into focus, is charged with a great responsibility. This individual must understand the creative, technical, and marketing process and help the project team to work toward a common goal.

Part II of this book examines the intricacies of building a Web site, from project life cycle to client management. After all, one can find many technical documents on building a Web site, but what about the business side of building a Web site?

It's all well and good if a graphic artist can produce eye candy that will knock the user's socks off, but if the client's company is having trouble deciding on a creative direction, the skills of the graphic designer cannot be capitalized on. Project management is about managing the client through situations like these so that the project does not bog down.

It's very easy to lose money in the process of Web development. This book focuses on how to satisfy clients through clear and precise communication. By adhering to this process, a project manager may not avoid 100% of the project pitfalls, but he or she may be able to avoid 90% while preserving the reputation of his or her Web firm.

WHAT YOU WILL NEED

You will need a networked PC with access to the Internet. The faster the connection the less time you spend on the World Wide Wait. You will also need a Web browser with as many plug-ins as you can support to experience as much marketing media as possible and on e-mail client with an account. In your browser preferences you should enable cookies.

HOW THIS BOOK IS ORGANIZED

In this book, and the others in this series, you are presented with a series of interactive labs. Each lab begins with learning objectives that define what exercises (or tasks) are covered in that lab. This is followed by an overview of the concepts that will be further explored through the exercises, which are the heart of each lab.

Each exercise consists of either a series of steps that you will follow to perform a specific task or a presentation of a particular scenario. Questions that are designed to help you discover the important things on your own are then asked of you. The answers to these questions are given at the end of the exercises, along with more in-depth discussion of the concepts explored.

At the end of each lab is a series of multiple-choice self-review questions, which are designed to bolster your learning experience by providing opportunities to check your absorbtion of important material. The answers to these questions appear in Appendix A of each part of the book. There are also additional self-review questions at this book's companion Web site, found at `http://www.phptr.com/phptrinteractive/`.

Finally, at the end of each chapter you will find a Test Your Thinking section, which consists of a series of projects designed to solidify all of the skills you have learned in the chapter. If you have successfully completed all of the labs in the chapter, you should be able to tackle these projects with few problems. There are not always "answers" to these projects, but, where appropriate, you will find guidance and/or solutions at the companion Web site.

The final element of this book actually doesn't appear in the book at all. It is the companion Web site and it is located at: http://www.phptr.com/phptrinteractive/. This companion Web site is closely integrated with the content of this book, and we encourage you to visit often. It is designed to provide a unique interactive online experience that will enhance your education. As mentioned, you will find guidance and solutions that will help you complete the projects found in the Test Your Thinking section of each chapter.

You will also find additional self-review questions for each chapter, which are meant to give you more opportunities to become familiar with terminology and concepts presented in the publications. In the Author's Corner, you will find additional information that we think will interest you, including updates to the information presented in these publications and discussion about the constantly changing technology Webmasters must stay involved in.

Finally, you will find a Message Board, which you can think of as a virtual study lounge. Here, you can interact with other Foundations of Web site Architecture Series readers, share, and discuss your projects.

NOTES TO THE STUDENT

This publication and the others in the Web Site Architecture series are endorsed by the World Organization of Webmasters. The series is a training curriculum designed to provide aspiring Webmasters with the skills they need to perform in the marketplace. The skill sets included in the Web Site Architecture series were initially collected and defined by this international trade association to create a set of core competencies for students, professionals, trainers, and employers.

NOTES TO THE INSTRUCTOR

Chances are that you are a pioneer in the education field whether you want to be one or not. Due to the explosive nature of the Internet's growth, very few Webmaster training programs are currently in existence. But while you read this, many colleges, community colleges, technical institutes, and corporate and commercial training environments are introducing this material into curriculums worldwide.

Chances are, however, that you are instructing new material in a new program. But don't fret, this publication and series are designed as a comprehensive introductory curriculum in this field. Students successfully completing this program of study will be fully prepared to assume the responsibilities of a Webmaster in the field or to engage in further training and certification the Internet communications field.

Each chapter in this book is broken down into sections. All questions and projects have the answers and discussions associated with them. The labs and question/answer formats used in this book provide excellent opportunities for group discussions and dialogue between students, instructors, and each other. In addition, many answers and their discussions are abbreviated in this publication for space reasons. Any comments, ideas, or suggestions would be greatly appreciated.

ACKNOWLEDGMENTS

This publication's seventh chapter discussing legal issues was created and authored by Susan Joyce with input from practicing attorneys. Susan is an instructor in the Merrimack College Webmaster Certification Program and President of Netability, a Web consultancy and development firm based in Marlboro, Massachusetts.

I'd like to thank the following people and parties for making this book a reality:

- Bill Cullifer WOW Executive Director, for believing in training, sticking with the model, and building WOW to its prominent place.
- Bebo White, for setting up the first Web server in North America and for taking time away from physics to keep us on track.
- The Merrimack College writing team of Arlyn Hubbel, Eric Larson, Kim Round, Brian Stephens, and Susan Joyce, for writing through the summer of 1999 after waiting through the fall, winter, and spring to begin and for being the best instructors a Program Director could ever hope for or bribe. (You too Cassie, Jim, Michelle, and Perry!)
- Karen McLean at Prentice Hall PTR, for driving this project forward and putting up with us simultaneously.
- Anneliese Mueller for being there so many, many times.
- Dawn Foss, for listening and supporting me through the challenging and chaotic moments.
- Diane Spatafore, for providing innumerable welcomed diversions and snacks.
- Leslie Dengel, for initially launching the Merrimack College Program.
- Jessica Delgaudio and Jan Brink, for keeping things running with or without me.
- And Julie Goldberg, for chatting with me.

—Donny Emerick

My chapters in Exploring Web Marketing and Project Management have truly been a Round family team effort. So it is my pleasure first to acknowledge my husband, Bruce, for all of the encouragement and support he has given me, without complaint. Because of Bruce's optimistic and supportive attitude, our young sons followed suit and have been consistently positive. I could not have started my part without the inspiration that they constantly give me to try new things, nor could I have finished it if my family had not been committed to it as well.

There are also several clients with whom I've worked closely, who have been kind enough to offer reflections and ideas for the book. Charlie Bleau of Disabilitynews.net, Mark Frisch of New England Digital Computers, Alan McAnally of Commonwealth Sales Consulting, Christine Pasternek of Battleship Cove, and Phil Sullivan of Design Write Partners all contributed time out of their busy schedules.

I'd like to thank Doug Smith, Matt Guay (a proud new Dad to son, Riley), Jamie Boudreau, and all the guys at Netway, a great Internet service provider with whom we've worked closely. You guys are the best!

Cindy Moore and Nancy Carroll, members of the Surf's Up Web Development team, also played supportive roles in getting these sections finished.

Last, but not least, I would like to thank my coauthor, Donny Emerick, and my editor, Karen McLean at Prentice Hall, for the opportunity to address project management issues in this form. When I first began building Web sites, one could find ten books on one version of Java but very little material on how to walk a client through a Web build in an organized fashion. A few wonderful books have been published since, which I have valued greatly. I hope this book can add further perspective for the budding Web developer.

—Kim Round

ABOUT THE AUTHORS

Donny Emerick is a communications expert who has applied his oral and written communications skills in a number of fields. Literally growing up in the Business-to-Business Direct Marketing field, he has worked in the private and nonprofit sectors in high-tech marketing, education, and environmental activism, always talking, writing, and doing.

Graduating with a degree in Journalism in 1991, he started out writing news for a local daily newspaper on the North Shore of Massachusetts. Later that year the call of the West beckoned and he relocated to the San Francisco Bay area. He consulted with Digital Equipment Corporation, facilitating lead generation marketing campaigns with technology partners and value-added re-sellers (VARs). He then organized consumers against tropical rainforest destruction and University of California students against tuition increases and social injustices.

After a brief stint in political campaigns, he returned the East Coast in 1994 to help start Receptive Marketing Inc., a Web marketing company, and the Netplaza, a shopping portal. (This was before, when they were called Internet malls.) Since most business development involved explaining the Internet and its uses in business communication, a natural shift moved Donny to training marketers in this field.

He then spent two years on the national seminar circuits as author and trainer of *Marketing on the Internet*, produced by Data-tech Inc. He realized another personal goal by joining the staff of Greenpeace U.S. and traveling extensively in support of campaign and fund-raising efforts. He also began teaching for Merrimack College's Professional Education Center and its fledgling Webmaster Program, which he began directing in 1996.

The Merrimack College Webmaster Certification Program was adopted as a training model by the World Organization of Webmasters in early 1997, and Donny assumed the post of Education Coordinator for WOW in the same time frame.

Donny has a Bachelor of Arts in English/Journalism from the University of New Hampshire and has recently begun graduate courses in Business Education at New Hampshire College. His other pursuits include music production, sea kayaking, and alpine skiing. He lives in Portsmouth, New Hampshire.

Kimberlee Round is a 1986 graduate of Merrimack College, with a B.S. in Electrical Engineering. Having spent several years as a project manager in the software development realm, Kim gravitated toward the Web from its earliest inception. The merging of creative ideas with technical skill held a fascination for her, and Kim began to build Web sites as a freelance developer. This part-time endeavor grew into a full-time business, now called Surf's Up Web Development, Inc. (www.surfsupweb.com), which is located in North Andover, Massachusetts.

In 1998, after having built over forty Web sites, Kim developed a Web project management course for Merrimack College, her alma mater. She counts herself very fortunate to have the opportunity to interact with the students in the Webmaster certification program there.

On the home front, Kim has been happily married to her husband, Bruce, for thirteen years. Together, they have two sons, Christopher and Jeffrey, and a golden retriever named, Murphy. It has been rumored that Murphy truly is the CEO of Surf's Up Web Development, Inc., but this remains unsubstantiated. When not teaching at Merrimack or building Web sites, Kim enjoys her sons' activities, her husband's sense of humor, having tea with her mother, reading, and boating.

CHAPTER 1

INTERNET MARKETING BASICS

The Internet is a worldwide network of computers that provides a highly interactive system for marketing communication. Nothing more and nothing less.

—Donny Emerick

The primary objective of this chapter is to understand the communication options and marketing techniques that are available to Webmasters. More importantly, this chapter begins to demonstrate how these communication options can be utilized to facilitate and enhance business communication and marketing using the Internet and World Wide Web to develop successful marketing relationships.

L A B   1 . 1

THE INTERNET AS A COMMUNICATIONS TOOL

LAB OBJECTIVES

After this Lab, you will be able to

- Evaluate How Your Organization Communicates
- Evaluate How a Live Web Site Communicates

The World Wide Web is a client-server application that provides a graphical user interface for information presentation and interactive communication. What this means is that we can communicate in almost any way imaginable over a network of computers. And the computers add previously unprecedented functionality to the situation.

That said, the primary goal in marketing communication is to add value to a product in the eyes of a prospective or current customer. Another way to say this is the fulfillment of wants, needs, and desires. The Web is an exciting opportunity for us as marketers to add value to products and services and fulfill wants, needs, and desires through the use of interactive information presentations and transaction systems. Over time we can build successful marketing relationships through this process.

These systems can be highly effective for marketing communication. The best systems duplicate successful physical world models. Buying books over the Web just duplicates a highly successful model of direct catalog marketing. All the Web can really do is provide an interface for information retrieval, interaction, and transactions. But this is a powerful situation for marketers as the Web empowers customers by giving them what they want, how they want it, and when they want it.

But let's not forget that the Internet and Web is a communications tool. It is not a business solution but instead provides communications tools that can facilitate business and interaction. The technology is not the answer. Using the technology effectively provides customers with answers to their questions. And that is what marketing is all about.

LAB 1.1 EXERCISES

1.1.1 EVALUATE HOW YOUR ORGANIZATION COMMUNICATES

To begin thinking about the Internet as a communications tool, let's start by answering a few questions about our own communication methods.

a) When you communicate professionally, what's your primary method of communication?

_____

_____

b) What is your secondary method?

_____

_____

c) What kinds of information do you communicate?

_____

_____

d) When you are asked a question by a customer or colleague, where do you find the answer?

_____

_____

1.1.2   EVALUATE HOW A LIVE WEB SITE COMMUNICATES

Using a computer connected to the Internet, your first lab assignment in this section is to purchase a book over the Internet. You are a consumer with a want, need, and desire. You want to purchase a book. To do so, follow these steps:

Point your browser to amazon.com, an on-line bookseller.

a) Have you ever visited amazon.com before?

_____

_____

Search the Web site for any book you wish. If you need a suggestion, try looking for the book titled "Versed in Country Things."

b) Which book title did you search for?

_____

_____

Complete the steps necessary to purchase the book until the last possible option to buy is presented. You don't need to purchase a book to complete this lab exercise. But do everything up to the point of purchase, including completing the customer account information requested by the Web site if you haven't done so previously.

c) Record the steps that are involved and the information exchanges that take place in the purchase of a book over the Internet.

_____

_____

Terminate your visit to the on-line bookseller. Check out the news at cnn.com.

LAB 1.1 EXERCISE ANSWERS

1.1.1 ANSWERS

a) When you communicate professionally, what's your primary method of communication?

Answer: Though we may not realize it, our primary communication tool at work or home is probably the telephone. This involves voice communication in a synchronous environment.

Unfortunately, the problems associated with synchronous communication grow every day. It is becoming increasingly rare that two parties are available for voice communication spontaneously. Along with phone appointments and conference calls, this situation has led to the frustrating growth of voice mail communication.

Voice mail could be called asynchronous voice communication. But problems occur when converting this type of communication to text. This is necessary for the actual use of information. There is a better way. An asynchronous method of personal and professional communication using text, which is my primary method of business communication, is electronic mail.

More and more people are using e-mail every day. It is a direct, personal, text-based communications channel that is instantaneous and inexpensive—a perfect channel for marketing and communications in general.

b) What is your secondary method?

Answer: After phones and e-mail, communication usually involves hard copy vehicles for text and graphics.

This includes everything from internal memos and operations forms to external marketing materials and annual reports. Just think about how many pieces of hard copy printed material literally covered with text and graphical information are available for your review at any moment in the office. We spend billions of dollars and hours creating, printing, writing, approving, editing, mailing, distributing, filing, and tossing hard copy materials every day.

The good news is that the growth of the World Wide Web has created a hyperlinked publishing environment that duplicates and actually increases the functionality of written material. The Web interface is more interactive, dynamic, and flexible than the current hard copy examples. And Web-based information can be distributed at relatively low cost, requires virtually no storage, and can be changed and customized instantly.

c)   What kinds of information do you communicate?

Answer: Obviously, your answer will vary here. The following represents the type of information that this question should have yielded for you.

On a daily basis I respond to external communication from current and prospective students with marketing and operational information. I respond to my staff and colleagues with different operational and sometimes personal information. I process two piles of incoming hard copy information (mail). I constantly create new versions of both operational (memos and internal forms) and marketing materials in hard copy for later distribution and internal functioning. I also constantly convert voice mail messages to more voice mail messages and respond to a constant stream of personal and professional conversations via e-mail.

Except for reading my mail, which usually involves a flick of the wrist into the circular file, almost every one of these information transfers either can be converted to Internet technology or already is. Communication between myself, my students, and my staff is almost exclusively by e-mail. The writing of this book was accomplished using e-mail and File Transfer Protocols (FTP).

Internal operations between departments involve e-mail and paper-based forms that could be converted easily to Web-based formats. Any information retrieval I do is accomplished via the Web. I get almost all of my professional information from this source. And every purchasing decision I make, from airline tickets to projection equipment, involves Web-based information. Though I am a Web proponent, there is no reason to believe that the rest of the business world is moving in a similar direction. If we use these Internet and Web communication tools effectively, which will probably involve nothing more than developing them as we use them ourselves, as marketers we will benefit greatly.

d)   When you are asked a question by a customer or colleague, where do you find the answer?

Answer: Unless you know the answer from memory, you probably have to look it up somewhere. Hard copy storage of information involves files, manuals, and good old-fashioned books. But more and more information retrieval involves databases.

While books and files are static databases themselves, business information is usually stored in databases for operational and logical reasons.

Information can be shared, developed, and manipulated by more people in a dynamic fashion and can be compiled and reviewed on demand.

When a customer contacts me with a question about billing or course grades, I refer to our internal database, which I access via a network from my desktop computer. This takes my time and energy. If I made this database available to the students directly, they could answer their own questions, which would make them happy. I would also have more time to do other things and theoretically save money through postage and lost time, which would make me happy.

If I put my internal database on the Web for student access, I'd save time and money and make the students happy. This is why the Web is good news for marketers and communicators.

1.1.2 ANSWERS

Point your browser to an on-line bookseller. A popular Web site for this type of commerce is amazon.com.

a)   Have you ever visited amazon.com before?

Answer: Your answer will vary, but if you frequent amazon.com or have purchased from it in the past, your experience will be slightly different from that of somebody who has never visited the site.

I accessed this Web site via the amazon.com home page. I'd always heard good things about this site but hadn't yet participated out of loyalty to my local book shop. You will see as we progress through this exercise how this Web site is an excellent example of relationship marketing over the Web.

Search the Web site for any book you wish. If you need a suggestion, try looking for the book titled "Versed in Country Things."

b)   Which book title did you search for?

Answer: Your answer will vary. Here's mine:

I searched for a publication of Frost's poetry by typing the book title into the search field. The Web site returned a description of the exact book with pricing, availability, and even a little thumbnail picture. The thumbnail helps out with the lack of tactile interaction and is a replacement for the physical process involved with traditional retail shopping.

Two options were also presented to purchase the book: putting the book into a traditional on-line shopping cart or using a single-step process.

Complete the steps necessary to purchase the book until the last possible option to buy is presented. You don't need to purchase a book to complete this lab exercise. But do everything up the point of purchase, including completing the customer account information requested by the Web site if you haven't done so previously.

c)   Record the steps that are involved and the information exchanges that take place in the purchase of a book over the Internet.

Answer: The following is an account of my experience. Yours should be similar.

I tried the quick method but wasn't an existing account holder. After attempting to change an account that didn't yet exist, I was given the option to create a new account. If I hadn't been persistent, I could have gotten frustrated and abandoned the effort. After a couple of redundant screens were overcome, I was able to create a new account. It involved first setting up an account name and password and then inputting contact and credit card information. A confirmation screen displayed my new account information and gave me the opportunity to return to browsing. This link brought me back to the home page. But now things on this index page were subtly different. I now had a customized message welcoming me by e-mail username and an option to view book recommendations.

Setting up an account and purchasing a book involved approximately eight different, linked Web pages. Every screen requested my choice of action, and two involved completing forms to input my contact, payment, and shipping information. The amount of time was minimal.

This situation was driven by me, the end user, at my convenience, though the Web site presentation dictated the interactions necessary to complete the transaction. The effort was completed by me on my schedule.

This is an important distinction in Internet communication and Web marketing. As Web marketers, we receive the communication from the customer. Like traditional direct marketing, we dictate the actions, but it is up to the prospective customer to complete the actions. The great thing about the Web, however, is that end users are empowered by the technology interfaces and can receive an immediate response to their actions. And they can participate at their leisure.

One of the fundamental goals in Web marketing is to empower end users in their interactions with us. We benefit from a lack of overhead in conducting transactions with computers instead of traditional methods, and the customers benefit by engaging marketers on the customers' own terms and receiving immediate informational and transactional responses. Web marketing is good news for both parties involved.

Terminate your visit to the on-line bookseller. Check out the news at cnn.com.

The purpose of this last step is to terminate your connection with the amazon.com server.

LAB 1.1 SELF-REVIEW QUESTIONS

In order to test your progress, you should be able to answer the following questions:

1) Which of the following is NOT an example of relationship marketing at the amazon.com Web site?
   a) _____ Customized welcome page for repeat visitors
   b) _____ Discount over retail price of product
   c) _____ Offering book recommendations
   d) _____ One-click ordering
   e) _____ All of these are examples of relationship marketing at amazon.com.

2) Which of the following is the most effective means of communication today?
   a) _____ Telephone
   b) _____ Postal mail
   c) _____ Electronic mail
   d) _____ Voice mail

3) It is not likely that the Internet will ever become a primary source of marketing and/or communication.
   a) _____ True
   b) _____ False

Quiz answers appear in Appendix A, Section 1.1.

L A B   1 . 2

ROLES OF DIRECT MARKETING AND RELATIONSHIP MARKETING

LAB OBJECTIVES

After this Lab, you will be able to

- Understand the Roles of Direct Marketing and Relationship Marketing
- Understand the Concept of Customization
- Understand the Simple Mechanics of Internet Marketing
- Identify and Evaluate Your Favorite Web Site

Let's take a look at the traditional definitions of direct marketing and its latest incarnation, relationship marketing. The Internet provides exciting marketing communication opportunities using these methods to customize presentations and exchange information with end users. Looking at our favorite Web sites also demonstrates the direct communication methods that the Internet supplies.

We usually think of direct marketing as junk mail and dinner-time telemarketing efforts, but the methods are much more in depth than we may realize. Simply put, direct marketing involves direct sales to a buyer by a seller. More important, direct marketing generally involves at least five distinct elements in any program or effort:

- Promotional materials
- Databases
- Analysis
- Marketing with offers (response driven)
- Fulfillment

Promotional materials carry the marketing message to the end user. They may be mail packages, catalogs, phone scripts, fax letters, postcards, or e-mail messages. Any material, from four-color glossy to spoken words and even television infomercials, can be considered the promotional materials of a direct marketing effort. These materials are then deliverd to the prospect or customer using some method. The script being read by the telemarketer at the other end of the phone during dinner is an example of direct marketing promotional material. The method of delivery in this case is outbound telemarketing.

Databases are electronic information storage and manipulation files. They are used at a basic level to provide contact information for the promotional materials to be forwarded to. A simple list of addresses for a mailing or names and phone numbers for a telemarketing effort can be considered a direct marketing database. Real direct marketers, however, use databases over time to create contact, prospect, and customer files for ongoing business development and customer service efforts. Every communication to and from a prospective or current customer is recorded. This is why modern direct marketing is sometimes called database marketing. The telemarketer called you during dinner because you are included in a database of information. Your contact information was probably purchased from a database company that specializes in consumer home contact information.

Direct marketers analyze database information before, during, and after each program they run to better use resources and further target offerings to prospects and customers. This is how direct marketing is developed and how it is measured. Using the telemarketing example, you are being called because you have demonstrated your willingness to do whatever the telemarketer is asking you to do. You may be a well-qualified prospect. Being a responsible credit card customer is one reason you get called during dinner with offers for more credit cards.

Whatever the reason you are contacted, that reason was determined by a direct marketer. And you were chosen to receive that call through analysis of a database. If you do speak with the telemarketer and sign up for the credit card, then you have advanced from qualified prospect to customer. Later, when the program is analyzed for success, the costs to run the program and the number of new customers can be compared and evaluated. Though those telemarketing calls may seem random, and sometimes they are, a company is paying for the call and the caller. A company can't afford to call every person who has a phone. You are being called because a database was analyzed at some level and your name and contact was provided as a prospective customer.

That call almost always involves an offer. And an offer is included in direct marketing communication to solicit and motivate response. Response is a communication action taken by the recipient of the offer. Offers work on the age-old psychological principle of "What's in it for me?" Offers can be anything included in a marketing message that sweetens the deal enough to solicit response. They might be free gifts, special pricing, time-sensitive discounts, and standing offers like money-back guarantees and risk-free trials. Direct marketing always contains some form of call-to-action that can be responded to. In the telemarketing call, the offer is usually a discounted finance charge and an introductory interest rate. You may have been offered a special credit card carrying a particular set of benefits important to you based on some type of affinity, like an alumni association or frequent flyer program. This offer was developed based on deeper analysis of your contact or customer database file. The response is verbal during the call.

Once a response is captured by a direct marketer, some type of fulfillment is executed. If a product is purchased directly from a catalog, then fulfillment involves charging the cutomer's credit card account and shipping the appropriate product to the correct address. A request for information is fulfilled in the appropriate manner. A credit card account is created and opened and the cards are shipped to the new customer. A record of this transaction is recorded in the direct marketing database for analysis and later use.

Use of these methods over time is now defined as relationship marketing. In a relationship marketing model, every communication between the customer and marketer is recorded in the database. And every department in a company has access to that same information, from sales to customer service to shipping and accounts receivable. In this type of marketing every person or department that has contact with the customer shares the same information. This creates a higher level of customer service, satisfaction, and efficiency in every interaction with the customer.

Greater use and sharing of information helps companies build and keep relationships with their individual customers.

As this information is captured and analyzed, special offers are being developed that are specifically targeted to the individual based on his or her demonstrated needs and buying history. This process builds a relationship between buyer and seller. Buyers get what they want, when they want it. Sellers deliver what is wanted at the right time. Both participants are engaged in a positive commercial relationship.

This customization is very successful in the marketplace, and it has been said that all marketing will eventually become direct relationship marketing between individuals and companies. Customization of marketing messages involves traditional elements, like personalization of promotional materials. But more important, it includes offers of products and services specifically designed to meet the wants, needs, and desires of the customer involved. These offers can be delivered in a customized presentation using personalization and targeted solicitation.

The Internet and Web are excellent communications methods for all of these aspects of direct and relationship marketing. The dynamic aspect of this media also makes individual customization of presentations available and powerful. Using the Internet as a relationship marketing tool incorporates the five elements of direct marketing to build relationships over time and deliver customized presentations and marketing messages to individual users.

Promotional materials. The Web can be used as an interactive promotional medium displaying text, graphics, and any other media available that is practical for communicating to prospects and customers. E-mail can serve the same role as traditional mail and phone communication. It could be said that every Web site is promoting something to some audience.

Databases. The nature of this medium, based on computer technology, provides the marketer with immediate interactions between users and databases of information. Information can be captured and manipulated instantaneously and utilized to provide solutions to wants, needs, and desires. A perfect example is the availability of Federal Express package tracking on the Web.

Analysis. Again this can be done immediately to provide value for the end user. Information can also be captured for later review, reporting, and improved targeting of information. This process is done automatically and behind the scenes of a Web site.

Marketing with offers (response driven). Successful Internet marketing involves the use of targeted offers. In any situation on the Web special offers can be made to solicit immediate response. And the Web provides an immediate, interactive response device that can capture and exchange information instantly. Offers can be individual for particular customers or specific products or services, such as special discounts for certain airline tickets purchased on-line. They can be available only on the Web or otherwise. Many heavily discounted airline offers can't be purchased any other way. Some offers in traditional media can be further strengthened by adding a Web response option. A recent mailing offered frequent flyer miles for completing an airline survey. The number of miles awarded was increased if the survey was completed on the Web.

Fulfillment. In some situations, including software, information products, and services like on-line trading transactions, fulfillment can be completed immediately over the Internet. Many research reports and software tools can be downloaded immediately after purchase. Internet stock trading is another example. Other products and services require fulfillment through traditional channels, including shipping of Web-based catalog purchases. But parts of the process can be automated using the Web. Credit card processing can be facilitated and fulfillment information can supplied to the customer. Order status (i.e., processing or back order) can be displayed on demand and an e-mail message can be sent when a package has been shipped.

As all of these processes are completed over time, an individual profile of each customer and his or her interactions over the Internet can be compiled. This information can be made available internally, inside the company, using a Web interface for facilitation of customer interactions. It can be added to existing customer databases and used in other media as well.

Most important, these compiled information profiles can be used to create customized presentations for each customer, further enhancing the customer/marketer relationship. As the profile grows, with more information added during each interaction, the marketer can build customized interfaces and offers that are specifically targeted to the customer. We'll look at examples of this activity in the following exercises.

We'll also start looking at the simple mechanics of the information exchanges that can take place over the Web. Information is solicited by marketers and supplied by the end user. Information captured by the marketer can then be used to build marketing relationships and fulfill wants, needs, and desires.

Some of these concepts also become apparent when we look at our personal favorites on the World Wide Web. Our favorite Web sites usually supply something we want—either information, products, or services. Looking at these sites helps us to start thinking about targeting Web presentations to audiences. And that is the subject of the next chapter.

LAB 1.2 EXERCISES

1.2.1 UNDERSTAND THE ROLES OF DIRECT MARKETING AND RELATIONSHIP MARKETING

a) Identify an example of direct marketing in your personal or professional life.

_____

_____

b) Define the elements that make up direct marketing as a marketing technique.

_____

_____

c) Describe an ongoing business relationship that you participate in.

_____

_____

d) Try to define relationship marketing as a marketing technique.

_____

_____

**LAB
1.2**

1.2.2 UNDERSTAND THE CONCEPT OF CUSTOMIZATION

This exercise involves returning to the amazon.com Web site that you visited in Exercise 1.1.2. If you didn't actually leave, please do so at this time. You're now returning as a customer.

Point your browser back to www.amazon.com.

> **a)** What do you notice that is different from your last visit?
>
> _____
>
> _____

A number of suggestions will be made by the Web site for additional titles you may want to check out. Do so.

> **b)** Record what you notice from a marketing perspective about this experience.
>
> _____
>
> _____

> **c)** What other elements of the Web site presentation are customized to you as a customer?
>
> _____
>
> _____

> **d)** How does this affect you emotionally as a consumer? Do you think you'll return here again to complete the same type of transaction? Why?
>
> _____
>
> _____

1.2.3 UNDERSTAND THE SIMPLE MECHANICS OF INTERNET MARKETING

Thinking about the whole book buying experience, please complete the following questions:

a) What information was supplied by the Web site?

_____

_____

b) What information did the Web site capture from you?

_____

_____

c) How was the information used by the Web site initially and later during your second visit?

_____

_____

d) What types of Internet communications technology were involved in these transactions?

_____

_____

**LAB
1.2**

1.2.4   IDENTIFY AND EVALUATE YOUR FAVORITE WEB SITE

Referring back to your Internet-connected computer, this next lab exercise is probably simplified by the use of your bookmark file in your Web browser.

Point your Web browser to your favorite Web site.

a) What is it and why is it your favorite Web site?

_____

_____

b) What information do you regularly retrieve from this Web site?

_____

_____

If this Web site is not bookmarked by your browser, do so now. We'll be referring to it again.

LAB 1.2 EXERCISE ANSWERS

1.2.1   ANSWERS

a)   Identify an example of direct marketing in your personal or professional life.

Answer: Almost every piece of mail you receive at work and home is an example of direct marketing.

For discussion purposes, let's talk about my favorite direct marketing company. L.L. Bean is a consumer-oriented catalog marketer.

b)   Define the elements that make up direct marketing as a marketing technique.

Answer: Most people recognize the basics of direct marketing—that it involves direct communication between marketers and customers—as opposed to retail marketing, which involves physical locations, and sales representation, which involves a personal conduit between parties. The Web is a direct marketing medium. Looking at traditional direct marketing can help us prepare for Web marketing.

The definable elements of direct marketing include promotional materials, databases, analysis, marketing with offers, and fulfillment. L.L. Bean distributes a variety of four-color promotional catalogs. They use advanced database techniques to develop and service customers through regular mailings of these catalogs. Analysis of response and purchasing records by the people at L.L. Bean leads to further targeting of materials and offers to appropriate audiences. If I purchase outdoor equipment, I receive the outdoor equipment catalog. If I purchase housewares, I receive the seasonal housewares catalog based on analysis of my responses.

The long-time offer from L.L. Bean is a 100% no questions asked guarantee. If you buy something from them you can return it at any time for a replacement or for the money you spent. I had a friend who returned a broken pair of sunglasses years after purchase and was refunded the amount the sunglasses were selling for when she returned them. This offer has worked for L.L. Bean because purchasers have much lower risk when buying. L.L. Bean also offers discounts, special shipping, and targeted products. Fulfillment of catalog requests is efficient, and the shipping of purchased goods is equally professional. L.L. Bean is a successful direct marketing company. We can learn much from looking at L.L. Bean's use of these techniques and how they can be adapted in Web marketing and communication.

c) Describe an ongoing business relationship that you participate in.

Answer: Your answers will vary. Following is mine:

Many of my own business relationships are based on mutually positive experiences. I get something I need, and the company involved makes it worth my while to keep the business relationship going. I drive a car and need gasoline. I regularly purchase Mobil gasoline because Mobil provides a direct payment system that is very convenient. In addition, Mobil offers a loyalty program that gives me discounted ski tickets after purchasing a certain amount of gasoline. In addition to getting something I need, I also get good service and something additional that I want, which gives me incentive to keep the relationship going.

My business relationships are similar. I use list brokers and a mail house for direct marketing of the Merrimack College Webmaster Training Program. After purchasing a new list from a broker, the broker sent me a fruit basket at work. In addition to providing a good product at a competitive price and delivering it in an efficient manner, the vendor also did something to enhance a personal relationship. Who do you think I'm going to call the next time I need a list?

I use the same mail house because the vendor is a nice person who does a good job and provides excellent customer service, doing extra work if needed to complete projects. These situations all involve positive relationships beyond the traditional buyer and seller model. Web technology allows us to enhance traditional marketing models and build relationships.

**LAB
1.2**

d)   Try to define relationship marketing as a marketing technique.

Answer: Relationship marketing is an advanced model of direct marketing using the previously discussed elements. The basic premises of relationship marketing involve capturing, analyzing, and sharing customer-supplied information between all parties within a company. Information is captured and stored in every single customer communication initiated by the buyer or seller. This process further involves developing and executing customized marketing and customer service programs for individual customers based on this information.

Let's look again at the L.L. Bean example. When I call L.L. Bean to order some new flannel pajamas for a gift, the sales rep pulls up my entire customer history. The representative knows immediately what pajamas I bought last year, the gift recipient information I previously supplied, my method of payment, and shipping information. The phone rep is able to suggest products based on previous history to complete the transaction efficiently. This simplifies the buying process and builds an ongoing relationship between us. If I call with a question, the customer service representative knows all the same information. This applies to billing or shipping questions as well.

This type of marketing communication can be duplicated over the Web. The Web also provides further enhancement by allowing buyers to initiate, control, and benefit from the communication.

1.2.2   ANSWERS

Point your browser back to the same Web site you just visited.

a)   What do you notice that is different from your last visit?

Answer: The following summarizes my account of what is different.

Upon return, I now have a customized greeting on the home page of the merchant. The merchant is now building a relationship with the customer. And relationship marketing is the key to success in today's highly competitive business environment.

A number of suggestions will be made by the Web site for additional titles you may want to check out. Do so.

b) Record what you notice from a marketing perspective about this experience.

Answer: Your answer will vary. Here's what my experience was like.

Clicking on the link to book recommendations brings up a whole section that provides further customization of the presentation I see as a consumer. This is smart Web marketing. The Web site continuously profiles me as a customer in a number of ways.

By comparing my purchases with other customers who have purchased the same titles or products, the site gives me additional choices based on patterns in customer records. If customers have similar tastes, demonstrated by purchasing the exact same thing, maybe other matches will work also. The site gives us the option to provide information about books we own and about our interests. And we can tell the site what we already own or don't like. Every piece of information we give to the site is captured and used to further customize our presentation and add to our relationship with the merchant. Our goal as Web marketers is to harness these same concepts when building on-line marketing and communication efforts.

c) What other elements of the Web site presentation are customized to you as a customer?

Answer: After completing the account setup process, our shipping information is stored and brought up when necessary. This can be changed if needed. The system is extremely easy to use, and purchasing requires only a mouse click. When an end user wants to purchase something, doing so is extremely simple and immediately gratifying.

d) How does this affect you emotionally as a consumer? Do you think you'll return here again to complete the same type of transaction? Why?

Answer: While I can probably safely assume that you had a positive experience like I did, your answer here will obviously vary.

I greatly enjoyed this on-line book-buying experience. I will certainly return when planning to purchase books, as this on-line merchant completely fulfilled my wants, needs and desires. The process is simple, quick, hassle-free, saves money, adds value to the products, and provides immediate results. Granted, I still enjoy retail shopping at bookstores and will continue to support my local book merchant. But if I have an immediate need and not much time, this Web marketing effort will garner my business.

1.2.3 ANSWERS

Let's take a look at the mechanics behind this type of marketing communication.

a) What information was supplied by the Web site?

Answer: The Web site supplied a whole range of presentations involving selling products and driving transactions to do so. The majority of the information was text and was supported by presentation graphics and minimal product representation.

b) What information did the Web site capture from you?

Answer: The Web site captured contact, shipping, and payment information over a secure, encrypted connection. Relationship-building information was captured using a number of forms and drill-down techniques. In addition, this Web site electronically coded my client browser software by setting a cookie on my hard drive.

This software transaction individually identifies each customer and allows the marketer's server to present customized presentations each time the client logs on. A cookie is actually a short text code written into a file on the client computer by the server computer. Each code is distinct making the client computer discernable by the server computer in each ensuing interaction. This electronic identity badge also provides a system to track the activity of the client over time and helps build relationships.

c) How was the information used by the Web site initially and later during your second visit?

Answer: When I filled out the initial account information, the Web site immediately customized by presentation and provided opportunities to add information in the recommendation process. When I returned to the site the server read my cookie file, accessed my customer account information, and served Web pages with the appropriate customization.

d) What types of Internet communications technology were involved in these transactions?

Answer: The technology involved in these transactions was the same two client-server–based applications available to us as Web marketers. World Wide Web servers and client browsers played a primary role for presentation and interactively between parties. E-mail served a secondary role to confirm the purchase transactions.

The power behind the scenes comes from the use of database technology for the storage, searching, and customized presentation of product information. Web pages produced and supported by database technology also capture customer information to complete the transactions and further customize the interactions.

In this situation and others on the Internet, the Web interface allows individual customers and other end users to access, manipulate, retrieve, and benefit from databased information. They can do this at their convenience in situations where they have control of the interaction and receive an immediate positive response. In addition, these database-driven interactions are more cost effective and more productive than many traditional communications channels. Database-driven Web communication is an achievable goal for any Web marketing and communication effort.

1.2.4 ANSWERS

Point your Web browser to your favorite Web site.

a) What is it and why is it your favorite Web site?

Answer: Your answer will vary.

I consider the Cable News Network site (cnn.com) to be my favorite Web site. I originally studied journalism in college and ever since have been kind of a news junkie. I like to know what is going on nationally and in the high-tech business sector. I also like the space coverage and the random features available on that site. Most important, a weather report and forecast is also available based on my hometown zip code. Your favorite site probably involves a personal interest.

b) What information do you regularly retrieve from this Web site?

Answer: Again, your answer here will vary. Here's mine.

I do a lot of outdoor stuff when I have the time, and knowing the immediate forecast is helpful in the inconsistent weather of New England, where I live. This is quite useful for me personally, and I go to my favorite site a couple of times a week. I'll bet that you access your favorite site at least weekly for some type of information you either want or need to see.

I have this resource bookmarked, and with one mouse double click I can get current weather conditions and a four-day forecast. I like doing so. It makes me happy, and I don't mind taking the action to retrieve this information that I value highly. Marketers and communicators can leverage such relationships using the Web as a communications tool.

LAB 1.2 SELF-REVIEW QUESTIONS

In order to test your progress, you should be able to answer the following questions:

1) Which are technologies used in creating customer relationships at amazon.com?
   a) _____ Client-server information exchange
   b) _____ Writing and reading cookie files
   c) _____ Databases of customer and product information
   d) _____ Customized Web pages created for each customer interaction
   e) _____ All of these are utilized.

2) Which are the elements of direct and relationship marketing?
   a) _____ Promotional materials
   b) _____ Offers, response devices, and fulfillment
   c) _____ Databases and analysis of information
   d) _____ Sales calls and branding campaigns

3) Which is the reason you access a particular Web site regularly?
   a) _____ Because it provides information I want easily and quickly
   b) _____ Because it has cool graphics and lots of banner ads for products I want

Quiz answers appear in Appendix A, Section 1.2.

C H A P T E R 1

TEST YOUR THINKING

The projects in this section use the skills you've acquired in this chapter. The answers to these projects are available to instructors only through a Prentice Hall sales representative and are intended to be used in classroom discussion and assessment.

1) Evaluate your current marketing efforts. How do you currently fulfill wants, needs, and desires?

2) Identify any direct and relationship marketing activities. Do you build relationships with customers through information capture and targeted communication?

3) Look for opportunities to develop database interfaces that will develop and sustain Web marketing relationships. Where can the use of this technology increase customer satisfaction while decreasing operational activity?

CHAPTER 2

INTERNET MARKETING: PLANNING, TARGETING, AND EVOLVING

 Are we there yet?

—backseat child (or adult)

CHAPTER OBJECTIVES

In this chapter, you will learn about

The objectives of this chapter are to understand the planning of an Internet marketing effort. This chapter stresses the importance of planning in any marketing program to facilitate initial development and later measurement. A model using the five W's of journalism writing is utilized for planning purposes. Defining the audience in Internet marketing is both explained and demonstrated. The evolution of Internet marketing efforts is also introduced to describe and facilitate the planning process.

L A B   2 . 1

THE IMPORTANCE OF PLANNING AN INTERNET MARKETING EFFORT

LAB OBJECTIVES

After this Lab, you will be able to

- Understand Why Planning Is Important in Web Communication
- Utilize the Five Ws and One Big H of Web Communication

The simple truth of Web communication and marketing is that any information can be communicated to anybody with Internet access at any time. This is good for Web marketers but requires a serious planning effort before any actual Web development work is begun. Of course, this is not the case in most situations. Many Web sites are thrown together with little or no previous planning, and then Web developers are held responsible for the enormous expense and minimal results.

Whether you are starting from scratch or revamping a Web effort already under way, it is never too late to make a plan for your Web communication efforts. Why do this? For two very significant reasons:

1. Without some type of plan, it is virtually impossible to measure the progress, success, or failure of a Web effort.
2. A lot of options are available in Web communication.

Without some type of plan in place regarding our Web marketing and communication efforts, we have no way to benchmark where we stand at any given point. Unless we are working for ourselves, we will probably be held accountable for a budget and how money is spent on Web communication. A plan helps justify and explain how money is used and the communication it funds.

A plan also gives us a course of action. Because of the technical nature of Web communication, it is very easy to get involved in technology usage issues while losing sight of an overall objective. Technology for technology's sake is a reoccurring problem in the marketplace. As Web communicators, we need to drive Web development efforts toward a communications goal. And to do so we must come up with a goal or series of goals in the first place.

Keep in mind that we are not talking about project management issues in this chapter. Those issues are covered elsewhere in this book. Instead we are talking about examining all of the communication options available to us and then developing a communications plan to execute and measure against.

To discuss this concept, I'd like to utilize the traditional journalism model of who, what, where, when, why, and how. This is a formula used by generations of writers to develop news reports. We can also use it to begin planning Internet marketing and communication efforts. In this discussion,

> *Who* defines the audience.
>
> *What* defines the information exchange taking place with each audience.
>
> *Where* defines the physical location of the audience members, which may or may not be important.
>
> *When* describes the time issues involved with the information exchange.
>
> *Why* describes the planned outcome of the exchange.
>
> *How* defines the structure and Internet communication applications being used to communicate to the audience.

The first term, *who*, is probably the most important aspect of such a plan. Since every user of the Internet is a potential audience member, this question must be determined first and foremost. Who are we planning to communicate with? The answer to this question can be defined as an audience, a group of users we wish to communicate with. A myriad of potential audiences exist on the Internet, but here are some likely groups for our efforts:

- *Current customers.* People or companies you regularly do business with using other media to communicate. A relationship already exists.

- *New customers.* People or businesses you didn't do business with before using other media but wish to now using the Internet. This is a new opportunity to build a relationship.

- *A variety of customers from different products or lines.* Some companies sell a variety of products to the same customers; an example could be an office supply company that specializes in products for the legal industry.

- *A variety of customers from different vertical industries or a horizontal market.* Some companies provide the same solutions to a number of vertical markets. An example is a PC maker who sells to all businesses, regardless of industry.

- *Offer respondents generated in other media.* Users who are coming to a Web site to respond to an offer made in a radio spot, direct mail piece, or space advertisement.

- *Offer respondents generated on the Internet.* These users are probably linked to your site somehow from another location. Maybe a search engine, banner advertisement, or another Web site that you have a relationship with was the initiator of the communication.

- *Shareholders in public companies.* Any users owning stock may want to access the Web site belonging to their investment.

- *Internal employees.* An intranet is designed for use by employees of a company.

- *External employees, vendors, and partners.* An extranet or private Web site is developed for these audiences.

- *International markets and consumers.* Any company or organization on the Web becomes an international player since the Internet is available worldwide.

What is the next question we must answer in an Internet marketing and communication plan. Each of the audiences listed previously will require a different information presentation and exchange effort. For example,

- Current customers are familiar with your company and need updated pricing or technical information and an on-line transaction system to order more efficiently. Maybe they need order status information for orders placed in other channels or a way to change their contact information.

- New customers may be looking for products they can't find in traditional channels, like specialty foods or goods, or maybe they are looking for a more convienient way to purchase products, like at amazon.com.

- A variety of customers from different products or lines. In this situation an on-line catalog of office supply products would be presented for a specific audience of office managers and supply buyers in this industry. Transaction and information exchange systems would be geared toward the needs of this particular audience.

- A variety of customers from different products or lines. In this situation a PC maker may want to present different products and pricing for different vertical markets, like specific education, consumer, and business presentations, and then use a universal transaction system for all users if it is possible to do so.

- Offer respondents generated in other media. These people are looking for whatever your offer promised and are so motivated by the offer that they have initiated communication to your Internet marketing effort. They require immediate fulfillment of wants, needs, and desires. These respondents are self-qualifying themselves based on your offer.

- Offer respondents generated on the Internet are the same as those generated in other media but slightly less self-qualified as they know they can always hit the back button on their browser if your offer does not meet their needs. Some users following a link may be highly interested in your offer as well.

- Shareholders in public companies may be looking for current stock prices or more detailed financial or annual reports.

- Internal employees will have a number of information needs that are very different from those of customers or prospects, including human resources, benefits, product training, operations information, and contact information.

- External employees, vendors, and partners may be looking to continue existing relations and information exchanges using the Internet as the communication channel.

- International markets and consumers may be seeking information about products or pricing that are not available in their location.

All or some of these different information presentations may need to be included in a comprehensive Internet communication effort. Each audience requires a different approach, but all can and should be served.

Where is a relatively easy question to answer in this process. In front of some type of computer terminal with access to the Internet, World Wide Web, and e-mail service is where this communication will take place. Geography is not important for many Internet-based communication efforts.

However, in some situations where that communication takes place might be an issue to consider. Delivery of products and services may not be available in some areas. Shipping of products may be priced based on geography. Employees working on a manufacturing floor may not have Internet access at work but can be encouraged and assisted in home access. Doing business with international customers brings in a whole series of issues, including currency, export laws, and shipping.

When is another easy answer with a big catch. The Internet is available all the time, seven days a week. That means a Web site can be accessed "24/7," to use a familiar buzzword. But if your audience requires individual, person-to-person interaction, that might mean a shift in business operations to a 24-hour cycle. If an e-mail message sent in by a customer or prospect won't be answered until the next business day, then that day must be defined for the Internet audience.

The same is true for any type of fulfillment on or off the Web. Due to the instantaneous nature of Internet communication, users expect fast results. Your company or organization must define its ability to fulfil information, products, and services and then execute that fulfillment as promised. If you commit to shipping a personalized product within 24 hours of the time the order was received, then that should happen. If it isn't possible to do so, then it is better to change the fulfillment schedules than not deliver as promised. A broken commitment is no way to begin or continue a business relationship.

Why this interaction is taking place has probably been discussed in the answer to the *what* question. But a planned outcome for each information exchange with the appropriate audience member helps further define the plan for development and measurement of an Internet marketing effort. This *why* answer can be a benchmark for Web site activity. If the planned outcome is a sale to a new customer or an information exchange with an employee, then a later comparison of actual sales versus new Web site visitors or measurement of information fulfillment is an excellent tool for analysis.

The answer to the *why* question also helps further develop a plan for the next question: *How* do we communicate using the variety of options available on the Internet? The answer to this question will probably involve a variety of technology options and information interface decisions.

Traditional marketing materials used text, graphics, and multimedia to identify, explain, display, and demonstrate products and services. The Internet provides opportunities to duplicate such efforts on the Web. The Web also provides opportunities to capture information using forms processors embedded into Web pages. If each user requires individual confirmation of an order or an answer to a specific question, then e-mail can probably be used. E-mail can also be used to replace relationship-continuing efforts like hard copy mailings and regular phone calls.

If your audience needs access to a database of information, then a Web-based database interface must be designed with the specific needs of each audience participant in mind. A complete sales cycle must be envisioned first and then an interface must be developed that accomplishes the goal of the interaction. The amazon.com Web site is an example of a interface designed to sell products and uses databases behind the scenes to deliver, capture, and exchange information with the user. The whole interaction is designed to facilitate the purchase and fulfillment of products.

LAB 2.1 EXERCISES

2.1.1   THE IMPORTANCE OF PLANNING

To understand the importance of planning in Internet marketing, let's use a hypothetical example from the physical world. Let's assume for the sake of discussion that you have been instructed by a supervisor to communicate face to face with the five biggest customers your hypothetical company has, asking each what their projected growth is for next year. Let's assume you have to complete this task in five days. You have to travel out of state to do so, and your company requires preauthorization for travel money. Your supervisor wants daily updates on your communication and how you spend travel money.

a) Using the five Ws, what is the first question you need to answer for yourself to complete this assignment?

_____

_____

b) What is your next step in going to see these people?

_____

_____

c) On the third day the supervisor calls you in a hotel and wants to know how much money you have spent and whom you have spoken with. Based on the information given in (a) and (b), what do you tell him or her?

_____

_____

d) Upon return to the home office you must submit an accounting of your travel expenses compared to the original authorization and estimate an average cost for this type of activity in the future. How do you do this?

_____

_____

2.1.2 UTILIZE THE FIVE WS AND ONE BIG H IN WEB COMMUNICATION

Let's now examine some basic planning ideas by reverse engineering a successful Web site. Using a computer connected to the Internet, return to the amazon.com Web site that you visited earlier. We won't know the exact answers to these questions, but we can make some general assumptions to address these concepts.

a) Who are some of the audiences this Web site plans to address?

_____

_____

b) What information is planned to be exchanged at this Web site with its audiences?

_____

_____

c) Where are these interactions taking place?

_____

_____

d) Does physical location play any role in this interaction? If so, what role?

_____

_____

e) Does the concept of *when* apply on this Web site? If so, how?

_____

_____

f) Why are these interactions taking place?

_____

_____

g) How are these interactions taking place using Internet technology?

_____

_____

LAB 2.1 EXERCISE ANSWERS

2.1.1 ANSWERS

a) Using the five Ws, what is the first question you need to answer for yourself to complete this assignment?

Answer: Your answers may vary, but you probably need to determine exactly whom you need to speak to.

You have a general understanding of your audience in this assignment. You need to communicate with the five biggest customers, but you don't know who they are. A quick check on sales numbers will give you the answer and, hopefully, the contact information you need.

This is the first step in developing a plan for communication with this audience. You already know what to ask these contacts. And you know the why and how of the situation. Your goal at the end of the interaction is to know the customer's plans for next year. You plan to visit each person personally to complete this interaction, answering the how question as well.

b) What is your next step in going to see these people?

Answer: Again, this is a broad question, but your answer should include development of a plan to travel to and communicate with these contacts. Since travel requires preauthorization in this hypothetical situation, you need to make arrangements in advance.

Regardless of the need for preauthorization, most people like to plan travel in advance and create an itinerary that includes all the stops and transportation issues involved with the trip. In this situation planning is imperative for most people. Plane tickets and hotel room reservations are usually purchased and reserved in advance to save money and secure availibility. Some things, like airport transit and dining choices, can be determined in each situation, but many of the larger details are planned in advance. In this situation money must be budgeted for these activities as well.

Overall, this effort requires an action plan of some kind. If you only have five days and need to visit five people, then one hypothetical plan would be to visit one each day. A plan will be developed to determine travel issues and make sure you get to each place at the appropriate time. A plan also helps you determine costs in advance and ensures that you don't spend the night in an airport.

c) On the third day the supervisor calls you in a hotel and wants to know how much money you have spent and whom you have spoken with. Based on the information given in (a) and (b), what do you tell him or her?

Answer: Answers will vary, but based on the discussion so far, you could tell the supervisor that you have visited with three customers, give their names, and state your conclusions based on your interactions, the amount of money you have actually spent, and your plans for the rest of the trip.

This demonstrates why planning is so important in any marketing effort. Planning gives us an opportunity to measure our activities and analyze expenses based on these measurements. With a travel plan in place, we can report actual results and accurate costs to our supervisor when it is requested. It is the same in Internet marketing and communication. A course of action, a record of interactions, and an accounting of costs gives us the opportunity to measure the performance of our efforts and compare results and expenses.

d) Upon return to the home office you must submit an accounting of your travel expenses compared to the original authorization and estimate an average cost for this type of activity in the future. How do you do this?

Answer: To complete this action you would add up all your travel costs and compare them to your budgeted amounts. You would also divide these costs by 5 to develop an average cost for this type of activity.

While this activity seems quite simple, the implication of this step is that a plan has established a benchmark for later analysis. The plan has also provided a basic analysis that can be used for determination of success and for a later allocation of resources. Though this communication plan was basic and dealt more with travel logistics than customer interaction, this exercise helps define the importace of plannning.

Quite simply, without planning we don't know how to get somewhere or how much it will cost. Planning gives us the opportunity to ascertain where we are at any given time, what it cost to get there, and a way to analyze results and costs in the same context.

2.1.2 ANSWERS

Let's now examine some basic planning ideas by reverse engineering a successful Web site. Using a computer connected to the Internet, return to the amazon.com Web site that you visited earlier. We won't know the exact answers to this question, but we can make some general assumptions to demonstrate these planning concepts.

a) Who are some of the audiences this Internet marketing effort plans to address?

Answer: Your answers will vary but could include a description such as this: A wide variety of customers from a horizontal representation of the Internet audience, meaning almost anyone on the Internet. This audience is interested in directly purchasing books, music, or other media and has demonstrated a desire to do so using the Web as a communication channel. Both current and new customers could be members of this audience, and prospects could be responding to on-line and traditional media offers.

b) What information is planned to be exchanged at this Web site with its audiences?

Answer: We discussed this in the previous chapter. The very simple answers to this question include: product information customized for returning visitors; special offers based on particular products; detailed information explaining the business transactions available; and updated customer accounts including contact, payment, product preferences and interest, and shipping information, which is all captured and utilized instantaneously.

It is important to note that this Internet marketing example does not have a traditional media component. The whole company is based primarily on the Internet communication model, which can be analyzed to define the importance of planning in such efforts. Many of the options available to us as Internet marketers are used on this site, and it serves as an excellent model to see all the types of information that can be exchanged over the Web.

c)   Where are these interactions taking place?

Answer: Again your actual answers will vary, but it can be assumed that the interactions are taking place on the Web, with users communicating from home or work via some kind of networked device.

d)   Does physical location play any role in this interaction? If so, what role?

Answer: The physical location doesn't necessarily affect the information exchange, but it does affect the transaction that is completed in this marketing activity.

Physical location is very important in the fulfillment process and affects the pricing structure for shipping costs and for international customers.

Another aspect of where this exchange takes place involves users and their relationship with the computer they are using to access the Internet. The customization aspects of the Web presentation use cookie technology to identify the client computer with the captured customer data. If the person using the computer shares that same machine with a number of users, who in turn access the site, then that cookie and ID will be incorrect.

In this situation the *where* and *who* definitions are in conflict. No solution exists for this issue, but the amazon.com Web site is not wholly dependent on cookie ID processes and instead uses individual usernames and passwords to identify customers.

e)   Does the concept of *when* apply in this marketing effort ? If so, how?

Answer: This marketing activity and the information exchange on this site is available at all times, 24 hours a day, and seven days a week, so when is only important for fulfillment activities.

Again, this involves shipping time for a variety of audience locations and the cost of that shipping. Express delivery is more expensive than ground transportation. International delivery takes longer than domestic. In addition, telephone-based communication is available for customer service in this effort, so this communications channel must be staffed 24/7 as well.

f)   Why are these interactions taking place?

Answer: These interactions are taking place for the specific reason of selling books and other materials using an on-line direct marketing model.

Though information gathering is a part of this process, the reason why this marketing effort has been put together is the direct sale of product. The entire effort was planned and produced to facilitate purchase and fulfillment of goods. The Web site is similar to a consumer catalog effort in traditional media.

g)   How are these interactions taking place using Internet technology?

Answer: Internet technologies being utilized include a front-end dynamic Web site supported by back-end database technology and e-mail for direct follow-up communication.

A lot of information is being exchanged on this Web site, but the technology being used is the same available to any interested Internet marketer. The Web site is dynamic because almost all of the actual Web pages displayed to the user are created from databased information as they are needed and as the interactions between users and sites develop. The information capture occurs via forms, and the information and graphics are displayed after instant retrieval from the databases where they are stored. E-mail is generated automatically when transactions are completed by the same database technology.

Though we don't know the exact development process involved, we can assume that this whole effort was planned and executed, at least in part, using these types of definitions. The same process can and should be used when developing any Internet marketing effort.

Planning is generally a common-sense practice in our personal lives. But this same common sense is sometimes overlooked in the confusing world of technology-based business. This can and will lead to inadvertant and expensive mistakes. A better practice involves defining the who, what, where, when, why, and how of our communication goals first and then planning and developing an Internet marketing effort to execute these definitions. Such a plan also helps us set a course of action and provides a point of reference for measurement and expense.

LAB 2.1 SELF-REVIEW QUESTIONS

In order to test your progress, you should be able to answer the following questions:

1) Which are two reasons to develop an Internet marketing plan before beginning any effort?
   a) _____ The large number of options available to Web marketers
   b) _____ The extended time frames involved with these types of projects
   c) _____ The inability for this type of communication to change later
   d) _____ The need for benchmarks in measuring success
   e) _____ The knowledge that Web sites are always sucessful

2) What are the five Ws and one H we should consider when planning a Web communication effort?
   a)
   b)
   c)
   d)
   e)
   f)

3) Planning is always considered first in Web communication development.
   a) _____ True
   b) _____ False

Quiz answers appear in Appendix A, Section 2.1.

L A B   2 . 2

DEFINING AUDIENCES AND TARGETING INFORMATION ON THE WEB

LAB OBJECTIVES

After this Lab, you will be able to

- Understand the Concept of Defining an Audience
- Understand the Targeting of Your Favorite Web Site
- Understand How Targeting is Used on the Web

Let's take a look at some traditional communication methods to learn more about defining and targeting. These are important steps in any type of communication and vitally important on the Internet because any person accessing the network is a potential audience member.

Internet users must initiate the communication activity by visiting our Web site and joining our communication efforts. In a way we are in a receptive position in this type of communication, and the only way we can initiate it is to attract customers or other interested parties. The end users can and will choose to communicate based on their needs. Our strongest method in this process is the development of engaging content for the end user.

But to do so we must first know who it is we wish to communicate with. Defining our prospective audience involves looking at our current customers, if possible, and determining why they are our customers and how and what we communicate with them now. If we don't have a current communication model, we can develop a model for the end user we wish to engage. Deciding who we wish to communicate with is vital on the Internet.

Once we know who we are trying to interact with, we can then determine what we are trying to communicate about. Then we can target information and presentations in an appropriate manner. If we are trying to sell a particular product to a known audience, then we can build a Web site that provides the information and transaction systems to do so. If we know our audience is looking for detailed information, we can supply it.

This is true in any media, not just the Internet. The first question a writer, speaker, or producer asks is, "Who is the audience?" Everything else is based on this answer. Successful marketing and communication efforts are targeted at specific audiences. Television advertising campaigns are excellent examples, though these are general and very stereotypical. Daytime television shows carry ads for domestic products targeted at homemakers. Children's cartoon shows carry advertising for toys targeted at children. Sports programs generally carry ads for tools and trucks targeted at the generally male audiences of these programs. Television ads are very expensive to produce and distribute, so they must be used in appropriate media channels to justify their use. They are targeted at specific audiences by the programming they are run with.

Our favorite Web sites contain information and other presentations that are valuable to us for some reason. They engage us with their content and provide something that keeps us returning to their addresses. These Web sites have been targeted to specific audiences of which we are members.

On the Internet we must target information presentations to the audience we wish to reach. Doing so will attract and sustain communication with these audience members. With so many choices for communication available to the end user, it is very important that our Web sites and other efforts provide the information the audience is looking for. Serving the needs of the targeted audience is a primary goal in Internet communication and will result in positive communication for all parties.

LAB 2.2 EXERCISES

2.2.1 UNDERSTAND THE CONCEPT OF DEFINING AN AUDIENCE

**LAB
2.2**

For discussion purposes, let's do another hypothetical exercise. Let's assume you have been given another assignment. This time you are asked to create and deliver a very short presentation about the favorite hobby of an unspecified audience. You are to give this talk at the end of the week, at an undisclosed location, using verbal communication and audiovisual technology support. You are doing this because this exercise asks you to. Using this information, answer the following three questions:

a) Identify the subject matter of your talk.

b) Define three different topics or subjects you wish to cover.

c) What is the single biggest question still unanswered at this point?

2.2.2 UNDERSTAND THE TARGETING OF YOUR FAVORITE WEB SITE

This exercise will help demonstrate the way information and presentations are targeted toward you on the Web. Answer the following questions:

a) Referring back to the previous chapter, what is your favorite Web site?

b) Why is it your favorite site?

c) What audience are you a member of if this site is your favorite?

d) How is this site specifically targeted at you? What information exchange is available that serves you as an audience member?

2.2.3 UNDERSTAND HOW TARGETING IS USED ON THE WEB

This exercise involves visiting a number of Web sites and investigating the ways they are targeted to specific audiences.

Point your browser to these Web site addresses and answer the same three questions in a general way for each of them.

a) `www.stopandshop.com`

What audience is targeted by this site?

How is this site specifically targeted at this audience?

What information exchange is available that serves this audience?

b) `www.more.com`

What audience is targeted by this site?

How is this site specifically targeted at this audience?

What information exchange is available that serves this audience?

c) `www.nasdaq.com`

What audience is targeted by this site?

How is this site specifically targeted at this audience?

What information exchange is available that serves this audience?

d) `www.firsttrade.com`

What audience is targeted by this site?

How is this site specifically targeted at this audience?

What information exchange is available that serves this audience?

e) `www.altavista.com`

What audience is targeted by this site?

How is this site specifically targeted at this audience?

What information exchange is available that serves this audience?

f) `www.artcom.com`

What audience is targeted by this site?

How is this site specifically targeted at this audience?

What information exchange is available that serves this audience?

LAB 2.2 EXERCISE ANSWERS

2.2.1   ANSWERS

For discussion purposes, let's do another hypothetical exercise. Let's assume you have been given another assignment. This time you are asked to create and deliver a very short presentation about the favorite hobby of an unspecified audience. You are to give this talk at the end of the week, at an undisclosed location, using verbal communication and audiovisual technology support. You are doing this because this exercise asks you to. Using this information, answer the following three questions:

a)   Identify the subject matter of your talk.

Answer: Your answer will depend on the interests of the audience involved.

Without knowing who the audience is that we are supposed to address, we cannot proceed with this assignment.

b)   Define three different topics or subjects you wish to cover.

Answer: Your answer will again depend on the interests of the audience involved.

Once we know the audience in this situation, we can define the favorite hobbies of its membership. Only then can the different topics of subjects for the presentation be determined.

c)   What is the single biggest question still unanswered at this point?

Answer: Looking at the information that is supplied initially, the biggest question yet unanswered is the audience for this talk (the who).

If I were to give this talk to a group of school children, the presentation would be very different from that for a senior citizens organization. The what is fully dependent on the who. And I must know the who to determine the what. The where, when, why, and how can be used with any audience. The audiovisual equipment could be the same, the undisclosed location would not matter, and the time frame could stay the same.

But the audience plays a vital role in the situation. Without knowing the audience I have no idea what content or subject matter to include in my presentation. The presentation must be targeted to its audience.

The same is true for Web communication. The flexibility of the communications medium and the massive variety of information available on the Web mean that a successful presentation must be specifically targeted to the audience it is meant to serve.

2.2.2   ANSWERS

This exercise will help demonstrate the way information and presentations are targeted toward you on the Web. Answer the following questions:

a)   Referring back to the previous chapter, what is your favorite Web site?

Answer: Your answer will include your favorite Web site. Mine is used for discussion.

My favorite Web site is operated by the Cable News Network, cnn.com.

b)   Why is it your favorite site?

Answer: Your answer will again be dependent on your interests. Mine is again used for discussion.

I like the instant access to domestic and international news, the overview of the technology marketplace, and the ability to access local weather on demand. I like to know what is going on regarding important issues and require weather information for my outdoor activities. This information is available at cnn.com and is refreshed on a regular basis, giving me reason to return often.

c)   What audience are you a member of if this site is your favorite?

Answer: Your answer will define you as an audience member specific to your favorite Web site. Since cnn.com is my favorite, I am a member of the cnn.com audience.

This audience is very broad and reaches horizontally across the entire user audience of the Internet. This audience desires news from an international source and may be educated or at least aware of the world in general.

d)   How is this site specifically targeted at you? What information exchange is available that serves you as an audience member?

Answer: Your answer will be specific to your favorite Web site. Refer to cnn.com to discuss mine.

Since I'm interested in a number of topics, I like the large and varied amount of information available at this Web site. The home pages lists hundreds of articles and topics that I can browse and links to a variety of news stories and features that I may want to read. The customized information choices are also attractive and are accomplished using database interfaces.

This site is full of information that I want to know. The information is presented in a well-organized fashion and is updated regularly, which keeps me coming back daily or more often if a dynamic situation is happening in the world. I can access this information whenever I wish, and thus I am a satisfied member of this Web site audience.

2.2.3 ANSWERS

This exercise involves visiting a number of Web sites and investigating the ways they are targeted to specific audiences.
Point your browser to these Web site addresses and answer the same three questions in a general way for each of them.

a) www.stopandshop.com

What audience is targeted by this site?

Answer: Regular shoppers at a retail grocery chain.

How is this site specifically targeted at this audience?

Answer: Content is specifically targeted the broad audience of people who shop for groceries and have Internet access at home or work. The site serves Internet users in the geographical regions served by the retail stores.

What information exchange is available that serves this audience?

Answer: Information about special offers made at the retail sites and made through the Web site using downloadable coupons. A loyalty program for frequent users offering rebates based on usage is also available.

b) www.more.com

What audience is targeted by this site?

Answer: Internet users at home or work who are interested in health products and information.

How is this site specifically targeted at this audience?

Answer: It supplies appropriate information on health issues and supplies related products in a direct sales model.

What information exchange is available that serves this audience?

Answer: A database interface makes customization available for regular users. Specialized information presentations and simplified on-line transactions based on captured data are created, similar to the amazon.com customer interface model.

c)   `www.nasdaq.com`

What audience is targeted by this site?

Answer: A broad group of end users interested in highly detailed information on current stock prices and activity on this and other stock markets.

How is this site specifically targeted at this audience?

Answer: It provides a comprehensive overview and detailed reporting ability on this market and its listings in real time (delayed by 15 minutes for proprietary reasons) as well as background and historical data.

What information exchange is available that serves this audience?

Answer: Since information is being captured in a database system in real time as the market operates and a lot of other information about the market itself is stored and updated, this data is made available through Web interface for end users.

d)   `www.firsttrade.com`

What audience is targeted by this site?

Answer: Serving a similar but more specific audience, this Web site is targeted to individuals that want to trade their own stocks and other financial instruments on the financial markets.

How is this site specifically targeted at this audience?

Answer: All of the in-depth information resources on this site are geared toward providing an inexpensive financial instrument trading service and assisting the customers of this service.

What information exchange is available that serves this audience ?

Answer: A transaction system using database technology provides interactive customized interfaces for each customer and trading functionality for on-line buying and selling of financial instruments.

e)   `www.altavista.com`

What audience is targeted by this site?

Answer: A broad audience of Internet users who seek information on the Web.

How is this site specifically targeted at this audience?

Answer: Users can search for information using a key word search engine.

What information exchange is available that serves this audience?

Answer: A database containing text from every publicly available Web site is captured and stored in a powerful database. End users initiate searches through a Web interface using key words, which are returned by the database in the form of links to Web pages.

f) www.artcom.com

What audience is targeted by this site?

Answer: A specific audience of Internet users who are interested in fine art showings and exhibitions.

How is this site specifically targeted at this audience?

Answer: Users can find listings and information about art exhibits in galleries and museums around the world.

What information exchange is available that serves this audience?

Answer: Limited exchange is available, but updated information and a large number of images are presented using static Web pages and links.

LAB 2.2 SELF-REVIEW QUESTIONS

In order to test your progress, you should be able to answer the following questions:

1) What is the first question in any Internet communication effort?
   a) _____ What am I trying to say?
   b) _____ How much money can I spend?
   c) _____ Who am I trying to communicate with?
   d) _____ What is my quest?

2) How is information presentation developed for Internet communication?
   a) _____ Based on the previous marketing materials
   b) _____ Based on the needs of the targeted audience
   c) _____ Based on the experience of others

3) Which is the best way to build communication over the Internet?
   a) _____ Offering lots of free stuff on your Web site
   b) _____ Attracting appropriate users with targeted content

Quiz answers appear in Appendix A, Section 2.2.

L A B   2 . 3

THE EVOLUTION OF INTERNET MARKETING EFFORTS

LAB OBJECTIVES

After this Lab, you will be able to

- Understand the Evolution of Internet Communications

Generally speaking, Internet marketing efforts have traditionally followed a pattern of development similar to other media. The purpose of this lab is to examine these patterns as part of our Internet marketing efforts.

Though every Internet communication effort is different, a pattern in the evolution of Internet communication has become evident that helps us plan and create such efforts. The use of the Internet by companies and other organizations generally involves a hierarchy of six stages of development. These six stages are discussed next.

Level I—Advertisement. This entry level is the use of the World Wide Web (WWW) to display a home page and a few associated or linked pages. Most companies putting up an initial Web page have overly enthusiastic dreams of being overwhelmed by new business inquiries. The truth is that having a home page on the WWW is like putting a billboard in your basement. The home page may have emotional value for the company owners, but users don't know about or gain any value from this type of effort. The typical home page is usually linked to information like pictures of the company building and a message from the president complete with his or her picture. Useful information for a targeted audience is not included. Often a phone number is listed for contact with the company.

Level II—Promotion. The relative ease of developing static Web pages has led to extensive conversion of existing brochures and promotional materials from desktop publishing applications (electronic format) to WWW electronic pages. This caused an explosion in the number of pages on a Web site without increasing the relative value of the communication effort for the user. Often called brochureware, this expansion of the number of pages in the company site added to the personal pleasure of owners and managers but, like the first level, did nothing to generate additional business inquiries, supply useful information exchange, or increase relationships. Though they may provide a minimal amount of direct communication via e-mail links, these sites don't respond to this communication quickly. While promoting the company was the intent of this phase, it can more aptly be called the time-wasting phase for end users who dig around a Web site searching for needed information and end up frustrated and feeling like they should have just called or gone to the retail shop instead. These types of communication efforts may cause more harm than good.

Level III—Interaction. This phase of Internet use is the first that provides value for a prospect or customer by offering meaningful information exchange. Visitors to the Web site can receive information about something that is of concern to them and not information about the company. Once prospects or customers have located your Web site, they can learn about your products, capture information about a solution, and even determine how to purchase a specific solution to their problem. A customer can access the company site to download appropriate information that was previously available only from customer service. Using database-enabled presentations, this interactive level allows prospects or customers to provide information to the Web site and gain desired information when they want it with no delay or hassle. The interactive level satisfies customer wants, needs, and desires and lowers costs by reducing demands on customer service. One example, the Federal Express Web site, allows a customer to determine the status of an overnight delivery. Customers, using their air bill number, can access the location of the package, delivery status, and even the name of the person who signed the delivery receipt. In essence, the overnight delivery company has hired its customers to perform their own customer service.

Level IV—Transaction. At this level the prospect or customer can initiate action and complete transactions beyond information exchange over the Internet. The prospect can respond to and accept an offer made by the company in another media. For example, a space ad may carry a

Web site address for response. That Web site address is specifically targeted to that offer and captures customer contact information to complete the transaction on-line. The customer can order a product or request a technical support visit from your company at this level of interaction. Customers or prospects may be able to order on-line using some form of credit, or customers may have a preestablished relationship and receive a bill for their purchase. At the transaction level the company can significantly reduce selling costs for acquiring new customers and improve customer service for current customers. Interactions in traditional media, including mail, phone, and personal, are moved onto the Internet. L.L. Bean still mails catalogs, answers the phone when customers call, and operates retail stores. But in this example, the availability of the Internet communication channel has moved customer transactions into a less expensive model and increased customer service in the process. The effect on return on investment (ROI) can be substantial, with decreased costs and increased revenue.

Level V—Transformation. At this level the relationship between the company and its markets has moved from traditional to electronic. In addition, the use of this communication has affected the internal operations of the company or organization. The Internet is not used occasionally but has become the accepted and preferred form of communication between the company and its customers. Because it does not operate in any other model, amazon.com has transformed a certain audience of media buyers into customer relationships. In the early days of Internet communication you might have had to call someone to tell them you had sent them an e-mail. Most of us have now transformed far enough that we no longer call to make e-mail notification. We send the e-mail in lieu of calling or any other form of contact.

Transformation can have a disruptive effect. It can cause the realignment or restructuring of the relationship between a distribution channel and its markets. For example, a manufacturer can eliminate one or more channel levels, opting to use the Internet to sell directly to an end user. When a manufacturer like Dell Computer Inc. sells PCs directly over the Internet, then the chain stores like Comp USA sell less. We don't yet know the impact of amazon.com on local or national chain booksellers.

Level VI—Community. At this highest level of Internet progression a group of people with common interests are bound together by emotional involvement. The emotional connection can range from personal commitment to a subject, like a health issue, to a professional group supporting each other through information transfer. The community is a group of people with common interests in a topic or issue who may not otherwise come together. Generally speaking, communities encourage audience members to communicate with each other as well as with the organizing body. Communities can be based on Web site presentations and then use mailing lists (e-mail subscription), collaboration forums, bulletin boards, chat rooms, IRC (Internet relay chat), or any combination of these to communicate among members. Many affinity groups have successful communities over the Internet. Clubs, organizations, religious groups, political organizations, and hobbyists with every variety of interest have established international communities over the Internet. A company or organization can set up a community, but expecting it to flourish may be problematic. The energy of the community comes from the participants. It can be fostered or supported by a sponsoring company, but it will only be successful if it is of emotional value to the members. Many commercial Web sites have some type of forum or bulletin board; most are unused. Software user groups supported by the development company are a good example of a commercial community. The America Online audience that communicates internally is also a very large community. The efforts by amazon.com to solicit and publish individual reviews is an effort in this direction, as are companies that build e-mail lists of active customers and use them to foster communication.

As we mentioned earlier, many companies evolve in their use of the Internet and seem to follow the progression just described. Evaluating expansion on the Internet within your company or organization is another part of the planning process. Consider where you are today and where you would like to go in the future, utilizing the flexibility and communication opportunities the Internet can provide.

LAB 2.3 EXERCISES

2.3.1 UNDERSTANDING THE EVOLUTION OF INTERNET MARKETING EFFORTS

To build a further understanding of this evolution process, let's examine communication efforts in the off-line world. Describe real-life or traditional media examples of these Internet communication evolution levels:

a) Advertisement

b) Promotion

c) Interaction

d) Transaction

e) Transformation

f) Community

2.3. ANSWERS

To build a further understanding of this evolution process, let's examine communication efforts in the off-line world. Describe real-life or traditional media examples of these Internet communication evolution levels:

a) Advertisement

Answer: Your answers will vary. An example of this type of communication is bulk mail pieces that are sent to current resident address contacts, including flyers from the local dry cleaner or optometrist.

Another could be general advertising space advertisements in untargeted publications with varying distribution. Many mass media television ads are also an example of this type of communication.

This type of advertising is not appropriately targeted to any audience. It provides no offer or response device or useful information for a customer or prospect. It is not useful or cost effective for most marketing activity.

Some companies do see value in traditional, mass media advertising. Millions are spent every year on television, other broadcasting, billboard, and space advertising efforts. But these efforts are successful due to massive size and reach. And their goals are generally based on building brand awareness, not direct relationships with customers.

The Internet is not a mass media. It is a direct media. Putting up a home page is like putting a billboard in a dark jungle. It will only be seen if found and gives no reason for end user involvement. A lot of Web sites start out at this level: a few pages acting as a billboard in cyberspace. They accomplish little except possibly frustrating prospective communicators.

b) Promotion

Answer: Your answers will vary. A great example of this type of marketing effort is the colorful collateral material sent as part of sales packages or picked up at trade shows.

This brochure-oriented material is big on flowery language and four-color artwork but not useful for the customer or prospect. Vague assurances about total solutions and industry-leading positions do not fulfill wants, needs, and desires. Often these types of materials are more useful in making internal management feel good about glossy pictures than in building relationships with customers.

Too many Web sites have been developed at this level of communication. Though some value can be seen in providing information to the end user via the Web, many of these sites lack the details that would make them useful for the customer. These cluttered Web sites have little audience targeting and few response mechanisms. They also tend to be full of broad information and graphics, using up development dollars and looking good for management without providing solutions for customers or prospects. And they may even frustrate these users.

c) Interaction

> *Answer: Your answers will vary. An example of this type of communication in traditional media is a direct marketing letter package that provides an immediate response device.*

A donation solicitation from a nonprofit group requesting money and providing a self-addressed, stamped envelope (SASE) for response is a good model. A personalized business letter package with a toll-free response number is another. These both provide direct one-to-one communication of an offer to a targeted audience chosen from a database. Both also provide an easy way to answer the sender. In this way, a resolution of some type is available using the communication method.

Web sites designed at this level are better targeted to specific audiences and might provide different content areas based on audience needs. They also provide forms or e-mail options for users to communicate with the company or organization. Requests for detailed response or specific data may be made on-line and answered in a asynchronous model, hopefully within 24 hours but maybe on the next business day (depending on geography). A Web site that provides detailed product information with a toll-free number to call and order and a form for requesting a catalog would be a good example.

d) Transaction

> *Answer: Your answers will vary. A traditional example of this level of communication would be a consumer or business catalog.*

All of the elements required to complete a transaction are present. A targeted group of products, prices, and details about them are available. A complete set of ordering instructions and a written and telephone response option for contact, product, and payment information are immediate usable by the consumer. Shipping details and other information are also involved.

Web sites with on-line ordering and other transaction options have been developed at this level of communication. Sites like this usually access databases for information capture and transfer to the end user. These Web sites enable end users to complete transactions on-line, fulfilling wants, needs, and desires immediately without additional human interaction from the company or organization.

e)   Transformation

A year or two ago, most people did not use e-mail regularly. Some researchers or technical people did, but the general business population did not use e-mail as a primary means of communication. This situation is now completely different. Many people use e-mail as a primary means of communication for internal purposes, often replacing the internal traditional memo process. Many people also use this communication method for personal and social reasons and stay in better contact at significantly lower cost than using phone or mail.

E-mail has transformed how people communicate with each other. It is cheaper and more efficient than other methods and has become a standard way to operate as business and personal communicators. Once we begin using the Internet and Web for operational purposes, we are transforming our communication methods to a new level. Often, this new Internet-based method becomes the primary means of communication and replaces older ways of doing business.

Web sites functioning at this level of evolution provide detailed information to targeted audiences. These efforts use interactive methods, giving end users access to databases of information and providing a high level of functionality to facilitate their use. Web marketing efforts at this level are replacing traditional marketing communication channels and transforming the way customers do business with the company. The growth and use of on-line stock trading and on-line travel bookings is an excellent example of this level of communication.

f) Community

Answer: Again, your answers will vary, but a good example of community in traditional communication is the gathering of professional or social affinity groups at trade shows, conferences, and events.

In these settings a number of people with common interests meet to further their mutual goals. At trade shows manufacturers, suppliers, vendors, and customers all interact for business and social reasons. The same type of community exists at conferences and other events. All participants put effort and money into attendance, and all achieve some type of benefit for doing so, usually by strengthening relationships of some kind.

Though this level of communication is difficult to achieve for a very large or broad audience using the Internet, smaller segments and audiences may get involved if they see benefits. And any mutually dependent audiences, including suppliers and manufacturers or even regular customers, may be interested in such an opportunity to communicate. Parties building on-line transactions systems with each other and other groups already involved in building relationships over the Internet are further examples of this level of communication.

LAB 2.3 SELF-REVIEW QUESTIONS

In order to test your progress, you should be able to answer the following questions:

1) What is the first level of Internet communication that provides value to the end user?
   a) _____ Promotion
   b) _____ Transaction
   c) _____ Interaction

2) All Internet marketing and communication efforts must progress through each of these levels.
   a) _____ True
   b) _____ False

3) Which is an example of Internet communication transforming a traditional communication model?
   a) _____ The use of e-mail in regular business and personal communication
   b) _____ The purchasing of products from on-line catalogs
   c) _____ The use of the Web instead of travel agents to research travel options

Quiz answers appear in Appendix A, Section 2.2.

C H A P T E R   2

TEST YOUR THINKING

The projects in this section use the skills you've acquired in this chapter. The answers to these projects are available to instructors only through a Prentice Hall sales representative and are intended to be used in classroom discussion and assessment.

1) Look at your current communication efforts. Who is the current audience served by your organization's traditional media activities?

2) Looking at a particular communication activity, how is the information presentation targeted to a specific audience and how does it meet the needs of this audience?

3) Look for opportunities to develop Web communication models that replace or transform existing models to Internet-based communication.

DEVELOPING AND INTEGRATING INTERNET COMMUNICATION STRATEGY

"Though this may be madness, yet there is method in it."

—Polonius in *Hamlet*,
William Shakespeare

In this chapter, we will expand our discussion of Internet communication development to include the larger-picture issues found in a business unit or organization. The effective use of Internet communication includes addressing a variety of internal and external issues, which involve and affect people and businesses both inside and outside the organization developing the effort.

The first lab of this chapter will discuss four broad issues that affect almost any project but are especially prevalent in this new electronic communication medium. The remaining three labs will discuss topics that can be combined with the previous chapter, on planning and audience targeting, to create a basic but comprehensive strategic plan for Internet communications.

The three strategic components in this chapter involve business justification, internal assessment and strategy, and external assessment and strategy. The use of Web-based commerce usually requires the use of external vendors, which is also included in the discussion of external strategy.

L A B   3 . 1

FOUR FORCES AFFECTING WEB COMMUNICATION

LAB OBJECTIVES

After this Lab, you will be able to

- Determine Strategy/Vision, Needs/Use, Tactics, and Economics
- Understand the Business Application of These Four Issues

Developing and utilizing an Internet communications effort does not happen in a vacuum. As with any project, a number of forces from within an organization and outside it will affect the project. As we have discussed, the Internet communications options are numerous and can replace and enhance almost any information flow, at any level, between any participants in any relationship.

But Internet communications will be affected by four different forces acting on the effort simultaneously: strategy/vision, needs/use, tactics, and economics (i.e., cost and ROI). These four forces will affect the justification of this communications model from a business standpoint and will lead to either effective implementation or stagnant acceptance of the efforts inside and outside an organization.

The first force, strategy, should be the initial driving force behind the effort. The strategy or vision for use of the Internet should be developed as the best possible options for using technology to enhance relationships via communication. The use of the Internet to increase customer satisfaction through better customer service using desired information presentations could be a sample strategy. This strategy should be realistic while creating a best case scenario. Completely shifting customer service communication to the Internet in its first three months of use is an unrealistic vision for its use.

The second force affecting Internet communication can be defined as need/use. This concept describes both the needs that can be fulfilled for audiences using the Internet and the use of the communications methods by these audiences. The communications efforts must fulfill wants, needs, and desires. Providing appropriate customer service information will fulfill the needs of a customer audience.

At the same time, use of the communications by the appropriate audience will dictate the success, failure, adjustment, and expansion of these efforts. If the effort does not supply appropriate information, for example, it won't be used. And a Web site that is not used is difficult to justify and fund in any organization.

The third factor affecting a Web communication effort is the tactics used in the effort. While a strategy/vision describes where you would like to go over the longer term, tactics are the things you do to execute a strategy. Building a Web interface to appropriate databases of information is a tactic used as part of a strategy to better serve the audience's customer service needs. The primary differences between strategies and tactics are scope and the dimension of the undertaking. The strategy is the war while tactics are the individual battles.

The fourth force affecting Internet communication involves economics. This is the strongest of these factors and will define the others. Increasing customer service through Internet communication is a good strategy because it is a justifiable expense. (Justifiable expenses will be discussed in detail in the next lab.) But if audience needs are not met because incorrect tactics are applied, then the expense is not justified and the effort will fail due to internal economic pressures. Let's say the strategy is to increase customer service using the Web. But a database-driven system is not built and a static system is used instead as a tactic. This system does not fulfill needs and doesn't get used. It is hard to continue to fund a project that is not being used.

From another perspective, while a strategy may be realistic and fulfill needs, a lack of economic support will limit or prevent any tactics from being utilized. In the preceding example, if the database system is not funded, then that tactic can't be used even though it is the correct one. The solution here would be to use a tactic that can be funded and that will serve some needs. The use of this tactic by the correct audience and a partial success of the strategy could lead to increased economic support and the use of more expensive tactics to meet more needs.

These four factors strike a delicate balance and are interdependent. It's important to understand strategy, tactics, needs/use, and economics when developing Internet communication efforts because they will affect those efforts in the short and long term.

LAB 3.1 EXERCISES

3.1.1 DETERMINE STRATEGY/VISION, NEEDS/USE, TACTICS, AND ECONOMICS

These four factors come into play in almost any buying decision. For this exercise let's utilize a personal example. The purchase of a vehicle is a major buying decision for most people. Let's assume you need to purchase a new vehicle.

a) If you were to purchase a new vehicle that was generally within your means, what car would you purchase to fit your personal needs?

b) Why did you pick this particular car model?

c) What would this purchase cost?

d) What car would or did you recently purchase based on your current financial situation?

e) Generally speaking, why will or did you make this purchase? How will/did the vehicle fit your needs?

f) How did you research, arrange, and finance this purchase?

g) Can you afford this purchase?

3.1.2   UNDERSTAND THE BUSINESS APPLICATION OF THESE FOUR ISSUES

Using these same four factors, let's apply them to a general discussion of Web communication in your company or organization. If you aren't affiliated with a company or organization, consider one you are familiar with.

> **a)** What is your overall Internet communication strategy?

> **b)** Using the Internet to communicate in these ways fulfills what audience needs?

> **c)** What tactics would make this effort happen?

> **d)** Would all the people you communicate with use these Internet communication methods?

> **e)** How do economics affect your current situation or envisioned strategy?

> **f)** If you are currently utilizing the Web in some way, how do the actual effort's needs, usage, tactics, and economic factors reflect your envisioned strategy?

LAB 3.1 EXERCISE ANSWERS

3.1.1   ANSWERS

These four factors come into play in almost any buying decision. For this exercise let's utilize a personal example. The purchase of a vehicle is a major buying decision for most people. Let's assume you need to purchase a new vehicle.

a) If you were to purchase a new vehicle that was generally within your means, what car would you purchase to fit your personal needs?

Answer: Your answers will vary. My choice of a vehicle, if I were to get a new one, would be a Volkswagon Passat station wagon.

For this discussion this is my vision, the thing I'd like to achieve. Owning this vehicle is a goal of mine and a significant part of my personal transportation strategy. Though this may not be a very glamorous vision for some, it is a vehicle that suits my needs exactly and is eventually achievable.

These are two important parts of any strategy. A strategy is an overall goal encompassing many smaller aspects. But this strategy must be achievable and fulfill your needs.

b) Why did you pick this particular car model?

Answer: Again your answers will vary widely, but I picked this particular car for several reasons, all having to do with my use of the vehicle.

I commute 80 miles a day and am dependent on my vehicle to get to my office. Since I am in the car so much, comfort and consistent reliability are important. This brand of cars is comfortable and reliable. As I commute and drive a lot otherwise, I need a vehicle that will handle high mileage over time without needing replacement. These vehicles are known to have long lifetimes and can travel many, many miles.

But why a station wagon? Because sea kayaking and other pursuits involve a lot of gear, which this vehicle can carry. Why not get a truck? Comfort and gas mileage, which this vehicle provides and which address the commuting issue. All these reasons are based on my use of this car to suit my needs. Needs exist in the future as well. I would need to be able to maintain this car myself, and the reliability and inexpensive maintenance over time add to the suitability of this car for my personal use.

A similar situation exists in the use of the Internet for communication. Need drives the use of this technology. If Internet communication can fill a need, it will be used within an organization. A vision or strategy can be developed that fills needs. But doing so requires knowledge of needs.

c) What would this purchase cost?

Answer: Again, your answer will vary. A brand new Volkswagon Passat Wagon costs about $25,000. Though I'd eventually like to own this vehicle, I could not meet the financial need it required at the time I purchased my most recent car.

Enter economics, the other major factor in any business or organizational situation. Though my strategy is solid for meeting my needs and use, it is affected by the economics of my life.

d) What car would or did you recently purchase based on your current financial situation? If you haven't ever purchased a car, then imagine doing so within your means.

Answer: Your answers will vary and if you haven't purchased a car, that's OK too. My most recent car purchase was a used Subaru Legacy Wagon.

Your answer to the first question in this exercise may be the same as this one. If that is the case then your strategy, usage needs, and economics are all in line with each other.

e) Generally speaking, why will or did you make this purchase? How will/did the vehicle fit your needs?

Answer: Your answers will vary, but mine are based on the same set of circumstances discussed in the previous discussion about my vision for a vehicle. I need a reliable, fuel-efficient car that can handle high mileage and carry a lot of stuff. This vehicle fit all these needs.

Again, if your answers are the same for both questions, then your strategy solved your usage needs and you could afford the appropriate vehicle to complete the strategy. You have demonstrated a successful and coordinated vehicle ownership.

f) How did you research, arrange, and finance this purchase?

Answer: Your answers will again vary, but if you purchased a vehicle you may have shared some of these experiences. I first decided generally what I wanted. My strategy, based on my needs, was to find a used station wagon. I then spent many hours looking at classifieds listings, visiting dealerships, talking with salespeople, and calling around looking for a car that matched my vision and that I could afford. Regarding finances, my strategy was to fund this purchase with my savings account.

These efforts were all tactics that helped me complete my goal. Tactics are actions that lead to or complete a strategy. In a general analogy, my personal mission or strategy was to purchase a vehicle that fit my needs. The actions I took, including research, traveling around town, test driving vehicles, and checking prices, were the tactics I used to achieve that goal.

g) Can you afford this purchase?

Answer: If you made a purchase, we can assume you could afford it. In my case I found a vehicle that fit my needs and that I could afford. I was able to buy it in cash using my savings at the time. I did not want to finance this purchase as I was entering graduate school at the time. I wanted the Volkswagon but settled for the Subaru based solely on economics.

Any buying situation is affected by many factors at once. In this case my strategy was affected by economic factors. Use of the vehicle and its ability to fulfill my needs led to the original strategy. Tactics were utilized to complete the strategy and balance economic factors with use and needs.

3.1.2 ANSWERS

Using these same four factors, let's apply them to a general discussion of Web communication in your company or organization.

a)   What is your overall Internet communication strategy?

Answer: Your answers will vary widely, but don't be concerned about setting unrealistic goals. We are initially discussing vision and strategy. Economics will always play a role but shouldn't act as an initial damper to communication planning.

In my case, I direct a training program and I would use the Internet to communicate any and all information from the program with all interested parties. I would communicate program descriptions, requirements, class listings, schedules, grades, financial information, and everything else over the Web. I would capture questions, registrations, and student contact information in a similar Web interface. I would also like eventually to develop a Web-based delivery method for the program's classes, and this is being currently developed for this publication. I would use e-mail to communicate directly with students, instructors, vendors, and prospects.

Though all of this communication may not all be feasible immediately, these elements make up an overall vision for Internet communication. A strategy for development of this communication has been created.

b)   Using the Internet to communicate in these ways fulfills what audience needs?

Answer: Your answers will again vary but should discuss your needs and how the Internet can be used to fulfill those needs. Here's my answer:

Running a training program involves publishing a lot of detailed general information for all interested students (e.g., class schedules), capturing individual registration and financial information from students (e.g., student registrations), and publishing individual-specific information (e.g., class lists for instructors or student grades).

All of these things are now done using paper-based systems with forms, receipts, lists, and letters But it could all be done using the Web. This would fulfill the needs of the students and instructors who want this type of information on a regular basis. It would make it easier for them to get what they need at their convenience, and it would positively impact the needs of myself and the departmental support staff, who must now process all of this paper to supply information and make the program operate. Using e-mail is also easier and more efficient for all parties due to it asynchronous nature.

Web-based delivery is more complicated, technology speaking, but would greatly increase student and instructor satisfaction by eliminating travel, traffic, and time pressure. It would also increase the program's marketability because geography would not be important in the training process.

In my own case, an Internet communication strategy fulfills the needs of all parties involved with the program in a number of ways. Your answers should also build a strategy by fulfilling needs.

c)   What tactics would make this effort happen?

Answer: Your answers will vary but should involve a short discussion of tactics you can use to develop the strategy based on the preceding questions. Review mine as an example.

The tactics I could utilize could involve several efforts. I could develop and publish a Web site that contains all of the information traditionally included in program catalogs. As courses are changed or added, this information can be updated. In addition, schedules can be published dynamically using the Web. Prospective students can request information fulfillment as well.

I use a customized database system to operate my training program. It contains and manipulates almost all of the information I use, including student records, class registrations, instructor information, and financial data.

Building a secure Web interface for individual student and instructor access to this database would fulfill a majority of the needs and desires of students and staff. Just moving my registration process into an on-line model would simplify that process and cut down on paper-based problems. Shifting individual communication to e-mail is another tactic that uses the Internet in a successful fashion.

Developing a Web-based delivery method is a more involved process but could be accomplished by partnering with a technology partner or vendor that could facilitate this process.

d)   Would all the people you communicate with use these Internet communication methods?

Answer: Your answers will vary but should discuss the use of Internet communication after development and availability. Again, here is my answer.

In my field, all of the parties involved with my program are adept at Internet communication and have Internet access at home or work. I have always communicated directly with my instructor audience via e-mail. I have worked to move student communication into e-mail, but some situations, including new prospects and conflict resolutions, require communicating via telephone.

In other audiences and markets, the Internet may not be as highly used and accepted. The usage of the Internet will be impacted by the audiences it is intended to reach. Consider both initial and long-term usage potential as part of a communication strategy. This is difficult since usage will change over time and can't be measured until Internet communication is attempted. But usage can and should be involved in justification and measurement of communication efforts.

In my case, many students want hard copy course catalogs for reference purposes and require hard copy documents for records and processing needs. Additionally, a Web-based delivery option may be good for a specific audience, but the students who attend classes now are doing so because they want an instructor-led classroom environment—something they can't get on the Web at this point. In these cases traditional communication methods can't be completely replaced by Web communication because the traditional methods are being used successfully to fulfill current usage needs.

Though Internet communication is generally better for all parties that use it, it may not be used initially by all parties involved. Usage can and should affect Internet communication strategy before and after the strategy is implemented.

e) How do economics affect your current situation or envisioned strategy?

Answer: Your answers will vary according to your current involvement levels. This question is hard to answer if you aren't working at using the Internet to communicate, but some general points can be made. Most important, economics will always affect your strategy and use of Internet communication, either positively or negatively.

Though Internet generally makes communication less expensive, development costs will be incurred. These economic factors will impact your implementation of Internet communication strategy. Economics will always be involved when discussing usage of any effort.

In my case, the development of an on-line catalog with schedules, information, and contact options was very inexpensive and easy to accomplish using student and instructor expertise. I was also able to piggyback my efforts onto the Web site already developed and funded by the college where I operate. In addition, I have an e-mail system that was developed and funded by the college's Information Systems (IS) department.

Building a customized Web-based interface for my program is not possible due to economic factors. I am not budgeted for this expense, even though almost every student and other party would probably use the system if it were developed. The same is true for a Web-based delivery system at my school. Though it would probably be successful as well, it is not being funded at this time. Economics are constraining my program's Internet communications strategy.

f)   If you are currently utilizing the Web in some way, how does the actual effort's needs, usage, tactics, and economic factors reflect your envisioned strategy?

Answer: Again, your answers will vary based on your current activity level. In my case, portions of the Internet communications strategy have been developed using a number of tactics.

I have developed a Web site that serves as an on-line catalog. It has attracted and informed prospective students who use its contact options. Current students access schedules as well. A majority of direct communication between myself, students, and instructors has been shifted from telephone to e-mail. These tactics fulfill the needs of the audiences they are targeted to reach and are used by them.

Other parts of the strategy have not happened due to economic factors. Development of direct, individual information exchanges for students and instructors and Web-based delivery have not been developed.

Regardless of your current use of Internet communication, these four issues will affect an Internet communications effort. The strategy's vision should encapsulate the best possible, yet generally feasible, situation. It should fulfill the wants, needs, and desires of audiences. This strategy will be affected by the usage of the communications effort after it is deployed. Most important, the communications effort will always be limited by the economic factors of the situation. As usage increases, economic justification can be increased. Tactics can also be employed over time to fulfill needs, match usage, and meet economic needs in stages.

LAB 3.1 SELF-REVIEW QUESTIONS

In order to test your progress, you should be able to answer the following questions:

1) Searching the classifieds for the car you want is a
   a) _____ Tactic
   b) _____ Strategy

2) Which of the four factors will always drive the other three?
   a) _____ Strategy
   b) _____ Needs/Use
   c) _____ Economics
   d) _____ Tactics

3) After the development of an Internet communications effort the factor that will be used to justify economics and influence strategy is use.
   a) _____ True
   b) _____ False

4) Given that economics will play a role, tactics should be applied in Internet communication to
   a) _____ Complete a strategy
   b) _____ Fulfill wants, needs, and desires
   c) _____ Provide useful information and transactions
   d) _____ All of the above

L A B   3 . 2

EXPENSE JUSTIFICATION AND RETURN ON INVESTMENT

LAB OBJECTIVES

After this Lab, you will be able to

- Understand the Cost of Communication
- Assign Value to Communication
- Understand Fixed Versus Variable Delivery Costs of Communication in Traditional Versus Internet Communication
- Justify Internet Communication Based on Delivery Costs and Value
- Assign Costs to Traditional Media
- Justify Internet Communication Based on Replacing Current Communication Efforts

---

A significant aspect in planning and executing Internet communications efforts involves the economic forces introduced in the previous lab. It is safe to say that economics drive most projects in a company or organization. Part of driving an Internet communications effort is justifying the expenses involved in developing and operating the effort.

Justification involves answering the question, Is it worth the money? In a business or organization the answer to this question will influence project funding and the future of Internet communications.

We face these types of decisions every day in any buying cycle. In the grocery store, for example, I must constantly decide if the item I am contemplating purchasing will provide a solution that justifies the purchase price of the item. Often these decisions are easy and automatic. But as prices increase (e.g., for specialty foods), the justification of the expense becomes more involved.

Another way this issue is discussed is in terms of ROI (return on investment). Building Internet communications efforts does cost money. This investment of funds and personnel resources requires some type of return to the organization to justify the effort. For example, building a basic Web site with limited database features could cost about $10,000. This is a significant investment for any company or organization. After putting this money into the effort, will the communication it provides justify the expense? Will it return valuable communication for the investment it required?

The answer to this question is yes. But providing expense justification and determining ROI are actions that you'll probably have to be involved in with your own Internet communications effort. The powers that be probably won't take my word for it.

Answering this question and others like it on your own involves examining several factors in an expense justification and ROI analysis. A large part this process involves comparing Internet communication costs and the value of that communication to other traditional media costs and types.

First you need to break down communication costs to a comparable level for each communication transaction that takes place in each specific media. Doing so is called determining the delivery cost of communication. A very basic but useful method for determining the delivery cost of communication is simply to divide the expense involved in executing a particular media effort by the number of contacts or people that are communicated with in the media effort.

For example, in a direct mail campaign that reaches 100 contacts and costs $50 to produce, the cost of communication is 50 cents each. That was calculated by dividing $50 (media costs) by 100 (number of contacts). This gave us a cost/contact of 50 cents.

Assigning value to a communications effort is another useful tool in the justification process. Value is an estimation of quality of communications. Some communication types provide a higher level of quality or value than others. Value is relative to the receiver of the communication, but properties like specific information; satisfaction of wants, needs, and desires; and personal or customized interactions will increase the value of a communication method.

Though this is not an exact science, it can be accomplished by listing all the media types used by an organization. The media types can then be ranked in value relative to the other items on the list.

The three ways I communicate most are by phone, e-mail, and traditional mail. Looking at this list, I'd say phone is of the highest value to the end user because it is personal and supplies specific fulfillment to specific needs in real time. Second would be probably be e-mail because it provides the same properties in a slightly less personal way. In some situations, e-mail may be of higher value because synchronous communication is not needed and text and other documents can be transferred easily The third method, mail, has the lowest value due to time factors and personalization factors. But mailing documents is important to some of my audiences, so that situation is also relative.

Communication value must be considered when looking at communication costs. A low-cost communication method probably delivers low-value communication. A high-cost method probably delivers high-value communication. The trick is to balance communication value against its cost. Due to the customizable and asynchronous, on-demand nature of the Internet, Internet communication is relatively high in value while low in cost.

One of the major factors contributing to the low cost of Internet communication can be defined by looking at the difference between fixed and variable communication costs. A fixed cost is an expense that stays the same in each billing cycle. At home my mortgage payment is the same predetermined amount each month. It is a fixed cost for my personal living arrangement. A variable cost for is an expense item that changes, either rising or falling, based on usage. The more it is used, the more it costs. A variable cost me at home is my personal phone bill. The more I use my phone, the more the bill costs at the end of the month.

In another example, people's salaries and the amounts necessary to design direct mail pieces or advertisements are fixed costs in an organization. But travel and other expenses are variable costs. The more the employees travel, the more travel costs. This is the case for most traditional communication methods. As space ads are placed, mail pieces are printed and sent out, phone calls are made, and travel is completed the communication costs rise. Costs are amortized and discounted at higher quantities, but, generally speaking, as communication increases so do the variable costs involved.

Internet communication is highly attractive because it does not involve variable costs. Internet communication can be funded at a fixed level for development and operation, including staffing and updating. That funding amount will not change as the amount of communication increases. The $10,000 Web site mentioned previously can serve 100 people or 10,000 people at the same expense. Communication costs are fixed and do not rise at the same rate as usage does.

Granted, significant increases in use will require added technology expenses. If a Web site is so successful that it is swamped by users, then increased server capacity and Internet connectivity must be paid for. But this is, again, an increase in fixed costs to operate at a higher level. Once it is funded appropriately, the technology can serve the same size or even larger audience indefinitely with no need for further investment. This is a very important issue to consider when looking at ROI for Internet communication.

Looking at the communication delivery cost for each contact, the value of that communication, and the impact of fixed versus variable costs, we start to see positive reasons for justifying Internet communication. The Internet provides a low communication cost for each contact. The Internet delivers relatively high value in these communication efforts. And the Internet can be classified as a fixed cost that does not rise as communication usage increases, unlike other types of communication methods.

Using the Internet for communication could be equated to having a phone line that is never busy for the end user and is billed for each month regardless of use. The number of callers does not affect the cost. And every caller receives the same level of individual fulfillment by using the line. The Internet is good news for communication.

Another piece of good news is that Internet communication can be further justified by replacing existing media efforts and saving money by doing so. Developing and operating Internet communications efforts does incur expenses. Much of this expense is needed in the initial phases, before any communication can take place. But as Internet communication begins, it can replace other types of more expensive communication. For every e-mail message I send, I am making one less phone call or mailing one less letter.

This is an excellent justification for Internet communication. Tracking Internet use can further help justification efforts when it is directly compared to decreases in other communication media. From this perspective, Internet communication begins returning on its investment as soon as its operation begins replacing other communication methods.

Not even considering the increases in value to the end user, the use of Internet communication can be justified by comparing its fixed costs to the variable costs of the other media. Eventually, the fixed delivery cost per contact on the Internet will drop below the variable cost per contact in other methods.

A $10,000 Web site serving 100 customers once seems expensive. That's $100 for each contact. But those contacts replaced 100 phone calls at $3.50 each, or $350, so that amount of money can be seen as contributing to the expense of the Internet effort. Once this Web site has replaced about 2860 phone calls, it has paid for itself ($10,000 fixed cost/$3.50 for each phone call replaced = 2857 calls to cover the fixed cost). Once that level of communication has been achieved, the Web site is saving money for the company or organization while supplying valuable communication in the process.

Another way of looking at this point is the amortization or spreading of Internet development costs over time as usage increases. A $10,000 Web site used once by 100 people is providing a high delivery cost of $100 for each contact. But a Web site serving the needs of 1000 people 10 times has now delivered a delivery cost per contact of $1 each. And the same Web site serving the needs of 1000 people 100 times has delivered a delivery cost per contact of 10 cents each.

While other media methods would increase in cost based on their variable delivery costs, the Internet actually becomes cheaper the more it is used. For this reason and the ones discussed earlier, the Internet is justifiable economically and from the standpoint of adding value to relationships. Both issues provide return on investment for Internet communications methods.

LAB 3.2 EXERCISES

3.2.1 UNDERSTAND THE COST OF COMMUNICATION

Determine the cost of communication for each contact in the following scenarios:

a) A print advertisement that costs $200 to produce and $550 to place once a week for four months in a newspaper with a circulation of 30,000 people

b) A direct mail campaign with 10,000 targets that costs $7500 to produce

c) Visiting three prospects in person in two days by a salesperson who, in doing so, spends about $1200 in travel expenses and wages

d) Telephone customer service calls that average 7 minutes (5 on hold, 2 in communication) at $.05/minute for the call and $.45/minute in salary and benefits for the employee

e) Communicating with 200 customers once a week for four months using a Web site that cost $10,000 to develop

f) Communicating with 2000 customers once a week for four months using a Web site that cost $10,000 to develop and maintain in that time frame

3.2.2 ASSIGN VALUE TO COMMUNICATION

Determine the relative value of each communication method:

a) Space advertising

b) Direct mail

c) Personal sales calls

d) Telephone customer service

e) Internet communication

3.2.3 UNDERSTAND FIXED VERSUS VARIABLE COSTS IN TRADITIONAL AND INTERNET COMMUNICATION

Identify the fixed and variable costs for each communication medium:

a) Space advertising

b) Direct mail

c) Personal sales calls

d) Telephone customer service

e) Internet communication

3.2.4 JUSTIFY INTERNET COMMUNICATION BASED ON DELIVERY COSTS AND VALUE

Answer the following questions:

a) How does the old adage of quality versus quantity play a role in this discussion?

b) Is the variable delivery cost of Internet communication low?

c) Does the low variable cost and relatively high quality of Internet communication justify its use?

3.2.5 ASSIGN COSTS TO TRADITIONAL MEDIA

Base your answers on Exercise 3.2.1.

a) What was the cost of each contact for space advertising?

b) What was the cost of each contact for direct mail?

c) What was the cost of each contact for personal sales calls?

d) What was the cost of each contact for telephone customer service?

e) What was the first cost of each contact for Internet communication?

f) What was the second cost of each contact for Internet communication?

3.2.6 **JUSTIFYING INTERNET COMMUNICATION BASED ON REPLACING CURRENT COMMUNICATION EFFORTS**

a) Can Internet communication replace the four other methods discussed so far in this lab?

b) Will replacing communication methods which are viable to do so, make communication cheaper?

c) Does this situation justify Internet communication financially?

LAB 3.2 EXERCISE ANSWERS

3.2.1 **ANSWERS**

Determine the cost of communication for each contact in the following scenarios:

a)   A print advertisement that costs $200 to produce and $550 to place once a week for four months in a newspaper with a circulation of 30,000 people

Answer: The cost for each contact is about $.19. This is computed by multiplying the $550 cost by 16, the frequency of placement, and adding the production cost of $200 to equal $9000 (550 x 4 x 4 + 200 = 9000) Multiplying 30,000 by 16 equals 480,000, the total number of contacts. Dividing $9000 by 480,000 equals $.01875.

b)   A direct mail campaign with 10,000 targets that costs $7500 to produce

Answer: Dividing the cost of $7500 by the number of contacts gives us a cost per contact of $.75 ($7500/10000).

c)   Visiting three prospects in person in two days by a salesperson who, in doing so, spends about $1200 in travel expenses and wages

Answer: Dividing the cost of $1200 by the number of contacts gives the cost per contact of $400 ($1200/3).

d)   Telephone customer service calls that average 7 minutes (5 on hold, 2 in communication) at $.05/minute for the call and $.45/minute in salary and benefits for the employee

Answer: The cost per contact is $3.50. Adding together the communications costs equals $.50 per minute ($.05 + .45). Multiplying this cost by the number of minutes gives us an average cost per contact ($.5 x 7 = $3.50).

e)   Communicating with 200 customers once a week for four months using a Web site that cost $10,000 to develop

Answer: The cost per contact in this scenario is $3.125. It is found by first multiplying the 200 customer contacts by the frequency of 16 to calculate the total number of contacts. Then divide the $10,000 cost by the total number of contacts to get the cost per contact ($10,000/200 x 16 = $3.125).

f)   Communicating with 2000 customers once a week for four months using a Web site that cost $10,000 to develop and maintain in that time frame.

Answer: Using the same equation with an increased number of customers drops the costs to $.31 for each customer contact ($10,000/200 x 16 = $.3125).

3.2.2   ANSWERS

Determine the relative value of each communication method:

a)   Space advertising

Answer: The relative value of this type of communication is the lowest of this group.

Though space advertising can reach a large number of contacts, only a very small percentage of the audience actually looks at or reads the advertisement. Of that small percentage, an even smaller amount may be members of the actual audience you are trying to communicate with. As it is not personalized, this method is not very useful for building relationships beyond initial levels.

b)   Direct mail

Answer: The relative value of this type of communication is much higher than space advertising and not as high as more personal methods.

It is personalized and targeted at a specific member of a specific audience. Though it may not be read by that audience member, it is at least delivered to the right person and can carry an offer aimed at that person's audience. It can be used to build and continue relationships in general ways.

c) Personal sales calls

Answer: This type of communication has the highest value possible.

Face-to-face personal communication provides opportunities to build and maintain professional relationships and deliver targeted offers and information. This does require scheduling meetings, and the communication is controlled by the availability of the parties involved. Though this is the most valuable type of communication, outside factors, including time and money, make this type of communication increasingly difficult.

d) Telephone customer service

Answer: This type of communication is probably second in relative value after sales calls.

It is personal in nature and provides opportunities for individual attention. It allows for individual fulfillment of wants, needs, and desires. But this method does tend to frustrate the customer if these needs can't be met efficiently, the process is dependent on the company's needs regarding time and availability of service. Customers can get what they want but not when they want it.

e) Internet communication

Answer: This type of communication is relatively high in value. Depending on the situation, it may be as valuable as telephone or even personal sales calls.

Though every situation is different, Internet communication may be as high in value as telephone customer service or even higher. Though Internet communication may not bring the same personal value to communication, customized interfaces can provide immediate fulfillment of wants, needs, and desires. More important, these efforts are driven by the end users, giving them immediate involvement and satisfaction.

3.2.3 ANSWERS

Identify the fixed and variable costs for each communication medium:

a) Space advertising

Answer: The fixed cost of space advertising is the expense of producing the advertisement. The variable cost is the money spent for each placement of the ad in a publication.

Though it wasn't mentioned earlier, the fixed cost should include the salary of the person coordinating the effort. Space advertising utilizes frequency of placement in publications to reach audiences. Each time the ad runs, the publisher charges a fee. These fees are discounted for frequent placement. A one-time placement may cost $500. But a three-time placement may be discounted to $400 each.

Regardless of the discount, the higher the frequency of placement, the higher the cost. As this communication increases, the variable costs increase as well.

b) Direct mail

Answer: The fixed cost of direct mail also involves, salaries and production costs, such as graphic design and copy writing. Variable costs involve printing, mailing, database purchasing, and postage charges.

Developing a direct mail campaign costs the same regardless of the number of pieces being sent. The piece must be written and designed. But the variable costs increase for each piece sent. Again, discounting occurs as quantity increases. But, generally speaking, as communication increases so does the cost involved. Each piece must be printed, addressed from a database, mailed, and carry postage.

c) Personal sales calls

Answer: Fixed costs include the salary and benefits of the sales representative. All other costs are variable.

As the salesperson travels to meet with customers, costs are incurred. The more meetings that take place, the higher the variable costs. This type of communication is extremely expensive since the amount of people that can meet face to face is small, time available to do so is limited, and travel time and expense is considerable. If the number of salespeople is increased to meet customer needs, these costs increase exponentially.

d) Telephone customer service.

Answer: Fixed costs involve the salary of the representative. Variable costs center around the phone call. Increasing service to meet customer needs also involves increasing employees and salaries, making salaries a variable cost as well.

This communication method is similar to the personal sales call except that people can communicate with significantly more customers at much lesser expense. But as communication increases, variable expenses increase as well.

e) Internet communication

Answer: Internet communication primarily involves fixed costs.

Unlike other types of communication, the Internet does not incur variable costs. Developing and maintaining Internet communication are fixed costs. As communication increases, these costs do not increase. If communication becomes so frequent that technology upgrades are needed to meet demand, then costs will increase. But these increases will involve higher fixed costs.

LAB 3.2

3.2.4 ANSWERS

Answer the following questions:

a) How does the old adage of quality versus quantity play a role in this discussion?

Answer: Your answers will vary, but here's mine. The Internet provides a high quality of communication in large quantities.

A Web site can be visited by millions of people, 24 hours a day, and each one can receive the information he or she seeks. The medium can serve one person and one million people in the same way, with each person receiving individual attention and fulfillment as long as the effort is developed to do so.

b) Is the variable delivery cost of Internet communication low?

Answer: Yes. The variable cost of Internet communication is nonexistent.

The more you communicate, the more you amortize the initial development and operating costs. Successful situations may require technology upgrades to meet demand. But increases involve fixed costs and are low relative to the amount of communication they enable.

c) Does the low variable cost and relatively high quality of Internet communication justify its use?

Answer: Hopefully, your answer is yes.

The basic justification of Internet communication is its delivery of valuable communication with no variable cost increases. Though other types of communication are more personal, the Internet delivers individual attention and customizable interfaces to information in an on-demand format for the end user.

As the number of users who access this information increases, the costs to deliver the information do not. No other method communication method can deliver this high-value, low-variable-cost formula. In any other communication method, costs increase with use.

3.2.5 ANSWERS

Base your answers on Exercise 3.2.1.

a) What was the cost of each contact for space advertising?

Answer: The cost per contact was $.01875.

b) What was the cost of each contact for direct mail?

Answer: The cost per contact was $1.33.

c) What was the cost of each contact for personal sales calls?

Answer: The cost per contact was $400.

d) What was the cost of each contact for telephone customer service?

Answer: The cost per contact was $3.50.

e) What was the first cost of each contact for Internet communication?

Answer: The cost per contact with 200 customers was $3.125.

f) What was the second cost of each contact for Internet communication?

Answer: The cost per contact with 2000 customers was $.3125.

Note that in this scenario the cost per contact was developed using the fixed costs of development and use. In the other situations variable costs were heavily involved in the equation. In this last scenario (f) communication costs decreased 100% from the previous scenario (e). The amount of communication, however, increased 100% from the previous scenario (e). This is not possible in any other method discussed.

3.2.6 ANSWERS

a) Can Internet communication replace the four other methods discussed in this lab?

Answer: The answer is a qualified yes. Though not all uses of these media can be completely replaced, many communication functions can be shifted to Internet methods.

Space advertising can be eliminated except for new business solicitation. The same is true for direct mail. Customers can be contacted via e-mail instead of traditional mailings. Personal sales visits can be decreased by using individual interfaces via the Web. Interpersonal relationships can be maintained in less frequent but more satisfying meetings, with additional communication via e-mail as well. Customer service needs can be served almost completely via the Internet, with an option for telephone communication available for special circumstances, although e-mail is probably a better, more satisfying option for the customer due to its asynchronous aspects.

**LAB
3.2**

b) Will replacing communication methods, which are viable to do so, make communication cheaper?

Answer: The answer is yes. Looking at the previous exercise shows us that shifting each communication activity to the Internet makes it cheaper to communicate overall.

Shifting communication to the Internet helps in two ways: (1) by decreasing the variable costs incurred in traditional methods, and (2) by further amortizing the fixed costs of Internet communication.

c) Does this situation justify Internet communication financially?

Answer: Another yes answer. The basic justification of Internet communication is its delivery of valuable communication with no variable cost increases. The more advanced justification involves the replacement of other, more expensive, and less effective communication methods with cheaper, more valuable Internet communication.

Though not all traditional communication costs can be eliminated completely, every interaction completed over the Internet can decrease the variable costs in other media while adding value to the relationships involved.

LAB 3.2 SELF-REVIEW QUESTIONS

In order to test your progress, you should be able to answer the following questions:

1) What is the cheapest communications method based on delivery cost per contact?
   a) _____ Personal sales calls
   b) _____ Telephone customer service
   c) _____ Web site communication
   d) _____ Space advertising

**LAB
3.2**

2) What method of communication is least valuable relative to the others?

   a) _____ Personal sales calls

   b) _____ Web site communication

   c) _____ Telephone customer service

   d) _____ Space advertising

3) Internet communication delivers relatively_____.

   a) _____ High cost and high value

   b) _____ Low cost and high value

   c) _____ Low cost and low value

4) Internet communication involves variable costs.

   a) _____ True

   b) _____ False

5) Internet communication can replace existing communications methods.

   a) _____ True

   b) _____ False

6) Internet communication can cut communication costs while increasing communication value.

   a) _____ True

   b) _____ False

L A B   3 . 3

ADDRESSING INTERNAL ISSUES IN A BASIC STRATEGIC INTERNET COMMUNICATIONS PLAN

LAB OBJECTIVES

After this Lab, you will be able to

- Assess and Strategize Internet Communication for Your Organization
- Assess and Strategize Existing Internal and Competitive Use of the Internet
- Assess and Strategize Internal Staffing and Capabilities
- Assess and Strategize Enhancing Functional Processes Using Internet Communication

---

This lab discusses a number of issues inside an organization that should be addressed in a strategic Internet communications plan. Some outside issues, such as competition, can also be included, but these are looked at from the perspective of how they affect internal issues. As previously discussed, strategy involves a long-term objective for Internet communication. Discussing actual tactics to execute Internet communication strategies should be avoided at this level.

Before developing a future strategy, it is necessary to assess current situations. First we look at where we are using Internet communication. Then we can decide how we want to use this communications method to affect the future. Strategic planning can take many forms, and a comprehensive plan should include audience targeting information from the previous chapter and financial justification from the previous lab. A basic strategic plan should also assess and strategize internal issues in the following four categories:

Organizational history and big picture overview

Current internal and competitive use of the Internet

Staffing and capabilities within an organization and needs for outsourcing

Automation of functional processes using the Internet

Organizational aspects, the big picture for a company or organization, is the first topic to be assessed and addressed in this part of the strategic planning process. Assessment and strategy topics issues should first include a brief history and a very general "30,000 feet" overview. This overview has nothing to do with the Internet but just identifies your organization's mission. A strategy can then be named that uses the Internet to further that mission.

A general look at how current operations are completed by your organization could include a discussion of the number of products or services you supply and the sizes of the audiences involved. Again, this does not mention the Internet at first. Then a possible strategy on Internet enhancement of these operations can be completed. Looking at your organization's current status in its marketplace or other universe and then how Internet communication could affect this situation can be included in a strategic plan. All of these discussions can be very general and broad in scope and act as an introduction to the next three subject areas.

Existing internal and competitive usage of the Internet is the second, more specific subject area. Looking at how the Internet is being used right now by your organization and others like it can lead to a strategy for how better to use the communication methods. For example, if you are using e-mail internally but not to communicate with members of your audiences, a strategy could be to increase this type of Internet communication.

Using the evolution levels from the previous chapter is also helpful for analyzing your current use of the Internet and any competitors' or other similar organizations' usage. Evolution levels can also be used as strategy targets for increasing efforts. For example, if your organization is at an informative level and another organization is at a transaction level, your strategy could be to increase your efforts to match your competitor.

The third, even more specific area in this part of a strategic plan involves internal and external responsibilities. Quite simply, who will be responsible for Internet communication within your organization? Will it be marketing, technology, or other personnel? It should be marketing or other communication people, but this is not always the case.

What capabilities does internal staff have to develop and maintain Internet communication and what will require outsourcing to outside help? You may have people inside that can contribute to an Internet effort. If you are reading this publication, maybe it is you. Maybe a number of people can be involved. Maybe front-end HTML and graphics development can be done inside while back-end database application building will require an outside vendor or consultant. Maybe internal technology staff can handle all aspects, with direction from the marketing and communication people. If staffing will require training to support Internet communication, then this should also be included.

A fourth area should discuss specific strategies for automating and transforming business processes. These strategies could include automation of information exchanges between employees inside and audience members outside an organization. Wherever information exchange takes place, a strategy for transforming that exchange to Internet communication could be developed.

For example, internal use of a database could be transformed to a Web-based model for easier access and use. Hard copy mailings of information to an outside audience could be transformed to electronic formats. Regardless of the information content, exchanges of information can be assessed. Then a strategy for using Internet communication to accomplish the same things can be created.

Information exchanges may or may not involve proprietary or personal information. This and other kinds of information may require some type of secure environment. This issue should also be addressed in the fourth subject area. Again, actual tactics for securing information (passwords, encryption, etc.) need not be discussed. But the transformation of information exchanges that need secure environments should be assessed and then included in an Internet communications strategy.

LAB 3.3 EXERCISES

3.3.1   ASSESSING AND STRATEGIZE FOR YOUR ORGANIZATION

Answer the following questions based on your current organization. If you are self-employed or a student, use an organization you are familiar with.

a) What is your organizational history?

b) What is your organization's big picture strategy for using the Internet?

c) What are your current operations?

d) What is a possible strategy for using the Internet to enhance operations?

e) What is your status in the marketplace?

f) What is your strategy to affect your status in the marketplace?

3.3.2   ASSESS AND STRATEGIZE EXISTING INTERNAL AND COMPETITIVE USE OF THE INTERNET

Answer the following questions based on your current organization. If you are self-employed or a student, use an organization you are familiar with.

a) Using the evolution of Internet communication from the previous chapter, what is your existing internal situation regarding Internet communication?

b) At what evolution level are your competitors' or other similar organizations' Internet communications activities?

c) What is your strategy regarding competitive efforts?

3.3.3 ASSESS AND STRATEGIZE INTERNAL STAFFING AND CAPABILITIES

Answer the following questions based on your current organization. If you are self-employed or a student, use an organization you are familiar with.

a) How will you assign organizational responsibilities for Internet communication?

b) What is your strategy regarding organizational responsibilities?

c) What are your internal capabilities for Web and Internet communications development?

d) What is your strategy for outsourcing development efforts?

e) Is training of staff required?

f) What is your training strategy?

LAB
3.3

3.3.4 ASSESS AND STRATEGIZE ENHANCING FUNCTIONAL PROCESSES USING INTERNET COMMUNICATION

Answer the following questions based on your current organization. If you are self-employed or a student, use an organization you are familiar with.

a) What are your strategies for transforming external business processes?

b) What are your strategies for automating existing internal processes using the Internet?

c) What are your strategies for securing information?

LAB 3.3 EXERCISE ANSWERS

3.3.1 ANSWERS

Answer the following questions based on your current organization. If you are self-employed or a student, use an organization you are familiar with.

a) What is your organizational history?

Answer: Your answers will vary. Your organization should be briefly described in a context relative to the largest element of the organization it is part of. Your answer should include relative time frames for your industry.

This information is helpful is setting strategic goals. By looking at where we came from, we can begin to decide where we want to go.

The Merrimack College Webmaster Certification Program has been in existence for three years and has increased in size and scope each year. One of the first programs of this type in the country, it is part of a professional education center that has been operating for six years and was established to provide noncredit professional education to vertical industry segments. The center is an independent department within a traditional four-year undergraduate academic institution. It originally served the training needs of local manufacturers but has recently been successful in offering educational products that serve the financial and technology marketplaces.

b) What is your organization's big picture strategy for using the Internet?

Answer: Your answers will vary. For a future strategy in my program, we can utilize the Internet to serve the training needs of financial and technology companies through better marketing, customer service, and delivery methods.

c) What are your current operations?

Answer: Your answers will vary to your situation. Your answer should discuss how your organization operates, the numbers of customers or products involved, and how information is stored and used to perform the organization's functions. This information is helpful in determining where Internet communication can be utilized to automate existing systems.

Briefly, the Webmaster Certificate Program operates dozens of courses in six sessions during each year. We have several hundred students taking one or more classes at a time. We use two database systems: one that is operated locally by our center that contains all course, instructor, registration, and financial information; and a second that contains only financial information for the college's accounting processes.

d) What is a possible strategy for using the Internet to enhance operations?

Answer: Your answers will vary widely. Since all operations involve some type of communication and information exchange, the Internet can be used somewhere to facilitate operations.

A possible strategy for us is to automate information capture and presentation to better serve and communicate with our students. This automation process using the Internet will also facilitate internal information flow and communication.

e) What is your status in the marketplace?

Answer: Your answers will vary widely. But some attention should be focused on how your organization relates to others in a pertinent universe or competitive marketplace. This information is useful in setting strategic goals by looking for ways that Internet communication can increase market share or cut operating costs in competitive environments.

The Merrimack College Webmaster Certification program seeks students from the same geography as several programs run by other academic institutions in the college-rich Northeast. At this point, all have independent curricula and differ in many elements, including delivery models and approaches.

LAB
3.3

f) What is your strategy to affect your status in the marketplace?

Answer: Again, your answers will vary. Any answer should address a slightly specific perspective on how Internet communication can affect your organization's status in its marketplace or other grouping by increasing market share, providing better value, or enhancing its services to its audiences.

Using the Internet, the Webmaster Certificate Program can look for ways to expand market share in this field outside our traditional geography using the Internet. We can also serve local students better through more efficient internal information exchange and increased communication quality with our students.

3.3.2 ANSWERS

Answer the following questions based on your current organization. If you are self-employed or a student, use an organization you are familiar with.

a) Using the evolution of Internet communication from the previous chapter, what is your existing internal situation regarding Internet communication?

Answer: Your answers will vary. Due to the explosion of Internet communication, your organization may already be involved in some way. Looking at current status can help in setting a strategy for eventual use of the Internet.

The Webmaster Certification Program is operating at an interaction level. The program has a section on the college Web site for program information and schedules, a prospect capture form that forwards via e-mail, and a registration system that is not tied directly to our database system. Registrations are captured using a form and are forwarded in text using e-mail. We use e-mail effectively to communicate between employees and students.

b)   At what evolution level are your competitors' or other similar organizations' Internet communications activities?

Answer: Your answers will vary widely based on your situation. Since Internet use is becoming so widespread, we can learn from other's use of the technology.

Many of the schools that offer similar programs near the Merrimack College are at about the same level of communication. They inform and interact with students using the Internet but conduct transactions using other methods. Of course, we do not know their internal use of the technology.

c)   What is your strategy regarding competitive efforts?

Answer: Again, your answers will vary.

Our strategy regarding competition will be to keep abreast of Internet communication use by other parties. As we are all in a service industry, our students will need to get the same level of service available at other programs.

3.3.3 ANSWERS

Answer the following questions based on your current organization. If you are self-employed or a student, use an organization you are familiar with.

a)   How will you assign organizational responsibilities for Internet communication?

Answer: Your answers will vary but should include both communications or marketing staff and technically oriented staff. It is crucial, however, that the communications-related people in your organization retain decision-making involvement. It is a common but misdirected practice that Internet communication be assigned to a technology department because of the technology involved.

As earlier chapters have demonstrated, the Internet is a communication medium. Communications-related people must drive the process, as they are the ones that can best formulate communications interchanges.

In my organization a small committee was formed with representatives from the marketing department and the IS department. The marketing director for the institution chairs the committee and has final decision-making ability. She oversaw the original development project using an outside vendor. She now manages a small part-time staff of people, who have been adding to and updating the Web site for the college.

b) What is your strategy regarding organizational responsibilities?

Answer: Your organization may use a different model, but communications people must be involved. This could be part of a new strategy.

Our strategy on this issue is to keep marketing and IS personnel working together under direction of the vice president (VP) of marketing. We are also seeking funding to staff the Web site full time. A staff position titled Webmaster will eventually be created and report to the VP of marketing and director of IS.

c) What are your internal capabilities for Web and Internet communications development?

Answer: Your answers will be based on your organization. Your situation may range from no internal capabilities except providing content to full development abilities, including both presentations and back-end database technology.

At Merrimack we originally had no capabilities. Training was then sought for internal personnel to take over minor front-end updating. Later, students from the Webmaster Certification Program helped expand the presentations.

c) What is your strategy for outsourcing development efforts?

Answer: This answer will depend on your situation. Web and Internet development companies run from small local development operations and consultants to international advertising agencies. Vendors can be chosen to assist in any aspect of Web communications.

Merrimack College originally contracted a specialized direct marketing agency with some experience developing Web sites for nonprofit institutions. This vendor built the original Web site, with input and direction from the VP of marketing. This site has been updated and expanded by internal efforts, discussed previously.

d) What is your training strategy?

Answer: Your answers will vary. But since you are reading this book, you must be interested in training. Identifying and training personnel responsible for Internet communication is necessary.

In our organization staff from IS and marketing communications received training on Web development and split updating and expansion work accordingly. Our strategy is to continue to train people as the effort expands so that the workload can be assigned fairly.

LAB 3.3

3.3.4 ANSWERS

Answer the following questions based on your current organization. If you are self-employed or a student, use an organization you are familiar with.

a) What are your strategies for transforming external business processes?

Answer: Your answers will vary widely but should touch on basic ideas for shifting business communication activities between your organization and your customers or other audience members to the Internet. This transformation is the justifiable goal of Internet communications evolution.

LAB
3.3

The Internet is useful for traditional marketing and advertising efforts. But the use of Internet communication to automate existing business processes is a powerful method for cutting communication delivery costs in other media. Many automation strategies may initially involve using the Internet to provide better customer service for current audience members.

Our strategy at Merrimack is to develop a Web-based transaction system that can capture registration information from students and present course, class, and other information from the current operational database to our audience members. Basically we want to put a Web front end on our current database. E-mail can also be used more effectively to communicate with students.

Eventually, the development and use of a database-driven system can transform our traditional communication methods to Internet based. This will be more efficient for all parties involved and allow our program to serve more students at a higher level than is currently possible. Use of this system and a possible Web-based education delivery model will eventually lead to a community of students, educator, and administrators using the Internet to communicate more effectively and efficiently. This community already exists but will be enhanced by replacing traditional communication with Internet communication.

b) What are your strategies for automating existing internal processes using the Internet?

Answer: Your answers will again vary. But using Internet communication to transform internal communication processes is another excellent method for justification of such efforts.

Strategies could include automation of sales force communication using a Web-based interface and distribution of internal information using e-mail lists and intranet Web sites.

Our strategy is to better utilize communication internally to process questions and comments from students as well as for traditional internal communication such as memos, budget documents, and reports. In addition, a Web-based system for our internal financial database could also be tied directly to our operational database for more efficient transfer of information.

c) What are your strategies for securing information?

Answer: Your answers will vary but should include acknowledgment of information security needs and what information requires security in the automated Internet communication systems.

Personal contact data, financial information, credit card information, individual accounts, sensitive product information, and proprietary information products are some of the information types that require some type of security arrangements in Internet communications. The techniques and technologies behind the security processes are discussed in another publication in this series (*Administering Web Servers, Security, and Maintenance,* Prentice Hall PTR.), but it is important to identify what information requires security in the development process.

In the Merrimack College project, each student would require his or her own secure access to grades, registration, and financial status information. Sensitive information and credit card or purchase order (PO) information would require a secure transfer system. In addition, the database systems where this information is stored would require protection from unwanted access while providing information to appropriate users.

LAB 3.3 SELF-REVIEW QUESTIONS

In order to test your progress, you should be able to answer the following questions:

1) Before developing a section of a strategic Internet communications plan, we need to
   a) _____ Devise tactics to achieve the strategy.
   b) _____ Assess the current status of the issues involved.
   c) _____ Decide how much money we have.
   d) _____ None of the above

2) Comparing Internet communication evolution levels is useful when assessing
  a) _____ Internal use of the Internet
  b) _____ Competitive use of the Internet
  c) _____ Both of these
  d) _____ Neither of these

3) A strategy for assigning responsibility for Internet communications should involve
  a) _____ Only technology people
  b) _____ Only marketing or communications people
  c) _____ A combination of both with communications people in charge
  d) _____ A combination of both with technology people in charge

4) Automating information exchange systems can enhance communications for audiences that are
  a) _____ Inside your organization
  b) _____ Outside your organization
  c) _____ Interested in information that must be secured
  d) _____ None of these
  e) _____ All of these

LAB
3.3

LAB 3.4

ADDRESSING EXTERNAL ISSUES IN A BASIC STRATEGIC INTERNET COMMUNICATIONS PLAN

LAB OBJECTIVES

After this Lab, you will be able to

*   Assess the Strategies of External Parties
*   Involve E-Commerce Vendors

Another area for assessment and strategizing as part of a basic Internet communication plan involves external parties and organizations that may add value, gain information, or help support your Internet communications efforts. While the previous lab discussed internal parties and issues, this lab addresses parties outside an organization. These could include participants from several groups: existing relationships, partnerships, and channel participants.

These external parties can also be included in audience targeting activities, discussed earlier. They are included here again because they should be included in a strategic planning process. Building Internet communications with these parties may involve building an extranet, an information system using the Internet built for external parties but not for the general Internet audience.

Existing relationships could include external employees, contractors, vendors, suppliers, and other parties that help your organization conduct its operations. In each of these situations direct benefits can be received by all organizations involved. Providing information and transactions using the Internet facilitates communication to these external parties that would be required in another medium. For example, companies or organizations that use the same print vendor or office supplier can build an Internet communication system to facilitate regular transactions.

Partnerships with other organizations could include trade associations, business partnerships, referral activities, or any situation that provides a more indirect benefit. These types of external parties may be seen as an example of "We'll help you and you'll help us." Perhaps two companies that provide different services to the same customer will work together to support each other's activities. A flower shop, caterer, and photographer in the wedding business are examples. Mutually positive contributions can be supplied through Internet communication for each external party involved.

Channel participants are individual external companies that supply, buy, or sell you your products or services. In these situations, mutual benefits can be provided for both parties through Internet communication. Though these are also existing relationships, they may be grouped separately in a strategic plan as they may require different communication systems. They are mentioned here because they are external parties. Channel participants are usually customers and may also be addressed in the audience targeting section of a strategic plan.

For each of these external parties a brief strategic discussion should involve several topics. An identification of the outside party and the nature of the relationship that exists should come first, followed by a look at the external parties' information needs and what information could be supplied to meet these needs, and a look at possible transactions that can be conducted over the Internet.

For a flower shop external parties could include the following:

- Flower suppliers are an existing direct relationship. Information exchanges could include product and account information. Transactions could include buying wholesale flowers daily.

- Funeral homes are a regular channel, reselling flowers on the shop's behalf. They could be considered a customer as well. Information includes available flower products and special requests from families. Transactions could include purchasing flowers as needed for services.

- Wedding planners are separate parties that act as partners. Information includes special packages, sample work, and schedules. Transactions could be referrals of contact information. Reselling floral services would make the planner a channel participant.

**LAB
3.4**

A fourth type of external party should also be introduced in a strategic Internet communications plan. E-commerce vendors and strategies for their involvement need to be addressed. These types of vendors may be needed if your organization is interested in completing transactions over the Internet and if those transactions require fulfillment of products using traditional methods.

These types of vendors can serve three significant roles and have experience doing so from other types of direct marketing activities, including catalogs and other mail and phone order efforts.

The first part of an e-commerce transaction that may require an outside vendor is the capture and processing of information from the end user. In the amazon.com example, this information includes product selection, customer contact, shipping, and payment information. This information is captured and stored in a database operated by amazon.com. If your organization is interested in capturing orders, a database-enabled Web site should be utilized. An outside vendor can be utilized to supply and operate a database-enabled Web site on your organization's behalf if your organization does not do so.

The second aspect of e-commerce transactions that may require an outside vendor involves processing the financial side. Many direct consumer transactions involve credit cards. Accepting and processing credit card orders requires the involvement of a vendor in the form of a bank or credit card processing company to facilitate the transactions. When you utilize a credit card to make a purchase in a retail setting, the clerk usually forwards your credit card information electronically using the cash register or other electronic device. The company at the other end of that communication, which immediately approves or denies your transaction, is some type of credit card processing vendor. The same is needed for Internet-based transactions. If you already conduct credit card transactions, then you may be able to utilize the same vendor in your Internet communications.

If your organization is interested in other types of financial arrangements, then a customized financial system may be built. For example, many companies and government organizations complete transactions using requests for quotations (RFQs), requests for proposals (RFPs), purchase orders, and invoices. These systems usually involve existing relationships and could involve development of customized communication applications using the Internet to complete these transactions.

A third e-commerce element that could involve an outside vendor is fulfillment or distribution of products. If an order for a specific item is completed over the Internet, then that item is usually shipped directly to the customer. This process can be handled by an internal shipping department, or an outside distribution vendor could be utilized. This vendor stores your inventory on your behalf and ships it to your customers based on contact information and shipping details you supply.

LAB 3.4 EXERCISES

3.4.1 ASSESS THE STRATEGIES OF EXTERNAL PARTIES

Answer the following questions based on your current organization. If you are self-employed or a student, use an organization you are familiar with.

a) Describe existing external relationships for your organization.

b) What are their needs?

c) What information can be supplied via the Internet?

d) What transactions or e-commerce can be conducted?

e) Describe current or possible partnerships.

f) What are their needs?

g) What information can be supplied via the Internet?

h) What transactions or e-commerce can be conducted?

i) Assess channel participants.

j) What are their needs?

k) What information can be supplied via the Internet?

l) What transactions or e-commerce can be conducted?

3.4.2 INVOLVE E-COMMERCE VENDORS

Answer the following questions based on your current organization. If you are self-employed or a student, use an organization you are familiar with.

a) How will your Internet communication effort capture orders and other information to conduct e-commerce?

b) Will a vendor be required to process the transactions?

c) Will a fulfillment center be required, or is this done internally?

LAB 3.4 EXERCISE ANSWERS

3.4.1 ANSWERS

Answer the following questions based on your current organization. If you are self-employed or a student, use an organization you are familiar with.

a) Describe existing external relationships for your organization.

Answer: Your answers will vary widely depending on your individual situations. Relationships could involve external employees, regular vendors, and any number of other parties that would benefit from Internet communication to facilitate your interactions.

My Webmaster Certification Program at Merrimack College is entirely dependent on external relationships for its operation. The instructors in the program work outside the college in the Internet communications field. These people are contracted to teach the courses in the program and need access to the information presentations created for the program.

b) What are their needs?

Answer: Your answers will vary widely depending on your individual situations. Regardless of the actual relationship, some need for information access and exchange will probably exist.

My instructors' needs include class composition lists, class times, and class locations. They also need the ability update this information as changes occur and to submit grades for completed courses.

c) What information can be supplied via the Internet?

Answer: Your answers will again vary widely depending on your individual situations. But almost any information can be communicated using the Internet.

All of the information my instructors may need could be published, updated, and captured using Web-enabled database technology in an extranet environment.

d) What transactions or e-commerce can be conducted?

Answer: Your answers will vary widely depending on your individual situations. In my situation instructors must sign contracts for payment of their services. This process could be conducted using a Web-based system using individual identification and confirmation processes.

e) Describe current or possible partnerships.

Answer: Your answers will vary. My program operates in partnership with the World Organization of Webmasters (WOW), the trade association that has coordinated the Webmaster training program of which this publication is part.

f) What are their needs?

Answer: Your answers are dependent on your situation. The WOW partnership requires the use of the Merrimack College Webmaster training program as an example of a successfully operating training program for other schools and training organizations to review. This partnership also provides opportunities for cross-marketing between the two organizations and requires the capture and forwarding of prospect contacts data. In addition, it provides a regular information exchange between the two organizations and their respective members regarding education, experience, and professional opportunities.

g) What information can be supplied via the Internet?

Answer: Your situation is individual. Almost any partnership would involve mutually beneficial information exchanges. In my situation program information can be linked between the two organizations and communication can be facilitated between organization members.

Appropriate captured data from end users seeking more information or communication could also be forwarded to either party. In addition, communities of educators, students, and professionals can be built around Web-based publishing, interactive discussions, and even Web-based training delivery systems.

h)   What transactions or e-commerce can be conducted?

Answer: Again, your situation is independent of mine. However, you may see opportunities to complete business transactions with partners using Internet communication.

Though it may not be needed, it would be possible, using the Internet, for both my organization and WOW to complete transactions for each other. WOW could conduct on-line registrations for my program's courses and Merrimack College could capture on-line WOW memberships.

This would require strong relationships and communication regarding financial information. For this reason, completing transactions for partners may not be feasible or practical. It would probably be better for each organization to participate in a joint Web presentation but operate separately behind the scenes. Separate transaction screens could be operated on our respective Web sites linked from the joint site. Other partnerships may be able to integrate operations on the same site.

i)   Assess channel participants.

Answer: Your answers will depend on the nature and product distribution of your business or organizational model. Channel distribution models include multiple parties buying and selling products from each other in a linear fashion.

For example, many products are made by manufacturers. These manufacturers sell the products to distributors. Distributors then sell the products to wholesalers. Wholesalers sell the product to retailers. Retailers sell to consumers of the products.

The Merrimack College Webmaster Program does not participate in a traditional channel environment, but we have acquired course registrations in a similar manner. Some private training companies have forwarded registrations into the program. In this case, students pay their registration costs to the training company. That company then pays the college the appropriate registration fee for the course, which is usually discounted in a distribution arrangement. In this case, the training company is acting as a channel participant with the college by reselling a course offered by the college.

j)   What are their needs?

Answer: Your needs will vary significantly depending on your channel activity. This runs the gamut from product information and pricing to order status, inventory availability, and financial transactions and reporting. When private systems are built for channel participants, the systems are considered to be extranet, or information systems using the Internet built for external parties but not for the general Internet audience.

In the Merrimack College example, the channel participant would need public information, including course offerings, times, and locations. Channel participants would also require customized pricing information and real-time space availability data.

k)   What information can be supplied via the Internet?

Answer: Again, your answers will vary. Any information that would normally be distributed and communicated between channel participants could be done so over the Internet.

As channel participants are already in a business relationship, it is relatively simplistic to determine what information is regularly exchanged and then to develop Internet communication systems to conduct this communication. Keep in mind that the flexibility of Internet communication could mean that channel participants could have an individual presentation of information based on their needs and pricing structures.

Merrimack College could provide course details and availability information through a customized interface, secured for use only by the channel participant. This could be considered an extranet application.

l)   What transactions or e-commerce can be conducted?

Answer: Your answers will vary. If you are currently involved in regular transactions with any number of channel participants, then Internet communication can be conducted at the transaction level to facilitate and economize these activities. Payment or purchase order information can be communicated as part of the process, but the variety of different financial systems will have to be considered in the development process.

The Merrimack College example could involve the channel participant capturing registrations and forwarding them directly into the Merrimack College registration system via e-mail. Or a customized interface into the same system could be deployed using the Web.

3.4.2 ANSWERS

Answer the following questions based on your current organization. If you are self-employed or a student, use an organization you are familiar with.

a) How will your Internet communication effort capture orders and other information to conduct e-commerce?

> *Answer: Your answer will vary based on your situation. If you are planning on conducting some type of transaction using the Internet, then you will need to capture information, process it, and return information to the end user.*

If Merrimack College implements an on-line registrations system, then registrations can be captured via the Web site in a secure environment. Students can create accounts initially and then register later using an account and password system similar to amazon.com. This system can be built on the Merrimack College Web site, which is hosted by a third-party Web hosting company that can support database-enabled Web sites.

LAB
3.4

b) Will a vendor be required to process the transactions?

> *Answer: Again, your answers will vary widely. But if you plan on conducting e-commerce directly with end users, then you will probably need to accept and process credit card transactions. Other types of transactions, including purchase orders or extension of payment with invoices, would require customized transaction applications tied into your existing systems.*

If you do elect to accept credit card transactions, then you will need to involve some type of vendor to process these transactions on your behalf. This vendor may be a bank or a specialized credit card processor or another financial institution that confirms the availability of funds and debits the appropriate account on your behalf.

If your company or organization currently accepts these types of transactions, then you might already have a vendor for these services. If not, you may need to set up a merchant account or other relationship with this type of company. This vendor will need to be included in the tactical development of your Web communication efforts because information on transactions will need to be forwarded to that vendor securely as it is captured over the Internet.

Merrimack College has a relationship with a bank, which handles our credit card transactions now. In the e-commerce system, our vendor can supply a preexisting application that will be run on the Web server. After capture on the Web, credit card information is encoded and forwarded to the bank using a dedicated data communication method. These transactions are approved or denied and returned to the Web database application, instantly, to continue the transaction.

c)   Will a fulfillment or distribution center be required?

Answer: Your answers will depend on your situation. If you are conducting e-commerce and providing products of some kind to a customer, then you need to fulfill orders. Depending on volume, many companies utilize internal fulfillment operations. Other companies and organizations outsource this function to distribution centers or fulfillment houses.

In this model your company or organization would purchase the products from your suppliers and forward them to the distribution center. Products are coded for sophisticated inventory control systems. Orders would be forwarded electronically after capture and processing by your company. Fulfillment and shipping would be handled by the distribution center, which charges a fee and shipping expenses back to your company. Many distribution centers are vary large operations that fulfill orders for many companies and are located in centralized locations near transportation hubs.

Since the Webmaster Certification Program delivers training on our campus, we don't require these services. But if you ordered this book or any other product from an on-line merchant, it was probably sent to you in a similar manner.

LAB 3.4 SELF-REVIEW QUESTIONS

In order to test your progress, you should be able to answer the following questions:

1)   Examples of external parties don't include:
- **a)** _____ Companies that resell our products
- **b)** _____ The IS department
- **c)** _____ Trade associations in our industry
- **d)** _____ Vendors we regularly do business with

2)   Channel participants may also be considered as customers.
- **a)** _____ True
- **b)** _____ False

3) Before creating a strategy to use Internet communication with an external party, we should
   a) _____ Call in a consultant
   b) _____ Develop tactics for communication
   c) _____ Asses communication needs
   d) _____ Create security systems

4) External parties may have both information and transaction needs that can be automated through Internet communication.
   a) _____ True
   b) _____ False

5) Merrimack College has examples of which of the following?
   a) _____ Partnerships
   b) _____ Existing relationships
   c) _____ Credit card transaction vendors
   d) _____ Distribution vendors
   e) _____ All of these

6) Possible external e-commerce vendors include:
   a) _____ Database hosting services
   b) _____ Credit card processing companies
   c) _____ Product distribution companies
   d) _____ All of these

LAB
3.4

C H A P T E R   3

TEST YOUR THINKING

The projects in this section use the skills you've acquired in this chapter. The answers to these projects are available to instructors only through a Prentice Hall sales representative and are intended to be used in a classroom discussion and assessment.

1) Assess current internal organizational situations, including operations, competition, current usage, staffing responsibilities, and opportunities for transforming business processes. Assembling these topics into a single report, what is a possible overall strategy for utilization of Internet communications?

2) Assess external parties, including existing relationships, partnerships, channel participants, and e-commerce vendors. Assemble these topics into the same report and add it to a possible overall strategy for utilization of Internet communications.

3) With a strategy now in place, consider current internal economics and add that to the plan. Will the current financial situation affect the strategy?

4) Assess financial justification for Internet communication based on the replacement of traditional variable-cost media with fixed-cost Internet communications. Compare this assessment to the economic strategy mentioned in item 3. Can the justification affect the strategy?

CHAPTER 4

WEB SITE ARCHITECTURE

Hold a mirror up to Nature.

—*Hamlet*, William Shakespeare

In this chapter, we return to the details of building Internet communications. The quote from *Hamlet* must be given strong consideration in this process. Successful Web communication should reflect successful traditional communication activities.

Internet communication must be based on the basics discussed earlier in this book. Audience wants, needs, and desires must be fulfilled. To build or design Web sites and other elements requires a foundation based on audiences and their information goals. If this is accomplished, then the audience will participate in the effort.

This chapter introduces a process that is useful for building Internet communication efforts that will be used by audiences. The first lab helps draw a comparison between mapping physical movements and movements on a Web site. The second lab uses a scenario to document current successful communication as a way to build Internet communication models. The third lab introduces a reversed method of building Web sites based on the audience information objective.

LAB 4.1

USING MAPPING TO BUILD PRESENTATIONS

LAB OBJECTIVES

After this lab, you will be able to

- Describe Movements in the Physical World
- Map in the Physical World
- Provide Directions on the Internet
- Map a Web Site Visit

The Internet is rife with road analogies for good reason. Though it is really made up of clients, networks, and servers, the road analogy works well for envisioning the information exchanges that take place. A road analogy is useful for envisioning and describing movements through information and transaction presentations.

Presenting information and interactivity on the Internet is similar in many ways to giving directions to a driver trying to find a specific physical location. Like the driver of a car trying to find an address, end users on the Internet must be presented with an easy-to-follow route to their information goal.

The road analogy can be used to help describe and build Web site interactions. Every Web site has a URL (uniform resource locator) or address that is particular to that site. This address can be found by anyone on the Internet and brings up the Web site's home or index page. This address is similar to a major interstate highway that any driver can find on a map. From there an exit is usually involved to bring drivers off the main highway into a smaller section of roads in a town or neighborhood. Links off a home page serve a similar role on the Internet, bringing users closer to the information they seek based on their audience needs. From this point, a series of turns or other directions lead a driver to the desired location. The same is true on the Internet, though the number of steps should be as small as possible to facilitate the process and not frustrate or confuse the end users.

Navigational aides, such as landmarks and road signs are usually included in driving directions as well. These types of elements can and should be involved in the construction of an Internet communications effort to facilitate audience access to information goals.

Directions are usually given from the perspective of the driver. The same is true with Web sites. They must be designed for the convenience of the end user. Different drivers may have different routes and different goals. The same is true on the Internet. Different audiences will have different goals requiring different presentations directing them to their goals.

Building Internet communications efforts can be facilitated through the use of flow charts to document information presentations. The end user's travel, route, or journey through the presentation can be designed using this system. A reverse engineering process will be used in this chapter to demonstrate these concepts. Reverse engineering is a process in which a final version of a project is deconstructed into its smaller parts to see how it was built. A currently active Web site can be reverse engineered to demonstrate the information goals sought by a particular audience and the route an audience member must take to reach that goal. We can look at existing Web sites and build directions and flow charts based on their presentations.

LAB 4.1 EXERCISES

4.1.1 DESCRIBE MOVEMENTS IN THE PHYSICAL WORLD

To demonstrate mapping Internet communication, let's take a look at how mapping is done in the physical world. Write down directions to a physical location like your house, school, or workplace from a major interstate highway.

a) What is the interstate highway?

b) What exit do you use to get to your location and what does the exit sign say?

c) What are the rest of the directions and landmarks involved?

d) Is there a more complicated route that you are not explaining?

e) What is the final location?

4.1.2 MAP IN THE PHYSICAL WORLD

Now let's create a diagram or flow chart of this set of directions. Fill in the squares and connect them according to the directions listed in the previous exercise. If necessary, disregard unneeded boxes or add more.

a) Write the interstate highway number in the square in the upper left square. What does the flow chart look like?

b) Write the final location in the bottom right square. What does the flow chart look like?

c) Fill in the exit number and what the signs say next to the highway number box and connect the two boxes with an arrow. What does the flow chart look like?

d) Fill in the rest of the directions and any landmarks, with each direction in separate squares. How does this affect the flow chart?

e) Connect the squares in order until you reach the final location. What does the flow chart look like?

4.1.3 PROVIDE DIRECTIONS ON THE INTERNET

Now let's begin mapping on the Internet by describing a set of directions to the information we regularly access.

Point your Web browser to the home page of your favorite Web site.

a) Who operates the Web site?

b) What is the URL or Web site address?

c) What is the first link you click to access your information objective?

d) What are the additional links or steps you took to reach your information objective?

List any icons or other landmarks that you could or did use to reach your information objective.

a) How can they be described?

b) What was your information objective?

4.1.4 MAP A WEB SITE VISIT

Using the same grid of boxes, build a flow chart of your visit to the Web site.

a) Fill in the Web site home page in the upper left box. What does the flow chart look like?

b) Write your information objective in the lower right box. What does the flow chart look like?

c) Add the first link or other action you took to reach your information objective. How does this affect the appearance of the flow chart?

d) Add any additional links or steps you took to reach your information objective to individual boxes and connect the boxes in a linear fashion. What does the flow chart look like now?

e) Add any icons or other landmarks that you could or did use to reach your information objective in the appropriate box. How does this add to the appearance of the flow chart?

LAB 4.1 EXERCISE ANSWERS

4.1.1 ANSWERS

To demonstrate mapping Internet communication, let's take a look at how mapping is done in the physical world. Write down directions to a physical location like your house, school, or workplace from a major interstate highway.

a) What is the interstate highway?

Answer: Your situation will be specific to your physical location. In describing the directions to my school, the closest interstate highway is Rt. 495 in Massachusetts. This is the best route for people coming from the north, east, and west. Another major highway is Rt. 93. This is the best route for people coming from the south.

In my situation, two different audiences utilize two different sets of directions to get to the same place. It is apparent that different audiences require different routes to reach their goals. This is also true in Web site presentations. Different audiences require different presentations to meet their communication goals.

b) What exit do you use to get to your location and what does the exit sign say?

Answer: Your answer will be different. My answer for the first set of directions is exit 42A, which is Rt. 114 East. The second set of directions would be exit 41, which connects to Rt. 125 North.

c) What are the rest of the directions and landmarks involved?

Answer: Again, your answers will vary. My directions for the first group are to proceed straight through a number of traffic lights and the college campus will be on the right. Landmarks include a large hill and an Italian restraunt on the left before the campus on the right. In the second set the driver is to take a right off the exit. Next the driver proceeds several miles to the junction of Rt. 114 and Rt. 125, where the college is on the left. I usually tell people to start anticipating the intersection once development starts after a long undeveloped stretch of road.

d) Is there a more complicated route that you are not explaining?

Answer: Your answers will vary from mine. For both sets of directions, other routes exist that may be shorter or more direct coming from other directions.

These different routes involve more complicated steps, including multiple turns and confusing intersections. Often directions that are given to a driver provide the easiest route to a location. And that easiest set of directions is given from the driver's perspective. It is the people giving directions that decide the easiest route based on the driver's needs, not their own.

This is also our role in building Internet communications systems. They should be built to present information in the easiest fashion, from the end user's perspective.

e) What is the final location?

Answer: Your answer will be based on your situation. The final location for my directions is Merrimack College in North Andover, Massachusetts.

The final location for Web end users should be their information objective. It is up to us as Web communications experts to facilitate that objective as much as possible.

4.1.2 ANSWERS

Now let's create a diagram or flow chart of this set of directions. Fill in the squares and connect them according to the directions listed in the previous exercise. If necessary, disregard unneeded boxes or add more.

a) Write the interstate highway number in the square in the upper left square. What does the flow chart look like?

Answer: Yours will vary. I've included both sets of directions in this exercise so mine looks like this:

b) Write the final location in the bottom right square. What does the flow chart look like?

Answer: Again yours will vary. Here's mine:

c) Fill in the exit number and what the signs say next to the highway number box and connect the two boxes with an arrow. What does the flow chart look like?

Answer: Yours will be based on your situation but will look similar to this:

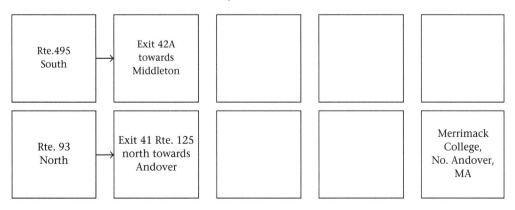

d)   Fill in the rest of the directions and any landmarks, with each direction in separate squares. How does this affect the flow chart?

Answer: Your answer will vary but should look something like this:

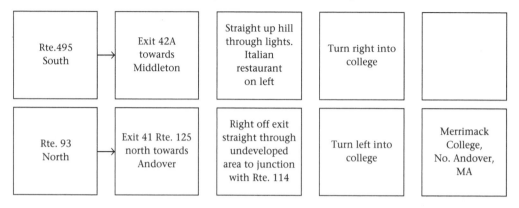

e)   Connect them in order until you reach the final location. What does the flow chart look like?

Answer: Again, your answer will differ. Mine looks like this:

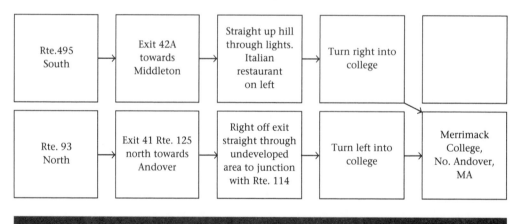

4.1.3   ANSWERS

Now let's look at mapping on the Internet by building a set of directions to the information we regularly access.

Point your Web browser to the home page of your favorite Web site.

a)   Who operates the Web site?

Answer: Your answer will be different based on your favorite Web site. My answer is CNN's Web site.

b) What is the URL or Web site address?

Answer: Yours will vary accordingly. Mine is www.cnn.com

c) What is the first link you click to access your information objective?

Answer: Your answer will be based on your specifications. In my situation I clicked on a link to the weather section.

d) What are the additional links or steps you took to reach your information objective?

Answer: You will have a different experience. In my situation a screen came up that provided a form to fill in my zip code or closest city, which I did. After pressing the submit button, a database interaction produced a screen with the latest weather information and a forecast for my city.

List any icons or other landmarks that you could or did use to reach your information objective.

a) How can they be described?

Answer: Your answer will differ. In my situation, I clicked on the word "weather" in a list of general topics on the index page of the site. The next screen I saw had a heading, text, graphics, and advertisements related to weather.

b) What was your information objective?

Answer: Your answer will define why this is your favorite site; mine is the local weather.

4.1.4 ANSWERS

Using the same grid of boxes, build a flow chart of your visit to the Web site.

a) Fill in the Web site home page in the upper left box. What does your flow chart look like?

Answer: Yours will vary but should look similiar to this:

**LAB
4.1**

Pulling up a Web site can be likened to a subset of linked pages on the information superhighway. The first step in giving physical directions to describe a single, large location that any person can find on a map. When mapping a Web site visit, the index or home page can serve as that initial starting point. There is only one URL like it on the Internet, and anyone can find it.

b) Write your information objective in the lower right box. What does the flow chart look like?

Answer: Your answer will be different. My flow chart now looks like this:

When building Web sites for Internet communication, it is imperative that the architecture be based on the information objectives of the audience. That is why we listed our objectives on the flow chart first in this exercise.

c) Add the first link or other action you took to reach your information objective. How does this affect the appearance of your flow chart?

Answer: Your answers will vary. My answer was to click on a link to a weather section.

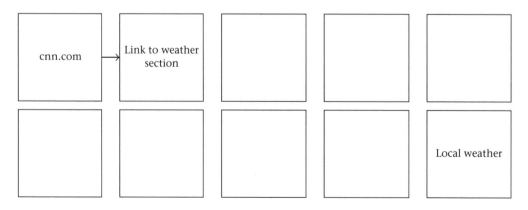

The second step I took here, after pulling up the URL, was to choose a specific grouping of information. Referring to the previous exercise, this can be compared to the exit off the highway. This exit off the index page sends us into a smaller subgroup of information close to our objective.

d) Add any additional links or steps you took to reach your information objective to individual boxes and connect the boxes in a linear fashion. What does the flow chart look like now?

Answer: Your answer will differ. Mine looks like this:

```
┌─────────┐   ┌──────────────┐   ┌──────────────┐   ┌─────────┐   ┌─────────┐
│         │   │              │   │   Weather    │   │         │   │         │
│ cnn.com │──▶│ Link to      │──▶│   database   │   │         │   │         │
│         │   │ weather      │   │   interface  │   │         │   │         │
│         │   │ section      │   │   form       │   │         │   │         │
└─────────┘   └──────────────┘   └──────────────┘   └─────────┘   └─────────┘
                                         └──────────────────────────────▶
┌─────────┐   ┌─────────┐   ┌─────────┐   ┌─────────┐   ┌──────────────┐
│         │   │         │   │         │   │         │   │              │
│         │   │         │   │         │   │         │   │ Local weather│
│         │   │         │   │         │   │         │   │              │
└─────────┘   └─────────┘   └─────────┘   └─────────┘   └──────────────┘
```

This next step actually involved a couple of substeps, which are combined here for clarity's sake. I entered a zip code and pressed the submit button. The database returned the information I was seeking. This is also similar to a physical set of directions that usually include a number of small course changes upon nearing the desired location. Also similar to physical directions, the route to the information goal should be very easy for the end user.

e) Add any icons or other landmarks that you could or did use to reach your information objective in the appropriate box. How does this add to the appearance of the flow chart?

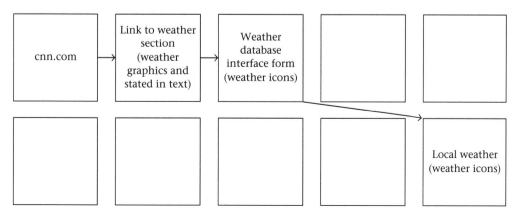

As with landmarks in the physical world, we can help end users of Web sites to locate their information goals with clear and obvious navigational aids. We can also provide appropriate icons, graphics, and information to help identify what information presentations they are currently seeing and how to access other types of information and interaction.

LAB 4.1 SELF-REVIEW QUESTIONS

In order to test your progress, you should be able to answer the following questions:

1) An Internet communications presentation can be described
   a) _____ Using a road directions analogy
   b) _____ Using a flow chart to document and design interactions
   c) _____ By reverse engineering an existing Web site
   d) _____ All of the above

2) Road directions are given from the perspective of the person giving the directions.
   a) _____ True
   b) _____ False

3) A highway exit is similar to
   a) _____ A fork in the road
   b) _____ An communications goal
   c) _____ A link from an index page for an audience to reach a goal
   d) _____ A Web-based transaction system

4) A communications goal is similar to
   a) _____ A link to a subgroup of information
   b) _____ A sought physical location
   c) _____ A search engine
   d) _____ A Web site address

5) When mapping a presentation, the following are useful:
   a) _____ Flow charts
   b) _____ Arrows directing the end user's movements
   c) _____ Documenting the information presentations and exchanges
   d) _____ None of these
   e) _____ All of these

6) Building a successful communications effort requires
   a) _____ A lot of cool graphics
   b) _____ As many Web pages as possible
   c) _____ The use of many clever ideas
   d) _____ Delivery of audience communication goals

L A B   4 . 2

DETERMINING AND MAPPING INFORMATION EXCHANGES AND PRESENTATIONS

LAB OBJECTIVES

After this lab, you will be able to

- Catalog Current Successful Communications
- Map Current Communications
- Convert Traditional Information Exchanges to Internet Exchanges

---

Moving forward in Internet communication construction, we can begin to build new communications systems using the mapping concepts from the previous lab. Again, this process must include the audience involved and the communications goal of that audience.

An excellent tool for many Web communicators is to catalog and map current successful communications. A flow chart can be used for each audience. This process involves documenting each interaction with a customer or audience member.

The information exchange that takes place is included in each box of a flow chart. Informational content is included as the subject matter involved in each exchange. Captured or supplied information, such as customer contact information or product details, should also be included in this cataloging process. Communications techniques, including phone, fax, mail, etc., that are utilized in each interchange should also be documented in the appropriate part of the flow chart or map.

Once this is completed for every step in a communications model, communications goals can be determined for each audience involved. These communications goals serve as the final box in a mapped communication effort.

This mapping of current efforts is then used to develop communications efforts, ideas, and solutions that shift traditional communication efforts communication onto the Internet. Internet technology can be applied to specific situations to build Internet communications systems that replicate traditional media efforts and fulfill audience goals.

LAB 4.2 EXERCISES

4.2.1 CATALOG CURRENT SUCCESSFUL COMMUNICATIONS

Refer to this scenario from the Webmaster Certificate Program at Merrimack College when answering the following questions.

One of the audiences that we communicate with regularly in the operation of the Webmaster Certificate Program at Merrimack College is prospective students who are responding to a referral or other type of advertising about the program. They are interested in the program when they contact us by phone or e-mail. They usually communicate with us in three separate communications using the same methods. The objective of our information exchanges is a class registration based on their needs.

The first time they contact us they are interested in general information. The most prevalent questions pertain to costs, class meeting formats, length of commitment to receive a certificate, and what skills are taught. After capturing their contact information we forward a catalog and schedule of classes by mail.

Once this information is in our database, we forward regular mailings of new schedules and class information. If we do not hear from a prospective student again, we try to follow up with a phone call after a reasonable amount of time, usually 2-3 weeks.

When we do hear from students again, the second interaction usually involves academic advising. Students ask specific questions about what classes they should take. Answers are given based on their education goals and existing skill sets.

Next, a student moves forward in the cycle and registers for a class. This happens two ways in our program. Many students register over the phone by updating any incomplete contact information, supplying a social security number, and paying tuition using a credit card. Some students register using a tuition extension model that involves a contractual commitment. Normally students request the appropriate form, which is specific for each course, and receive the form by fax. They then return the completed form to complete the transaction. A confirmation letter is forwarded via mail after the registration is completed.

> **a)** Who is the audience involved in this communications cycle?
>
> **b)** What information is captured in the first interaction with prospective students?
>
> **c)** What are the questions and answers in the first interaction?
>
> **d)** What are the vehicles for the first information exchange?
>
> **e)** What communication may take place between the first and second interaction?
>
> **f)** What is the content exchanged in the second interaction?
>
> **g)** What are the vehicles for this exchange?
>
> **h)** What is the content exchanged in the third interaction?
>
> **i)** What are the vehicles for this interaction?
>
> **j)** What is the final outcome of this interaction?
>
> **k)** What is the last communication?

4.2.2 MAP CURRENT COMMUNICATIONS

Referring to the previous lab, which discussed mapping of information presentations, build a map of the information described in Exercise 4.2.1 using traditional media. Utilize the flow chart and the information from the previous exercise to complete this exercise.

a) What is the audience of this information exchange?

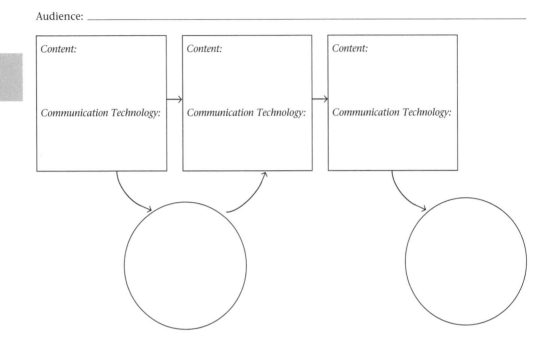

b) Based on the first exchange in the previous exercise, what is the information content in the first box of this diagram?

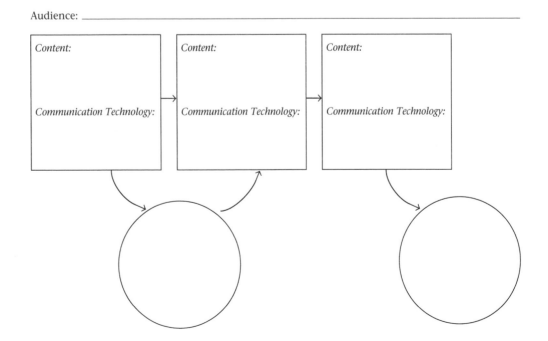

c) What are the communication technologies used in the first box?

Audience: _____

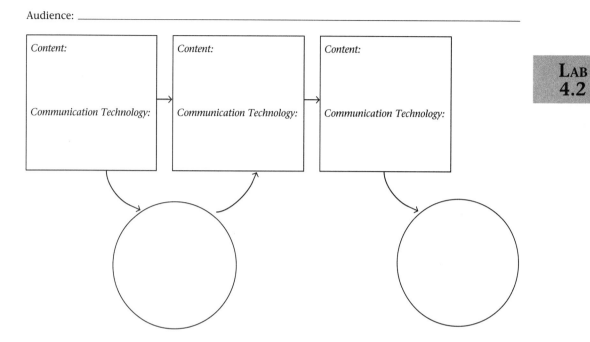

d) What communications activity could be included in the small circle adjacent to the first box?

Audience: _____

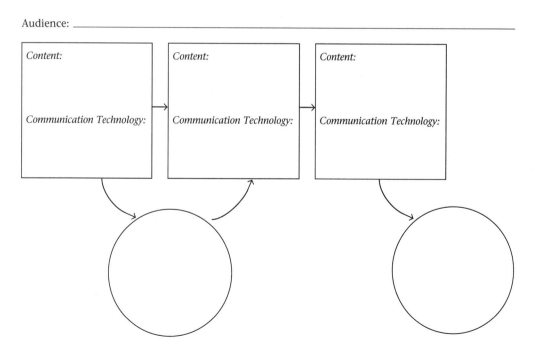

e) Based on the second exchange in the previous exercise, what is the informational content of the second box?

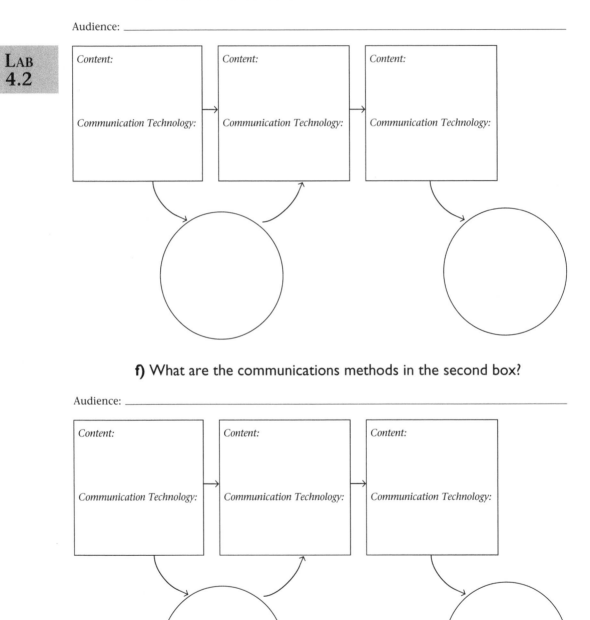

Audience: _____

Content:

Communication Technology:

Content:

Communication Technology:

Content:

Communication Technology:

f) What are the communications methods in the second box?

Audience: _____

Content:

Communication Technology:

Content:

Communication Technology:

Content:

Communication Technology:

g) Based on the third exchange in the previous exercise, what is the informational content of the third box?

Audience: _____

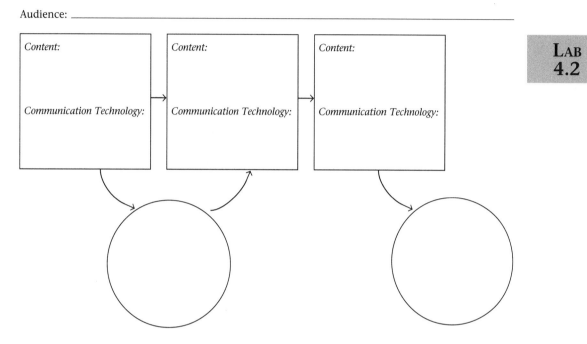

h) What are the communications methods in the third box?

Audience: _____

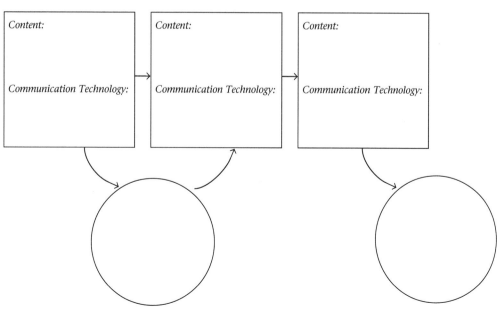

i) What is the purpose behind the last box's interactions?

_____

_____

j) What communication could be included in the small circle adjacent to the third box?

Audience: _____

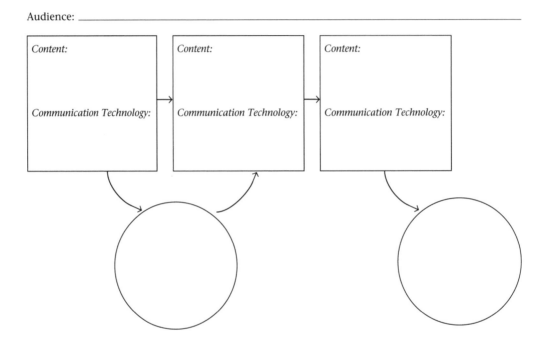

4.2.3 CONVERT TRADITIONAL INFORMATION EXCHANGES TO INTERNET EXCHANGES

a) What is the potential Web audience involved in this communications cycle?

b) How can the Internet be used to facilitate the first exchange?

c) How can the Internet be used to facilitate the smaller boxes in the map?

d) How can the Internet be used to facilitate the second exchange?

e) How can the Internet be used to facilitate the third exchange?

f) How can the Internet be used to complete the overall goal of the interchanges?

LAB 4.2 EXERCISE ANSWERS

4.2.1 ANSWERS

Refer to this scenario from the Webmaster Certificate Program at Merrimack College when answering the following questions.

One of the audiences that we communicate with regularly in the operation of the Webmaster Certificate Program at Merrimack College is prospective students who are responding to a referral or other type of advertising about the program. They are interested in the program when they contact us by phone or e-mail. They usually communicate with us in three separate communications using the same methods. The objective of our information exchanges is a class registration based on their needs.

The first time they contact us they are interested in general information. The most prevalent questions pertain to costs, class meeting formats, length of commitment to receive a certificate, and what skills are taught. After capturing their contact information we forward a catalog and schedule of classes by mail.

Once this information is in our database, we forward regular mailings of new schedules and class information. If we do not hear from a prospective student again, we try to follow up with a phone call after a reasonable time, usually 2-3 weeks.

When we do hear from students again, the second interaction usually involves academic advising. Students ask specific questions about what classes they should take. Answers are given based on their education goals and existing skill sets.

Next, a student moves forward in the cycle and registers for a class. This happens two ways in our program. Many students register over the phone by updating any incomplete contact information, supplying a social security number, and paying tuition using a credit card. Some students register using a tuition extension model that involves a contractual commitment. Normally students request the appropriate form, which is specific for each course, and receive the form by fax. They then return the completed form to complete the transaction. In both methods, a confirmation letter is forwarded via mail after the registration is completed.

a)   Who is the audience involved in this communications cycle?

Answer: The audience in this communications example is prospective students for the Webmaster Certificate Program responding to a marketing program.

b)   What information is captured in the first interaction with prospective students?

Answer: Contact information is captured.

c)   What are the questions and answers in the first interaction?

Answer: Questions and answers include costs, class meeting formats, length of commitment to receive a certificate, and what skills are taught.

d)   What are the vehicles for the first information exchange?

Answer: The vehicles for information exchange are phone and e-mail for direct communication and traditional mail for hard copy fulfillment of catalog and schedule materials.

e)   What communication may take place between the first and second interaction?

Answer: If a prospective student responds to a marketing effort but does not contact us again, we follow up with a phone call.

f)   What is the content exchanged in the second interaction?

Answer: The second interaction involves academic advising based on the student's situation, goals, and current skill sets.

g)   What are the vehicles for this exchange?

Answer: The vehicles for this exchange are phone and e-mail.

h)   What is the content exchanged in the third interaction?

Answer: The third interaction involves course registrations. Interactions include either capturing contact, course selection, and payment information or the exchange of a registration and tuition extension form.

i) What are the vehicles for this interaction?

Answer: The vehicles for this communication are situational and include phone, e-mail, fax, and mail.

j) What is the final outcome of this interaction?

Answer: The final outcome of this interaction is a completed course registration.

k) What is the last communication?

Answer: The last communication in this cycle is the forwarding of a confirmation letter to the student via mail based on the outcome of the registration.

LAB
4.2

4.2.2 ANSWERS

Referring to the previous lab, which discussed mapping of information presentations, build a map of the information described in Exercise 4.2.1 using traditional media. Utilize the flow chart and the information from the previous lab to complete this exercise.

a) What is the audience of this information exchange?

Answer: Prospective students can be added to the title of this flow chart.

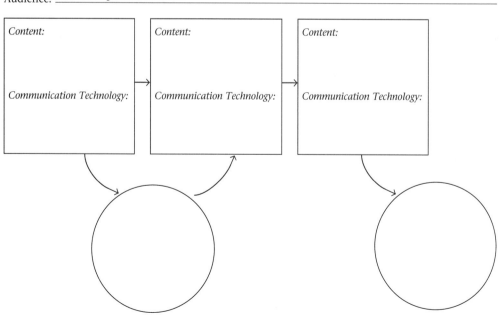

Audience: _____ Prospective students _____

| Content: | Content: | Content: |

| Communication Technology: | Communication Technology: | Communication Technology: |

b) Based on the first exchange in the previous exercise, what is the information content in the first box of this diagram?

Answer: Contact information is captured. Information exchanged in the first box is basic information answering prevalent questions including costs, class meeting formats, length of commitment to receive a certificate, and what skills are taught.

Audience: _____ Prospective students _____

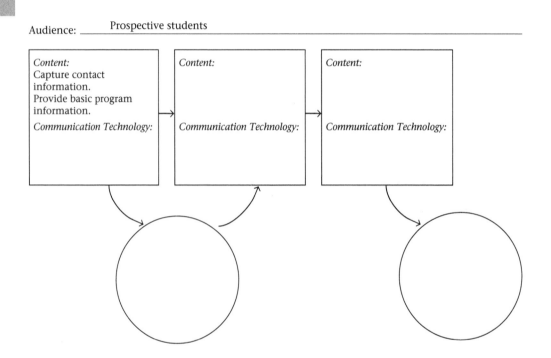

c) What are the communication technologies used in the first box?

Answer: Currently, this communication is completed by phone, e-mail, and hard copy fulfillment of catalogs and schedules.

Audience: _____ Prospective students

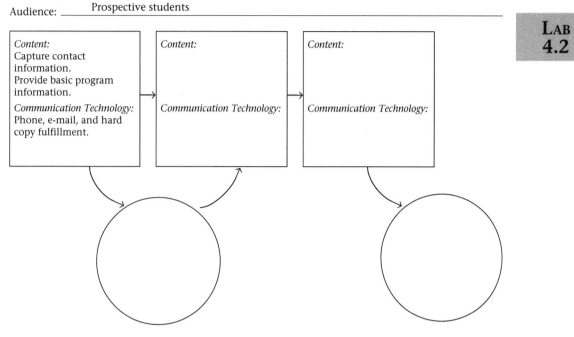

d) What communications activity could be included in the small circle adjacent to the first box?

Audience: _____ Prospective students

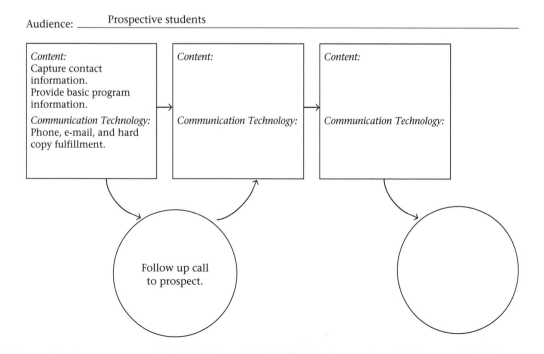

e) Based on the second exchange in the previous exercise, what is the informational content of the second box?

Answer: The second box includes academic information discussing individual course choices based on student needs and skill levels.

LAB 4.2

Audience:  Prospective students

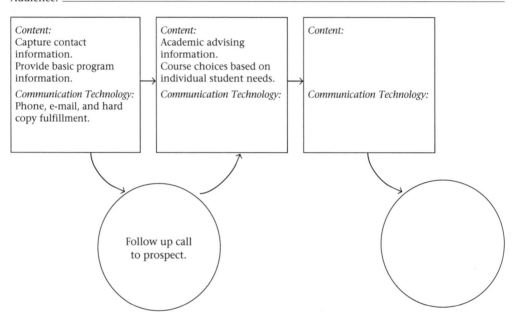

Content:
Capture contact information.
Provide basic program information.

Communication Technology:
Phone, e-mail, and hard copy fulfillment.

Content:
Academic advising information.
Course choices based on individual student needs.

Communication Technology:

Content:

Communication Technology:

Follow up call to prospect.

f)   What are the communications methods in the second box?

Answer: The communications methods used now are phone and e-mail.

Audience: _____ Prospective students _____

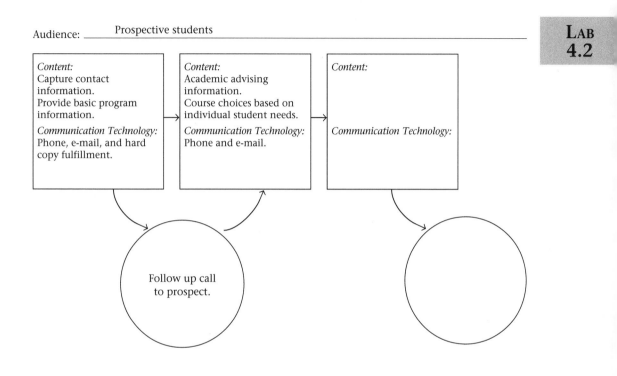

Content:
Capture contact
information.
Provide basic program
information.

Communication Technology:
Phone, e-mail, and hard
copy fulfillment.

Content:
Academic advising
information.
Course choices based on
individual student needs.

Communication Technology:
Phone and e-mail.

Content:

Communication Technology:

Follow up call
to prospect.

g) Based on the third exchange in the previous exercise, what is the informational content of the third box?

Answer: The third box involves registration. Additional information is captured and completed, including course selections, payments, and contractual agreements.

LAB 4.2

Audience: _____ Prospective students _____

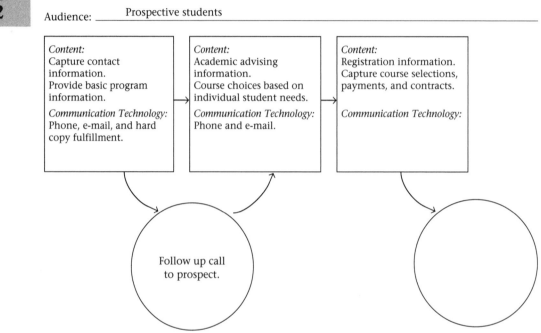

h) What are the communications methods in the third box?

Answer: This process involves phone, e-mail, and faxing of documents.

Audience: _____ Prospective students _____

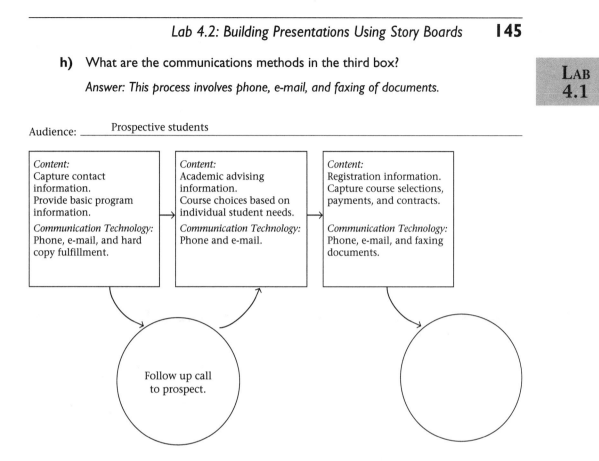

| Content: Capture contact information. Provide basic program information. *Communication Technology:* Phone, e-mail, and hard copy fulfillment. |
| Content: Academic advising information. Course choices based on individual student needs. *Communication Technology:* Phone and e-mail. |
| Content: Registration information. Capture course selections, payments, and contracts. *Communication Technology:* Phone, e-mail, and faxing documents. |

Follow up call to prospect.

i) What is the purpose behind the last box's interactions?

Answer: The purpose behind the last interactions and the whole process is to complete student registrations.

**LAB
4.1**

j)   What communication could be included in the small circle adjacent to the third box?

Answer: The forwarding of individual confirmation letters by mail.

Audience: _____ Prospective students _____

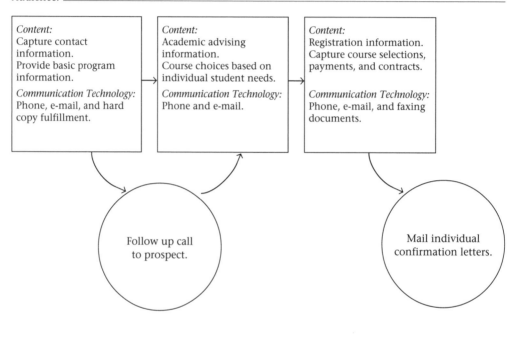

4.2.3 ANSWERS

a)   What is the potential Web audience involved in this communications cycle?

Answer: Any prospective student who also has Internet access, which is likely.

b)   How can the Internet be used to facilitate the first exchange?

Answer: The first exchange involves information capture and presentation. Both can be accomplished over the Internet.

A form can be utilized to capture contact information in the student database. Course catalogs, schedules, and information answering the prevalent questions can be presented in text or graphic formats.

c) How can the Internet be used to facilitate the circles in the map?

Answer: In both situations, e-mail can be substituted for the communication. A follow-up e-mail could be automatically generated based on the time involved. A course confirmation can be created and forwarded via e-mail, replacing the hard copy version now created by the database and forwarded via mail.

d) How can the Internet be used to facilitate the second exchange?

Answer: A Web presentation could be designed to present academic advising information and course recommendations based on current skill levels and goals.

A static system with scenarios could be presented or a question and answer format could be presented utilizing forms and a database. E-mail could also be used for individual attention.

e) How can the Internet be used to facilitate the third exchange?

Answer: The third exchange could be accomplished via the Web using forms and the student database, similar to the transaction model from amazon.com. If a contract is needed, a Web page could be used for authorization and be printable for student records. A downloadable or printable page that could be returned by fax could be used as well.

f) How can the Internet be used to complete the overall goal of the interchanges?

Answer: The goal of the interchange is to complete registration transactions, and these can be facilitated and completed using Internet communication.

LAB 4.2 SELF-REVIEW QUESTIONS

In order to test your progress, you should be able to answer the following questions:

1) An excellent tool for developing Web site architecture is
    a) _____ A cool-looking home page
    b) _____ A flow chart documenting current communication activiites
    c) _____ A strategic plan for incorporating partnerships
    d) _____ A mandate from upper management on company structure

2) The communications goal of the audience member is not included in the mapping process.
    a) _____ True
    b) _____ False

3) Mapping current communications efforts should include
   a) _____ Audiences involved
   b) _____ Informational content involved in each interchange
   c) _____ Communications methods used
   d) _____ All of these

4) Mapping current efforts can lead to
   a) _____ Flow charts of information exchanges
   b) _____ Development of audience communications goals
   c) _____ A process to shift communication to Internet methods
   d) _____ All of these

5) Internet communication can replace
   a) _____ Hard copy fulfillment of materials
   b) _____Traditional letters
   c) _____ Informational presentations
   d) _____ Traditional transaction processes like phone purchasing
   e) _____ All of these

LAB 4.3

BUILDING PRESENTATIONS USING STORY BOARDS

LAB OBJECTIVES

After this lab, you will be able to

- Put Audience Objectives First
- Create Story Boards
- Use Story Boards for Internet Presentations

The next steps in building Internet communications efforts after mapping current activities include two major parts. The first activity utilizes a planning device to make sure that audience communication goals are the most significant part of any Web site or other effort. The second activity involves the development of actual story boards of the Web presentation involved.

When pulling together the architecture of a Web site, it is useful to refer to the four major aspects of the audience being targeted with Web communication:

Who—the identification of the audience members

What—the information they are seeking

Why—the communications objective of the audience member, which may be defined as information but also could be a transaction of some kind

How—the communications technologies being utilized to complete the exchange

These audience-targeting concepts should be well defined and documented when building a Web site to meet audience needs. Every step in the development of Web communications should continue to recognize audience goals. They are the primary purpose of building the presentation. A useful planning device is to design the presentation by starting at the audience goal and working backward to the beginning of the interchange. This way, the goal comes first and the rest of the presentation is built to facilitate this goal.

Looking back at the flow charts from the previous exercises, an easy way to demonstrate this concept is to reverse the arrows on the charts, especially that in Exercise 4.1.4. Reversing the flow of the information exchange puts the goal first and the index page last in the flow chart.

Building Web architecture can also utilize a concept from the film industry, story boards. Story boards are used to develop visual scenes in movies and other presentations. Directors draw a series of pictures to tell a story and then shoot film that re-creates this story. This process is also used in multimedia presentations. A modified version using flow charts to design Web presentations is discussed here. Some Web developers also create visual representations of Web pages to further define the presentations while building a site.

These story boards are titled with the audience they are designed to reach and contain three significant elements:

Informational content of each exchange with the audience members

Communications technologies involved

Navigational aids involved

Additional elements, such as e-mail interactions, should also be included when appropriate. Navigational elements involve icons and links that help the end users reach their communication goals easily and move around the presentation to reach other information. Like landmarks and street signs, navigational aides should be developed from the audience perspective.

LAB 4.3 EXERCISES

4.3.1 PUT AUDIENCE OBJECTIVES FIRST

Let's revisit targeting audience communication objectives to begin the process of constructing a Web site. Answer the following questions in regard to your favorite Web sites.

a) What audience are you a member of when you visit this site?

b) What specific information are you seeking?

c) What outcome are you looking for in this communication?

d) How is the information presented?

e) What, therefore, is the primary purpose of this section of your favorite Web site?

f) Where should you begin when constructing an Internet communications effort?

4.3.2 CREATE STORY BOARDS

To demonstrate how Web sites and Internet interactions can be constructed from the objective of the audience members, reverse engineer the flow chart from Exercise 4.1.4, depicting your visit to your favorite Web site. Use the following grid to build story boards of the Web site by including the information objectives, the presentations you saw, the ways that the information was presented, and the navigation options available. *Hint:* Reverse the arrows on the flow chart and start in the bottom right corner.

a) Who is the audience targeted by this presentation?

b) What information is now in the first box in the flow chart?

c) What presentation technology was involved?

d) What navigational elements were present?

e) What appears in the last box in the flow chart?

f) What navigational elements were present? (You don't need to list every one here but may want to in an actual construction situation.)

g) What presentation technology was involved?

h) What are the steps in between?

i) What presentation technologies were involved at each step?

j) What navigational elements were present at each step?

4.3.3 USE STORY BOARDS FOR INTERNET PRESENTATION ARCHITECTURE

Create a Web site story board of the information interchanges from the previous lab. Suggest possible information exchange technologies and navigational options.

Audience: _____

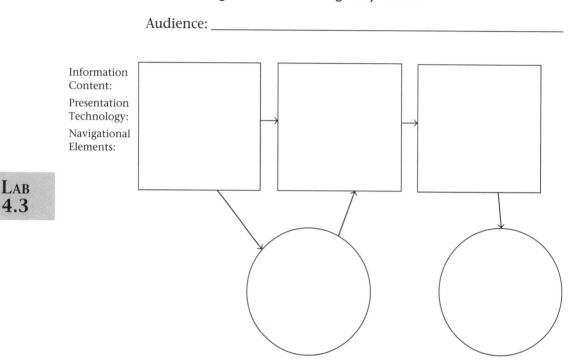

Information
Content:

Presentation
Technology:

Navigational
Elements:

**LAB
4.3**

a) Who is the audience targeted by this presentation?

b) What information content should be listed in the first box?

c) What communication technologies should be listed in the first box?

d) What navigational elements could be listed in the first box?

e) What about the smaller circles?

f) What information content should be listed in the second box?

g) What presentation technologies should be listed in the second box?

h) What navigational elements could be listed in the second box?

i) What information content should be listed in the third box?

j) What presentation technologies should be listed in the third box?

k) What navigational elements could be listed in the third box?

LAB 4.3 EXERCISE ANSWERS

4.3.1 ANSWERS

Let's revisit targeting audience communication objectives to begin the process of constructing a Web site. Answer the following questions in regard to your favorite Web sites.

a)   What audience are you a member of when you visit this site?

Answer: Your answer will vary. I am a member of the general Internet audience interested in updated weather information.

This was explained as the *who* in Chapter 2. The audience is always the first issue in building Internet communications systems.

b)   What specific information are you seeking?

Answer: Your answer will probably be different. Mine is the immediate and extended weather forecast for my physical location.

This was discussed as the *what* in Chapter 2—the information that fulfills the audience's wants, needs, and desires.

c)   What outcome are you looking for in this communication?

Answer: My outcome is to receive the information I am seeking. This is my communication goal. Your outcome may be information as well or it may be a transaction of some kind.

This communication goal was explained as the *why* in Chapter 2. The outcome may be informational, which is the case in this example. Or the outcome my be a transaction, as it was in the previous lab. Either way, this goal must be considered when building Internet communications efforts.

d)   How is the information presented?

Answer: Your answer will depend on the Web site involved. In my situation, the information is presented by a database using text, graphics of weather maps, and a small video file showing maps with moving weather patterns.

This answer documents how the information was presented. Determining information presentation to serve the audience goals is another vital part of this process.

e) What, therefore, is the primary purpose of this section of your favorite Web site?

Answer: Your answer will be based on your communication goal. In my case the primary purpose for this section of the cnn.com site is to deliver pertinent weather information.

Our objective in creating effective Web and Internet communication systems is to deliver the information sought by the audience as quickly and as easily as possible.

f) Where should you begin when constructing an Internet communications effort?

Answer: The construction of an Internet communications effort should begin at the point where information or other goals are delivered to the audience that seeks them.

Everything else in a Web site or other type of effort should be geared toward facilitating this goal. This involves building efficient and effective delivery mechanisms and presentations that provide the information goals for the audiences involved. An excellent way to begin building Web site presentations is first to determine the who, what, why, and how of the information exchanges and then work outward from these goals using story boards.

4.3.2 ANSWERS

To demonstrate how Web sites and Internet interactions can be constructed from the objective of the audience members, reverse engineer the flow chart from Exercise 4.1.4, depicting your visit to your favorite Web site. Use the following grid to build story boards of the Web site by including the information objectives, the presentations you saw, the ways that the information was presented, and the navigation options available. *Hint:* Reverse the arrows on the flow chart and start in the bottom right corner.

a)   Who is the audience targeted by this presentation?

Answer: Individual Internet users, like myself, who seek weather information for their specific location.

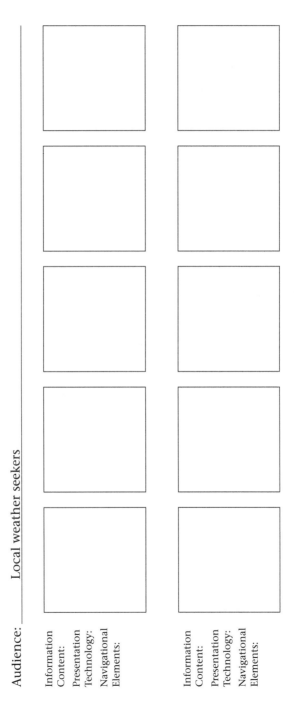

Audience: _____ Local weather seekers

Information Content:
Presentation Technology:
Navigational Elements:

Information Content:
Presentation Technology:
Navigational Elements:

b) What information is now in the first box in the flow chart?

Answer: Weather information based on my geography.

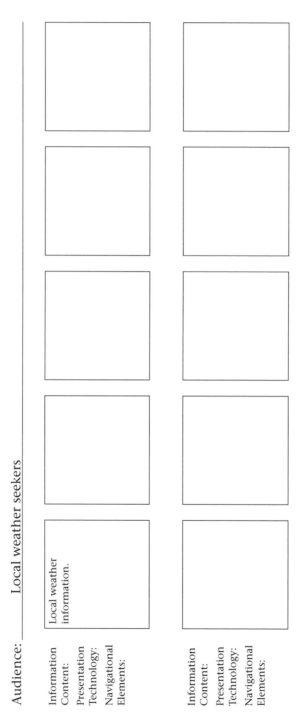

c) What presentation technology was involved?

Answer: A Web page presenting text, graphics, and video culled from a database of information.

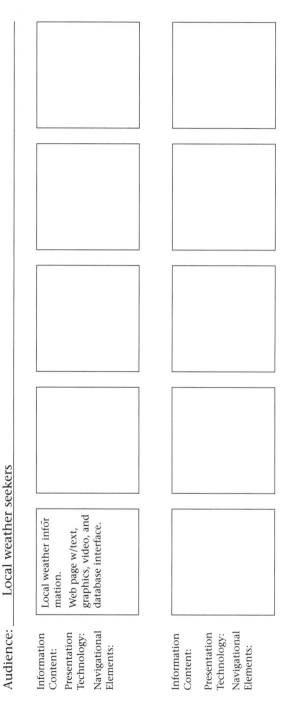

Audience: _____ Local weather seekers

Information Content: Local weather information.

Presentation Technology: Web page w/text, graphics, video, and database interface.

Navigational Elements:

Information Content:

Presentation Technology:

Navigational Elements:

d) What navigational elements were present?

Answer: *Your answer will vary from mine. On the cnn.com site icons and links to other information involved with weather were prevalent as well as links to other topics on the site.*

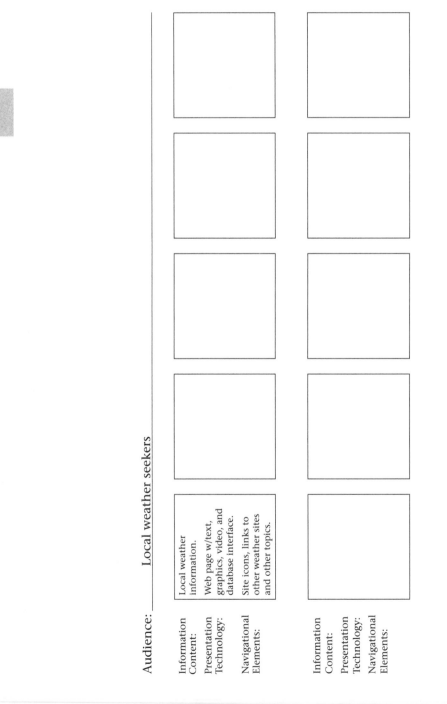

Audience: ___ Local weather seekers

Information Content: Local weather information.

Presentation Technology: Web page w/text, graphics, video, and database interface.

Navigational Elements: Site icons, links to other weather sites and other topics.

Information Content:

Presentation Technology:

Navigational Elements:

A variety of links were available to other information topics on the site, and a consistent graphic appears on each page presented by the site. Sometimes called a navigation bar, this type of navigational tool is used on many Web sites.

e) What appears in the last box in the flow chart?

Answer: Your answer should be the home page of your favorite site. Mine is the index page for cnn.com

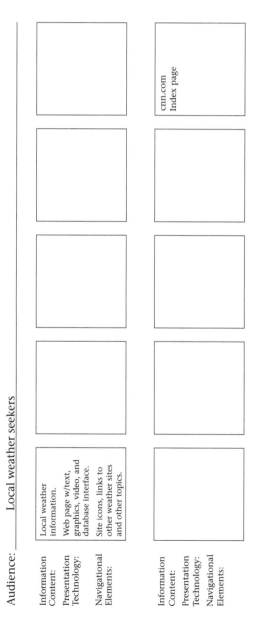

f) What navigational elements were present? (You don't need to list every one here but may want to in an actual construction situation.)

Answer: Your answers will vary. On the cnn.com the navigation bar appears on the first page.

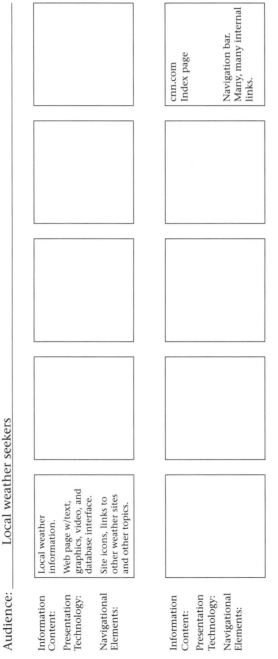

g) What presentation technology was involved?

Answer: The presentation was conducted using a Web page carrying graphics and a form for a search engine.

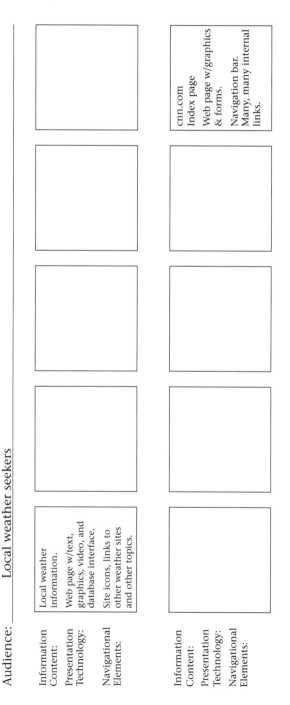

Audience: ___ Local weather seekers

Information Content: Local weather information.

Presentation Technology: Web page w/text, graphics, video, and database interface.

Navigational Elements: Site icons, links to other weather sites and other topics.

Information Content: cnn.com Index page

Presentation Technology: Web page w/graphics & forms.

Navigational Elements: Navigation bar. Many, many internal links.

**LAB
4.3**

h) What are the steps in between?

Answer: Your answer will be based on your flow chart. My steps were very short, just one link to the weather section. A database query form on that page returned my communication goal.

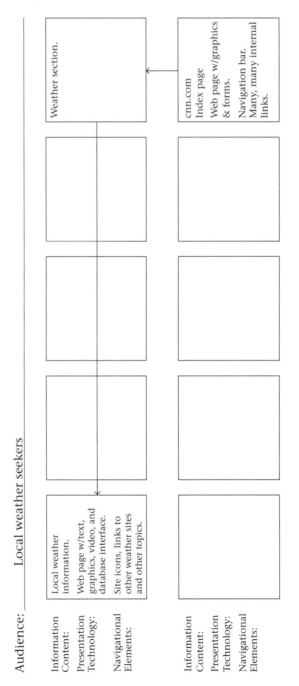

On my flow chart, the middle step was only one step. This is an example of a well-designed Web presentation as the information I sought was delivered to me in an extremely efficient manner.

i) What presentation technologies were involved at each step?

Answer: The information presentation in the middle step was a Web page serving as an interface to a database on weather information.

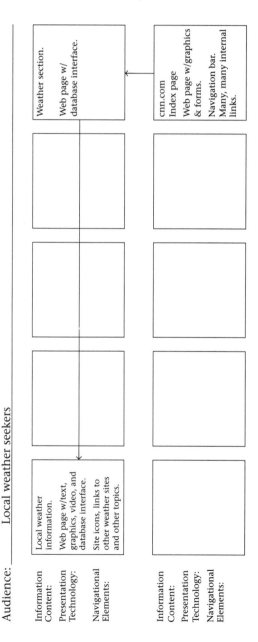

j) What navigational elements were present at each step?

Answer: Your answer will be based on your Web site. In mine, the navigation bar was present on every presentation.

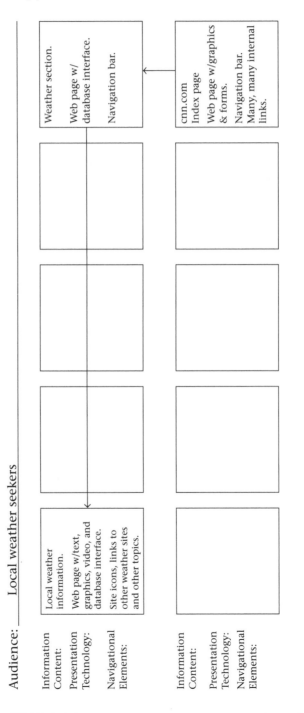

Audience: Local weather seekers

Information Content: Local weather information.

Presentation Technology: Web page w/text, graphics, video, and database interface.

Navigational Elements: Site icons, links to other weather sites and other topics.

Information Content:

Presentation Technology:

Navigational Elements:

Weather section.

Web page w/ database interface.

Navigation bar.

cnn.com
Index page

Web page w/graphics & forms.

Navigation bar.
Many, many internal links.

This flow chart is now serving as a story board of this information exchange. Information, presentation technologies, and navigational information are present for each page in this presentation.

4.3.3 ANSWERS

Create a Web site story board of the information interchanges from the previous lab. Suggest possible information exchange technologies and navigational options.

a)   Who is the audience targeted by this presentation?

Answer: The audience is prospective students.

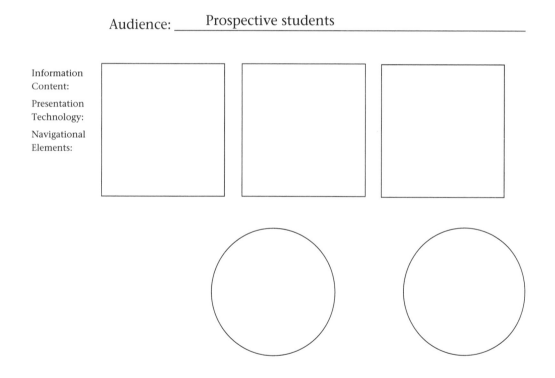

Audience: Prospective students

Information
Content:

Presentation
Technology:

Navigational
Elements:

b) What information content should be listed in the first box?

Answer: The capture of a course registration is the communication goal of this audience. Captured information should include course, contact, and payment information. An option for contractual agreements must also be present.

Audience: ___Prospective students_____

LAB 4.3

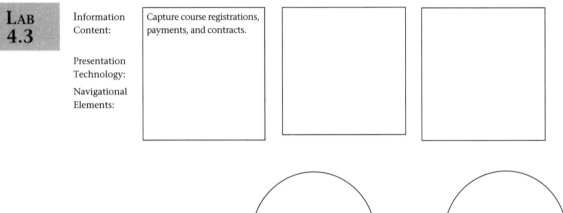

Information Content:

Presentation Technology:

Navigational Elements:

Capture course registrations, payments, and contracts.

c) What communication technologies should be listed in the first box?

Answer: A Web page carrying a form to capture the appropriate information and interact with the student database.

Audience: _____Prospective students_____

Information
Content:

Presentation
Technology:

Navigational
Elements:

Capture course registrations, payments, and contracts.

Web page w/form to interface w/student database.

d) What navigational elements could be listed in the first box?

Answer: A navigation bar leading to other areas of the Web site could be involved. Links to other areas pertinent for this audience, especially back to the previous (or next in this flow chart) presentation providing academic advising information, should also be prevalent.

Audience: _____Prospective students_____

LAB 4.3

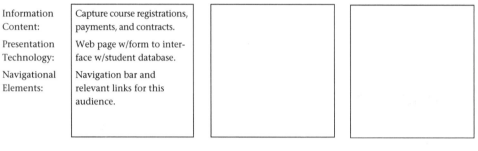

Information Content: Capture course registrations, payments, and contracts.

Presentation Technology: Web page w/form to inter-face w/student database.

Navigational Elements: Navigation bar and relevant links for this audience.

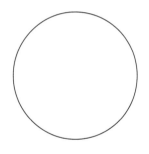

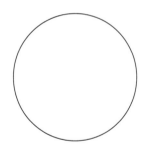

e) What about the circles?

Answer: These circles should include e-mail confirmation in the first and e-mail prospect follow-up in the second.

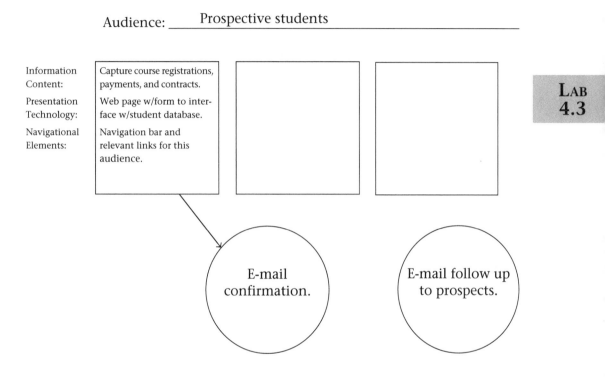

Audience: _____ Prospective students _____

Information Content:

Presentation Technology:

Navigational Elements:

Capture course registrations, payments, and contracts.

Web page w/form to interface w/student database.

Navigation bar and relevant links for this audience.

E-mail confirmation.

E-mail follow up to prospects.

LAB 4.3

f) What information content should be listed in the second box?

Answer: This information presentation should explain course offerings based on audience members' needs and experience. A static presentation could utilize scenarios. A dynamic presentation could use questions and answers from a database.

Audience: ___Prospective students_____

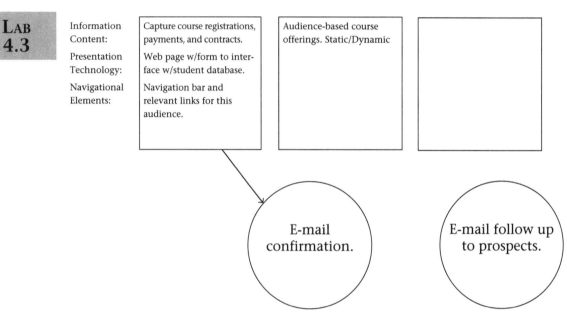

LAB
4.3

Information Content:

Presentation Technology:

Navigational Elements:

Capture course registrations, payments, and contracts.

Web page w/form to interface w/student database.

Navigation bar and relevant links for this audience.

Audience-based course offerings. Static/Dynamic

E-mail confirmation.

E-mail follow up to prospects.

g) What presentation technologies should be listed in the second box?

Answer: Web pages will be used to present textual information. Graphics may be incorporated, and a database interface would be required for a dynamic presentation.

Audience: ___Prospective students_____

Information Content: Presentation Technology: Navigational Elements:	Capture course registrations, payments, and contracts. Web page w/form to interface w/student database. Navigation bar and relevant links for this audience.	Audience-based course offerings. Static/Dynamic Web pages w/text, graphics. Dynamic uses database interfaces.	

LAB 4.3

E-mail confirmation.

E-mail follow up to prospects.

h) What navigational elements could be listed in the second box?

Answer: A navigation bar could be displayed for other sections of the Web site. A link to the registration presentation should be very significant. Links to additional information on the suggested courses are important.

Audience: _____Prospective students_____

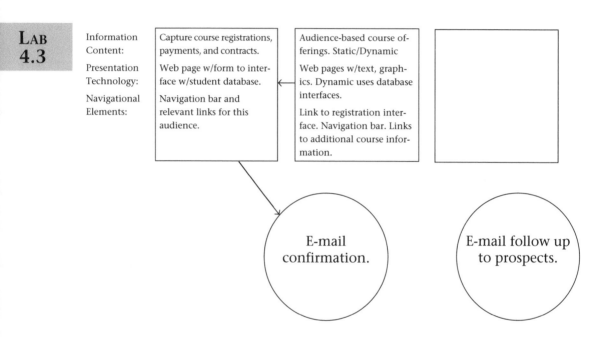

LAB
4.3

Information Content: Capture course registrations, payments, and contracts.

Presentation Technology: Web page w/form to interface w/student database.

Navigational Elements: Navigation bar and relevant links for this audience.

Audience-based course offerings. Static/Dynamic

Web pages w/text, graphics. Dynamic uses database interfaces.

Link to registration interface. Navigation bar. Links to additional course information.

E-mail confirmation.

E-mail follow up to prospects.

i) What information content should be listed in the third box?

Answer: The third box in this set of story boards should include the index page for the program Web site. This should include information and links targeted to any interested audience member.

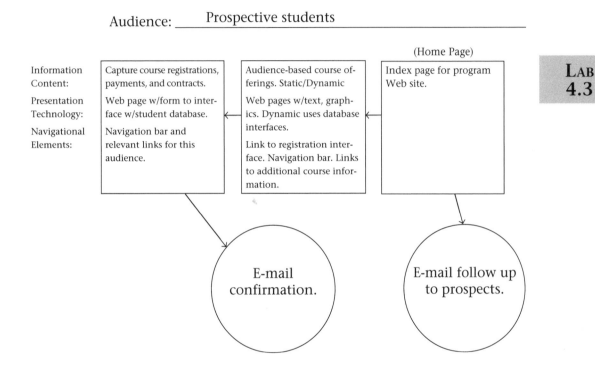

j)   What presentation technologies should be listed in the third box?

Answer: A Web page with text and graphics will probably do the trick. Perhaps a database interface could be included to serve other audience needs as well.

Audience: Prospective students

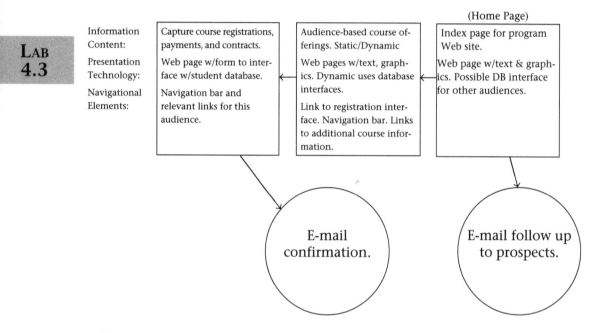

Information Content: | Capture course registrations, payments, and contracts.
Presentation Technology: | Web page w/form to interface w/student database.
Navigational Elements: | Navigation bar and relevant links for this audience.

Audience-based course offerings. Static/Dynamic
Web pages w/text, graphics. Dynamic uses database interfaces.
Link to registration interface. Navigation bar. Links to additional course information.

(Home Page)
Index page for program Web site.
Web page w/text & graphics. Possible DB interface for other audiences.

E-mail confirmation.

E-mail follow up to prospects.

k) What navigational elements could be listed in the third box?

Answer: The navigation bar could be introduced. A significant link for new or prospective students would lead to the presentation described in the second box in this exercise.

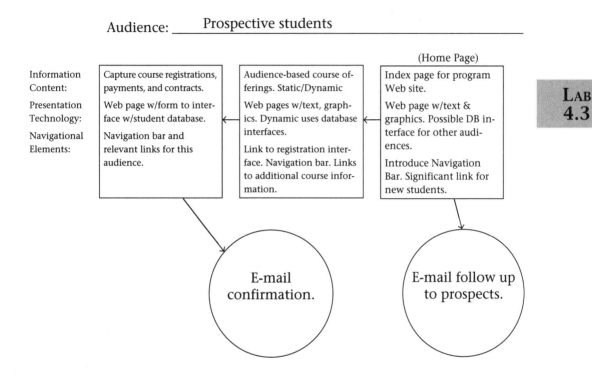

Audience: ___Prospective students___

			(Home Page)
Information Content:	Capture course registrations, payments, and contracts.	Audience-based course offerings. Static/Dynamic	Index page for program Web site.
Presentation Technology:	Web page w/form to interface w/student database.	Web pages w/text, graphics. Dynamic uses database interfaces.	Web page w/text & graphics. Possible DB interface for other audiences.
Navigational Elements:	Navigation bar and relevant links for this audience.	Link to registration interface. Navigation bar. Links to additional course information.	Introduce Navigation Bar. Significant link for new students.

E-mail confirmation.

E-mail follow up to prospects.

LAB 4.3

Navigational elements on the index page are very important because they are the exits off the Web site to present audience-based information. Grouping information and determining appropriate navigational terms is further facilitated by this process of creating story boards from the communication objective back to the index page. It is significantly easier to decide where you need to go once you know where that is.

LAB 4.3 SELF-REVIEW QUESTIONS

In order to test your progress, you should be able to answer the following questions:

1) When building a Web site presentation, it is imperative first to
   a) _____ Decide on logos and other graphics
   b) _____ Define audience targeting elements
   c) _____ Establish hosting vendors
   d) _____ Determine navigational aides

2) Major audience targeting elements include
   a) _____ Who the audience is
   b) _____ What information the audience seeks
   c) _____ Why the audience is communicating
   d) _____ All of these
   e) _____ None of these

3) Reversing the traditional flow of information exchanges in the development process helps
   a) _____ To confuse the management team involved
   b) _____ To justify development expenses
   c) _____ To prioritize audience communication goals in the process
   d) _____ To clarify confusion in the IS department

4) Story boards should document
   a) _____ Informational content of every interchange
   b) _____ Communications technologies of every interchange
   c) _____ Navigational aids in every interchange
   d) _____ None of these
   e) _____ All of these

5) Navigational aids serve audiences by facilitating access to information they seek.
   a) _____ True
   b) _____ False

LAB 4.3

C H A P T E R   4

TEST YOUR THINKING

The projects in this section use the skills you've acquired in this chapter. The answers to these projects are available to instructors only through a Prentice Hall sales representative and are intended to be used in classroom discussion and assessment.

1)   Who are your audiences?

2)   What are the communications goals of your audiences (*what* and *why*)?

3)   What are the information or content areas of your story boards based on audience objectives?

4)   What information will be presented at each information interchange?

5)   What communications technologies will be utilized to conduct these exchanges (*how*)?

6)   What navigational aids will be added to your story boards and effort?

CHAPTER 5

CREATIVE STRATEGIES

 It is always hard to go beyond your public. If they are satisfied with cheap performances, you will not easily arrive at better. If they know what is good, and require it, you will aspire and burn until you achieve it.

—Ralph Waldo Emerson

CHAPTER OBJECTIVES

In this chapter, you will learn about

In this chapter, we will continue to look at the actual development of Internet communication efforts by primarily focusing on the creative presentation of information.

We have thoroughly discussed the development of information presentations and the necessity of targeting this content at appropriate audiences. This chapter deals with the presentation of this content—what it should look like. Creative concepts support audience targeting by making information presentations appealing to their audiences. Like the content they provide, creative presentations engage the end user.

Our role as Webmasters may not involve the creative development of Web sites. This responsibility usually lies with more artsy people. But it's important to understand some general creative development concepts and terminology taken from traditional marketing methods. We will look at a set of Web sites to identify basic creative development concepts. These sites will also be visited to assess the use of creative elements and to critique Web presentations. We will also briefly discuss creative development issues.

Multimedia elements, including sound, video, and animation, are not discussed in this chapter, though all could eventually be used in creative delivery of information. But the basic creative concepts discussed in the chapter are applicable to them as well. At the time of this book's publication, these media elements are becoming standardized but are not fully developed. Many of them are not immediately available to all Web audience members. As Web usage increases, so will the use of these technologies. And the general concepts we discuss in this chapter will be useful in making those technologies part of Internet communication.

LAB 5.1

IDENTIFYING CREATIVE CONCEPTS

LAB OBJECTIVES

After this Lab, you will be able to

- Understand Look, Feel, and the Big Idea
- Identify Audience Appeal and Engagement
- Identify Branding Activities

Creative concepts involve the presentation of information. Web pages can be considered as blank pages. When building engaging communication systems, the content of the information is the most important factor. But presenting these information exchanges in an appropriate manner is also important. Creative concepts are executed on these blank pages to make text, graphics, and other visual elements more appealing to the target audience involved.

Marketing people have been using the phrase "look and feel" to describe creative concepts for some time now. The look and feel of a presentation describes the appearance of a presentation and the emotional response the presentation is aiming to trigger in the target audience.

Think about a TV advertisement for laundry detergent. The look of such an ad usually involves happy consumers in clean, tasteful, colorful surroundings. These ads make us feel comfortable, domestic, and happy about clean clothes. They inspire us to purchase these products with these looks and feelings. A creative development team did this on purpose.

Now think about the many TV advertisements for technology companies. They look modern, fast, high-tech, and usually include businesspeople or other people they are targeting. Technology companies are basically providing business solutions. Their advertisements usually try to make us feel as like they understand our problems, can solve our problems, and will make us happy and rich by doing so. Again, the look and feel of these ads was developed to appeal to the target audiences.

Identifying the look and feel of a presentation can be accomplished using adjectives. Descriptive terms can be used to explain the appearance and emotional involvement that a presentation is geared toward.

A single sentence, called a big idea or theme, can be used to identify the look and feel of a presentation. This single statement should represent the creative aspects of the presentation. It acts as a summary of the look and feel. Once developed, this theme can be used in the creative process as a benchmark for every aspect of a presentation.

Engaging communication is the objective on the Web and in other media. For presentations to be engaging, they must appeal to the target audience. Creative elements such as color, text, and images must match the needs of the identified audiences.

Of course, knowledge about the target audience is needed to create presentations that will appeal to that audience. And each audience probably needs information presented a certain way. Presentations for children will be designed differently than for adults. Serious information and subjects require a different approach than entertainment and lifestyle fulfillment. Text, images, and other media elements can all be used in different ways to engage the audience they are trying to reach.

Branding is another aspect of creative strategy that is very important in traditional advertising and now in interactive communication. Branding describes the process of developing customer identification and recognition of products and companies over time. This is usually accomplished, in part, by utilizing consistent images, colors, and messages in multimedia advertising and promotion. TV, print, billboards, promotional items, signage, and interactive images all contain the same icons and creative presentations to build recognition among their audiences.

Large and small companies spend millions of dollars building brand recognition in the marketplace. For example, the Coca-Cola and Anhauser-Bush companies spend millions every year to keep their company and product brand names fresh in the consumer mind. Their brand-building activities are so successful that the color and logo for Coke™

and Budweiser™ beer is instantly recognized by millions of people around the world.

Internet-based interactive communication systems should include branding elements if the company is involved in such activities. Logos, color choices, and other corporate identity elements can be included in the presentation to leverage branding activities in other media and continue efforts on-line.

LAB 5.1 EXERCISES

5.1.1 UNDERSTAND LOOK, FEEL, AND THE BIG IDEA

To complete this exercise, log onto the home or index page of the following Web sites and answer the questions for each site. You may want to bookmark these Web sites as we will return to them in the following exercises.

`www.disney.com`

a) What three adjectives can be used to describe the look and feel of this Web site?

b) What is a single-sentence description that identifies the big idea or theme behind the creative aspects of this Web site presentation?

`www.gouldshawmut.com`

a) What three adjectives can be used to describe the look and feel of this Web site?

b) What is a single-sentence description that identifies the big idea or theme behind the creative aspects of this Web site presentation?

`www.putnaminvestments.com`

a) What three adjectives can be used to describe the look and feel of this Web site?

b) What is a single-sentence description that identifies the big idea or theme behind the creative aspects of this Web site presentation?

`www.llbean.com`

a) What three adjectives can be used to describe the look and feel of this Web site?

b) What is a single-sentence description that identifies the big idea or theme behind the creative aspects of this Web site presentation?

`www.vw.com`

a) What three adjectives can be used to describe the look and feel of this Web site?

b) What is a single-sentence description that identifies the big idea or theme behind the creative aspects of this Web site presentation?

`www.aarp.org`

a) What three adjectives can be used to describe the look and feel of this Web site?

b) What is a single-sentence description that identifies the big idea or theme behind the creative aspects of this Web site presentation?

5.1.2   IDENTIFY AUDIENCE APPEAL AND ENGAGEMENT

Return to the index page of each site and answer these questions.

`www.disney.com`

a) What is the general target audience for this Web site?

b) How do the creative aspects of this site appeal to the target audience and engage it?

`www.gouldshawmut.com`

a) What is the general target audience for this Web site?

b) How do the creative aspects of this site appeal to the target audience and engage it?

`www.putnaminvestments.com`

a) What is the general target audience for this Web site?

b) How do the creative aspects of this site appeal to the target audience and engage it?

`www.llbean.com`

a) What is the general target audience for this Web site?

b) How do the creative aspects of this site appeal to the target audience and engage it?

`www.vw.com`

a) What is the general target audience for this Web site?

b) How do the creative aspects of this site appeal to the target audience and engage it?

`www.aarp.org`

a) What is the general target audience for this Web site?

b) How do the creative aspects of this site appeal to the target audience and engage it?

5.1.3 IDENTIFY BRANDING ACTIVITIES

Return to the Web sites discussed previously to assess branding activities on the index page of each site.

`www.disney.com`

a) What branding activities are immediately apparent on this Web site?

`www.gouldshawmut.com`

a) What branding activities are immediately apparent on this Web site?

`www.putnaminvestments.com`

a) What branding activities are immediately apparent on this Web site?

`www.llbean.com`

a) What branding activities are immediately apparent on this Web site?

`www.vw.com`

a) What branding activities are immediately apparent on this Web site?

`www.aarp.org`

a) What branding activities are immediately apparent on this Web site?

LAB 5.1 EXERCISE ANSWERS

5.1.1 ANSWERS

To complete this exercise, log onto the home or index page of the following Web sites and answer the questions for each site. You may want to bookmark these Web sites as we will return to them in the following exercises.

`www.disney.com`

a) What three adjectives can be used to describe the look and feel of this Web site?

Answer: Yours will vary, but mine are fun, entertaining, *and* colorful.

b) What is a single-sentence description that identifies the big idea or theme behind the creative aspects of this Web site presentation?

Answer: Your answer will vary but could be something like this: Disney provides fun and entertainment using old characters and new stories.

Though this is a rather obvious statement, it provides a basic theme that represents the information presentation on the Web. All of the creative elements support and complement this theme.

`www.gouldshawmut.com`

a) What three adjectives can be used to describe the look and feel of this Web site?

Answer: Yours will vary, but mine are solid, standard, *and* functional.

b)   What is a single-sentence description that identifies the big idea or theme behind the creative aspects of this Web site presentation?

*Answer: Your answer will vary but could be something like this: Standard solutions that
you can count on.*

Though this Web site does not provide much eye candy, it does have a
creative theme reflective of the company and products involved.

www.putnaminvestments.com

a)   What three adjectives can be used to describe the look and feel of this Web
site?

Answer: Yours will again vary, but mine are precise, conservative, and informative.

b)   What is a single-sentence description that identifies the big idea or theme behind the creative aspects of this Web site presentation?

*Answer: Your answer will vary but could be something like this: Information you can
trust.*

Again, the lack of creativity in this presentation is successful in producing
a sparse, banklike presentation theme that is appropriate for this company.

www.llbean.com

a)   What three adjectives can be used to describe the look and feel of this Web
site?

*Answer: Yours will probably differ, but mine are wholesome, relaxing, and tradi-
tional.*

b)   What is a single-sentence description that identifies the big idea or theme behind the creative aspects of this Web site presentation?

*Answer: Your answer will vary but could be something like this: Wholesome products
and traditional business practices in an on-line shopping experience.*

This company has a solid reputation and loyal customer base for its
wholesome products and traditional business practices in retail and catalog direct marketing. These concepts are presented in the appearance of
this Web site.

www.vw.com

a) What three adjectives can be used to describe the look and feel of this Web site?

Answer: Yours will vary but mine are hip, slick, *and* cool.

b) What is a single-sentence description that identifies the big idea or theme behind the creative aspects of this Web site presentation?

Answer: Your answer will again vary but could be something like this: Hip, slick, and cool vehicles for hip, slick, and cool people.

Interactive information and communications are presented in the same highly creative fashion as the company's advertising efforts in traditional media.

www.aarp.org

a) What three adjectives can be used to describe the look and feel of this Web site?

Answer: Yours may differ, but mine include uplifting, organized, *and* patriotic.

b) What is a single-sentence description that identifies the big idea or theme behind the creative aspects of this Web site presentation?

Answer: Your answer will vary but could be something like this: News and benefits people can use to be happier in retirement.

This national association for retired persons utilizes a creative presentation similar to a newsletter for its membership.

5.1.2 ANSWERS

Return to the index page of each site and answer these questions.

www.disney.com

a) What is the general target audience for this Web site?

Answer: The target audience is Disney fans, mostly children and other family members.

b) How do the creative aspects of this site appeal to the target audience and engage it?

Answer: The colorful aspects, cartoon characters, and Disney icons are all appealing to these audiences and engage this audience through recognition.

www.gouldshawmut.com

a) What is the general target audience for this Web site?

Answer: The target audience for this fuse manufacturing company is buyers of fuses and related products.

b) How do the creative aspects of this site appeal to the target audience and engage it?

Answer: The audience is seeking dependable devices for electrical systems. The no-frills approach to this information presentation supports the standardization and trustworthy solutions provided by this company.

Industrial supplies are not very flashy, but people buying them are not looking for highly creative presentations. What they are looking for is dependable, standard, and valuable products. This site is engaging to this audience by providing a presentation reflective of these concepts and consistent with the needs of the audience.

www.putnaminvestments.com

a) What is the general target audience for this Web site?

Answer: The target audience includes individuals, advisors, and monetary managers seeking information about the management of theirs and other people's financial investments.

b) How do the creative aspects of this site appeal to the target audience and engage it?

Answer: The presentation appears intelligent, informative, and conservative, which are appealing traits when the management of investments is being discussed.

This site engages the audience by appearing boring, secure, and noncreative, just as traditional banks have done for decades. This is highly appropriate and effective for the audience this information is targeted at. Cartoons are good for some, but people's money is being discussed at this site.

`www.llbean.com`

a)   What is the general target audience for this Web site?

Answer: The target audience includes current and prospective customers seeking consumer clothing, housewares, and outdoor activity products.

b)   How do the creative aspects of this site appeal to the target audience and engage it?

Answer: The audience for this site is engaged by the outdoor scenery and activity representations, which they find appealing. This presentation also uses icons and text recognized by the audience.

The creative presentation of this transaction-based site is very similar to the catalogs produced by this company for decades. An outdoor, adventuresome, and country lifestyle is reinforced. Traditional elements used for years also help support the company's reputation in the marketplace.

`www.vw.com`

a)   What is the general target audience for this Web site?

Answer: The target audience is prospective buyers and owners of Volkswagen vehicles.

b)   How do the creative aspects of this site appeal to the target audience and engage it?

Answer: The extremely modern, hip, and cool presentation is appealing to the young, successful, and progressive audience targeted by this company.

This company sells a lifestyle as part of its ongoing marketing efforts to sell vehicles. It engages people interested in joining this lifestyle by purchasing a vehicle and reinforces a my-car-is-cool-and-so-am-I concept in this presentation.

`www.aarp.org`

a)   What is the general target audience for this Web site?

Answer: The audience for this site is current and prospective members of the American Association of Retired Persons, who are Americans over the age of 50 years old.

b)   How do the creative aspects of this site appeal to the target audience and engage it?

Answer: This site appeals to the audience by providing an information-rich presentation in an easy-to-read, uplifting, and patriotic manner.

5.1.3 ANSWERS

Return to the Web sites discussed previously to assess branding activities on the index page of each site.

www.disney.com

a) What branding activities are immediately apparent on this Web site?

Answer: The company's logo and internationally recognized rodent mascot are displayed prominently. Other well-known images and phrases also reinforce the branding effort.

www.gouldshawmut.com

a) What branding activities are immediately apparent on this Web site?

Answer: Color, logos, and slogans are incorporated in the presentation.

www.putnaminvestments.com

a) What branding activities are immediately apparent on this Web site?

Answer: Corporate logos and other identity elements are included to reinforce this company's brand in the marketplace.

www.llbean.com

a) What branding activities are immediately apparent on this Web site?

Answer: Company logos, outdoor images, and icons taken from the company's other media efforts support a continuing branding effort.

www.vw.com

a) What branding activities are immediately apparent on this Web site?

Answer: This site is particularly strong as a branding tool, serving as an on-line extension of branding campaigns in other media. Logos, slogans, and graphics are utilized in the same manner as the company's extensive brand-building strategy.

www.aarp.org

a) What branding activities are immediately apparent on this Web site?

Answer: Logos and colors are used to tie this Web site to the organization's other communication efforts and to make the site consistent for member recognition.

LAB 5.1

LAB 5.1 SELF-REVIEW QUESTIONS

In order to test your progress, you should be able to answer the following questions:

1) The big idea for a creative presentation does what?
   a) _____ Identifies the creative aspects
   b) _____ Summarizes the look and feel of the presentation
   c) _____ Acts as a benchmark for the creative development process
   d) _____ All of these
   e) _____ None of these

2) The look and feel of a presentation involves which concepts?
   a) _____ General appearance
   b) _____ HTML coding
   c) _____ Database interfaces
   d) _____ Emotional triggers
   e) _____ Astrophysics

3) Branding is the process of directly selling products to consumers.
   a) _____ True
   b) _____ False

4) Branding is the process of building company and product recognition with an audience over time.
   a) _____ True
   b) _____ False

5) Creative elements of a Web presentation should do what?
   a) _____ Look cool regardless of download speed
   b) _____ Have flashing text
   c) _____ Engage and appeal to the target audience
   d) _____ Differ from traditional media
   e) _____ Inspire devotion

LAB 5.2

CREATIVE EVALUATION

LAB OBJECTIVES

After this lab, you will be able to

- Identify Text Usage in a Creative Strategy
- Assess Visuals in a Creative Strategy

Web-based presentations are primarily a visual experience. The basic building blocks of creative content are the same as traditional printed materials. These can be described in two distinct groups: text and visuals. This lab evaluates the use of these two elements to demonstrate their use in Web creative strategy.

Text includes words, phrases, slogans, headlines, captions, etc. Visuals include almost everything else, such as color, images, photographs, drawings, graphics, and icons. Placement of these elements, including textual elements, is also a visual discussion. Text-based logos can usually be considered a visual element, especially if the logo is used in a branding effort.

A magazine page is a good example. Most magazine pages contain a combination of text and visual elements. The editorial content is presented in text using columns on the page. The size and kind of the actual typeface, or font, used is probably targeted to the audience of the magazine. Visual elements may include photographs or other images. The amount of white space and the use of color on the page are both important visual elements. Smaller graphics may help identify the section of the magazine or add to the look and feel of the presentation in some way. Even page numbers and their appearance are considered in the creative theme of the magazine.

Newspapers use the same two elements in a variety of different ways to present information and advertising messages. Compare the front pages of your local paper with *USA Today*. Text and images are probably used differently in each to create a look and feel for each publication. Even if they are delivering the same information, the two publications will demonstrate two distinct creative strategies based on their respective audiences.

Richer media, including sound, video, and animation, are becoming more widespread on the Internet but are primarily used at this point to augment the initial text and graphics of a presentation. Except for sound, most multimedia elements can also be considered visual items.

A Web page, especially the home page of a Web site, uses the same two elements in the creative aspects of it presentation. Starting from a hypothetical blank page, an information presentation is built that engages the audience by appealing to its wants, needs, and desires. Utilizing a big idea or creative theme, a combination of text and visuals is used to present the communications effort.

In some situations, text plays a primary role is supporting the creative theme and targeting the audience. In others, visual imagery is the driving force behind look and feel development. In either situation, appealing to the end user is the creative strategy goal.

LAB 5.2 EXERCISES

5.2.1 IDENTIFY TEXT USAGE IN CREATIVE STRATEGY

Describe the use of text on the home page of these Web sites.

> `www.disney.com`
>
> **a)** How is text used in this Web site presentation?
>
> `www.gouldshawmut.com`
>
> **a)** How is text used in this Web site presentation?
>
> `www.putnaminvestments.com`
>
> **a)** How is text used in this Web site presentation?
>
> `www.llbean.com`
>
> **a)** How is text used in this Web site presentation?

`www.vw.com`

a) How is text used in this Web site presentation?

`www.aarp.com`

a) How is text used in this Web site presentation?

5.2.2   ASSESS VISUALS IN CREATIVE STRATEGY

Return to these Web sites and describe the use of graphics and other visual elements on the home page of these sites.

`www.disney.com`

a) How are graphics utilized in this Web site presentation?

`www.gouldshawmut.com`

a) How are graphics utilized in this Web site presentation?

`www.putnaminvestments.com`

a) How are graphics utilized in this Web site presentation?

`www.llbean.com`

a) How are graphics utilized in this Web site presentation?

`www.vw.com`

a) How are graphics utilized in this Web site presentation?

`www.aarp.com`

a) How are graphics utilized in this Web site presentation?

LAB 5.2 EXERCISE ANSWERS

5.2.1 ANSWERS

Describe the use of text on the home page of these Web sites.

www.disney.com

a) How is text used in this Web site presentation?

Answer: Your answer will vary. The following is mine:

A lot of text is used but it is secondary to images. The text is used for identification of subject matter and for navigational links to information. Text is not necessarily included for reading in a traditional sense but instead serves a functional purpose.

www.gouldshawmut.com

a) How is text used in this Web site presentation?

Answer: Again, your answer will vary. Mine follows.

Quite different from the previous example, this presentation is based on text. Like an informative brochure, easily read text is the primary content and is also used for navigational purposes. This helps drives the theme of the presentation, which is a dependable solution.

www.putnaminvestments.com

a) How is text used in this Web site presentation?

Answer: Your answer will be in your own words. Here is mine.

This is another example where text is the primary factor in the content of this presentation. Presented in a professional, concise, and straightforward manner, this text-based content drives the presentation toward its conservative and informative theme.

www.llbean.com

a) How is text used in this Web site presentation?

Answer: Your answer will vary but might include aspects of mine.

This Web presentation utilizes text primarily for headlines and for captions to graphics, similar to a catalog. The text is less important than the images. Text is used for navigational purposes and is present in the logo. But it is not as significant a factor in delivering the theme as visual images are.

www.vw.com

a) How is text used in this Web site presentation?

Answer: Your answer will be based on your perspective. Here is mine.

Text is used in this presentation in an intelligent and informative fashion to explain navigation and deliver content. It plays an equally significant part of the presentation as do visual images. The use of text is slick, like rest of the material.

www.aarp.com

a) How is text used in this Web site presentation?

Answer: Yours will vary but may be similar to mine.

This informative presentation is dependent on text to support the site's newsletter look, deliver its content, and provide internal navigation. The text is also especially easy to read, which is an important consideration for its audience.

5.2.2 ANSWERS

Return to these Web sites and describe the use of graphics and other visual elements on the home page of these sites.

www.disney.com

a) How are graphics utilized in this Web site presentation?

Answer: Your answer will be based on your interpretation of this and the other sites. Here is mine.

Graphics are significant, as the whole presentation is very colorful and rich with recognizable images. This use of visual images seems quite appropriate considering the entertainment subject matter and helps support the animated fun of the creative theme.

`www.gouldshawmut.com`

a)   How are graphics utilized in this Web site presentation?

Answer: Again, your answer will vary from mine.

Graphics do not play a significant role on this site except to reinforce branding activities. Limited variation in color helps support the creative theme of standardization and simplicity.

`www.putnaminvestments.com`

a)   How are graphics utilized in this Web site presentation?

Answer: The following is my answer.

This site uses almost no graphics and little color. Beside very basic logos, the site content and navigation are text based, which supports the serious nature of the subject matter.

`www.llbean.com`

a)   How are graphics utilized in this Web site presentation?

Answer: Yours will vary but should include some of the following.

This site utilizes visual imagery and appropriate colors to engage the audience in a similar fashion as other media. Outdoor images and seasonal color variations are prevalent, which drive the creative content of the presentation. Product images are given precedence over text explanations.

`www.vw.com`

a)   How are graphics utilized in this Web site presentation?

Answer: Again, your answers will vary from mine.

Logos, product images, and targeted audience images play a major role in this presentation. Graphical elements support navigation. Speed and quickness are also incorporated into images to support the product benefits. Colors are cool.

`www.aarp.com`

a)   How are graphics utilized in this Web site presentation?

Answer: Here is my perspective.

Logos and limited images to aid identification for the audiences are included in a limited fashion. Colors are patriotic.

LAB 5.2 SELF-REVIEW QUESTIONS

In order to test your progress, you should be able to answer the following questions:

1) The building blocks of a Web site's creative presentation are which?
   a) _____ Headlines
   b) _____ Text
   c) _____ Sound files
   d) _____ Visuals
   e) _____ Logos

2) Navigational aides are provided on Web sites using which?
   a) _____ Text
   b) _____ Graphics
   c) _____ Both
   d) _____ Neither

3) The use of color is not important in Web creative strategy.
   a) _____ True
   b) _____ False

4) Text is sometimes used to execute the creative theme of a Web presentation.
   a) _____ True
   b) _____ False

5) The creative theme or big idea of a Web presentation should do what?
   a) _____ Appeal to the target audience
   b) _____ Involve a lot of pretty pictures
   c) _____ Engage the target audience
   d) _____ Sell a lot of widgets
   e) _____ Involve massive expense

LAB 5.3

CREATIVE DEVELOPMENT

LAB OBJECTIVES

After this lab you will be able to

- Brainstorm the Evaluation of a Product or Organization
- Brainstorm the Targeted Audience Solutions
- Build Connections and Visualization
- Repurpose Information
- Understand the Importance of Copy Writing

In this lab, we will look at some basic concepts that are helpful when developing the creative elements of a Web presentation.

The previous two labs highlighted the continuing theme of targeting creative strategy to the intended audience. Developing a targeted strategy can be accomplished in three steps:

Identify product/organization issues defined as features and benefits.

Identify audience issues that include the audience's wants, needs, and desires and solutions for them.

Build connections between these two sets of issues to create appeal and engagement and develop visualization.

In this model, features are facts or ideas that can be attributed directly to the product or company being discussed. Benefits are statements that explain how this product or company will satisfy wants, needs, and desires for the customer or audience. Both sets of statements are written from the company or products perspective. This evaluation helps marketers determine what they've got to communicate about.

Audience issues are written from their own perspective as well. First the audience is identified and described. Then audience wants, needs, and desires are written from an objective perspective without any consideration of the product or company being discussed. Audience solutions are also listed without initial consideration of the product or company. This step helps marketers determine exactly what the targeted customer wants.

The third step builds connections between the first two lists. Marketers look at what they have first. Then they look at what the audience needs. Developing ways to portray the company or product as what the audience wants, needs, and desires is fundamentally what marketing is based on.

Matching features and benefits with the wants, needs, and desires of the audience creates appeal and engagement. Presentations can then be built that leverage these two concepts against each other.

Developing creative strategy for Web presentations requires textual and visual representation of these concepts. Textual statements are relatively straightforward. The use of text and other visual elements is dependent on the audience and issues involved.

In a true creative fashion, these steps should each involve a brainstorming session, in which any and every idea on a topic is communicated and captured. Brainstorming usually involves a small group of people stating ideas as they are conceived. A note taker or facilitator writes down every idea as it is announced. These ideas can later be reviewed and refined to develop an appropriate creative strategy.

For www.putnaminvestments.com, an example development effort could look like this:

- Organizational issues about this company could include the following:
    - Features—conservative, low-risk, professional, precise, dependable, smart, realistic, intelligent, informative, helpful, careful, wealthy, successful, traditional, etc.

- Benefits—company takes care of its clients; money is safe with company; company knows what to do with money; investments succeed; professional operation with experience and confidence; etc.

- Audiences are varied but all are investors. Investors want financial gain with minimal risk. They need security and serious consideration.

- Audience wants, needs, and desires include trustworthy and lucrative investment management; security about their financial future; intelligent decisions made on their behalf; information about the status of their investments; serious approach to a serious matter; etc.

- Connections can be made between the features and benefits and the audience wants, needs, and desires. Company provides intelligence, security, informed decisions, successful investments, and conservative approach to business for the customers—all things audience members want.

- Visualization of these connections appears on the site: a professional appearance stressing an informed, secure, and conservative approach that uses mostly text to represent this creative theme.

Another aspect of creative development involves the decision to repurpose information. Repurposing information involves using existing materials and graphics in a presentation to continue branding efforts, return continued impact for previous creative investment, and tie Internet communication with other media. The McDonald's golden arches are a repurposed image used to support branding activities.

Other uses of repurposed materials could be product information, technical data images, and graphics that were developed for other media but can be utilized in Internet communication as well. An e-mail newsletter may distribute informational content that was originally published in hard copy. This could be considered repurposed material.

Copy writing is the process of developing text-based marketing communication materials. Without going into a diatribe on the sinking quality of our civilization, let's just say that people don't read like they used to. People look but don't actually read most marketing copy.

Although books, magazines, and newspapers are read by millions of people every day (including you right now), the growth of other media and the overwhelming amount of images has shifted reading patterns in many people. Instead of actually reading text, many people just look at it.

The commitment to reading isn't present. Most text is skimmed or briefly reviewed. In-depth processing of text material is saved for entertainment novels or work-related material.

This means that marketing copy on the Web must be short and sweet. This situation was demonstrated on the Web sites we evaluated earlier. Headlines, captions, and short statements are the primary text formats in Web presentation development.

LAB 3.1 EXERCISES

5.3.1 BRAINSTORM THE EVALUATION OF A PRODUCT OR ORGANIZATION

To understand the basics of a creative brainstorming process, start by first evaluating the product or company issues. List as many features and benefits as possible about a product. Be sure to write down every idea you can come up with in the next few minutes in a true brainstorming fashion.

a) What are some of the features of water?

b) What are some of the benefits of water?

5.3.2 BRAINSTORM THE TARGETED AUDIENCE SOLUTIONS

Identify audience issues by determining as many solutions as possible that the target audience may be seeking for fulfillment of wants, needs, and desires. For this exercise the audience is marathon runners.

a) Who is the target audience?

b) How can you briefly describe the target audience?

c) What solutions to wants, needs, and desires does water provide for this audience?

5.3.3 BUILD CONNECTIONS AND VISUALIZATION

Identify ways to appeal to and engage this audience through creative content presentations. Review connections between the product evaluations and the audience solutions from the previous two exercises. Then develop a big idea that can be stated in one sentence, which describes the creative approach of this product presentation to this audience. Finally, list ideas for visually representing this creative strategy.

a) What connections can be built between the features and benefits of water and the wants, needs, and desires of marathon runners?

b) What is a big idea or theme that can be used as a creative strategy in a presentation on water for marathon runners?

c) How can this theme be represented visually in the creative content of the presentation?

5.3.4 REPURPOSE INFORMATION

To demonstrate the concept of repurposing materials, let's return to two of the Web sites from a previous lab and look for examples of repurposed information.

Log on to the home page of `www.disney.com`.

a) List examples of repurposed material that you recognize from other media efforts.

Log on to the home page of `www.llbean.com`.

a) List examples of repurposed material that you recognize from other media efforts.

5.3.5 UNDERSTAND THE IMPORTANCE OF COPY WRITING

To understand the real importance of copy writing in the creative development of visual presentations, complete the following exercise.

Read the following sentence once. While doing so, count the number of times the letter F appears. Please read the sentence only once at this time.

Finished files are the result of years of scientific evidence combined with the sharing of discoveries.

a) How many times does the letter F appear?

Now read the sentence again very slowly. Count the appearances of the letter F again.

a) Do you get a different number?

b) What does this tell us about the importance of copy writing in visual presentations?

LAB 5.3 EXERCISE ANSWERS

5.3.1 ANSWERS

To understand the basics of a creative brainstorming process, start by first evaluating the product or company issues. List as many features and benefits as possible about a product. Be sure to write down every idea you can come up with in the next few minutes in a true brainstorming fashion.

a) What are some of the features of water?

Answer: Yours will vary, but here are mine:

Wet, dampening, cooling, refreshing, available, elemental, natural, life giving, solution providing, thirst quenching, diluting, dissolving, soothing, calming, lubricating, insulating, heavy, healthy.

b) What are some of the benefits of water?

Answer: Yours will again vary, but could include the following:

Water provides dampness and replaces dryness. Living things need water to flourish and to replace water lost through processes. Water is refreshing and cooling in hot situations. Water is a naturally occurring element that provides and sustains life. Water dilutes and dissolves many substances and creates solutions.

5.3.2 ANSWERS

Identify audience issues by determining as many solutions as possible that the target audience may be seeking for fulfillment of wants, needs, and desires. For this exercise the audience is marathon runners.

a) Who is the target audience?

Answer: The target audience is marathon runners.

b) How can you briefly describe the target audience?

Answer: Your answer will vary, but mine follows.

Marathon runners are people who exercise frequently and run many, many miles on a regular basis. They are healthy. They perspire a lot. They also get very hot while running and exercising.

c) What solutions to wants, needs, and desires does water provide for this audience?

Marathon runners need a lot of water to replace the water they lose through perspiration. Runners of this type are very healthy, probably are engaged in a healthy lifestyle, and drinking water regularly is part of such a lifestyle. Water is also cooling and refreshing for runners while they exercise.

5.3.3 ANSWERS

Identify ways to appeal to and engage this audience through creative content presentations. Review connections between the product evaluations and the audience solutions from the previous two exercises. Then develop a big idea that can be stated in one sentence, which describes the creative approach of this product presentation to this audience. Finally, list ideas for visually representing this creative strategy.

a) What connections can be built between the features and benefits of water and the wants, needs, and desires of marathon runners?

Answer: Yours will vary, but here are mine.

Marathon runners need water to run. Runners get thirsty and water quenches thirst. Runners need water to replace lost fluids. They want water to be part of their healthy lifestyle. They desire water to be cool and refreshed. Connecting features, benefits, and audiences is the primary role of creative brainstorming efforts.

b) What is a big idea or theme that can be used as a creative strategy in a presentation on water for marathon runners?

Answer: Again, yours will vary but here are my big ideas.

Water is life for runners. Running is hot while water is not. Run a lot and drink a lot. Simple phrases like these are useful for identifying creative themes. These themes can then serve as benchmarks for presentation development. Every idea, image, or text item can be created and critiqued based on the selected theme.

c) How can this theme be represented visually in the creative content of the presentation?

Answer: Your answers will vary but could include the following:

Warm colors juxtaposed with cool colors. Water graphics. Natural water environments and scenery could be used in a visual presentation of these concepts. These visual concepts and other creative elements built into a Web presentation will appeal to the audience they were developed for. In this example, marathon runners will be engaged by a presentation created with their wants, needs, and desires in mind.

5.3.4 ANSWERS

To demonstrate the concept of repurposing materials, let's return to two of the Web sites from a previous lab and look for examples of repurposed information.

Log on to the home page of www.disney.com.

a) List examples of repurposed material that you recognize from other media efforts.

Answer: Your answers will vary but should include images taken from movies and other media developed by this company. The logo in use is probably utilized in other media, as well as the infamous Mickey Mouse character. Characters from recent movies and cartoons are also involved.

This use of repurposed material is to be expected at a Web site for a media company with recognized images as part of its brand identity. This company spends millions of dollars on advertising and promotion. These efforts increase and sustain recognition of these images in the consumer marketplace. Incorporating them on the Web site is a continuation of these efforts. In addition, the inclusion of newly developed images further leverages the investments made in other media activities to increase recognition and build awareness.

Log on to the home page of www.llbean.com

a) List examples of repurposed material that you recognize from other media efforts.

Answer: Again, your answers will vary. This home page displays images and text used in the company's traditional catalogs and other media.

Like the previous example, the inclusion of these materials provides continuing value for the investments made in advertising and direct marketing efforts. Usage also ties into the various catalog programs to build synergy between media.

Repurposed material also includes information and material developed and distributed in the printed catalogs. Product information, images, and technical specifications that currently exist in electronic formats are easily utilized in this Web presentation.

5.3.5 ANSWERS

To understand the real importance of copy writing in the creative development of visual presentations, complete the following exercise.

Read the following sentence once. While doing so, count the number of times the letter F appears. Please read the sentence only once at this time.

Finished files are the result of years of scientific evidence combined with the sharing of discoveries.

a) How many times does the letter F appear?

Answer: Most people notice the letter F three times in the first reading.

Now read the sentence again very slowly. Count the appearances of the letter F again.

a) Do you get a different number?

Answer: You probably noticed the presence of more Fs in the next reading. The actual number of times F appears is six.

b) What does this tell us about the importance of copy writing in visual presentations?

Answer: Your answer may be that people don't notice silent letters. But more important, this simple exercise helps demonstrate how fast most people read textual information and that extensive copy writing is not as important as many of us think.

Many creative development efforts are heavily geared to getting just the right series of words to describe, explain, or extol a product, service, or situation. But many of these agonizing decisions are not worth the time spent. Many people only look at text instead of actually reading it. Many phrases and thought-out text blocks in traditional communication efforts are not read by the audience members. They may be looked at but not read.

This is definitely the case in Internet communication, where the fast-paced nature and the shrinking patience level of most audience members add to the situation. In interactive media, the less text that is used to convey a message the better the chance it will be read.

This means that Web copy writing must be extremely concise and directly targeted to the audience involved. Images can be used instead of text in many situations. And text should probably exist as short statements and headlines instead of complete sentences.

Lab 5.3 Self-review Questions

In order to test your progress, you should be able to answer the following questions:

1) Evaluating a product or company for creative presentation involves looking at what?
   a) _____ Ownership and funding
   b) _____ Current efforts
   c) _____ Other sites
   d) _____ Features and benefits
   e) _____ Yellow pages

2) Assessing the target audience should be done from what perspective?
   a) _____ The company's perspective of the audience
   b) _____ A truly objective perspective
   c) _____ The perspective held by the targeted audience
   d) _____ None of these

3) Engaging creative presentation is based on connections between the audience and product or company.
   a) _____ True
   b) _____ False

4) Appealing to the audience wants, needs, and desires is not important in the creative theme of a Web presentation.
   a) _____ True
   b) _____ False

5) Large amounts of text should be developed and included in Web presentations.
   a) _____ True
   b) _____ False

6) Repurposed material could include which?
   a) _____ Logos and branding elements
   b) _____ Materials developed for distribution in other media
   c) _____ Product images and information
   d) _____ None of these
   e) _____ All of these

L A B 5 . 4

A WWW CRITIQUE MODEL

> ## LAB OBJECTIVES
>
> After this lab you will be able to
>
> * Rate a Good, Ugly, and Bad Web Site

This lab introduces a useful critique model for assessing Web sites and their creative presentations. The World Wide Web has been compared to the Wild Wild West in American history due to its quick expansion, unproven business models, the general wide open nature, and free-range spirit of this communication medium. One of my favorite films depicting this time frame and its outlaw characteristics is the movie *The Good, the Bad, and the Ugly*, starring Clint Eastwood.

Current Web presentations tend to fall into one of three categories: good, ugly, and bad. This process is not an exact science but rather a loose, fun, and very subjective way to think about Web site communication efforts:

* The good Web site looks good and delivers information wanted by an audience. Creative strategy engages the targeted audience and content presentation informs. This type of site looks a good and does a good job delivering appropriate interactive communication.

* The ugly Web site looks bad but delivers the goods. This type of site may not have an engaging creative strategy, but the presentation successfully informs and communicates with the audience.

* The bad Web site looks bad and doesn't deliver information wanted by the target audience. A bad Web site doesn't have an

engaging creative presentation and doesn't communicate successfully. Another type of bad Web site is one that looks good, with lots of appealing creative elements, but has no useful content. This version of the bad Web site is particularly frustrating due to overdone graphics and slow-loading multimedia elements that don't deliver any worthwhile interactive communication.

Another useful term for describing Web sites involves the level of stickiness. A sticky Web site is one that keeps its audience engaged with interactive communication presented in an appealing fashion. Good Web sites are sticky; end users can't leave because they are so well engaged and informed. Ugly Web sites are kind of sticky or maybe sticky enough with room for increases in stickiness. End users stay for a while but are not stuck there. Bad Web sites are not sticky. End users leave as soon as they can.

LAB 5.4 EXERCISES

5.4.1 RATING A GOOD, UGLY, AND BAD WEB SITE

Critique the Web sites listed here with a rating of good, bad, or ugly based on your interpretation of these definitions.

`www.disney.com`

a) Is this site good, bad, or ugly?

b) Why do you rate it this way?

`www.gouldshawmut.com`

a) Is this site good, bad, or ugly?

b) Why do you rate it this way?

`www.putnaminvestments.com`

a) Is this site good, bad, or ugly?

b) Why do you rate it this way?

`www.llbean.com`

a) Is this site good, bad, or ugly?

b) Why do you rate it this way?

`www.vw.com`

a) Is this site good, bad, or ugly?

b) Why do you rate it this way?

`www.aarp.org`

a) Is this site good, bad, or ugly?

b) Why do you rate it this way?

LAB 5.4 EXERCISE ANSWERS

5.4.1 ANSWERS

Critique the Web sites listed here with a rating of good, bad, or ugly based on your interpretation of these definitions.

`www.disney.com`

a) Is this site good, bad, or ugly?

Answer: Your ranking may be different, but I rank this Web site as good.

b) Why do you rate it this way?

Answer: Your answer is based on your ranking. I think that the creative aspects of this Web site are fun and engaging for its entertainment-seeking audience members, who are mostly children. The site is also packed with information and media presentations, making it highly informative and sticky as well.

`www.gouldshawmut.com`

a) Is this site good, bad, or ugly?

Answer: Your ranking is based on your opinion, but I would have to give this site an ugly ranking.

b) Why do you rate it this way?

Answer: Your answer is based on your perspective. Mine is based on the information-rich presentation geared toward that company's audience and presented in a boring, uncreative fashion. The site is ugly but delivers the information its audience wants. Not sticky but effective.

www.putnaminvestments.com

a) Is this site good, bad, or ugly?

Answer: My answer is to rank this site as good.

b) Why do you rate it this way?

Answer: Though the appearance is sparse, I believe the presentation is appropriate for the audience involved. This site is highly informative and provides relationship-building interactions that increase the sticky factor significantly.

www.llbean.com

a) Is this site good, bad, or ugly?

Answer: As an old school direct marketer, I must rate this site as good.

b) Why do you rate it this way?

Answer: Again my subjective opinion is that I find this site highly attractive to its loyal customer base while providing an interactive shopping experience. As an L.L. Bean guy, I find this site as sticky as a well-read catalog.

www.vw.com

a) Is this site good, bad, or ugly?

Answer: Though it should be quite obvious by now that I chose these Web sites as examples and therefore must like them, I also feel this is a good site using this ranking system.

b) Why do you rate it this way?

Answer: Engaging for hip, slick, and cool people with hip, slick, and cool creative presentations, this sticky site also informs, entertains, and builds relationships with potential and returning customers.

www.aarp.org

a) Is this site good, bad, or ugly?

Answer: Though you may not agree, I see this as another good site.

b) Why do you rate it this way?

Answer: Targeted to its audience with appropriate use of text and visuals, this site is also highly informative for its audience. Sticky for the retired set.

This exercise is lacking a bad Web site example. This was done for two distinct reasons. First, Web sites are dynamic and may not be bad by the time you are reading this book. Second, it's not very nice to comment negatively about a Web site in a publication such as this. Web communicators are doing the best they can in most situations.

I am confident that all Web users have visited a site that was not especially pleasant to look at and contained little valuable information. Some promotional sites even look quite good but contain no value. These sites might actually negatively affect relationships by frustrating the audience they are trying to reach. You can probably identify a bad site with little effort, unfortunately.

LAB 5.4 SELF-REVIEW QUESTIONS

LAB 5.4

In order to test your progress, you should be able to answer the following questions:

1) A good Web site has which traits?
   a) _____ Engaging presentation
   b) _____ Appropriate information and communication
   c) _____ Stickiness
   d) _____ All of these
   e) _____ None of these

2) A bad Web site has which traits?
   a) _____ Engaging presentation
   b) _____ Appropriate information and communication
   c) _____ Stickiness
   d) _____ All of these
   e) _____ None of these

3) An ugly Web site may look bad but still deliver appropriate communication exchanges for the target audience.
   a) _____ True
   b) _____ False

4) Stickiness describes keeping end users engaged at a Web site.
   a) _____ True
   b) _____ False

CHAPTER 5

TEST YOUR THINKING

The projects in this section use the skills you've acquired in this chapter. The answers to these projects are available to instructors only through a Prentice Hall sales representative and are intended to be used in classroom discussion and assessment.

1) Brainstorm connections between your audience and the solutions that the organization provides to its targeted audience. What connections exist that can be used to develop a creative strategy?

2) Develop a creative theme utilizing a look and feel that appeals to the target audience. What is the single sentence that describes your big idea?

3) Decide how text and visuals can be used in the creative presentation to fit the creative theme. Which will play a bigger role?

4) What branding elements may be included in the presentation?

5) Consider how your site engages and presents to its audience, making it a good Web site. Why will your site be sticky for its audience?

CHAPTER 6

PROMOTION AND MEASUREMENT

It pays to advertise; but you pay first.

—Anonymous

A hit, a very palpable hit.

—Osric, *Hamlet*, Shakespeare

CHAPTER OBJECTIVES

In this chapter, you will learn about

✔ Promoting Internet Communication Efforts   Page 221

✔ Measuring Internet Communication Activities   Page 243

In this chapter we will discuss some issues that become relevant after an Internet communication effort has been developed. Both discussions focus primarily on Web-based communications activities, but some of the concepts could be applied to e-mail activities as well.

The issues include the promotion of an Internet communications effort and the measurement of an effort once it is under way. Promotion describes the act of telling somebody about something. In this case, we need to tell our targeted audiences about a Web communication effort in order to engage them.

Measurement involves reviewing data from different sources to analyze the status of our efforts. Data can include technical data and impersonal and personal information captured through our communications activities. A positive aspect of Internet communication is that the technology provides several methods for in-depth capturing, profiling, and reviewing of activities. This captured information can be used to improve presentations, engage audiences, and fulfill wants, needs, and desires.

LAB 6.1

PROMOTING INTERNET COMMUNICATION EFFORTS

LAB OBJECTIVES

After this Lab, you will be able to

- Understand Traditional Media Promotion
- Understand Search Engine Positioning
- Understand Directory Listings
- Understand Banners and Buying Links
- Understand Relationship Links

Putting up a Web site is similar to building a billboard in your basement. It may look good, but unless somebody is searching for it, they will not see it. This lab introduces the primary options that are available to Webmasters planning to promote an Internet communications effort. The discussion centers on the promotion of Web-based communication efforts.

Promotion of an effort is important because it informs a current or potential audience member of your organization's efforts and provides an opportunity for end users to initiate communication with you. Since the Internet medium is driven by end-user motivation, it is necessary for your potential audiences to know how to communicate with your organization over the Internet.

The key to promotion, like everything else on the Internet, is targeting the correct audience. Promotion must be targeted at the audience the Internet effort is designed to reach. You must use the appropriate media to reach that audience and inform its members of the Web site and how it will fulfill their wants, needs, and desires.

Your existing audience may need notification of your organization's Internet communication efforts so they can begin transforming communication to this new method. Customers of a manufacturing company will need to be told they can seek product information and order status reports via the Web once those systems are set up. And if those same customers come onto the Web looking for a way to communicate with the company, it is important for the company to be listed in the various search engines and directories in use.

If your organization is seeking a new audience on the Internet, then it's necessary to promote your effort in a way that informs this new audience of your presence. A number of options are available to promote an Internet communications effort. These options fall into two categories: (1) efforts using traditional media and communication channels, and (2) activities that can be conducted on the Internet itself.

The first category includes any and all of the existing communication methods that are available off-line. These methods may or may not be in use for promotion or marketing activities by your organization. If they are in use, then the promotion of a Web site can be built into existing advertising and promotional activities.

If your organization is new or doesn't use traditional advertising methods, then it should consider promoting a Web communications effort. If you are operating a new business or other effort on the Internet, then traditional media channels can be used to drive end users onto a Web site.

Traditional media channels include the following options. Other methods exist as well, but these methods and their descriptions are a good place to begin promoting a Web communications effort.

- Mail-based communication, including postcards, letters, self-mailers, and catalogs, is the first medium to consider. This medium is the basis for most original direct marketing and is still very effective for communication with both customers and a prospective audience. Highly targetable and cost effective, mail is an excellent tool for promotion. One technique could involve making special offers to end users that require a Web-based response. Others could involve special discounts to catalog customers that use a Web transaction site.

- Broadcast media, including TV and radio, are very expensive but could be important if you need to reach a broad, mass-market audience. TV ads can easily carry Web addresses, and several large companies are including Web communication in national branding campaigns. An example is the Volkswagen effort discussed previously. Local TV ads are also available. I recently saw a local used car dealer carry a Web address on a TV spot.

- Radio promotion is easier to target than TV. Many business marketers use news radio ads to deliver offers to commuters during drive times. The use of this media could also be effective if a Web effort is targeted to this audience. Consumer marketers use radio promotion targeted at the demographics of the listening audiences of specific radio stations. Radio stations that have a young audience carry a lot of soft drink ads. Stations playing music for older listeners carry a lot of car advertisements. Web sites can be promoted using the same targeting criteria to reach specific audiences.

- Public relations is an indirect promotion effort. Public relations efforts involve media releases and press conferences to inform the media of an issue. These activities involve professionals who build relationships with media representatives and journalists. The objective is to gain "free media" or publicity and be included in the editorial content of magazines, newspapers, and broadcast journalism. This is difficult to accomplish without professional help on a national level. But locally, gaining media coverage about a Web communications effort may not be as difficult. In addition, trade magazines, publications, and newsletters that reach your targeted audience my be good places to focus public relations activities.

- Print media is driven by space advertising. This is another excellent method to promote an Internet communications effort. Promotion can be targeted at the readership of an appropriate publication. Specific space ads can be run carrying offers that drive readers onto a Web site. Addresses and e-mail can also be included as part of the ad's copy.

- Packaging for products or even informational packets is another vehicle for promotion. Since these materials are a necessary part of communicating with audience members, it's a good idea to promote Internet communication as well. Since people receiving these kinds of materials already have a relationship with your organization, these are excellent vehicles to begin transforming traditional customer service activities to Internet communication.

- Billboards and other signage are used by some companies and organizations for advertising and branding activities. These same efforts can be used to promote Web sites to the localized, mass-market audiences they reach.

On-line promotion is available to Webmasters wishing to promote a Web site or engage an audience. It is only useful in reaching the Internet audience, but that audience is growing daily.

This chapter discusses four areas ways to promote a Web site on-line. The first two activities involve search engines and Web directories. The second two methods involve creating links to a Web site by paying for them or sharing them with another Web site.

Search engines and Web directories are very similar and have a similar interface for the end user. But they are different as well. Both consist of information about Web pages taken from the actual Web pages stored on Web servers worldwide. Both store and catalog information about Web pages store the information in a database. And both provide opportunities for end users to search these databases, looking for the information they seek.

The primary difference between these two resources is how the information is originally stored in the databases. A search engine is sometimes called a search bot, or spider, because it uses a software tool to catalog the entire World Wide Web, following every link to every public Web site available and cataloging the text information on each Web page.

This information is then stored in a database or index. A search of this database requires the use of key words, meaning words that represent the subject of the search. A search will turn up pages that carry these key words. It is similar to looking up a phone number in the white pages. Altavista.com is an excellent example of this type of resource.

A Web directory is similar in many ways except that the information it provides was submitted to the administrators of the directory. Web sites are reviewed and categorized by human reviewers based on the content of the site. Searches of a directory yield results from the content of the directory, not the whole Web. And searches yield categories of information listed in the directories in addition to the individual Web pages involved. Directories can also be examined manually, like looking up a subject in the yellow pages, where information is stored in hierarchical fashion.

Unfortunately, the searching and storage systems for both of these types of resources are text-based. Written words are not the best ways to identify an idea or concept. The word *fly,* for instance, has many meanings. *To fly* is a verb involving soaring through the air. A *fly* is a noun describing an insect. A computer only sees one word, not the context it is written in.

The text issue is very apparent when using search engines. Searching for a key word will provide every Web page that contains that word. This means that a lot of matches won't be appropriate. Combinations of key words yield better results in search engines because pages that are found with the same words are probably related to the subject involved—but not always.

To provide better searching ability, the administrators of search engines are constantly improving the systems used to search, catalog, and store information found on Web pages. In addition, Web communicators are constantly trying to determine how the search engines are operating. Web communicators want their Web pages to be presented at the top of the results seen by end users searching the databases.

I think of this as a type of game: the search engines game. Administrators of search engines are constantly changing the formulas and systems they use to catalog Web pages. And they are altering the ways the information is presented to end users to make searching more useful. Meanwhile, Web communicators are trying to keep up and build their presentations to suit the systems in use by the search engines. The winner gets to be first in the search results. This is called good or high positioning.

Web directories do not create such a high-pressure situation. Web pages are reviewed and categorized by humans after being submitted by Web communicators. In this situation, the best recourse for communicators is to create targeted presentations and then suggest to the directories how best to classify the information. Communicators can't really beat the game since the directory administrators make the final decisions. These listings are important, however, and should be used to promote a Web presence.

The other prevalent types of on-line promotion involve linking between sites. Linking is a function of the World Wide Web that makes it possible to link any two pages or presentations existing on any public Web server. Links between content on different pages were the original reason for development of the Web and is the basis for its name.

Links promote a Web site by providing a direct connection to the site. For this reason, links are usually placed on high-traffic sites, meaning sites that get a lot of visitors. These links provide a connection to the site seeking promotion.

In these situations links are usually paid for by the site receiving the link. A form of advertising has been developed using banners, or small space ads, on Web sites. The banner ads promote the company or product they are representing and serve as link to the Web presentation by that company or organization. These banners are created by the advertisers and targeted to audiences based on the visitors to specific Web sites. Companies and organizations promote their Web sites on other Web sites that engage similar audience members.

Banner advertising is very similar to space advertising in traditional media. Banner ads are placed on sites with content targeted at appropriate audiences, just as space ads are placed in targeted publications. The Web sites for search engines, directories, and large media companies are some of the most visited Web sites. These sites can therefore charge the most money for banner ads linking from their sites. Banner ads also provide a direct response device by offering immediate linking to the advertiser and engagement of that end user in the process.

Another linking technique involves sharing links between Web sites that are in some type of relationship. In this type of arrangement, links are swapped by Web sites that are trying to help promote each other. These types of links are prevalent for noncommercial entities that want to provide informational resources and communities on the Web. They are used less by commercial operations.

Links provide an exit from a Web presentation. An organization may have to spend money or other resources engaging an audience member. If a link off the Web site is provided, an engaged visitor has a way to leave the presentation immediately. This issue must be considered. Technical solutions using additional browser windows have also been developed to alleviate this issue.

LAB 6.1 EXERCISES

6.1.1   UNDERSTAND TRADITIONAL MEDIA PROMOTION

To demonstrate the opportunities for promoting an Internet communication effort available in traditional media, review examples in your experience. You may not initially be able to complete all of these questions. Return to this exercise later if needed. Promotional efforts in traditional media may become more apparent once you start looking for them.

a) Where have you seen a reference to a Web site or e-mail address in a marketing piece you received in the mail?

b) Have you heard a Web site mentioned in a radio spot? If so, what was the subject matter?

c) Describe a Web site address from a TV advertisement.

d) What Web site address or e-mail contact have you seen in a space advertisement?

e) Have you noticed product packaging carrying a Web address?

f) Have you read an article or seen a mention of a Web site in a newspaper article or magazine listing?

g) How about in a billboard or other public signage?

6.1.2   UNDERSTAND SEARCH ENGINE POSITIONING

Log onto the index page www.altavista.com. This is the interface to the comprehensive database of Web pages and other information indexed by this popular Web search engine.

Type in the four key words: "peanut, butter, and jelly" with no commas.

a) What information is returned by the database?

b) What is the first item listed in the results?

c) What information is included in the first listing?

6.1.3 UNDERSTAND DIRECTORY LISTINGS

Examine directory listings by logging onto the index page for www.yahoo.com.

Find the category heading for education. Click on the subheading for colleges and universities.

a) What are some of your choices?

Click on the category identified as Colleges and Universities.

a) What are most of your choices?

Click on the United States item.

a) What choices are given now?

This is a set of more specific categories of universities and colleges in the United States.

Click on the letter M. Then click on Merrimack College.

a) What sites are listed?

Return to the index page and type "merrimack college" into the search engine for the site.

a) What are the results of the search?

Return to the index page at yahoo.com. At the bottom of the page click on the link titled "How to suggest a site."

a) What are the three steps involved with suggesting a Web site for inclusion in the Yahoo Web directory?

Log onto the index page at www.submit-it.com. Review the material on this page.

a) What service does this company provide?

6.1.4   UNDERSTAND BANNERS AND BUYING LINKS

To begin examining on-line promotion using banner ads, return to the index page of www.yahoo.com.

> **a)** What is the subject of the banner advertisement on the top of the page?

Hit the reload button on your Web browser to reload this page from the server.

> **a)** Is the banner advertisement different?

> **b)** Does the banner advertisement contain a direct marketing type of offer?

Click on the banner advertisement.

> **a)** Where does the link take you?

Return to the home page of yahoo.com. Click the link to the "Computers and the Internet" category.

> **a)** What is the subject of the advertisement on the top of this page?

6.1.5   UNDERSTAND RELATIONSHIP LINKS

Log onto the index page for the World Organization of Webmasters at www.world-webmasters.org. Click on the link for partners.

> **a)** How can you summarize the links that are listed here?

Log onto the Web page at this address: www.phish.com. Link to the contacts page. This is part of the Web site produced by a musical group named Phish. Click on the link to Phish.net.

> **a)** Where does this link take you?

Return to the www.world-webmaster.org/partner_index.html and click on the link for Prentice Hall publishing.

> **a)** Where does this link lead?

b) How is the appearance of this page different from the previous example?

LAB 6.1 EXERCISE ANSWERS

6.1.1 ANSWERS

To demonstrate the opportunities for promoting an Internet communication effort available in traditional media, review examples in your experience. You may not initially be able to complete all of these questions. Return to this exercise later if needed. Promotional efforts in traditional media may become more apparent once you start looking for them.

a) Where have you seen a reference to a Web site or e-mail address in a marketing piece you received in the mail?

Answer: Your answer will be based on your experience but might include the following.

A catalog that displays an on-line buying option. A letter package or postcard carrying a direct response offer with an e-mail or Web-based response device. A mailer for a large retailer that includes the corporate Web site address. A utility company may even include its Web address on the monthly billing statement, especially if it's providing an on-line payment option.

b) Have you heard a Web site mentioned in a radio spot? If so, what was the subject matter?

Answer: Your experience will vary, but here is mine.

I have noticed a growing number of radio spots that mention Web addresses, which is interesting considering that most radio advertising is targeted at people driving in cars. These spots usually involve high-tech companies and promotion of Web-based businesses such as amazon.com, mortgage.com, and priceline.com.

c) Describe a Web site address from a TV advertisement.

Answer: Your answer will again be based on your experience.

Web addresses are becoming prevalent on national advertising campaigns and branding efforts for many types of businesses. The large software and hardware companies, including Microsoft and Compaq, usually display Web addresses, which seems appropriate. Automotive manufacturers, large business consultants, and financial institutions have done so as well.

d)   What Web site address or e-mail contact have you seen in a space advertisement?

Answer: Your answers will vary.

In nationally distributed magazines carrying both business and consumer content, more ads carry Web addresses than don't. In my local paper, ads for training companies, credit unions, photo development shops, printers, restaurants, and even a local tourist attraction all carry e-mail or Web response vehicles.

e)   Have you noticed product packaging carrying a Web address?

Answer: Again, your answer is subjective.

I have noticed Web addresses on a variety of consumer and business products including office supplies, foods, and entertainment media.

f)   Have you read an article or seen a mention of a Web site in a newspaper article or magazine listing?

Answer: Your answer is based on your experience. Mine follows.

Though some journalists and editors do their own research about new interactive communication efforts, many rely on public relations (PR) activities that supply them with information and suggestions about these efforts. Public relations companies and consultants utilize press releases and media events to attract the attention of appropriate journalists. These efforts are expensive but can be rewarding if the media picks up a story in a well-read publication. Business publications are full of stories about new Web sites that were announced to the press using these methods.

g)   How about in a billboard or other public signage?

Answer: If you live in a major metropolitan area, you may have observed a billboard, bus, or taxi promoting a Web communication effort.

All of these examples demonstrate the use of traditional advertising as a method to promote interactive communication. All of the examples you have seen were executed to reach a particular audience and inform them of an Internet communications effort. Informing audience members, especially customers or other end users that have an existing relationship with your company or organization, is an important part of the promotion process.

Sometimes this step is overlooked in the rush to engage new prospects on the Internet. But informing and communicating with existing relationships should be a priority before seeking new end users to communicate with.

Some of the examples you have seen are part of ongoing advertising and branding efforts, and the general Web addresses were added to give additional return to the promotional investment.

Other examples may have provided specific Web or e-mail addresses tied into specific marketing campaigns. In these situations a Web site may be designed to tie into a certain advertising effort or direct marketing offer. A different e-mail address could be used for every magazine an ad runs in to track the responses based on readership.

Regardless of the level of complexity, companies and organizations need to inform their audiences of Internet communication efforts. If the audience is reachable through traditional media channels, then this is the place to start.

6.1.2 ANSWERS

Log onto the index page www.altavista.com. This is the interface to the comprehensive database of Web pages and other information indexed by this popular Web search engine.

Type in the four key words: "peanut, butter, and jelly" with no commas.

a)   What information is returned by the database?

Answer: The database returns a list of Web pages that contain the words peanut butter and jelly.

This list of links, called results, was pulled from a massive database created by this company's Web search engine. This engine is an automated system that systematically searches, analyzes, and records text from every Web page it can find about once a month. More than a dozen different search engines are currently operating. Popular ones inlcude Lycos, Excite, HotBot, and Infoseek. They are also sometimes called spiders or bots because they search and record text-based information on the Web automatically, following every link they come across.

When you make a key word request, a database, called an index, containing all this stored information is searched and the results are displayed. But at this point in time computers are not very good at identifying context, only words. That's why these types of key word searches can be frustrating. They turn up every page that is stored in the database and contains the words you requested. The pages are then ranked according to relevance.

Getting a high position in this ranking is a challenging process for Web communicators. The ranking is based on several elements of each Web page involved. In addition, each Web search engine uses its own system to search, store, and rank results, and these systems often change.

One of the reasons for this constant flux is the efforts of the search engine administrators to develop more advanced methods of information indexing and search functionality. Great progress has been made in this area, and search engines are getting better at delivering appropriate results to end users. Recent advances provide answers to questions posed by the end user instead of just key words.

b) What is the first item listed in the results?

Answer: Your answer might vary slightly but the first item on the list probably contains the key words peanut, butter, and jelly *in the title of the Web page.*

This title also serves as a link to the Web page. Although every search engine is different, most ranking is initially based on the key words in the title of the Web page. A title is very important for search engines. It serves as a headline for the rest of the page.

c) What information is included in the first listing?

Answer: A short description of this page is included in the listing. Other information includes the URL address and creation or updating of the page.

The appearance of this listing information is another important factor in the ranking of this page in this search engine's results. The description of the page is copied from the description meta tag on the HTML source code of the Web document involved. (Meta tags are part of the HTML code that is read by the server but not displayed to the end user accessing a Web document. Meta tags and HTML are examined in other publications in this series. *Understanding Web Development and Web Protocols,* Prentice Hall PTR.)

Depending on the search engine involved, the information that affects the ranking is the actual visible text from the Web document.

The search engines that index and display information in this manner all use proprietary algorithms to decide the importance, or weight, given to each of these factors when determining the results listings. How each item is weighted in the results process is also changed regularly.

Search engine administrators and Web page developers struggle to gain the upper hand over each other in this ranking game. I would only suggest getting involved in this game if your Web site business model is wholly dependent on being found by search engines and listed in the initial results presented to end users. And if that is the case, I suggest looking for additional promotional opportunities. I don't believe this game can truly be won.

A number of software products and services have been developed that claim assistance in this game. But a reliable source has informed me that there is really only one way to play this game and get a high position in search engine results. It involves learning each search engine's weighting algorithm by analyzing the results of a search on that engine. This is accomplished by looking at the key word density using a software tool called a text analyzer.

This process will show you the weight of particular key words in high-ranking documents. Reproduce the weight in your own documents and you should get the same high-ranking results on that engine. Of course, you'll have to repeat this process on a regular basis for each of the dozen or so search engines to keep up with the constantly changing rules of the game.

One practice being used by some Web publishers is called page swapping or page redirection. This involves the development of specific Web pages to match the needs of search engines during their inquiries and rank high in their results. However, these Web pages are not served to end users and instead redirect users to a different page. A refresh meta tag also accomplishes a similar situation, creating a doorway page for search engines that immediately reloads when the end user requests the page.

This process is very controversial in the Internet community, and many search engine administrators will blacklist a Web site if this practice is detected, banning inclusion in the database. Search engines are against the practice of searching, indexing, and providing links to pages that don't carry the content the end user is searching for.

Again, this search engine game is very complicated. The rules of the game are constantly changing and the results are questionable at best. Most companies and organizations would not count on their phone directory listing to be their primary method of promotion in the marketplace. That's basically what search engine listings provide.

Another interesting aspect of the search engine game is the development of Web sites that provide searches of multiple search engine databases through one interface. A popular search of searches can be accomplished at www.dogpile.com.

6.1.3 ANSWERS

Examine directory listings by logging onto the index page for www.yahoo.com.

Find the category heading for education. Click on the subheading for colleges and universities.

a) What are some of your choices?

Answer: A new listing of categories and a list of Web sites that don't fit well into categories.

This Web site operates an extensive Web directory service. Similar to a combined table of contents and an index for a book, information on Web sites is stored, referenced, and cross-referenced by category in a database.

This directory and others like it list Web sites, not just Web documents. It differs from a search engine because it does not search the Web on its own. Instead, this database is dependent on the submission of Web sites for consideration, categorization, and indexing.

This process actually involves human consideration of the Web sites involved. Humans review each submission to decide how a Web site will be listed in the directory and how it will be cross-referenced.

Click on the category identified as Colleges and Universities.

a) What are most of your choices?

Answer: The majority of the choices is an extensive list of countries.

The Web site information groupings are organized in a hierarchical fashion. This means that information about Web sites and links to them are stored in categories and subcategories from general to specific. In this case, the category for colleges and universities is subdivided into specific country subcategories.

Click on the United States item.

a) What choices are given now?

Answer: Letters and a number of other groupings, including private, public, men's, and women's colleges.

This a set of more specific categories of universities and colleges in the United States.

Click on the letter M. Then click on Merrimack College.

a)   What sites are listed?

Answer: Yours might vary but should include at least two options: the Merrimack College Web site and a site discussing men's hockey at Merrimack College.

These Web sites are the subject of this directory search: the college's official site and an unofficial site discussing the college's highly competitive hockey team. Note that the Merrimack College Web site is actually listed based on its physical location in North Andover, Massachusetts. It is cross-referenced as a college in the education categories. The hockey site is actually catagorized under sports and recreation and cross-referenced to education as well.

Return to the index page and type "merrimack college" into the search engine for the site.

a)   What are the results of the search?

Answer: Your answer may vary but should include the same two sites for the college and the hockey team.

This search turned up links to sites already stored in the directory's database of Web sites. Again, these sites were submitted to the directory and categorized by humans, not found by search engines.

Return to the index page at www.yahoo.com. At the bottom of the page click on the link titled "How to suggest a site."

a)   What are the three steps involved with suggesting a Web site for inclusion in the Yahoo Web directory?

Answer: 1. Check to see if your site is already listed in Yahoo!. 2. Find the appropriate category in Yahoo!. 3. Suggest your site from the appropriate category.

This Web document explains the steps involved with submitting a Web site to this directory for review, inclusion, and categorization by its staff. Click on the link to the "List of Important Pointers" to learn more about how submitted material is handled.

Log onto the index page at www.submit-it.com. Review the material on this page.

a)   What service does this company provide?

Answer: This company helps promote Web sites by submitting Web site listings to hundreds of directories and search engines.

This company charges a fee to distribute Web site listings on your behalf. It submits Web site listings to search engines, which will then come and search your site, and Web directories. A list of the hundreds of search engines and directories that are notified is available on the site as well.

Of course, each directory and search engine uses a different process to store and present this information to its end users. This service, and others like it, will also update this information and provides reports on the status of your listing with some of the popular search engines.

A number of software products are also available to automate the submitting process. They will submit listings at both Web directories and search engines. Some claim to submit Web site listings to over 900 different Web directories on your behalf.

Utilizing either of these of these methods to spread the word about a Web communication effort is an excellent way to begin reaching the Internet audience. And both save you time and effort in promoting your Web site on-line.

Most search engines and directories do not necessarily reach targeted audiences. But a Web communication effort should be included in them so prospective audience members can find your site if they are looking for the solutions you provide. Specific directories can also be investigated that may cater to a more specific audience that you wish to reach.

6.1.4 ANSWERS

To begin examining on-line promotion using banner ads, return to the index page of www.yahoo.com.

a) What is the subject of the banner advertisement on the top of the page?

Answer: Your answer will vary based on your experience. Mine follows.

I saw a direct response advertisement for an organization called cars.com. When this Web page was shown to me, this advertisement was included in the presentation. It was probably one of several banner ads that are being displayed by this site simultaneously.

Hit the reload button on your Web browser to reload this page from the server.

a) Is the banner advertisement different?

Answer: Yours may be different, but the answer is probably yes.

A different banner advertisement is presented each time a new user logs onto the site or when the page is reloaded from the server. The Web site is showing different ads based on a rotation of some kind so multiple advertisers can be presented by the site in the same time frames. The same practice is done in TV and radio advertising.

The display of this banner ad is called an impression. One end user saw this banner one time. The banner theoretically made one impression on one person.

Many Web sites charge advertisers on a cost-per-impression basis. This is called a Cost per Thousand (CPM) model, which is a term borrowed from traditional direct marketing list-buying terminology. Advertisers must pay the Web publisher a set amount of money for a set amount of impressions.

The published rates for the myway.com Web site, which engages a national audience of consumers on the Web seeking a personalized information resource, are between $25 and $35 for 1000 impressions. These numbers are discounted in quantity and vary widely based on the audience of the site involved, its traffic levels, and relationships between advertisers and Web sites.

This pricing structure may not be the best case scenario for promoting a Web site. Just because the banner ad is displayed does not mean that end users will respond to the offer on the banner ad.

b) Does the banner advertisement contain a direct marketing type of offer?

Answer: Your experience will probably differ from mine.

The banner ad did contain a direct response offer. The ad stated, "Win a 1-year car lease!" This offer acts as an enticement for me to click on the banner to find out how I can win. Banner ad copy is usually written to gain an immediate response from end users who see the ad. Banner ad creative efforts are extensive and usually involve multiple presentations for the same campaign.

Click on the banner advertisement.

a) Where does the link take you?

Answer: Your answer is based on your situation. Regardless of the specifics, the link took you to a Web page for the advertiser who was running the banner ad.

This Web page may be a specific presentation targeted at the audience responding to this promotion or offer. It might also be the home page for the company or organization. It might be another page or service offered by the Yahoo! company.

By linking to this Web page you have completed a click-through. You clicked through the banner ad to its sponsor and responded to the offer.

Another method Web sites use to charge advertisers to display banner ads is on a per-click-through basis. In this model, the advertiser pays the Web site for every response or click-through that is generated by the banner ads on that site. Costs for this type of model are currently running between $.01 to $.15 for each click-through. This is a better pricing model for Web marketers than straight CPM pricing as marketers only have to pay for results instead of space ads.

Return to the home page of www.yahoo.com. Click the link to the "Computers and the Internet" category.

a)   What is the subject of the advertisement on the top of this page?

Answer: Your answer will vary, but the ad banner probably has something to do with technology.

This ad was intentionally placed here to reach an audience interested in technology issues. The ads in this and other sections of the Web directory are targeted to particular audiences. Banner advertising on the Web provides opportunities for promotions to be placed on pages carrying related content. This means that end users interested in particular topics or information can be targeted with offers based on those topics. For example, a test preparation company can place ads on information pertaining to college entrance exams.

Purchasing banner advertising space is similar to buying space ads in traditional publications. A number of companies currently act as brokers in the marketplace and can place banner ads on different Web sites for a set amount of money. Some brokers represent groups, or networks, of Web sites. Others represent marketers.

Fortunately, it is very easy to test creative content, offers, and placement of banner ads on Web sites. Due to the immediate and dynamic nature of Web communication, the success or failure of banner ads becomes apparent quickly. Banners can be pulled from unsuccessful sites. Creative approaches can be tested simultaneously and the ones that work can be used to replace the ones that don't.

**LAB
6.1**

Overall, the use of banner ads to buy links and generate response to an Internet communications effort is an effective and expensive proposition. This type of on-line promotion may be necessary if the target audience for your effort is to be found on the Web.

6.1.5 ANSWERS

Log onto the index page for the World Organization of Webmasters at www.world-webmasters.org. Click on the link for partners.

a) How can you summarize the links that are listed here?

Answer: Your answers will vary. Here's mine.

This is a list of links to partners and organizations that the World Organization of Webmasters has some type of mutually beneficial relationship with. Most support the efforts of the organization in some way through promotions, financial assistance, or other means.

These links are included on the site to provide on-line promotion for these companies. This service is provided in return for the nice things these companies do for WOW.

Besides playing the search engine and directory game and buying links through banners on popular Web sites, another way to promote a Web-based communications effort is to seek links from other Web sites that you have a relationship with. These could include vendors, partners, affinity groups, and associations.

The nature of linking, however, means links only go one way. Links to your site have to be provided by the Web site linking to you. This may involve paying a Web site for a listing. Or it could involve shared linking or swapping. This is the Internet version of "I'll link from mine if you'll link from yours."

Log onto the Web page at this address: www.phish.com. This is the Web site produced by a musical group named Phish. Link to the contacts page. Click on the link to phish.net.

a) Where does this link take you?

Answer: Your answer will vary but could include something like this: To the index page at www.phish.net, a Web site serving an on-line community for fans of this band.

Scrolling down the page, you can find several links to the Official Phish Web Site on this index page. It is also linked twice in the disclaimer on the bottom of the page. This is an example of a shared link. Two sites with a relationship have swapped links with each other. In this case, the band is supporting the efforts of an organized fan community and the fans are enthusiastically (some may say extremely) supportive of the efforts of the band. Many other links are listed on this page as well, and most of them are provided as part of shared link arrangements between the site's creators as well.

Links can also be shared in the form of banners. Several programs exist in the marketplace that provide opportunities for Web communicators to exchange banners with each other. These banners will provide a similar type of shared link functionality. The Submit It service discussed previously is related to another service called Link Exchange, which arranges these types of situations.

Return to the www.world-webmaster.org/partner_index.html and click on the link for Prentice Hall publishing.

a) Where does this link lead?

Answer: This link takes you to the home page for Prentice Hall.

This company is the training materials publishing partner for the World Organization of Webmasters and the publisher of this book.

b) How is the appearance of this page different from the previous example?

Answer: In this example the Prentice Hall site opens within the browser window of the WOW site. In the previous example, the link brought us from the Phish.com site directly to the index page of the Phish.net site.

In the WOW example, the link brings up the Prentice Hall Web site while keeping end users engaged with the WOW site. This is done using frames as part of the HTML document, allowing different sections of the browser window to present different information. In other situations the linked site appears in a separate browser window. In the band and fan example, the link provides an exit from one site and an entrance to another site.

This can be a negative situation for Web marketers and communicators, who are attempting to engage an audience. Providing an exit for an end user to leave a site may not be a good idea if a lot of money and effort was spent to get that visitor. On the other hand, if the shared links bring a lot of traffic, then that contribution to promotion of the effort must be considered as well.

LAB 6.1 SELF-REVIEW QUESTIONS

In order to test your progress, you should be able to answer the following questions:

1) What is the best way to use traditional media to promote a Web presence?
   a) _____ Create cool TV ads that win advertising awards.
   b) _____ Take out space ads in the local paper.
   c) _____ Hire expensive PR people to shmooze for you.
   d) _____ Utilize the appropriate media to reach your target audience and inform them of your presence.
   e) _____ Tell your friends.

2) How do you win the search engine game?
   a) _____ By receiving a check in the mail
   b) _____ By receiving a high position in search engine results
   c) _____ By buying a lot of banner ads
   d) _____ By answering your door and seeing Ed McMahon

3) How do directories receive suggestions for Web site listings?
   a) _____ They use automated software to search the Web.
   b) _____ They solicit input from focus groups.
   c) _____ Sites are submitted by Web communicators and submission services.
   d) _____ Anonymous letters

4) How are banner ads similar to space advertisements?
   a) _____ They provide promotion for a Web site or product.
   b) _____ They are paid for by the advertiser.
   c) _____ They are placed on Web sites that have a targeted audience wanted by the advertiser.
   d) _____ None of these
   e) _____ All of these

L A B   6 . 2

MEASURING INTERNET COMMUNICATION ACTIVITIES

LAB OBJECTIVES

After this Lab, you will be able to

- Understand Web Site Usage Reporting
- Understand Cookies that Compile
- Profile People

In this lab, we will discuss three ways to measure activity in an Internet communications effort. These three methods appear in the order of quality. Each method provides useful information. Information that is specific to an individual audience member is more useful for marketers as it provides more opportunities to develop relationships based on individual wants, needs, and desires. But all of these methods provide data that can be used deliver targeted presentations to audiences.

The first method involves reviewing general information from server log files and reports. This is a useful method but is least effective from a marketing and communication perspective. The second method uses a software tool, called a cookie, that is built into the client-server computing model, which allows servers to track the activities of an individual PC. The third method, which is the most effective measurement tool, involves the review of the communication actually taking place through a Web communication effort.

The first method uses server logs to review activity on a Web site. Every time a client computer communicates with a server via the Web, a record of the transaction is recorded by the server. These log files contain a lot of useful information for measuring Web activity. This information can then be reported by the server itself using a reporting software tool. A number of third party services can also be utilized to track server activity and publish easy-to-read reports for Webmasters. A new tracking service called superstats.com is used as an example in this lab.

Captured and reported data can include many topics:

- Page views—records of what and when individual pages were viewed by end users and the history of this activity
- Unique visitors—the number of individual visitors to a page or site by hour, day, or month
- Referring documents—the pages that visitors linked from outside and inside the site
- Search engines that provide links to your site
- The operating systems of the end users' computers
- Browsers and plug-ins being used by the end users
- The domain names of the end users' computers
- Origin countries and languages being used by the end users

All of this information is useful for Web communicators. The popularity of a Web page can help determine the needs of a Web site audience and provide opportunities to improve a presentation. The link records can help determine how a visitor is interacting with a presentation and how it can be improved. Usage numbers can be compared to promotional activities. Client computer information is useful when improving presentation content.

The client-server computing model also provides another useful tool for tracking Web activity. A function built into the client and server software packages developed by Netscape and Microsoft allows Web communicators to set cookies into the client software when end users access servers. These cookies are text codes generated by the server and stored in a file on the PC. Cookies act as individual identifiers or name tags. When a PC logs onto a server using this method, the server checks for cookies. If one is present, the server can track the activity of that PC over time. If one isn't present, the server will try to create a new one. This process can be blocked by the end user, however.

This information is useful for marketers as it provides opportunities to track individual users of a Web site. In the first chapter we discussed the value of cookies as used by amazon.com. These individual identifiers can be combined with usage information to create comprehensive pictures of individual end users and their activity on a Web site. Historical data can be compiled to document users' wants, needs, and desires over time.

Unfortunately, this method does not immediately identify the actual person involved in the communication, just a PC. In the amazon.com example, the cookie identifier was matched with the end user account information to provide personalized greetings when I logged onto the Web site.

The best kind of measurement involves the review of actual communication completed with individuals over the Web or net. Direct communication with individual audience members is the purpose behind this type of communication. Measuring this type of activity involves reviewing the capturing of data and contact information from customers or prospective customers over time. The number of individual profiles built from direct, individual communication is the best type of information to measure. It is the most useful for building relationships.

Success or failure of a Web site or Internet communications effort should not be based on measurement of activity. Success is based on the goals of the effort, the information exchanges, and the audiences involved. The fulfillment of wants, needs, and desires is the motivation for marketing. Fulfillment of these issues via the Internet is the ultimate measurement of success.

LAB 6.2 EXERCISES

6.2.1   UNDERSTAND WEB SITE USAGE REPORTING

Let's look at an example of this type of activity. Log onto the Web site at this address: www.superstats.com. This site describes a service available to Webmasters that will track the usage of a Web site using HTML code embedded into the Web site's documents. This service stores and reports that information via a Web interface.

This service is provided free to Webmasters in exchange for the display of a banner ad on the Web site being tracked. This provides promotional opportunities and banner sales opportunities. This service may or may not be beneficial for Web marketers depending on the click-through opportunities and response of these banners. A paid tracking service is also available from super-stats.com and others.

On the index page, click on "Examples" or "Demo."

a) What three categories of information topics are tracked and reported by this service?

b) Why is this information helpful for Web communicators?

6.2.2   UNDERSTAND COOKIES THAT COMPILE

To examine a more specific measurement tool, conduct a search on your PC for a file with the word "Cookies" in it. This can be done with the Find tool in Windows or Find File on a Mac. Once the file is located, open it with a text editor.

a) What does this file contain?

b) Is the information gained by a Web server setting and tracking cookies more helpful than information from usage files?

6.2.3   PROFILE PEOPLE

Consider again the discussion in Chapter 1 regarding amazon.com. In that first chapter we discussed the process involved with purchasing a book from this on-line merchant.

a) What specific customer information can be captured and stored by this company?

b) What is the best kind of measurement discussed in this lab?

LAB 6.2 EXERCISE ANSWERS

6.2.1   ANSWERS

Let's look at an example of this type of activity. Log onto the Web site at this address: www.superstats.com. This site describes a service available to Webmasters that will track the usage of a Web site using HTML code embedded into the Web site's documents. This service stores and reports that information via a Web interface.

This service is provided free to Webmasters in exchange for the display of a banner ad on the Web site being tracked. This provides promotional opportunities and banner sales opportunities. This service may or may not be beneficial for Web marketers depending on the click-through opportunities and response of these banners. A paid tracking service is also available from superstats.com and others.

On the index page, click on "Examples" or "Demo."

a) What three categories of information topics are tracked and reported by this service?

Answer: Your answers will vary but should include the following topics: site traffic reports, visitor profile reports, and marketing reports (a very loose use of this term).

Without going into too much detail, a lot of information is available from looking at the usage of a Web site by end users. All of the information presented in this tracking service can be also gleaned directly from the Web server that is hosting a Web site.

Every interaction between a server and a client computer is recorded, or logged, by the server. Generally speaking, these logs record hits. A hit is the term used to describe a file download from the server to the client. These logs can be read directly but are not very simple to decipher and vary according to operating system and administrator.

Software products and services like the one shown here capture this log data and generate reports. This exercise is utilizing this service and its demonstration to show the types of information available from server log files.

b) Why is this information helpful for Web communicators?

Answer: Your answers will again vary. Here's mine.

This type of information is useful to measure the traffic activity on a Web site and to begin gauging the effectiveness of the presentations being made on it. These reports give a rough idea as to what end users are doing on your site. Deductions can be made about audience characteristics and what is working on a site versus what is not working.

For example, historical data can be compared to site promotion activities to see what efforts are successful. Individual page usage can identify what pages and subjects are popular and effective for the audience. Internal link records can demonstrate how users are interacting with your presentation and how it can be improved to meet their needs. External link records can tell you where users are coming from and influence decisions about on-line promotional activities. Client computer operating systems, browsers, and plug-in usage can help determine how best to present information to the audience. Domain addresses can help indicate if users are logging on from work or home.

It is important to note that none of this information tells you exactly who you are communicating with, just general activity. This type of information is valuable but not as useful as more specific information about individual end users. More specific ways to measure Web site use are discussed next.

6.2.2 ANSWERS

To examine a more specific measurement tool, conduct a search on your PC for a file with the word "Cookies" in it. This can be done with the Find tool in Windows or Find File on a Mac. Once the file is located, open it with a text editor.

a)   What does this file contain?

Answer: Your answer is subjective. Mine follows.

This file contains a series of text messages that represent cookies. If this file is empty, then this machine has not accepted cookies set by Web servers.

If the file contains text, then your PC has allowed cookies to be set. It probably looks like this: On the left side of the document are Web site addresses. On the right side of the document are a series of corresponding code strings.

Together this information acts as a kind of marker or identifier for this individual PC. This information was written here by the Web servers that are identified on the left side of the document. The code string is unique to this machine. Every time this machine logs onto the same server, the server checks for cookies. If a cookie is present here already, the machine can track the activities of this PC on that server. If a cookie isn't present, it creates one and writes it to this file. Cookies can be blocked and erased from a PC by an end user as well.

This cookie identifier allows a Web server to track this particular PC's activity on the server. Every repeat visit provides more information about the wants, needs, and desires of this PC.

b) Is the information gained by a Web server setting and tracking cookies more helpful than information from usage files?

Answer: The answer is yes.

This information is more advanced than the information taken from usage records because detailed information on an individual PC is captured. When combined with the information discussed in the previous exercise, a more in-depth picture of audience members can be created.

Granted, the server doesn't track a person. Cookies track PCs, and more than one person can use a PC. But data generated by tracking the movements, history, and activity of individual PC users is valuable for developing customized, engaging presentations and measuring results. The only thing more valuable for building relationships is to know the actual identity of the end user involved.

6.2.3 ANSWERS

Consider again the discussion in Chapter I regarding amazon.com. In that first chapter we discussed the process involved with purchasing a book from this on-line merchant.

a) What specific customer information can be captured and stored by this company?

Answer: Your answer will be clouded by all the information you've covered since that discussion, but it might sound something like mine.

When a customer purchases a book or other item from amazon.com, the customer's name, contact, payment, and shipping information is captured to process the order. In addition, specific product preferences are captured from the customer by providing opportunities to specify wants, needs, and desires. Remember the option for selecting your interests, likes, and dislikes on the amazon.com site? That site even suggested products based on the preferences of other customers.

All of this information is captured in a database and is updated with each visit or purchase. The company can then build a profile for each individual person. Relationship marketing can be developed, delivering offers to the specific wants, needs, and desires of this person.

b) What is the best kind of measurement discussed in this lab?

Answer: Your answer will vary but should identify individual responses from customers or prospects as the best kind of information to capture and measure.

Site usage reporting and cookie tracking are both valuable for measuring the results of a Web communication effort. But the best kind of measurement involves reviewing actual responses from prospective or current customers.

This is why we initiated Internet communication: To communicate directly with an audience. Therefore, the measurement of our success is based on the amount of direct communication we actually accomplish. Capturing information about the actual people we are communicating with allows us to continue the communication and to build profiles of the people we are communicating with over time.

Knowing how many people looked at a Web page is good. Knowing if the same people came back again and when is better. But knowing who they are and what their wants, needs, and desires are is the best.

With this information we can use Internet communication to build relationships. Capturing information from our individual audience members helps us find ways to serve their needs.

The actual success of an Internet communications effort can best be defined by looking at our original goals discussed in Chapter 2. If we are reaching them and communicating based on our original plan, then we are succeeding.

LAB 6.2 SELF-REVIEW QUESTIONS

In order to test your progress, you should be able to answer the following questions:

1) Traffic reports from a Web server are useful for gauging what?
   a) _____ The software packages in use by clients
   b) _____ Success of a promotional effort
   c) _____ The use of color on a Web site
   d) _____ All of these
   e) _____ None of these

2) Link histories and referring pages provide what information?
   a) _____ The software in use by clients
   b) _____ The record of a visitor's travel through a presentation
   c) _____ A record of a link provided by an on-line promotional effort
   d) _____ Both b and c

3) Cookies can identify the end user of a PC being tracked.
   a) _____ True
   b) _____ False

4) The best kind of information for measuring Internet communication is captured from what methods?
   a) _____ Reading server usage files and reports
   b) _____ Tracking cookies and building profiles
   c) _____ Reviewing information captured from direct communication with end users
   d) _____ None of these

CHAPTER 6

TEST YOUR THINKING

The projects in this section use the skills you've acquired in this chapter. The answers to these projects are available to instructors only through a Prentice Hall sales representative and are intended to be used in classroom discussion and assessment.

1) Identify what audience you need to inform of your effort. How will you promote the effort using traditional media channels?

2) Identify on-line promotional activities. Is it necessary to play the search engine games, or will submission efforts be enough to promote your site?

3) Identify linking options. Are shared linking options available? How will you utilize paid banner advertisement?

4) Consider measurement options for your effort. What information will you retrieve from server logs? What information will be captured to profile end users?

C H A P T E R 7

INTERNET MARKETING: LEGAL ISSUES

We have always known that heedless self-interest was bad morals; we know now that it is bad economics.

—Franklin Delano Roosevelt

CHAPTER OBJECTIVES

In this chapter, you will learn about

The objective of this chapter is to provide you with enough information to know that laws do apply to activities on the Web and to know that even common situations may have significant legal implications. Most of the situations discussed in this chapter are based on U.S. law, although international laws apply. International law is a complex area outside the scope of this book.

This chapter is not intended as a substitute for legal advice, nor does it contain professional legal advice. An attorney is best suited to respond to the specific circumstances of your situation.

253

Legality and illegality are based on the specifics of each unique situation combined with federal, state, and local laws and regulations and current case law. Do not hesitate to go to an attorney, and the earlier in the situation, the better. A good attorney prefers to practice preventative law rather than trying to practice much more expensive damage control in a courtroom. If your target audience is outside of the United States, select a law firm with expertise and experience in the laws of that country.

L A B   7 . 1

ESTABLISHING AND DOCUMENTING AGREEMENTS IN A CONTRACT

LAB OBJECTIVES

After this Lab, you will be able to

- Describe a Contract and Its Three Basic Elements
- Evaluate a Contract

Before you dive eagerly into your next (or first) Web site development project, as either an employer or as an independent consultant, you need to develop a strong foundation for that project. This is done through a development contract. It should describe what will be accomplished, how it will be accomplished (in general, usually, not the "bits and bytes"), when payments are earned and due, and who owns what. (Who owns what at the end of the project is extremely important, as you will see in Lab 7.2.) As questions arise during the implementation process, the contract will be the baseline of what was intended. If you are the employer, *don't pay* for any coding without it. If you are the developer, *don't do* any coding without it.

CONTRACTING FOR SUCCESS

A contract is the basic building block of business relationships. Fortunately or unfortunately, life cannot be conducted without contracts, both written and verbal. We enter into contracts all the time, whether we know it or not, and we will be more successful if

> We are aware that we are making a contract.
>
> We know the rules that apply.
>
> We understand the negotiation process.

If everything goes well, then the contract is just a piece of paper (or several!) with signatures on it. If things do not go well, or if a question arises during the course of implementation or paying for the service, then the contract is extremely useful (or *should* be). A written contract is more effective for obvious reasons ("I *never* agreed to *that!*"), and is highly recommended. In general, very few businesspeople object to contracts because they know that contracts usually prevent more misunderstandings than they cause, and a good fair contract protects all the parties. Of course, signing a contract will not make an honest person out of a dishonest one, but it can describe the penalties, or "remedies," if the terms and conditions ("t's and c's") of the contract are not met.

Often, the process of documenting the "deal" in the contract is extremely useful by itself. This is where everyone's assumptions should be described and examined. This documentation process helps eliminate many points of confusion that could become nasty disagreements if delineated *after* the project is started. The contract should truly reflect an up-front agreement among the parties about what is going to happen.

At a minimum, a Web development contract should describe

> Who has ownership, and when the ownership transfers
>
> What is to be accomplished
>
> Who is responsible for doing what
>
> The time frame, or time frames
>
> The price and terms of payment

With everything "out on the table," the parties should have a clearer understanding about what is going to happen and what is expected of everyone. There should be less confusion and more cooperation. The key is to agree on the terms and conditions. If there is something you do not like about an aspect of the deal, discuss it and negotiate something with which you can agree. Or walk away.

CONTRACT ELEMENTS

Traditionally, a contract is defined as an agreement among two or more parties, who know each other, and who promise to perform a transaction with each other. This is fairly clear in the real world. You know when you are buying a house, leasing an apartment, renting a car, or purchasing something with your credit card. In the real world, you deal directly with the people involved—the realtor, the landlord, the rental car agent, or the store salesperson. It isn't as clear in the virtual world of cyberspace.

A contract is comprised of three basic elements. If one of the elements is missing, then there is no contract. If all of the elements are in place, we have a contract.

1. An *offer* made by an offeror—the person (or entity) extending the offer

2. An *acceptance* made by an offeree—the person (or entity) accepting the offer

3. *Consideration*—an exchange of something of value, like money

You participate in contracts all the time, as an offeree or an offeror. The process is so well established in our world that we participate without even being aware that we have made and executed a contract. For example, you go to a computer store to shop for a new printer for your office. The store is making thousands of offers, constantly, by putting merchandise on display with price tags attached. The store hopes that offerees will come along and will accept its offer and exchange money for the products for sale.

Suppose that you find the exact printer that you want at the store, but the price is too high and the only one left in stock is the one on display. So you take the "floor sample" printer to the salesperson and make an offer to purchase that specific printer at a price lower than the posted purchase price. When you do that, you have exchanged roles with the store. You have become the offeror (by offering to purchase the printer at a price lower than the posted price) and the store has become the offeree. If the store clerk accepts your offer by agreeing to accept the lower price, you give the clerk your credit card; you sign the sales slip at the agreed-upon price; and you leave with your new printer. The transaction is completed. The store offered you the item at a specific price. You rejected that price and made a lower counteroffer. The store accepted your counter offer, and the transaction was completed. You actually negotiated a lower price in exchange for what could possibly be a less valuable item—the display model.

ORAL AND WRITTEN AGREEMENTS

A contract does not have to be in writing to be a contract. There is such a thing as verbal contract, but it is usually much harder to enforce than a written contract.

VISIBLE AND INVISIBLE CONTRACTS

Frequently, you sign some kind of slip of paper as you complete a transaction (like the credit card charge slip). That's a contract, or part of it! Often, you don't even notice the contract and its terms and conditions because they are such a common part of your daily life.

Some contracts are more noticeable than others. The contract is painfully obvious when you buy a house (tons of paperwork and lots of lawyers), less obvious with an apartment lease or car rental agreement, and nearly invisible with a charge slip. Hopefully, you read and understand *all* of them before you sign any of them. However, it is not easy to read all of the documents associated with the house purchase because much of the language is written by lawyers specifically for lawyers, with volumes of case law behind it all (that's why the lawyers are there).

The contract is also obvious, and usually much less intimidating, with the apartment lease—what size is the security deposit required, when do you get it back, what kind of apartment damage can result in losing that deposit, etc. The contract is at least partially obvious with the car rental agreement, where you initial your option choices (so that it can be proven that you did agree to those choices), offer your credit card, and sign at the bottom. The contract is much less obvious with your credit card slips, which usually do not appear to contain much text. In most cases, the real terms and conditions associated with your credit card purchases are written in *very tiny print* on small slips of paper included with your monthly statement or your actual credit card application.

ENFORCEABLE CONTRACTS

There are some requirements associated with contracts, to make them enforceable by a court if the need arises.

- An enforceable contract must be "legal." For example, movies have the bad guys "put out a contract" on one or more of the good guys, as though they were having attorneys draw up contracts for the bad guys to sign, documenting the terms and conditions for killing someone. While that situation is more of a Hollywood fantasy than anyone's reality, if such a contract was drawn up, it would not be enforceable by any recognized court of law. It is not legal, fortunately, to kill anyone, so such a contract would not be legal.

- Another requirement of enforceability is that some contracts must be in writing, signed by both parties. This makes sense. How could a court, or anyone else, determine who is right or wrong in a situation when the contract was verbal? Possibly, it could be video taped in front of unimpeachable witnesses, like a room full of U.S. Supreme Court justices, but such circumstances would be extremely rare for most people. It would be time consuming and expensive to prove that contract's terms and conditions, if you could. It is much easier to put those terms and conditions in writing.

- In addition, minors (usually defined as younger than 18 years of age) cannot participate in contracts, at least not enforceable ones. While children and teenagers do shop, frequently using their parents' credit cards for payment, they cannot *legally* do so.

NEGOTIATION PREPARATION

When beginning any type of business relationship with a client or vendor, the project and financial arrangements are usually informally discussed first. But it's a good idea to begin formal negotiations over a contract as soon as possible. In the hype and vapor world of Internet communication, discussing what, when, and how much is a very good idea. And since anything is possible using this communications method, defining projects and responsibilities is very important.

Once you've begun developing a new situation with a client or vendor and need to move forward, help your attorney draw up the contract that you want, or review a contract submitted to you, by outlining the "deal" and the important issues. Describe your goals, what you need to have included, what should not be included, etc. In addition, if you already have a contract draft from the other party, read it and highlight clauses that bring up questions or concerns.

The following are important points for everyone in a contract negotiation:

1. Whenever possible, be the party that originates the first draft of the contract. Yes, it *will* be more work (and, probably, expense). However, as a consequence, you will know the contract

extremely well, and you will have included all of your important requirements (as well as some of your "wants" and a couple of "give aways" for the negotiation).

Be sure to enlist the assistance of an attorney to draw up the contract. Do-it-yourself contracts (unless you are an attorney), or using a cookie-cutter contract out of a book or some software, can be dangerous because they are not developed with your situation and your point of view in mind.

Be prepared to have the other party dispute some contract clauses and come back to you with a revision to your draft contract. Ask them to highlight the changes that they made, and then read the contract, again, completely to see if any other changes were made. Again, the wisest way to proceed in such situations is to have your attorney review the revised contract, too. A change in words or even punctuation can appear meaningless to you but may, in fact, be significant.

If the other side prepares the first draft, you need to read it very carefully and thoroughly. Highlight anything that confuses you or that you do not like (because it is not fair to you, not doable, not realistic, etc.), and take it to an attorney for review. With your attorney, develop compromise positions to present to the contract's originators that address your issues or concerns.

Over time, you can develop your own standard contracts that contain the terms and conditions with which you are comfortable and under which you usually work.

2.   Only sign contracts that you have read completely (and understood!) yourself, preferably after your attorney has read and discussed them with you.

3.   When you make a concession in negotiation (like speeding up delivery, if you are the seller), ask for one from the other party in exchange (like a more complete specification or a single point of contact who will be responsible for answering all of your questions within 24 hours).

4.   Be prepared to walk away from an unfair situation or an unprofitable deal. Know what your "deal killers" are—those terms and conditions that are completely unacceptable (non-negotiable) for you. If the other side insists on one of those, walk away from the deal. Usually, a compromise position acceptable to both parties can be reached. Sometimes the other party will insist on something that is totally unacceptable to you, as a negotiation ploy to see how badly you want the deal. If they see that you are seriously ready to terminate the

negotiation and walk away from the deal, they *may* make a concession. But they may not! So you must truly be prepared to walk.

Also know what your price limit is, recognizing that things like payment terms, content source, or technology may affect the actual cost. It is most rational to think in terms of the overall total cost of the project, including not only the purchase price but also cost of maintenance, hosting, software, etc. Figure out your limit (as either the buyer or the seller), and know that going beyond that limit will turn the deal into something that you cannot afford.

5. Keep a "poker" face, in most negotiation situations (think how the car salesperson's eyes light up when you exclaim how much you love the new car!). Something that may be very important to you may not be important to the other parties. However, if they know how important it is to you, they may expect a large concession from you in exchange for it, regardless of its cost or actual importance to them.

6. Don't start a negotiation with your "final" position (or best offer). People usually expect to do some negotiation in a Web site development effort (and most other contracts as well), so build in some maneuver room for yourself.

The following are important points for the sellers in a negotiation:

1. Don't automatically drop your price as your first concession. Research has shown that price is *not* usually the buyer's biggest concern (or it shouldn't be). Buyers are usually more concerned with quality, reliability, and time to delivery, although every buyer and every situation is different. If the buyer indicates that the price is too high, ask what deliverable he or she would like to leave out to lower the price, assuming that your price is a fair one for the effort.

2. *Want* the business or the contract, but do not *need* the business! Know what your deal killers are and what your bottom line price is. If those are reached or crossed, walk away from the deal. You will be better off in the long run.

CONTRACT NEGOTIATION

Many businesspeople are not comfortable negotiating a contract, but unless you want to trust that everyone else will operate with your best interests at heart, you need to negotiate for yourself (or hire someone to do it for you, if you can, like an attorney). The best approach to negotiation is to look for a "win-win" solution, where all parties are satisfied with the outcome and the overall document is fair to all involved.

Unfortunately, some people and some companies, as part of their corporate culture, negotiate for a "win-lose" solution, where they "win" and you "lose." This negotiation strategy is not good for a long-term relationship among the parties. It can breed a basic dislike and distrust that can backfire.

- Most businesses depend on repeat business from satisfied customers. Customers on the wrong end of a "win-lose" negotiation are usually desperately seeking an alternative and will take their business elsewhere as soon as they are able. Research has shown that they will also let at least ten other people know how unhappy they are!
- Equally, suppliers or subcontractors on the wrong side of a "win-lose" negotiation will usually do their best to recover or get out of the situation/relationship. This "recovery" or "escape" can end up being much more expensive to the employer/contractor than a more equitable contract would have been.

Research and experience show that "win-lose" is usually transformed into "lose-lose" experience in the long run. "Win-win" is a better goal, both ethically and practically.

The best contract negotiation is actually just documentation, in proper format written (or at least reviewed) by an attorney representing each party, of the terms and conditions that have already been discussed and agreed to by all parties involved.

CYBERSPACE CONTRACTS

When you think about traditional contracts (interactions involving an offeror, an offeree, and consideration resulting in an agreement among two or more parties, who know each other, and who promise to perform a transaction with each other), you have many examples in daily life to guide you. In cyberspace, it starts to get more complicated. How often do the parties "know" each other and come to a meeting of the minds?

LAB 7.1 EXERCISES

7.1.1   DESCRIBE THE THREE BASIC ELEMENTS OF A CONTRACT

You are a Web developer and have a potential new client. After a couple of long discussions with you, the client has asked you for a proposal, delineating what the Web site will contain, how it will be organized, when it will be done, and how much it will cost. You also include some options for the client to consider—monthly maintenance, training, additional sections, and functionality (a shopping cart, an e-mailed newsletter). Each option is priced separately.

a) You do not have a contract yet, but you have some of the elements. What elements of a contract do you have?

_____

_____

b) What element is missing?

_____

_____

c) If the client likes your proposal but suggests a lower price, what has happened? What are your options?

_____

_____

d) You did not indicate an expiration date on your proposal. Do you have any long-term exposure as a result?

_____

_____

7.1.2 EVALUATE A CONTRACT

After reading most of a contract, you, as the developer, sign the contract, collect the agreed 30% deposit, and begin work. You immediately hire two subcontractors: a graphics designer to prepare graphics for the site and a Java programmer to develop a couple of custom applets. Thirty days later (when you are about 60% done with the initial development effort and your subcontractors have completed their efforts), the client submits their notice to cancel the contract in a week. They do not tell you why they are canceling, and they tell you that they don't need a reason. They reference a clause in the contract that you had not noticed:

"This Agreement may be terminated/cancelled by Client for its convenience on seven days prior written notice to Developer."

> **a)** Can they cancel this contract?

_____

_____

> **b)** Can they cancel the contract without telling you why?

_____

_____

> **c)** Assuming that you have already invested more than the 30% deposit, can you recover for the investment you made in the graphics and the Java development?

_____

_____

There are two other clauses in the contract that you missed when you reviewed it:

"Work may not be subcontracted or otherwise performed by third parties on behalf of Developer without the prior written permission of Client."

"Client shall reimburse Developer for reasonable out-of-pocket expenses incurred at the specific request of Client."

d) If you do not have the client's written approval to use the subcontractors, what are your chances of being reimbursed for the costs of their efforts? Why?

_____

_____

_____

_____

e) Will you read the *next* contract more carefully before you sign it? Are there some clauses that you would have negotiated "out" of the agreement? Are those clauses deal killers?

_____

LAB 7.1 EXERCISE ANSWERS

7.1.1 ANSWERS

a) You do not have a contract yet, but you have some of the elements. What elements of a contact do you have?

Answer: You have two of the three elements of a contract.

Contracts have three elements: an offer made by an offeror, an offeree who accepts the offer, and some consideration. You have made an offer (the proposal), and you have indicated the consideration (pricing) that you feel is appropriate.

b) What element is missing?

Answer: The only missing element is the acceptance by the offeree.

If you wanted to withdraw the proposal (say you made a mistake in the pricing), now would be the time—before the offeree has accepted it. If you discover the mistake after acceptance, you are dependent upon the cooperation of the offeree to allow you to correct your error. The offeree is not required to cooperate.

c) If the client likes your proposal, but suggests a lower price, what has happened? What are your options?

Answer: The offeree has, by proposing a new price, rejected your offer and made a counteroffer. So the roles are now reversed.

You are now the offeree and your client is now the offeror. When they make a counteroffer, you have several options: Accept their counteroffer, accept their counteroffer and request a change to something else (a lowered price may indicate less functionality), or reject the counteroffer. It's usually smart (and fair) to request a concession from the other party when you make a concession.

d) You did not indicate an expiration date on your proposal. Do you have any long-term exposure as a result?

Answer: If you have not limited the time frame that your offer is open, the client may accept it at any reasonable time.

Reasonable is not defined and is usually dependent on the circumstances. So you could be in the position of maintaining a very different Web site from that in the proposal but at the price in the proposal. An argument could be made that by rejecting your initial offer, the client also rejected the options. But since they were priced separately, the client could easily make an argument that it was only your main proposal that was rejected. So, be sure to indicate an expiration date or "offer, including options, effective until . . ." date in your proposal.

7.1.2 ANSWERS

a) Can they cancel this contract?

Answer: Unless there is something else in the contract that describes specific situations where this clause does not apply, the answer is yes. They definitely can cancel this contract.

b) Can they cancel the contract without telling you why?

Answer: Again, unless there is some other clause in the contract that is contrary to this one, they do not owe you any explanation. They are canceling for their convenience.

c) Assuming that you have already invested more than the 30% deposit, can you recover for the investment you made in the graphics and the Java development?

Answer: Maybe and maybe not. It depends on the rest of the contract (e.g., any progress payments terms).

d)   If you do not have the client's written approval to use the subcontractors, what are your chances of being reimbursed for the costs of their efforts? Why?

Answer: If you are in violation of the first clause, requiring prior written permission by the client, the chances of recovery may be slim to none.

Hopefully, you can pay for their efforts out of the 30% deposit. If not, you are probably out of luck. Obviously, you should have either objected to that clause *before you signed the contract* or complied with it and gotten the client's written permission first. It might be argued that the second clause, allowing reimbursement for reasonable expenses, should cover you. But the first clause is pretty clear.

e)   Will you read the *next* contract more carefully before you sign it? Are there some clauses that you would have negotiated "out" of the agreement? Are those clauses deal killers?

Answer: You should answer yes, yes, and maybe. A wise person would also indicate the need for an attorney to do a review of the contract prior to signing it.

Most developers would find the specified clauses unacceptable as they are written. You should be able to soften or eliminate them in a negotiation. In many cases these draconian clauses are included because they are "standard terms" included in *every* draft agreement. There may even be an expectation that they will be eliminated from the final agreement, as bargaining "chips" in the negotiation process.

They could also be included because the client always operates this way. Many very large companies and the U.S. federal government have these clauses in their contracts because they use the same draft terms and conditions over and over. They are also used because these very large customers have so many competitors who want their business that they can do business on whatever terms they choose. They can force acceptance of what is on the surface a "win-lose" situation. This has obvious consequences in the long term. You may decide that you do not want their business that badly. Or you may conclude, after some research, that since these clauses are seldom actually implemented in real life, the risk is acceptable. Be sure to run these contracts past an attorney who specializes in contracts before you sign one. At a minimum, the attorney should be able to point out the risks you will be taking and potentially acceptable alternative clauses or clauses that mitigate the effect of the more objectionable ones.

LAB 7.1 SELF-REVIEW QUESTIONS

In order to test your progress, you should be able to answer the following questions:

1) Which are two reasons to use a written and signed contract in a Web development project?
   a) _____ Attorneys need the business.
   b) _____ It should document the requirements, responsibilities, and price of the project.
   c) _____ If anything goes wrong, it can help clarify the situation.
   d) _____ It is required by the U.S. federal government and the IRS.
   e) _____ Written contracts are required by many state and local regulations.

2) You may withdraw an offer
   a) _____ After it is made, but before it is accepted.
   b) _____ After the contract is signed, but before work has started.
   c) _____ After it is made and accepted.
   d) _____ If they have not accepted it within 30 days of their receipt of the proposal.
   e) _____ Whenever you want to withdraw it.

3) A client may cancel a contract
   a) _____ Whenever they want to cancel.
   b) _____ After the proposal is made, but before it is accepted.
   c) _____ According to whatever is written in the contract about the client's ability to cancel.
   d) _____ After the contract is signed, but before work has started.
   e) _____ Whenever they want to cancel, as long as they pay all the expenses.

Quiz answers appear in Appendix A, Section 7.1.

LAB 7.2

DEVELOPING WEB CONTENT

LAB OBJECTIVES

After this Lab, you will be able to

- Define Copyright and Trademarks
- Describe the Five Basic Sources of Web Content
- Understand How to Develop a "Safe" Linking Strategy
- Advertise on the Internet

The Web has the reputation of being like the "Wild West" where normal rules don't apply:

> You can freely use anything from anyone's Web site, and vice versa, without penalty? (Not true.)

> Anything you publish on the Web can and will be "borrowed" by someone without your permission. (This is technologically true in most cases, but there are steps you can take to protect your work.)

> You can post anything on the Internet about any person or product, true or not, without fear of legal retribution? (Not true.)

Fortunately for the future of creativity and commerce, business rules apply on the Web, enabling creative and ambitious people who develop their ideas on the Web to reap the benefits of their work. Truth is still truth, on-line and off, so concepts like fraud, defamation, and liability transfer to the cyber world from the real world.

**LAB
7.2**

COPYRIGHT AND TRADEMARKS

COPYRIGHT

Copyright is just what it sounds like—the right to make copies of (reproduce) a work. Categories of creativity protected by copyright include computer programs, literary works, movies, graphics and art, photos, sound recordings, and audiovisual presentations. "An original work fixed in a tangible medium of expression" is automatically accorded copyright protection at the time of creation. We have all created many, many "copyrighted" things, from the time we scribbled with crayons in preschool to today, when we sent an e-mail to someone.

It is the tangible *expression* of an idea that is copyrightable, not the idea, itself. The *ideas* presented by the copyrighted material are *not* protected by the copyright. Your HTML code or JavaScript is protected by copyright, but the ideas presented by the code are not usually protected, unfortunately. Patents, which are another form of intellectual properties, protect ideas.

The ownership of a copyright may be the source of dispute. Usually, the creator is the owner of the copyright. Frequently, an employer owns the copyright of the results of an employee's work. Employer ownership is not automatic, however. If the employee performed the creation as a normal part of doing "the job" while working at "the office" using the employer's property, then this is probably classified as "work for hire" or "work product." The employer, who pays for the work that created the copyrighted material, usually owns the results. As usual, discussing this issue prior to initiating work and documenting that agreement in a written, signed contract, with the assistance of an attorney, is usually the safest course. Many times, as a part of the new employee "orientation" process, new employees sign a contract in which they waive their ownership of anything that they may create during the course of their employment.

It is a *very* good idea to put the world on notice that you own the copyright to your work, although in the United States, it is not a requirement. You notify the world of your copyright ownership by marking your work with the copyright symbol (the c in the circle, like this ©) or the word *copyright,* the year of the first publication, and the name of the owner. Frequently you will also see the words, "all rights reserved" as well:

"© Your Company, 1999. (*or* Copyright, Your Company, 1999.) All rights reserved."

(Many newer software products will automatically put a circle around the c for you when you type the c within a set of parentheses.)

In specific situations, you can use copyrighted materials. This limited use is called "fair use." This is a very sensitive area. Typically, fair use is use for reporting, education, and criticism. For these purposes, limited use of excerpts is allowed. A TV movie review show wouldn't be as interesting or as effective without the movie clips we see during the reviews. These clips are not usually used so extensively that we lose desire to see the movie, so there is no economic damage to the movie from the use of the clips. (The review may inflict economic damage, but that is another issue.) Do not assume that you can freely use copyrighted material under fair use. This is a very complex area, and the damages can be significant. Check out the Web site fairuse.stanford.edu for more information on fair use.

In late 1998, the U.S. Congress passed the Digital Millennium Copyright Act (DMCA) to update copyright laws and regulations. It has some provisions that may affect fair use. The primary focus appears to be offering some protection from copyright infringement liability to the businesses and individuals in the Internet information distribution chain. Basically, it allows Internet service providers (ISPs) to make copies of digital transmissions in the normal process of performing their transmission services without fear of infringing on the copyrights of the transmissions' contents. In addition, it also appears to release providers of information location tools (search engines) from liability for copyright infringement if use of their "tool" results in a link to a site that infringes on someone's copyright.

The DMCA does impose a new requirement on the Internet industry. It requires the registration of a designated agent to receive notification when someone has posted something objectionable (or infringing) on an organization's Internet resources. The recipient of this notification is then required to remove the offending material "expeditiously" or "to remove or disable access." This appears to address situations where someone puts infringing material on a Web site or posts infringing information on an electronic bulletin board or news group. The key here is to identify, and *register,* an individual to receive the complaints. The Register of Copyrights in the Copyright Office receives and retains this information.

Since the DMCA is so new, it is impossible to know what kind of rules, regulations, and case law will develop over time. So keep watching for more information about the DMCA and its impact on cyberspace.

TRADEMARKS

A trademark is different from a copyright. It is best to hire the services of a trademark or intellectual property attorney for federal registration.

Ownership of a copyright vests in the creator at the time of creation. Trademark ownership is *not* automatic. There is a complex application process, and research is required before an approval for trademark ownership is obtained.

You don't automatically receive a trademark just because you have requested it. First you must demonstrate that you are using the mark or have an immediate intent to use the mark. Then there must be a search to see if any other organization is using the same trademark in the same class of goods or services. There cannot be two registered trademarks for "widget" if both of them are in the same class (software, for example). The same trademark name may be used by differing organizations in differing categories—Digital Equipment Corporation registered the word "VAX" as the trademark for a computer. Another company registered the same word as the trademark of its vacuum cleaner. Both were acceptable registered trademarks because most people would not have confused the two.

A thorough search of trademarks is required (and the safest course of action). This is usually best done by an attorney who specializes in trademarks or in intellectual property (IP). You can do some checking yourself at Web sites like www.uspto.gov/tmdb/index.html.

The purpose of registering a trademark is to establish exclusive ownership of an identifiable trade name. A trademark may be a symbol, a graphic, a word or phrase, even a sound, and, rarely, a color. Once you have survived the process and been awarded your trademark registration, you must protect your trademark, or it could be lost.

For maximum protection in the United States, a trademark must be registered, either with a state registry or, preferably, with the U.S. Patent and Trademark Office, or both (ask your attorney). Once awarded, a registered trademark is usually viewed as a valuable company asset. Registering a trademark in the United States does *not* automatically give you an international registration, unfortunately.

After your trademark registration has been awarded by the U.S. Patent and Trademark Office, you are entitled (and very strongly encouraged) to mark your registered trademark with the R in the circle ® beside it. Only trademarks that have survived the registration process with the U.S. Patent and Trademark Office are entitled to use the ®, which indicates a registered trademark. If your trademark is not registered with the U.S. Patent and Trademark Office, do not use the ® mark beside it. You can use the TM while you are in the registration process even if you are not planning on registering immediately. But you must make sure that you are not interfering with someone else's mark.

If you have permission from a trademark owner to use their trademark on your Web site, ask them how they want it presented and then be sure to respect their requirements. For example, your company may have a business partner whose products you sell, and, assuming that those product names have registered trademarks, you will probably want to use those trademarks on your Web site, and your business partner will probably want you to use them. Many company logos are trademarks, and they are always a specific size or a specific height to width ratio, specific colors, specific fonts, etc. They may also be given to you as a graphic file.

Your business partner may require everyone who uses their logo to place the logo in the upper left side of each page (or lower right, or whatever). Whether the trademark is a graphic or a word, there is usually a required credit line at the bottom of the page giving the specific text used to reference the trademark. For example, "This is the registered trademark of the XXX Corporation." If you don't follow the guidelines for the use of your partner's trademark, you may be viewed as infringing on it. It's better not to use their trademarks at all rather than use them inappropriately or outside of the guidelines.

For more information about trademarks in general, go to www.uspto.gov/web/menu/tm.html.

TRADEMARKS AND META TAGS

In the endless games that Web developers and search engines play with each other, meta tags are an important component. Some developers and/or Web site owners have added a new wrinkle to this game that *seems* like smart search engine gamesmanship. They add the names of their competitors' products and services to the list of key words in the key word meta tag. For example, if your company's competitor had an extremely popular product named "Smith's Extra Fast Printer," your company would probably want to divert sales for that product to one of its own, "Jones' Equally Fast Printer." In this case, it *might* seem like a good idea to add the phrase "Smith's Extra Fast Printer" to the list of key words in the key word meta tag. But particularly if "Smith's Extra Fast Printer" was a registered trademark of Smith's company, your company could be making a very expensive mistake.

Do not make the mistake of assuming that the Smith company will never find out about this particular game. Companies are bombarded by services promising to move them "up" in the search engine results, so people are paying attention to what is happening with the search engines and their products or services. The Smith company will probably discover your company's games and not be happy with what is happening. They could easily take the view that you are infringing on their trademark, and they would appear to have a very good case. Your company could be quite expensively embarrassed.

FIVE BASIC SOURCES OF WEB CONTENT

As we have noted in earlier chapters, successful Web communications models are, in many cases, duplicates of successful physical models, like a comprehensive book or music catalog. In another parallel with the physical world, successful Web sites, from a legal point of view, are also built on the model of a business that is compliant with the applicable laws and regulations. To act otherwise is to put yourself and your organization at risk.

Once you have developed your plans and mapped out your audience interactions, you will start developing your Web site's contents. For the purposes of this chapter, we will define *Web content* as the text, graphics, and design of each page. Ownership of that content is extremely important, and this is when Web developers and Web site owners must exercise caution and good judgment. Using someone else's content without their written permission is as bad a decision on the Web as it is in the rest of the business world. To the best of your abilities, refrain from using material on your Web site for which you do not have the permission of the creator or owner. To do otherwise is to invite embarrassment and loss of reputation as well as to put significant amounts of money (and, maybe, your job!) at risk.

There are numerous sources of content, but, from an ownership point of view, it all boils down to five basic sources, and each has its own issues:

1. Original content developed by you or your organization's employees
2. Original content developed by an individual or organization *outside* of your organization at your direction (e.g., a Web developer or a graphics designer who works independently or for another organization).
3. Previously purchased content being repurposed for the Web site.
4. Borrowed content used without the need to pay the person who created it or the person or organization that legally "owns" it. This content may legally be used for free.
5. Borrowed content used with the specific permission of the owner to include it on the Web site in exchange for the payment of a fee or the purchase of a license to use the content.

The following is a detailed discussion of these five situations:

1. Original content may be created specifically for the Web site by company employees, or existing company-owned materials (e.g., the contents of the organization's personnel manual) may be modified for Web use. (For a discussion of repurposed material, see item 3.)

    If you are an employee of the organization, doing your job, the organization that pays your salary usually owns the output of your work. This situation is classified, in legal terms, as "work for hire" or "work product." You do not own the output of your work. Your employer does, and they have the right to use it. So anything that you create for your employer in the normal course of doing your job, your employer has the right to put on the Web site without your expressed permission.

2. Original content developed for the Web site by individuals or groups outside of the Web site owner's organization may be used on the Web site, in accordance with the terms and conditions of the agreement between the Web site owner and the outside organization.

    This content is also usually new, at least for this organization or Web site, and it may or may not have been developed specifically for this Web site. The Web site's owner usually pays to purchase or license this content, either with money or with some other form of compensation.

    This is also usually classified as "work for hire" or "work product," and ownership of the results of the work (the contents developed, in this case) resides in the organization that paid for its creation, not in the individuals who created it. In some cases, the originating organization continues to "own" the content, and the Web site's owner pays for a license to use it for a specified period of time.

    At the beginning of the Web site development process, both parties should sign a contract specifying the terms and conditions of the relationship between the two organizations. These terms and conditions should include when ownership of the content (copyright) transfers from the creator organization to the Web site owner organization, the price to be paid, deadlines for creation and payment, and who is responsible for what.

3. Repurposed content created for another purpose but used on the Web site. If existing company materials (e.g., the contents of the organization's personnel manual) are being modified for use on the Web site, check into the background of that mater-

ial if possible to see who owns what and for what specific use and time frame.

Your organization's staff probably created much of the material being repurposed at some point in the past. On the other hand, people or organizations from outside your organization may have also created some of it (e.g., the photography or some of the graphics). Before using material created by someone from outside of your organization, you need to check with the terms and conditions of purchase, or of the license to use, to see if using the material on the Web site is in compliance with those terms. In many cases, the materials were developed before the Web was even a glimmer on the horizon, and the terms of the agreement do not include permission to use the material on a Web site. Check with an attorney to see how you should proceed in this situation.

If the terms and conditions prohibit use of the material for anything other than the original purpose or certain other restrictions on use (maybe time frame, distribution method, or quantity produced), you will need to make a change. You should go back to the originator and get the permission that you need, through a new agreement or a modification of the existing one so that you are in compliance with it. Or, you need to find or develop a substitute if agreement cannot be reached.

Unless you know to the contrary, assume that you will be violating an old or existing contract by posting material on the Web site. Using the personnel manual as an example, there are companies and consultants who create personnel manuals for organizations as a product with a price tag and associated terms and conditions. Over the past few years, publishing the contents of an organization's personnel manual on the Web has become much more common (on an intranet, for example), so existing contracts may address the issue, like allowing the publication on an intranet but not a public Web site. If your personnel manual, or other content, was originally created several years ago, you would be very wise to check into the contract that was the basis of that work. In many cases you will find that distribution and copying are limited to the traditional forms. Check before you proceed.

4. Borrowed content that may be used without permission or payment is content in the public domain, like Shakespeare's works, many government documents, and other works whose author or creator has been dead for more than 70 years. You need to be very careful with this category as well. It is not as simple as

it looks. You can do some research into what is the public domain at lcweb.loc.gov/copyright/circs/circ22.pdf.

You might think that a very popular and ubiquitous cartoon mouse is in the public domain, but that character is also a famous company's trademark. Use that mouse or any other organization's trademark at your peril. Better yet, do not even think about using any trademark but your own on your Web site unless you have obtained written permission. It is best to use an attorney experienced in the field to research trademark ownership.

On the other hand, very rarely an owner or creator may grant a blanket permission to use their work without any compensation for its use. For example, there are some Web sites that offer "free" graphics for use on Web sites. You need to be cautious here, too, however, because usually that permission has a caveat that limits use without payment to noncommercial use only, and payment is required before commercial use. Typically, noncommercial use means use on personal Web sites, not the Web site of a for-profit or a nonprofit organization. Read the terms on the Web site to see how noncommercial use is defined to see if it applies to your proposed use. If noncommercial use is specified as approved but there is no definition of noncommercial use, *ask!* Even charities and other nonprofit organizations need to pay for some things. So don't assume that your church's or your PTA's Web site can freely use other people's works without permission *and* compensation.

5. Borrowed content may be used with the specific, usually compensated, permission of the owner/creator organization. This kind of content may be the trademark of a business partner, like the trademarked name of a product (which is usually provided for free if credited appropriately). It may be a quote or section from a book or article and must be used with permission and specific credit to the original source. There are organizations (with Web sites) where you can research the need for permission, the terms, and the associated costs. Check out www.copyright.com and www.icopyright.com for more information.

DEVELOPING A SAFE LINKING STRATEGY

Pointing to Web sites outside your organization's Web site is something to approach cautiously. Along with the obvious concerns about losing visitors and keeping outside links live, you should also be concerned about what the visitors might find at the linked site. Don't forget that, depending on how you approach this issue, the site that you are linking to may not be thrilled with your generosity.

Do not assume that your external linking strategy is your little secret. It's not. For some time, search engines like AltaVista (www.altavista.com) and HotBot (www.hotbot.com) have had the capability of doing a "reverse" search. This means that you can put a URL into the search field and have the search engine search for sites linking *to* that URL. (It's a little more complicated than that, but not much!) There are also Web-based services that "sweep" the Internet for Web site owners, gathering the URLs of Web sites that link *to* a specific URL. So the Web site owner *will* find out eventually.

UNPLEASANT SURPRISES

You may be providing links to other sites as a service to your visitors. If you do, it's usually a good idea to offer a fairly prominent disclaimer indicating that you are providing a service and have no control over what someone else puts on their Web site. Always offer visitors the opportunity to provide you with feedback, so that they can let you know if something is not appropriate or offends them. It is also a good idea to methodically and periodically review the content at the end of those links, just in case a new ownership has a new philosophy that differs from yours or from the original owner's.

UNHAPPY LINKEES

Most of the time, Web sites are thrilled, or at least pleased, to have "inbound" links (other Web sites that point visitors to their Web site). However, you can change that attitude very easily by the way that you provide those links. You will have unhappy "linkees" (sites to which you link from your Web site) if you

Link to their site solely for the purpose of "borrowing" a graphic

Disguise the identity of the site you are linking to (as in a frame) so that you get the credit and the revenue while someone else does the content development

Offer your visitors a link into a "members only" area to which the linkee is otherwise trying to limit access

Imply that there is more of a relationship between your two organizations than there actually is

For example, occasionally someone will find a graphic that they particularly admire and want to use on their site. They do not want to be accused of "stealing" it, so they just pull it into their site via a link from its home site. They use the <IMG> tag, pointing to the URL where the "live" image appears. This kind of action has created consternation. Most notably, a cartoonist had a fan link to a selection of the cartoonist's strips from the cartoonist's Web site. The link pulled those strips into the fan's Web site. Some might see this as flattering. However, copyright and trademark holders probably would not appreciate it. The cartoonist and his publisher felt that this link infringed on the cartoonist's copyright and also on the cartoonist's trademarked characters. Unprotected trademarks may be at risk of losing their trademark status, which would have put a big dent in the cartoonist's bank account. So you can imagine why the cartoonist was not pleased. He took action against his fan to protect both his copyright and his trademarks.

In another famous situation, a Web site focused on collecting the latest news from the best sources linked to many of the major news Web sites (CNN, etc.). These major news sites were not pleased with those inbound links because although their news pages were shown to a group of visitors, those visitors could not see which Web sites were actually the sources of the news. The news collection site was using frames, and frames technology displays only the parent URL in the browser location field. So the only URL displayed was the URL of the news collection site, not the news services sites that were the actual sources of the content. Thus, the framing Web site was generating revenue from the work of the true news services through the advertisers on his own site while hiding the URL of the news services. This practice was challenged as infringing on the copyright of the news services' Web sites, and the framer was forced to change his site.

Copyright and trademark owners are rightfully concerned about protecting against infringement on their property.

HAPPY LINKEES

At this time, it does not appear to be illegal to link to another site without asking permission first. (It may be bad "netiquette," but not, apparently, illegal.) To keep the recipients of your outbound links happy, respect their ownership of their own intellectual property (trademarks, copyright, etc.):

Use a basic link with the name of the company or organization spelled out and underlined, as usual.

Only use their trademark as a clickable icon (link) if you have their written permission to display their trademark on your Web site.

Do not put their content inside a frame. Many public service Web sites will offer you blanket permission to link to them as long as you don't do it using frames.

Politely ask permission to link to the linkee (a quaint practice, perhaps, but a nice one, as long as you are willing to accept a negative answer and act appropriately).

Bad netiquette will probably ultimately lead to bad economics, so "play together nicely," as your first-grade teacher taught you a long time ago.

ADVERTISING ON THE INTERNET

**LAB
7.2**

Many courts and governmental authorities are taking the view that the entire Web site is an advertisement, so the laws governing advertising, as well as the rules and regulations, are being applied to Web sites, too.

Truth in advertising applies to the Web as well as to the rest of the marketing communications world. Just as an unfair or deceptive commercial or print advertisement will get the advertiser into trouble in the real world, so will the same false claim get the advertiser into trouble on the Internet. The U.S. Federal Trade Commission (FTC) has documented its position that "Web site designers . . . also may be liable for making or disseminating deceptive representations."

Both inside and outside the United States, consumers are, in general, a protected group. In the United States, the Federal Trade Commission Act established the FTC, with broad responsibilities for business regulation. There are also many other different federal government agencies inside the United States protecting the consumers of different industries (e.g., the Food and Drug Administration focuses on food and drugs, the Securities and Exchange Commission focuses on the securities industry). Different laws affect various aspects of the purchasing process (e.g., Truth in Lending Act, Fair Credit Reporting Act). To the extent that a Web site participates in lending and credit reporting or sells food or securities, those same rules and regulations would probably also be applied to the Web site.

In the United States, state and local governments are also involved. The 50 states have state consumer protection laws, with rules and regulations enforced by the 50 state attorneys general. In addition, since the Web is worldwide, there are laws, rules, and regulations from outside the United States that may also be applied.

For some guidance, the FTC's Web site offers an amazing range of information and guidance. Check out the site at www.ftc.gov and also at www.ftc.gov/bcp/guides/guides.htm. In addition, the FDA also provides guidance on its rules and regulations at www.fda.gov/opacom/more-choices/transcript1096/fdainet1.html.

This lab will attempt to address only those regulations and requirements that seem to cross the most industries. Be sure to research what applies to your industry and geography, and get professional advice from an attorney familiar with that particular area.

The bottom line is that, assuming that your organization complies with all relevant local and federal advertising regulations in its other advertising, then those same rules and the people with that knowledge should be participating in the development of Web site content. The "wild card" in this is the international aspect that applies to the World Wide Web. If you have a question, or even a doubt, contact an attorney with relevant experience, and get professional advice.

TRUTH IN ADVERTISING APPLIES ON THE WEB

The U.S. Federal Trade Commission Act specifies the rules that apply to advertising at the national level. An advertiser cannot lie in an advertisement. Advertisers must back up the claims in their ads with some substantiation, and an advertisement cannot be unfair or deceptive.

UNFAIR OR DECEPTIVE ADVERTISING

To be compliant, advertising must be truthful and should not present the truth in a way that is misleading. An omission is viewed in much the same light as a misrepresentation. This means that omitting information relevant to the claim is not a good thing to do. For example, selling a "Swiss" watch that was not manufactured in Switzerland is deceptive. Omitting the information that the watch was manufactured in Thailand, *not* Switzerland, is, effectively, being untruthful, even if you actually bought the watch in Switzerland. The country of manufacture is relevant information for a consumer who wants to purchase a "Swiss" watch.

What is unfair or deceptive as defined by the FTC?

> An unfair ad is likely to cause an injury to a consumer that is substantial, not outweighed by other benefits, and not reasonably avoidable by the consumer.

> An ad is deceptive if it contains a statement that is likely to mislead a consumer by providing seemingly relevant and important information that should not be accepted at face value. It can also be deceptive by omitting to include relevant and important information.

If you have a disclaimer to make, do not hide it, and do not expect that, by itself, a disclaimer will protect you.

SUBSTANTIATED AND UNSUBSTANTIATED CLAIMS IN ADVERTISING

When it comes to claims relating to product/service performance, health benefits, and safety benefits, the FTC usually requires substantiation. The level of substantiation typically depends on the product/service and the nature of the claim. If an on-line advertisement claims that an automobile can go from 0 to 60 mph in 6.0 seconds, then it should have the test results that show that the automobile performs at that level. If the test automobile was modified to make it faster, then the claim may not be substantiated *unless* the ad clearly states that the car that reached that speed had been modified and is not the standard car being sold off the assembly line. That information should probably be included in a prominent disclaimer closely associated with the claim. As such, it would probably not be a claim worth making.

If the claim states that four out of five dentists recommend a product, then there should be substantiation that a survey, or some study, showed that specific result. A study involving five dentists who work for the product's manufacturer probably would not be good substantiation. Again, a disclaimer would probably be appropriate.

The FTC recommends that Web designers not depend on their client's (or, if working as an employee, their manager's) assurances that a claim is substantiated, but that they push back to see the substantiation for themselves. If they do not feel that the substantiation is sufficient, they should avoid making the claim.

If you are performing the function of the Web designer or the Web marketer, you should press to see proof that the claims being made are substantiated. Remember, the FTC currently believes that it may hold you responsible.

ADVERTISING AIMED AT CHILDREN

This is an area of particular attention and sensitivity because children, in general, are less sophisticated and skilled than adults in evaluating the information (or lack of information) being provided to them. Guidance on proper advertising to children is available from the Children's Advertising Revue Unit (CARU) of the Council of Better Business Bureaus at www.bbb.org/advertising/caruguid.html.

FREE PRODUCT OR SERVICE ADVERTISED

Offering something free is very powerful. However, advertising that you are giving away something for free is not as simple as it sounds. You must take great care not to deceive or to act unfairly toward consumers. In your ad, you must clearly specify the applicable terms and conditions. In addition, the product or service offered for free should be one that is typically sold at a standard price. So the "Buy One—Get One Free" statement should offer one item at no price when the same item, bought at the standard price (in effect during the 30 days prior to the offer), is purchased. See www.ftc.org.gov/bcp/guides/free.htm for the details.

FINANCIAL TRANSACTIONS

If you accept orders on your Web site, you should be paying attention to the rules and regulations that affect the world of financial transactions. For example, the Fair Credit Billing Act requires that you respond in writing to customer complaints, credit payments within a specified period of time, etc. For more details, see www.law.cornell.edu/uscode/15/1666.shtml.

If you accept orders for items to be shipped, then you are probably covered by the requirements of the FTC's Mail or Telephone Order Merchandise Rule. This requires that you either post an expected shipment time frame or, if you do not state a specific time frame, then you "reasonably" believe that you will be able to ship within 30 days. Should you need to postpone shipment for some reason and be unable to ship within the specified window, then there are consumer notification requirements, which may require that you receive permission from the consumer to delay shipment or offer the consumer the opportunity to cancel order. Again, more details are available on the Web at www.ftc.gov.

TESTIMONIALS AND ENDORSEMENTS

In general, you cannot substitute testimonials and endorsements as claim substantiation. If you post any testimonials or endorsements, they should be those of your "typical" customer—not the endorsement of the only satisfied customer that you have. Experts should have relied on their standard tests or other procedures. Or, if they are paid by your organization or otherwise connected (e.g., stockholder), that connection should be clearly disclosed. See www.ftc.gov/bcp/guides/endorse.htm for more information.

LAB 7.2 EXERCISES

7.2.1 COPYRIGHT AND TRADEMARKS

a) A copyright occurs when the creator

_____

_____

b) When you hire a consultant to write a booklet for you to distribute freely as part of your company's promotion efforts, you should own the copyright. In order to ensure that you own the copyright, you should

_____

_____

c) A trademark registered in the United States must be registered with

_____

_____

d) Before you initiate the process to register a trademark, you should do three things:

_____

_____

_____

e) Two organizations can own the same trademark (for example, a word) only if

_____

_____

7.2.2 THE FIVE BASIC SOURCES OF WEB CONTENT

a) The five basic sources of Web content are

_____

_____

_____

You are a Web developer working as a company employee on the company's new Web site. Content is being pulled from several areas of the company and people are busily working on it. You have been requested to repurpose a large brochure for one of your company's main product lines.

b) Assuming that this addition and the repurposing makes sense as part of your Web site development strategy and plan, what information do you need to collect before you start?

_____

_____

c) If you discover that the graphics used were outsourced five years ago, what is your next step?

_____

d) Who owns the rights to the new material that you create for the site? You, the employee, or your employer?

_____

_____

Additional content must be developed since the brochure is now out of date. No one from the company's marketing communications department is available right now, and you must proceed ASAP. So a decision to outsource has been made, and you have chosen a qualified writer from outside the company.

e) How do you ensure that your employer has the right to publish the outside writer's materials on the new Web site?

_____

_____

_____

The determination has been made to develop the new Web site from a Microsoft-centric point of view, so you need to add the Internet Explorer logo and the "Best viewed with Microsoft's Internet Explorer" statement on each page. You can easily get the Internet Explorer logo, but you see that it is also a Microsoft trademark.

f) Do you need permission to use the Internet Explorer logo? If you do, how do you get it? If you don't, why not?

_____

_____

_____

7.2.3 SAFE OUTBOUND LINKING STRATEGIES

a) Why should you be cautious about linking to a site outside your own?

_____

_____

_____

b) Most site owners will object to being pulled into a frame on your Web site. Why?

_____

_____

c) Is using a company's trademark as the clickable image a good practice? Why or why not?

_____

_____

7.2.4 ADVERTISING ON THE INTERNET

a) Why should Web designers and developers be concerned about truth in advertising on the Web?

_____

_____

b) If you can keep the Federal Trade Commission happy, what other governmental groups should concern you?

_____

_____

_____

_____

c) Would your board of directors be a sufficiently representative group of customers that you could use their testimonials about your product's effectiveness as substantiation for your claim that it helps middle-aged white men lose weight?

_____

_____

d) What kind of advertising claims should you be the most concerned about being able to substantiate?

_____

_____

e) If the "home library" is comprised of condensed books, rather than the full text, should you include a disclaimer about the contents when you advertise them for sale on the Web?

_____

_____

LAB 7.2 EXERCISE ANSWERS

7.2.1 ANSWERS

a) A copyright occurs when the creator

Answer: A copyright occurs when the creator creates the tangible expression of his or her idea. And it is only that tangible expression (a document, a song, a piece of artwork, etc.) that is copyrighted.

b) When you hire a consultant to write a booklet for you to distribute freely as part of your company's promotion efforts, you should own the copyright. In order to ensure that you own the copyright, you should

Answer: If you want to freely distribute that booklet, you must own the copyright, preferably, or possibly have a license from the copyright owner to distribute it freely.

If you paid the consultant to write the booklet, then you hopefully signed a contract with the writer before work began. In that contract, you should have specified that copyright ownership would transfer to your company at the completion of the contract, presumably after the consultant's bill was paid.

c) A trademark registered in the United States must be registered with

Answer: To register a trademark in the United States, you must submit an application to the U.S. Patent and Trademark Office, and then your application must be approved before it is officially registered.

d) Before you initiate the official trademark registration process, you should do three things:

Answer: You should probably do many things, but you should specifically do the following three.

Hire an attorney who specializes in intellectual property law.

Be using the proposed trademark for the intended purpose or have an immediate intent to use the trademark.

Have a professional research your proposed trademark to see if anyone else is using it. Your attorney or someone working for your attorney is probably the best person for this effort.

e) Two organizations can own the same trademark (for example, a word) only if

Answer: Two organizations can own the same trademark only if they are in different classes of goods or services, and such use would not confuse consumers or reduce the perceived value of either trademark.

7.2.2 ANSWERS

a) The five basic sources of Web content are

Answer: New original content created by employees. New original content created outside the company. Repurposed company-owned content. Borrowed content used without the need for permission or payment. Borrowed content used with the need for permission or payment.

- New original content developed by company employees. This content would most likely be owned by the company, as work for hire or work product, with no need for expressed permission from anyone to use it on the Web.

- New original content developed specifically for the company Web site by someone outside of the company. The company would purchase this content, presumably with the appropriate copyright allowing its use on the company Web site.

- Repurposed company-owned content. This content may have been created entirely by company employees, so it is likely safe to use on the Web. However, if someone created some part(s) of that content outside the company, the copyright for that material would need to be explored. If the material is pre-Web (1994 or earlier), it probably was not purchased with an expressly permitted right to use it on a Web site. But it may not have been expressly denied, either. So research would be necessary.

- Borrowed content used without the need for permission or payment. This material is commonly known as "in the public domain," and frequently it is hard to figure out exactly whether or not something is in the public domain. So do more research (or turn it over to your attorney to do!), and proceed cautiously until you know for sure that the material is "public domain."

- Borrowed content used with the need for permission and payment (usually). This content is typically not new, but it is content that you want to use on the Web site. Examples include the logos of business partners (who do not usually charge each other to use their respective logos) and excerpts from music, movies, books, articles, etc. (which probably will require both written permission to use as well as payment for that use).

b) Assuming that this addition and the repurposing make sense as part of your Web site development strategy and plan, what information do you need to collect before you start?

Answer: There is a great deal of information that will need to be collected.

Within that collection, the information most relevant to this lab is who developed the content, when it was developed, and who owns the copyright under what specific terms and conditions. This information should be found in contracts kept with the other material about the original project. Different organizations have differing filing systems and record retention requirements, so this may not be an easy task. The company legal department may keep a record and copies of all contracts, or, if outside counsel was used, that attorney (if known) may still have copies of those contracts.

c) If you discover that the graphics used were outsourced five years ago, what is your next step?

Answer: You need to find out what rights for reproduction were obtained in the original contract.

This will tell you whether or not you have the right to use them on the Web site, if you need them. You need to see the contracts, if any.

d) Who owns the rights to the new material that you create for the site? You, the employee, or your employer?

Answer: In this case, the answer is usually relatively uncomplicated. The owner of the material that you create while doing your job is usually your employer.

In some cases, people are working with an employment contract or other special arrangement that allows them to retain ownership of their own work. Check with an attorney before attempting to use something you created in a previous job.

e) How do you ensure that your employer has the right to publish the outside writer's materials on the new Web site?

Answer: Discuss the situation with the writer, making it clear that the material has no value to your employer unless the copyright provides express permission to use the materials on the Web site. Then, once you have agreement from the writer, work with an attorney to commit the agreement to writing. The agreement should be signed before work is begun, but certainly before payment is made.

f) Do you need permission to use the Internet Explorer logo? If you do, how do you get it? If you don't, why not?

Answer: At this point, you do not need Microsoft's permission to use the Internet Explorer logo on your Web site because Microsoft wants sites designed to the specifications of its browser, and it wants the world to know that you have designed your site specifically for Internet Explorer.

If you go to the Microsoft site, you will see a "grant" that allows you to use the logo (at msdn.microsoft.com/downloads/samples/Internet/imedia/netshow/smedia/NS3/logo/demo.htm).

7.2.3 ANSWERS

a) Why should you be cautious about linking to a site outside of your own?

Answer: There are many reasons.

Two of them are self-defense—first, the contents of the site, which were acceptable and appropriate when you first established the link, may become unacceptable and inappropriate over time if the site ownership or goals change over time. Second, because you have no control over these external Web sites, you may find that your outbound links go to dead ends because a file has moved, or been renamed, or the site has gone out of business. Other concerns include a negative reaction from the external site because it is not happy with the context of the link or what happens to its content when the link is selected.

b) Most site owners will object to being pulled into a frame on your Web site. Why?

Answer: They will object because their URL will be hidden from the visitors to your site by the way frames work.

This may impact their ability to gain revenue from their Web site and infringe on their copyright and/or trademarks.

c) Is using a company's trademark as the clickable image a good practice? Why or why not?

Answer: It is a good practice if you do not have permission from the trademark owner to use their trademark on your Web site. Most trademarks end up as graphics to keep them as consistent as possible.

On the other hand, usability studies have shown that often plain underlined text (an "old-fashioned" link) is less confusing to Web site visitors than a graphic.

7.2.4 ANSWERS

a) Why should Web designers and developers be concerned about truth in advertising on the Web?

Answer: Web designers and developers need to be concerned because the FTC has a stated position that they view that "Web site designers . . . also may be liable for making or disseminating deceptive representations."

b) If you can keep the Federal Trade Commission happy, what other governmental groups should concern you?

> Answer: It depends on your products or services, your industry, and where your customers are.

If you sell a food or drug, you also need to worry about the FDA; if you sell securities, you need to worry about the Securities and Exchange Commission (SEC). Because a Web site may be viewed by different authorities as being one large advertisement, you need to worry about all of the U.S. state and local governments' rules and regulations, as well as all the countries on the Internet and their federal and local governments.

c) Would your board of directors be a sufficiently representative group of customers that you could use their testimonials about your product's effectiveness as substantiation for your claim that it helps middle-aged white men lose weight?

> Answer: Your board of directors has a vested interest in seeing your company succeed, so they would not be particularly useful for testimonials. In addition, testimonials are specifically excluded as acceptable substantiation of advertising claims.

d) What kind of advertising claims should you be the most concerned about being able to substantiate?

> Answer: Claims related to health and safety benefits get particular scrutiny.

e) If the "home library" is comprised of condensed books, rather than the full text, should you include a disclaimer about the contents when you advertise them for sale on the Web?

> Answer: If you don't include a disclaimer or use an accurate description, you could be considered to be using deception to mislead consumers.

LAB 7.2 SELF-REVIEW QUESTIONS

In order to test your progress, you should be able to answer the following questions:

1) It is illegal to link to another Web site without the permission of that site.
   a) _____ True
   b) _____ False

2) An employee, in the normal course of doing his or her job, creates a document. Who owns the copyright to that document?
   a) _____ Work created by employees cannot be copyrighted, so no one owns it.
   b) _____ The employee always owns the copyright for his or her creation.
   c) _____ The employer always owns the copyright for the employee's creation.
   d) _____ The employee's attorney probably owns the copyright for the employee's creation.
   e) _____ The employer probably owns the copyright unless the employee has a contract with the employer that specifies otherwise.

3) If you own a trademark, you must protect it to keep it valid.
    a) _____ True
    b) _____ False

4) No permission is needed to use the Coca Cola trademark to add color to your company's Web site.
    a) _____ True
    b) _____ False

LAB 7.2

5) It is acceptable to borrow content off the Web for your Web site, for two of the following reasons:
    a) _____ You have permission to use the content, in writing, from the copyright owner.
    b) _____ You know that exactly the same content has been used by other Web sites.
    c) _____ You have researched the content's source and know that the content is in the public domain.
    d) _____ You believe that your use fits under the description of fair use because you are using the Web site to learn as much about Web site creation as you can.
    e) _____ The content was not marked with the © Copyright notice.

6) You cannot use someone's trademark on the visible part of your Web site, but using a competitor's name or the words comprising their trademark is appropriate for key word Meta tags.
    a) _____ True
    b) _____ False

Quiz answers appear in Appendix A, Section 7.2.

C H A P T E R   7

TEST YOUR THINKING

The projects in this section use the skills you've acquired in this chapter. The answers to these projects are available to instructors only through a Prentice Hall sales representative and are intended to be used in classroom discussion and assessment.

In this chapter's Test Your Thinking project, assume that you have completed the development of your own Web site. Go to 3 search engines to see when and where your site shows up. This also gives you a chance to do some competitive analysis and to see if anyone is infringing on your copyright or trademarks. In addition, check the "Legal Notices" section of the Amazon.com Web site for examples.

1) How does your contract define the completion of the Web site? When do you know you are done?

2) Develop a legal statement for your Web site covering the copyright issues to put on each page of your Web site.

3) Are there any other legal issues that should be covered for your Web site (check the Amazon.com Web site's example to see the kinds of things that might need to be covered)?

4) Do a search engine search on your Web site (or another one) and evaluate the results. How can you use those results to see if a competitor is infringing on a copyrighted or trademarked property?

CHAPTER 8

PROJECT LIFE CYCLE BASICS

"The road is not always to the swift . . . but to those who keep on running."

—Anonymous

CHAPTER OBJECTIVES

In this chapter, you will learn about

So you've gone to school for Web design. Or maybe you're looking to expand your advertising business to include an interactive division. You've heard all of the acronyms—ASP, HTML, and VB. You know that if a potential client says that he wants Java, he's not talking about a cup of coffee. You may know how to program in ten different Web languages, make eye-popping graphics, and build the Web server. However, undertaking the responsibility of someone else's company image and understanding their needs is a whole different arena. Doing so in a way that you don't end up losing your shirt could be considered an art.

Being a super Web developer does not immediately give insight into doing business as a Web developer. There's so much to learn the hard way. In this part of the book, you will investigate how to avoid some of these hard knocks, helping your firm to create a better product and build an excellent reputation. Hopefully, this will allow you to sleep better at night!

First, let me introduce myself. I'm Kim, and I own a Web firm in North Andover, Massachusetts. We probably have a lot in common because one day, after trying a course in Web site design, I decided that I liked it so much that I wanted to design Web sites for hire. Little did I know that learning the technology would be second to understanding how to address the client fairly, communicate the message successfully, and hire effective people to assist with production. My business grew organically, as many people picture their freelance business might do. No influx of venture capital for me. So when I was learning how to manage projects for the Web, my mistakes directly affected my wallet and my ability to grow my business. It didn't take long before I realized that a systematic approach to running Web projects was the only way to stay in the business. Every time since that I have been a little bit casual about this point, it costs the firm money.

In Part II of *Exploring Web Marketing and Project Management,* it is my pleasure to share my ideas about the successful management of Web site production. If you're thinking about starting a Web firm, are presently a Web design firm owner, wish to increase job stability because you manage Web projects for someone else, or are just curious about the business side of Web site development, I hope these concepts are helpful. The development process is always changing. It's a dynamic and exciting environment and a chance for people with an entrepreneurial spirit to try out new ideas. There are a lot of negative experiences that await a Web developer, but there are so many more to broaden the Web developer's personal and professional horizons.

In this chapter, we'll talk about the generalized concepts behind project management and how these concepts can be applied to the Web environment. Let's get started toward running more satisfying Web projects.

LAB 8.1

GOALS OF SUCCESSFUL PROJECT MANAGEMENT

LAB OBJECTIVES

After this lab, you will be able to

* Identify Client Goals
* Identify Contractor Goals

Project management assures that Web projects stay profitable. One can bring the best graphic artists, savvy programmers, and/or cutting-edge marketing people to a project, but if communication isn't adequate between all of the constituencies, money can be lost on a perfectly good opportunity.

TEAM DYNAMICS FOR WEB PROJECT MANAGEMENT INCLUDE THE FOLLOWING:

* Client management
* Budgeting and scheduling
* Logical work flow

All of these factors contribute to a successful project life cycle.

In a perfect world, project managers can avoid pitfalls by adhering to a disciplined development process. Unfortunately, communication, technology, and people are not always perfect. On the client side, upper management is often multitasking profit-centered activities while gathering materials for the company's Web site, but if communication isn't adequate between all of the constituencies, money can be lost on a perfectly good opportunity. The Web firm itself can become overburdened with too many projects going live at the same time. Despite these obstacles, the project manager must keep everyone centered and on track. Therefore, the process used becomes even more important.

It is a long way from project proposal to implementation. The project is not successful unless all constituencies have been satisfied. Is the client looking for a way to communicate to a new audience or better facilitate communication with an existing customer base? The Web firm needs to know this among many other things. After all, vague requirements from the client will spell death for the Web project. Throughout this part of the book, we will be discussing techniques to pin down the client requirements so the firm has a chance of meeting expectations.

Clients can be driven by deadlines, increased profitability, market conditions, and/or customer expectations. All are relying on the Web firm to take their business to the Web in the most effective way. Unfortunately, the client's goals are not always apparent. Some clients are better at communicating their objectives than others. The burden falls upon the Web firm to help clients clarify their requirements. We will investigate how to do this in all areas of Web site production. However, first you may need to understand the process involved with building a site.

On the contractor side, the project team desires to produce a Web site that meets the client's expectations and generates capital for the firm. These are the goals that can drive the Web firm. After all, if the client's needs are not met, the firm will suffer financial and emotional losses. The client may never see how depressed a project team can become when it has not hit the mark. However, the project manager will. In order to attract and keep good staff, the firm needs to maintain a successful track record. Surely, there will be some disappointing engagements along the way, but the majority of the projects a Web firm attracts must have a positive outcome.

Along the way, there can be a host of other objectives that need to be met. However, the right questions need to be asked. A project manager must try to put himself or herself in the client's place, understanding the client's point of view and making suggestions. You will investigate the best techniques for handling this challenge as you complete the upcoming exercises.

LAB 8.1 EXERCISES

8.1.1 IDENTIFY CLIENT GOALS

a) If you were contracting a Web firm to build a Web site based on your pet business idea, what would your general goals/concerns be? How would you measure success? Do not worry if you have never considered this possibility before. This exercise is meant to spur brainstorming on your part. After all, this is the same mind-set that your clients will have when they approach you.

_____

_____

_____

_____

b) The local bookstore has contracted you to build a Web site. What can a bookstore with a limited budget reasonably expect to achieve with its Web site?

_____

_____

_____

_____

c) Interview a small business owner about how he or she would see his or her business on the Web. Based on your experience as a Web developer, do these goals seem reasonable? What suggestions would you make?

_____

_____

_____

_____

**LAB
8.1**

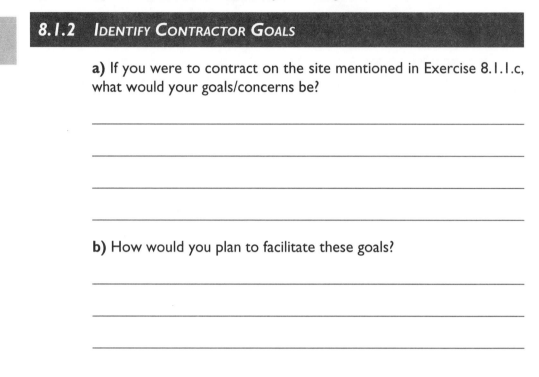

8.1.2   IDENTIFY CONTRACTOR GOALS

a) If you were to contract on the site mentioned in Exercise 8.1.1.c, what would your goals/concerns be?

_____

_____

_____

_____

b) How would you plan to facilitate these goals?

_____

_____

_____

_____

LAB 8.1 EXERCISE ANSWERS

8.1.1   ANSWERS

a)   If you were contracting a Web firm to build a Web site based on your pet business idea, what would your general goals/concerns be? How would you measure success?

Answer: Different types of Web sites can be built for different types of businesses. A commerce site that enables direct ordering of a product is quite different from an informational site that profiles a professional service (i.e., a law firm). I would want to contract a firm that had experience with all types of sites or specialized in sites for my type of business.

I would also want to see a written estimate with an expected delivery date. I would want to clarify the approval process with the contracting company so that I don't get stuck paying for a site that I do not like.

I would measure success by realizing increased sales equal to or exceeding the amount I paid for my Web site within a reasonable period of time.

b) The local bookstore has contracted you to build a Web site. What can a bookstore with a limited budget reasonably expect to achieve with its Web site?

Answer: Any Web site that is built to generate commerce must have a solid marketing plan. Most small businesses do not have an advertising budget equal to that of amazon.com. However, this does not mean the bookstore cannot have a profitable Web site and add to its bottom line.

I would ask the bookstore for a listing of all marketing/advertising vehicles currently in use for the store. I would evaluate how much traffic to the Web site could be internally generated through adding the URL to newsletters, catalogs, business cards, yellow pages ads, newspaper advertising, and so forth. If there are enough cross-marketing avenues available, chances are that traffic can be generated without contracting $1500/month banner advertising on Yahoo (which is totally out of the question, in this case).

Based on this foundation, I would suggest that the bookstore then build features into its Web site as profits are generated from it. The owner may want to grow traffic by putting revenues into additional Web advertising—banner advertising or optimized search-engine placement services.

Depending on the amount of money the bookstore wishes to generate, the time involved with building the Web site and its traffic organically can vary.

c) Interview a small business owner about how he or she would see his or her business on the Web. Based on your experience as a Web developer, do these goals seem reasonable? What suggestions would you make?

Answer: Obviously, this question has many answers. However, as a developer, I always beware of the client who has unrealistic expectations. Therefore, it's very important that anyone who is managing Web projects has a clear understanding of what a Web site will and will not do for a business.

The Web attracts entrepreneurs and "Get Rich Quickers." Unfortunately, this leads to unrealistic business plans. As a developer, you can just work on the project without regard for its eventual success. However, when the client realizes a few weeks down the road that he or she has just spent money on an unprofitable venture and the developer facilitated it, the client may lose respect for the developer. This is not a good way to build a firm's reputation—better to turn down the project than to risk tarnishing your firm's reputation.

8.1.2 ANSWERS

a) If you were to contract on the site mentioned in Exercise 8.1.1.c, what would your goals/concerns be?

Answer: My concerns/goals would be the following (in order of priority):

1. *I would want to be completely confident that resources existed within my firm to complete the task at hand. If any outsourcing was required, I would only do so with proven firms with which I had worked closely in the past.*

2. *I would not want to lose money for my firm.*

3. *I would want to produce a Web site that creates word of mouth referrals and encourages the client to become a long-term customer of my firm.*

4. *I would like to make money for my firm.*

5. *I would like to see my team's skills expand and rapport build.*

b) How would you plan to facilitate these goals?

Answer: I would facilitate these goals by doing the following:

1. *Assessing the customer requirements and meeting with my team and potential subcontractors to talk realistically about our ability to complete the project*

2. *Making sure that the lines of communication are clear between the client and the project team*

3. *Underpromising and overdelivering to the client*

4. *Implementing budgeting and scheduling tools that track expenses*

5. *Establishing an atmosphere where enthusiasm reigns*

LAB 8.1 SELF-REVIEW QUESTIONS

In order to test your progress, you should be able to answer the following questions:

1) Which of the following would be a goal of the client?
   a) _____ Getting the project completed for the least amount of money
   b) _____ Making the Web site launch date
   c) _____ Determining a schedule of payment
   d) _____ Incorporating existing company branding (i.e., logos)

2) Which of the following would be a goal of the contractor?
   a) _____ Getting the project completed for the least amount of money
   b) _____ Making the Web site launch date
   c) _____ Determining a schedule of payment
   d) _____ Incorporating existing company branding (i.e., logos)

L A B   8 . 2

COMPARING PROJECT MANAGEMENT IN VARIOUS INDUSTRIES

LAB OBJECTIVES

After this lab, you will be able to

- Compare Web Project Management to Construction Project Management
- Compare Web Project Management to Software Development Project Management

---

Management of projects differs in various industries. While the Web is a new medium, and it may seem like project developers need to reinvent the wheel, project management principles from established industries can apply to it.

Envision building a house. What kinds of factors impact that process? Are some factors unavoidable? In comparison, the Web is a much more controlled framework to build upon. Servers crash and news events can cause certain sections of the Internet to bog down. Still, how do these circumstances compare to the havoc an ill-timed blizzard can wreak upon a construction site?

Similar to constructing a skyscraper, developing a software database application can involve planning for a multitude of conditions. Many Web sites are static and uncomplicated. As time goes on, many more are offering interactivity reminiscent of the most sophisticated software applications. All of these processes can move forward within a rapid application development environment, with deadlines looming and financial limitations causing concern.

Whether one is building a mall off the interstate or on the information highway, many of the same engineering methodologies apply. The Web project manager can build upon these methodologies and refine them to produce effective Web sites that are scalable for future enhancements.

LAB 8.2 EXERCISES

8.2.1 COMPARE WEB PROJECT MANAGEMENT TO CONSTRUCTION PROJECT MANAGEMENT

a) When building a Web site versus a house, what processes do you feel are similar?

_____

_____

_____

_____

_____

_____

_____

_____

_____

_____

_____

_____

_____

_____

_____

_____

b) When building a Web site versus a house, what processes do you feel are different?

_____

_____

_____

_____

_____

_____

_____

_____

_____

_____

_____

_____

_____

_____

_____

**LAB
8.2**

8.2.2 COMPARE WEB PROJECT MANAGEMENT TO SOFTWARE DEVELOPMENT PROJECT MANAGEMENT

a) When building a software application versus a Web site, what processes do you feel are similar?

_____

_____

_____

_____

_____

_____

_____

_____

_____

_____

_____

_____

_____

_____

_____

_____

b) When building a software application versus a Web site, what processes do you feel are different?

_____

_____

_____

_____

_____

_____

_____

_____

_____

_____

_____

_____

_____

_____

_____

_____

_____

LAB 8.2 EXERCISE ANSWERS

This section gives you some suggested answers to the questions in Lab 8.2., with discussion related to those answers. Please post any alternative answers to these questions at the companion Web site for this book, located at http://www.phptr.com/phptrinteractive.

8.2.1 ANSWERS

a) When building a Web site versus a house, what processes do you feel are similar?

Answer: This may not have been an easy question for everybody to answer, but hopefully the following discussion will help you understand how building these two very different entities are very similar.

Most of the time when someone first approaches you to develop a site, they have a good idea that the Web is important for their application, but many clients don't understand how they are going to get from the analysis stage to implementation.

I often use the analogy that building a Web site is similar to building a house. I ask the client what steps he or she might expect to go through when building a house. The following are some questions that come to mind:

> How many rooms do I need?
>
> How do I want the house to look?
>
> What kind of appliances and conveniences do I want?
>
> What colors do I like?
>
> How long is it going to take?
>
> How much is it going to cost?

How many of you have ever built a house from scratch before with a builder? What kinds of things were you hoping he or she could do for you to guide you through the project? And who would you think you'd have on board when building your house? Most likely the team would consist of an architect, general contractor/project manager, plumbers, carpenters, electricians, and perhaps interior decorators.

After the architect puts together the plans, the general contractor will review how many people he or she will need to complete the house, how much it will cost, and when it will be complete. Delays can be caused by client availability to approve work completed or the client running out of funds. Therefore, plans need to be made for those kinds of eventualities.

In Web site design, instead of plumbers, carpenters, and electricians, your project team will consist of graphic designers, programmers, writers, and editors. Instead of the number of rooms, the client needs to determine how many sections he or she needs and how he or she wants the site to look. What type of functionality is required? How long is the Web site construction process going to take and how much is it going to cost?

b) When building a Web site versus a house, what processes do you feel are different?

Answer: There are obviously many differences between building a Web site and building a house. But in terms of project management, there are some key differences, as outlined in the following discussion.

Obviously, we're working in a different medium. When estimating project cost, the construction industry must incorporate the cost of materials and labor rates, whereas labor rates, site licenses, and software purchases tend to be the only consideration when costing a Web site.

One always runs the risk that no matter what has been agreed upon by the client and contractor, other opinions will be given from people outside the project loop that conflict with the original plan. These opinions can confuse the client. This is why project management is important, because if one follows the appropriate steps in the project life cycle, there is documentation that keeps track of approvals. Therefore, if a spouse or best friend or second cousin once removed hates the site, the burden of the changes still falls upon the client. Just as if someone says they want to paint a room yellow and then they come back and say they want it sky blue pink, who pays for the painter's time? The burden shouldn't fall on the general contractor.

But because Web site design is a new field, sometimes clients do not understand the labor involved with making changes.

8.2.2 ANSWERS

a) When building a software application versus a Web site, what processes do you feel are similar?

Answer: The engineering process is the same, as programming events are defined and flowcharted. Multiple conditions need to be tested before implementation.

b) When building a software application versus a Web site, what processes do you feel are different?

Answer: A Web site requires a graphical user interface that many software applications do not need to address. Therefore, the graphic design and approval process add complexity to the project. Also, the writing and editing requirements can be much more involved.

The biggest difference between a software application and a Web site is that most Web sites are deliverable to the masses. Most Web sites are built to be seen across platforms and to carry a message about a product or service. A software application is a tool that can be used in a more controlled environment. It doesn't necessarily have to reach across all system configurations.

LAB 8.2 SELF REVIEW QUESTIONS

In order to test your progress, you should be able to answer the following questions:

1) Which of the following scenarios could cause a contractor to stop work in the software development environment:
   a) _____ Rainy weather
   b) _____ Server hard drive crash
   c) _____ Nonremittance of scheduled payment
   d) _____ Sick employees
   e) _____ Labor strike

2) Which of the following scenarios could cause a contractor to stop work in the construction industry:
   a) _____ Rainy weather
   b) _____ Server hard drive crash
   c) _____ Nonremittance of scheduled payment
   d) _____ Sick employees
   e) _____ Labor strike

L A B   8 . 3

PROJECT TASKS

LAB OBJECTIVES

After this lab, you will be able to

- Identify Creative Tasks
- Identify Technical Tasks
- Identify Administrative Tasks
- Identify Marketing Tasks
- Identify Editorial Tasks

The skills required to develop a Web site are diverse. In most cases, Web sites involve a team approach. This is because an individual does not commonly possess the artistic, content-development, and technical abilities required to complete the project by himself or herself. It's unusual to find an engineer who also writes well, and it's also unusual to find a Web developer who is at the same time a high-level graphic designer, programmer, and editor.

Thus, most project managers find themselves dealing with a team of individuals with widely diverse skill sets. How that all comes together is a subject we will discuss in Chapter 9. However, for our purposes here, we will want to identify the project tasks involved with creating a Web site and determine under which category these tasks fall.

At this stage, when tasks are identified, the object is more to make a "shopping list" than to devise a highly specialized how-to document—a project specification. Once the tasks are identified, the project specification can then be authored by the project team (i.e., the artistic team head writes the creative specification; the programming team head writes the technical specification; and so forth). Therefore, the project manager needs to develop a "to-do" list. Once the team members have a chance to review it, specifications will be written, and from there the project manager can devise a budget and a schedule.

LAB 8.3 EXERCISES

For the following exercises, envision a project requiring the Web firm to build a school's Web site, which would include a database for the library. The school wishes to attract new students, provide a foundation through which students can learn about the Web, and provide information for the school community.

8.3.1 IDENTIFY CREATIVE TASKS

a) How would you identify the creative tasks involved in this site? What would they be? Do not be concerned if you have no experience with this. Look at a Web site. What elements might be contributed by people in traditionally creative roles?

_____

_____

_____

_____

_____

_____

_____

_____

_____

_____

_____

_____

b) What would you ask the client about how he or she would like the Web site to look if you had the opportunity?

8.3.2 IDENTIFY TECHNICAL TASKS

a) How would you identify the technical tasks involved in this site? What would they be? What type of contributions to the Web site might you expect from your programming team?

_____

_____

_____

_____

_____

_____

_____

_____

_____

_____

_____

_____

_____

_____

_____

_____

_____

_____

b) What would you ask the client about his or her technical goals if you had the opportunity?

_____

_____

_____

_____

_____

_____

_____

_____

_____

_____

_____

_____

_____

_____

**LAB
8.3**

8.3.3 IDENTIFY ADMINISTRATIVE TASKS

a) How would you identify the administrative tasks involved in this site? What would they be? Consider how an office is run. Are there some tasks, such as filing, answering client inquiries, and submitting the weekly payroll, that might have to take place in the background so that this project can continue in the foreground?

b) What questions would you ask the client that might impact on these administrative concerns?

_____

_____

_____

_____

_____

_____

_____

_____

_____

_____

_____

_____

_____

_____

8.3.4 IDENTIFY MARKETING TASKS

a) How would you identify the marketing tasks involved in this site? What would they be?

_____

_____

_____

**LAB
8.3**

_____

_____

_____

_____

_____

_____

_____

_____

_____

_____

_____

_____

_____

b) What would you ask the client about his or her marketing goals if you had the opportunity?

_____

_____

_____

_____

_____

_____

_____

LAB 8.3 EXERCISE ANSWERS

This section gives you some suggested answers to the questions in Lab 8.3, with discussion related to those answers. Please post any alternative answers to these questions at the companion Web site for this book, located at http://www.phptr.com/phptrinteractive.

8.3.1 ANSWERS

a) How would you identify the creative tasks involved in this site? What would they be?

Creative tasks can be defined by interviewing the client and discussing requirements with the creative team. A broad description of the creative tasks involved in developing this Web site includes the following:

- *Identify the content—What do we want to say in the Web site?*

- *Determine the deliverable schedule—When should all materials be supplied to the Web firm in order for the firm to make an implementation date?*

- *Graphic design—What do we want the Web site to look like?*

- *Develop the content—Write and create written and graphic composites.*

- *Edit the content—How would the written content read on the Web? Let's refine it.*

- *Create prototypes—Put composite graphics and written material together to create a working model of the site.*

- *Work with the technical team to implement finalized content into site—Refine the prototypes into the finalized version of the site.*

When building any Web site, there are graphical interfaces and content to be developed. Therefore, the developer needs to ascertain how the content is going to be delivered and how much original graphic design is required. The only way to do this is to require the school officials to organize their thoughts (see 8.3.1.b).

The developer understands that the site is being built for school families as well as for prospective students and their parents. Therefore, the audience visiting the site will have varying access speeds and may be running older browsers on their computers.

The graphic design must be attractive to both kids and adults, as well as make the best use of image size so that the pages will load quickly. Graphics should also make the best use of any school logos, colors, and mascots—things that are uniquely identifiable with the school.

Written content should be developed by the school administration, with editing contributed by the Web firm. Several Web sites are extremely helpful for editing Web-based communications, and Web site editors should be familiar with the concepts contained therein:

> *Yale C/AIM Web Style Guide: info.med.yale.edu/caim/manual*
>
> *Bobby Web Accessibility Analysis Tool: www.cast.org/bobby*
>
> *IU Web Site Design Guidelines: www.iuinfo.indiana.edu/policy*
>
> *All Things Web: www.pantos.org/atw*
>
> *Guide to Web Style: www.sun.com/styleguide*

b)   What would you ask the client if you had the opportunity?

> *Please define your basic goals for the Web site.*
>
> *What are the schedule requirements?*
>
> *Are there any existing collateral materials from which logos and content can be derived?*
>
> *Who will be supplying content?*
>
> *How often will content be updated? By whom?*
>
> *Which Web sites do you like from a graphical standpoint?*
>
> *Please storyboard your site and show how you envision it working.*

8.3.2 ANSWERS

a) How would you identify the technical tasks involved in this site? What would they be?

Technical tasks would be defined by interviewing the client and discussing require-ments with the technical team. A broad description of the technical tasks involved in developing this Web site includes the following:

> *Identify database requirements.*
>
> *Identify additional interactive elements.*
>
> *Identify server requirements.*
>
> *Program the site.*
>
> *Test the site.*
>
> *Stage the final site.*

A database programmer should evaluate the Web site requirements so that decisions can be made regarding the server, its operating system, and database middleware. NT platforms offer SQL server and Access database solutions. The preferred database for UNIX servers is Oracle or mySQL. Oracle can be used for databases with 80,000 records and above. However, the site license is expensive. MySQL is available as a free download and offers a stable environment for databases with up to 80,000 records. Based on database and any additional interactive requirements, a decision can be made regarding the server.

The following sites, particularly CAST.org, are very useful for developing a site that is widely accessible by the general public. A school Web site should pass the "Bobby" test—a Web-based tool that evaluates sites for accessibility to people with disabilities and international users and for compatibility with various browsers.

> *Bobby Web Accessibility Analysis Tool: www.cast.org/bobby*
>
> *IU Web Site Design Guidelines: www.iuinfo.indiana.edu/policy*
>
> *All Things Web: www.pantos.org/atw*
>
> *Web Content Accessibility Guidelines: www.w3.org/TR/WAI-WEBCONTENT*

b) What would you ask the client if you had the opportunity?

> *Please define your basic goals for the Web site.*
>
> *What are the schedule requirements?*
>
> *How often will content be updated? By whom?*
>
> *Which Web sites do you like from a technical standpoint?*

Please storyboard your site and show how you envision it working.

How many library records are there?

How would you like the database to be searched?

Do you have any requirements regarding the server the site must be staged upon? Or is Web hosting at the Web firm's discretion?

Are there any other interactive elements that you would like to include on the site (i.e., a bulletin board or chat room)?

LAB 8.3

8.3.3 ANSWERS

a) How would you identify the administrative tasks involved in this site? What would they be? Consider how an office is run. Are there some tasks, such as filing, answering client inquiries, and submitting weekly payroll that might have to take place in the background, so that this project can continue in the foreground?

Administrative tasks would be defined by interviewing the client, the Web firm owner (or whoever has authorization to allocate the firm's resources) and discussing requirements with the project team.

Defining the project

Estimating the project

Tracking contracts, work orders, and change orders

Developing project schedule/budget

Coordinating resources

Communicating with the client

Administrative tasks are traditionally performed by the project manager. Techniques for performing these functions will be examined in depth in later chapters.

b) What would you ask the client that might impact on these administrative concerns?

Please define your basic goals for the Web site.

What are the schedule requirements?

Are there any existing collateral materials from which logos and content can be derived?

Who will be supplying content?

How often will content be updated? By whom?

Which Web sites do you like from a graphical standpoint?

Please storyboard your site and show how you envision it working.

Which Web sites do you like from a technical standpoint?

How many library records are there?

How would you like the database to be searched?

Do you have any requirements regarding the server the site must be staged upon? Or is Web hosting at the Web firm's discretion?

Are there any other interactive elements that you would like to include on the site (i.e., a bulletin board or chat room)?

What is your budget for the site?

Do you require a flat bid or will you consider paying for time and materials?

What is your plan for marketing the site? Do you need the firm to facilitate and/or consult regarding marketing?

Are there plans for a later version of the site?

What is your availability for project meetings?

Who will be responsible for signing off on the work?

In other words, the project manager needs to have a broad view of the project so that he or she can adequately estimate the project and manage it cost-effectively. While the specifics can be micromanaged by creative, technical, and marketing team leaders, the project manager will need to be aware of all the schedule benchmarks and whether the project is progressing on budget, making adjustments as necessary.

8.3.4 ANSWERS

a) How would you identify the marketing tasks involved in this site? What would they be?

Marketing tasks would be defined by interviewing the client and discussing require-ments with the marketing team.

Analyzing current public relations

Recommending free on-line marketing options (i.e., search engines, reciprocal linking, banner swaps)

Identifying cost-effective marketing options (i.e., links from town page, tile and banner advertising, search engine placement, targeted e-mailing)

Writing press releases

Submitting the Web site to the seven major search engines

b) What would you ask the client about his or her marketing goals if you had the opportunity?

What kinds of marketing programs are already in place for the school that could be modified to include the Web site address?

What is the budget for marketing the site?

Since prospective students would come from local communities, are there any local Web sites that would drive traffic to the school site?

Are there any educational Web sites that might drive traffic to the school Web site?

What kind of traffic do you expect?

LAB 8.3 SELF-REVIEW QUESTIONS

In order to test your progress, you should be able to answer the following questions:

1) Which of the following creative tasks would need technical input:
    a) _____ Large animation on the front page
    b) _____ Buttons that change when the pointer is put over them
    c) _____ Inclusion of company logo
    d) _____ Embedding of multimedia objects
    e) _____ Inclusion of sales versus product information

2) Which of the following marketing tasks would require creative input:
    a) _____ Banner advertising on major search engines
    b) _____ Keyword identification
    c) _____ Exchange of links with noncompetitive Web sites
    d) _____ Identifying paid-for links with city- and industry-related guides (e.g., townonline.com)
    e) _____ Drafting of press releases

LAB 8.4

PROJECT LIFE
CYCLE FORMATS

LAB OBJECTIVES
After this lab, you will be able to
• Understand the Flow of Project Events • Identify the Team Members Involved with Each Project Phase

Coordinating a large Web project is a bit like ice skating. As the professional ice skater's movements are fluid and smooth, so are those of the seasoned project manager. Still, how many times did the ice skater fall while learning to land his triple Lutz? Many of us who have managed a lot of projects and find ourselves motivated to write books on the subject do so not because we started out managing projects perfectly. Rather, I can vividly remember my first extremely difficult client as well as the first time I ran into a tough technical glitch. Have I run into similar situations since? Absolutely! However, experience is a great teacher. A successful track record can do a lot to help a project manager smooth over moments of doubt and refocus on the problem.

While creative, technical, administrative, and marketing tasks are being undertaken, the timing of these events can be crucial. For example, the graphic designer should not complete a navigation scheme before all of the content is defined.

There are distinct phases to a Web project—definition, estimating/negotiating the contract, analysis, production, testing, launch, and postproject analysis. Postproject analysis can be best accomplished in an informal environment that lends itself to team building. The definition, estimating/negotiating, and analysis phase phases may need to be repeated as the project takes shape.

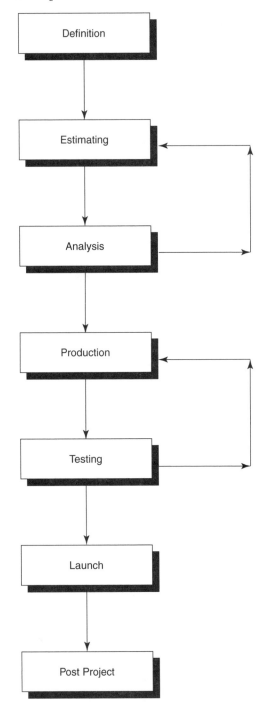

**LAB
8.4**

It is more cost-effective to reestimate and renegotiate a project should, upon further analysis, the project entail more expensive features to produce than originally included in the budget than to deal with this problem once the team is in the production phase. Conversely, testing may show errors made in production that need to be corrected. Thus, one phase does not always lead flawlessly into the other.

LAB 8.4 EXERCISES

Using the example of the school Web site in Lab 8.3 for the following exercises, determine which project management tasks might be performed in the various project phases and who would perform them.

8.4.1 UNDERSTAND THE FLOW OF PROJECT EVENTS

LAB 8.4

For each of the following phases, identify the project management tasks that you feel should be performed.

a) Definition Phase

_____

_____

_____

_____

_____

_____

_____

_____

_____

_____

_____

_____

_____

_____

_____

b) Estimating Phase

_____

_____

_____

_____

_____

_____

_____

_____

_____

_____

c) Analysis Phase

_____

_____

_____

_____

_____

_____

d) Production Phase

**LAB
8.4**

e) Testing Phase

f) Launch Phase

_____

_____

_____

_____

_____

_____

_____

_____

_____

_____

_____

_____

_____

_____

g) Postproject Analysis Phase

_____

_____

_____

_____

**LAB
8.4**

_____

_____

_____

_____

_____

_____

_____

_____

**LAB
8.4**

_____

_____

_____

_____

_____

8.4.2   IDENTIFY THE TEAM MEMBERS INVOLVED WITH EACH PROJECT PHASE

For each of the following phases, list the team members who you feel would be most appropriately involved.

a) Definition Phase

_____

_____

_____

_____

b) Estimating Phase

_____

_____

_____

_____

_____

c) Analysis Phase

_____

_____

_____

_____

_____

_____

**LAB
8.4**

d) Production Phase

_____

_____

_____

_____

_____

_____

_____

e) Testing Phase

_____

_____

_____

_____

_____

_____

f) Launch Phase

_____

_____

_____

_____

_____

g) Postproject Analysis Phase

_____

_____

_____

_____

_____

_____

LAB 8.4 EXERCISE ANSWERS

8.4.1 ANSWERS

For each of the following phases, identify the project management tasks that you feel should be performed.

a) Definition Phase

The definition phase entails only learning enough about the potential project to estimate cost. Many Web firms could spend a valuable part of each day drafting lengthy proposals and responding to RFPs (requests for proposals). This is a piece of the process that needs to be handled carefully, as the Web firm will be awarded only a percentage of the work that it is asked to bid upon. The time spent defining the potential project and drafting the bid is not billable. Therefore, this is not an income-generating task. While care should be taken to identify the scope of the project, Web firms would do well to establish a limit on time spent pursuing new business if the firm is busy.

Tasks in the definition phase might include

> *Reviewing the RFP, if available*
>
> *Interviewing the client*
>
> *Asking the client to complete a project questionnaire. (Most firms develop a standard questionnaire that is faxed to the potential client upon request for a bid.)*
>
> *Determining quality of competitor presence on the Web*

b) Estimating Phase

The estimating phase is crucial to creating profitable Web sites. No Web firm wants to find itself in the midst of an unprofitable, unending project with a difficult client. Renegotiating a new contract can be problematic and can be avoided by accurately evaluating the project and the costs involved up front.

While this is a crucial step in the process, estimating is also a phase, like the definition phase, where the Web firm is not being compensated for the time involved. Therefore, estimating must be done quickly and accurately. A project manager might want to develop his own system of determining price, which is constantly updated as each project is implemented. Also, many firms estimate a price and then build in a "fudge factor." Most of the time, unforeseen events will cause a project to become more expensive than originally planned for. It's best for the firm to cover itself with a percentage calculated over and above the estimated costs of the project.

Tasks in the estimating phase might include

- *Meeting with programmers, graphic designers, and editors to determine the amount of time involved creating the Web site as defined by the client*
- *Determining whether to flat bid (bid on the project using a flat fee for the whole project) or bid time and materials*
- *Determining whether the firm is in a competitive bidding situation*
- *Determining whether the prospective client is "high maintenance" or if the organization seems well prepared, knowledgeable, and motivated*
- *Evaluating how the client sees the Web and whether this project, as the company envisions it, could be a successful application of Web technology*
- *Determining method of billing*
- *Determining type of contract/agreement between the Web firm and client*
- *Writing a formalized bid detailing Web site features as the firm currently understands them, type of contract, and how billing will be done*
- *Upon acceptance of the bid, overseeing the signing of the contract and remittance of retainer/first payment*

c)   Analysis Phase

The analysis phase is where a detailed project specification is written and becomes the "Bible" for the Web project, used by both the client and the project team. The project specification is the written agreement between the client and the firm regarding exactly how the Web site will function.

Occasionally, while in the analysis phase, the client may decide to include value-added components not originally planned for in the first project bid. The firm will then either renegotiate the project or include the value-added components under a separate agreement. However, the project manager must be cautious when determining elements that were covered under the bid and those that were not. It's more cost-effective to identify these items now than to come to terms with them during production.

Tasks in the analysis phase might include

Writing the project specification with input from creative, technical, and marketing teams. The project specification includes the creative specification, the technical specification, and the marketing specification.

Renegotiating project price based upon value-added requirements.

Devising a project schedule.

Creating a project budget.

Determining the best way for the team to interface with each other and the client, as well as the method by which approvals will be obtained.

d) Production Phase

In a perfect world, all project issues would be ironed out in the analysis phase, before any team member touched a keyboard. This is what the project manager should be aiming for. Therefore, the production phase should encompass the physical building of the site. During this phase, it is important for the client to be available to approve work completed. All collateral materials must be received by the Web firm from the client. Otherwise, the penalties suffered due to lack of cooperation by the client should fall upon the client and not upon the Web firm. Likewise, the Web firm needs to meet its deadlines. Some clients insist that a clause be written into the contract that states that if the developer fails to meet the appointed deadline, the developer must forfeit a portion of the fee (typically 10%). Thus, strict adherence to the project schedule by all parties is desirable.

Tasks in the production phase might include:

Verifying receipt of collateral materials from client

Coordinating tasks performed by team members

Communicating with the client

Overseeing programming, graphic design, editing, and marketing tasks

Gaining approvals from client based on work performed by the project team

e) Testing Phase

Typically, most programmers feel that their code is perfect when it's turned over for testing. Being a programmer myself, I am always shocked to find errors in my code after testing. However, the key thing here is that someone else has interacted with my code. Up until this point, I have been the only "user."

The testing phase involves another person evaluating the site and trying to break it by inputting any and every condition. Given his fresh perspective, the tester is often able to identify coding problems of which the programming team was not initially aware. Many times this is because the programming team is too close to the project by the time it goes for testing. After a while, it becomes assumed that a user will behave in a certain fashion. However, users will interact with the site in a multitude of different ways—some planned for, others not.

The site should be proofread and tested in all browsers. Images should be evaluated for "weight"—the amount of memory they use. All of these tasks should be performed by individuals not involved in the production of the project.

Tasks in the testing phase might included:

Selecting testers not connected with the project to evaluate the site's functionality

Overseeing testing

Overseeing correction of errors by the team

f)   Launch Phase

Once the site is tested and all of the approvals are set, it's tempting to go ahead and set the site live. However, if the site is being uploaded to a new server, it will need to be retested. Also, the marketing plan is being implemented, with press releases going out to industry publications, the URL submitted to the search engines, banners sent to on-line advertisers, and links requested from strategic Web partners.

The Web firm may want to cement its relationship with the client at this time by celebrating the launch of the site, allowing for better communication in the future.

In addition, a maintenance plan or contract will need to be written, with the date for the first Web site review meeting agreed upon by the firm and the client. This procedure not only provides for continued business for the Web firm but will provide structure for the client. Most clients understand that the value of their Web site depends upon their ability to keep it current. However, the Web firm cannot expect the client to remember to contact them with changes on a regular basis. It's a bit like visiting the dentist—you know it's necessary, but it can become low on the priority list unless there's a major problem. Therefore, setting up a maintenance plan, preferably a maintenance contract with retainers in place, can provide this structure for the client.

Tasks in the launch phase might include:

> *Overseeing implementation of the marketing plan*
>
> *Negotiating a maintenance contract with the client*
>
> *Overseeing testing the final version of the Web site on the client's server*
>
> *Inviting team members and clients to the launch party*

g)   Postproject Analysis Phase

The postproject analysis phase is crucial to the Web firm's development. This is where the team conducts an internal audit of the project and all of its phases, discussing what went wrong, as well as which tasks went smoothly. MVPs (most valuable players) should be recognized and congratulated by the project team members, promoting camaraderie and, hopefully, smoothing over any ruffled feathers that might have occurred during the last push toward implementation.

Tasks in the postproject analysis phase might include:

> *Coordinating internal audit of the project*
>
> *Rewarding outstanding performance by deserving team members*

**LAB
8.4**

8.4.2 ANSWERS

For each of the following phases, list the team members who you feel would be most appropriately involved.

a) Definition Phase

Project Manager

b) Estimating Phase

Project Manager, Creative Team Manager, Technical Team Manager

c) Analysis Phase

All Team Members

d) Production Phase

Project Manager, Creative Team, Technical Team

e) Testing Phase

Project Manager, Quality Assurance Team

f) Launch Phase

Project Manager, Technical Team, Quality Assurance Team, Marketing Team

g) Postproject Analysis Phase

All Team Members

**LAB
8.4**

LAB 8.4 SELF-REVIEW QUESTIONS

In order to test your progress, you should be able to answer the following questions:

1) How do you see the project manager's role in the development of a Web site? Which of the following is he or she most similar to?
   a) _____ A coordinator
   b) _____ A negotiator
   c) _____ A team advisor
   d) _____ An administrative assistant
   e) _____ A multidisciplinary Web developer

2) Which of the following phases does the project manager *not* play a major role in?
   a) _____ Estimating
   b) _____ Analysis
   c) _____ Design
   d) _____ Production
   e) _____ All of the above

CHAPTER 8

TEST YOUR THINKING

The projects in this section use the skills you've acquired in this chapter. The answers to these projects are available to instructors only through a Prentice Hall sales representative and are intended to be used in classroom discussion and assessment.

1) How would you manage a situation in which the client begins bringing up definition/analysis issues while the project is in the production phase?

2) What kinds of documentation might help you to track what has been agreed upon by both the client and the developer?

C H A P T E R   9

THE PROJECT TEAM

 "The sum of its equal parts is greater than the whole."

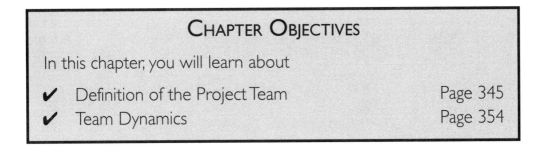

Before a Web firm can contract for projects, a solid working team must be in place. Some firms are made up of one or two people. However, as the projects themselves or the volume of projects get larger, the Web firm relies on more team members to roll them out. As the size of the firm grows, so does the number of human interfaces, which can either benefit a project or bog it down.

Speaking from experience, I can say that it takes a long time to build a reliable team that can react fluidly to project events. Finding talented individuals, who wish to enhance the firm, is difficult. However, as the firm's reputation builds, so do the reputations of the team members. Commitment to teamwork benefits everyone.

Members of the team may be coming from different places. Some may be subcontractors, brought in for a specific project. Others may be long-time employees. When assembling a team, the project manager must make the decision regarding human resources. However, I always follow the para-

343

digm to contract on the project first and then hire or subcontract the personnel later. One may want to keep abreast of which subcontractors are available at any given time. I'm often in touch with my subcontractors every week or so and am aware of their schedules. However, subcontractors get very tired of dealing with firms that take their time describing a project, ask about the subcontractor's schedule, and then award the contract elsewhere. I say very little or nothing to my subs until a project is ready to be contracted. I feel that to do otherwise falls into the same category of a potential client who keeps calling the firm, bending everyone's ear, but never will commit on contracting the project. After a while, no one takes them seriously. This subject is discussed in Chapter 10.

The project manager's leadership skills will come into play when dealing with all of these constituencies. He or she must be willing to listen, have excellent communication skills, be task oriented while satisfying the needs of the team members, model good team conduct, and be able to address negative undercurrents fairly. The project manager may not only find himself or herself as a mediator between the firm and the client, but between team members as well. Therefore, an ability to rise above a given conflict and not take issues personally is not only a desirable trait in a project manager but rather necessity to keep the team in working order.

I used to take criticism to heart. As the owner of a new Web site development business, I felt crushed whenever anyone had anything to say that was less than positive within my team. In several cases, I had to build the confidence to know whether I was dealing with my problem or someone else's. With experience comes a track record of success and an innate ability to determine the impetus for the disagreement. I am also much better at assembling my team now because I know what to look for in a potential team member.

It's quite simple—when I start thinking about the challenges of dealing with a particular team member more than the challenges that the projects are presenting, I know that it's time for that team member to go elsewhere. This comes with experience. The more you deal with Web development people, the easier it is to select individuals who will fit in best on certain projects.

LAB 9.1

DEFINITION OF THE PROJECT TEAM

LAB OBJECTIVES

After this lab, you will be able to

- Define the Writing Process
- Define the Artistic Process
- Define the Engineering Process
- Define the Marketing Process
- Determine How Divergent Processes Interface

A Web development team is made up of people. These people are not programming languages, skill sets, or marketing techniques. Rather, these people possess multidisciplinary experiences, which they must rely upon to converge with those of other team members and thus to build one Web site seamlessly. Therefore, despite multidisciplinary skills, each team member must be able to communicate and educate the others and have their own speciality, upon which they can be the last word.

Truly, the exciting point about project teams is their diversity. The various processes required when building a Web site involve different ways of thinking. This is an asset to a peer-to-peer supervised team, because these types of teams become goal oriented as opposed to self-oriented. Team members can appreciate one another's strengths without being threatened. Each team member has his or her own area of expertise, which cuts down on competition.

The graphic designer is concerned about how the Web site is going to look. The editor is focused on what the site communicates. The programmer wants to be sure that all of the programs work. Lastly, the marketing team leader is concerned about making users aware of the Web site's presence so that the client benefits from it.

People who specialize in these areas—graphic design, editing, programming, and marketing—rely primarily on different sides of their brains. People are primarily left- or righthanded, and many individuals favor different sides of their brain. The left brain hemisphere works primarily with analysis, language, reason, and computation; the right side processes intuitive, imaginative, and artistic operations.

Thus, the project manager must be aware of how the team is arriving at their conclusions and the process by which this happens.

The Whole Truth

A superior skill set for a project manager to possess would be writing, editing, graphic design, programming, and marketing experience. I often refer to someone who can accomplish all of these tasks well as being ambidextrous, in that the individual is equally comfortable with both left and right brain activity and does not seem to favor one over the other.

This ambidextrous trait can assist the project manager in understanding what is taking place within the project team. Considering the challenges each member faces and what motivates them allows the project manager to facilitate project tasks.

The project manager's job is not to supervise autocratically, but rather to coach, educate, and encourage team members, respecting each individual as an expert in his or her own field. By providing structure for the team to work as independently as possible, the project manager helps the team develop its mission and identify the goals it wishes to accomplish. As a football team has a coach and an orchestra has a conductor, a Web site development team has a project manager—a person with the view of the big picture, but who isn't necessarily running the ball or playing the violin. Thus, the project manager helps the team define its mission and provides benchmarks and clear goals through which the team can gauge its success.

The purpose of the following exercises is for the project manager to understand the various processes involved within the team. This by no means assumes that the project manager has to be an expert writer/editor/graphic designer/programmer/marketer, but rather that he or she gives thought to the challenges faced by team members performing these tasks.

LAB 9.1 EXERCISES

9.1.1 DEFINE THE WRITING PROCESS

Write a simple paragraph that details the Internet services your brand new (fictional) Web firm offers. After the paragraph is complete, describe how you created it.

_____

_____

_____

_____

_____

_____

_____

9.1.2 DEFINE THE ARTISTIC PROCESS

Draw a company logo for your brand new (fictional) Web firm. Describe how you created it.

_____

_____

_____

_____

_____

_____

9.1.3 DEFINE THE ENGINEERING PROCESS

If you wanted to show prospective customers how to your Web firm can produce cutting-edge programs, how would you accomplish this? Describe the process by which you determined the technical requirements.

_____

_____

_____

_____

_____

_____

_____

_____

_____

9.1.4 DEFINE THE MARKETING PROCESS

If you were to market your new firm's Web site, how would you do so? Then detail the process through which you determined the marketing requirements.

_____

_____

_____

_____

_____

_____

_____

_____

9.1.5 DETERMINE HOW DIVERGENT PROCESSES INTERFACE

Describe strategies through which you would incorporate these writing, artistic, engineering, and marketing processes.

_____

_____

_____

_____

_____

_____

LAB 9.1 EXERCISE ANSWERS

9.1.1 ANSWERS

a) Write a simple paragraph that details the Internet services your brand new (fictional) Web firm offers. After the paragraph is complete, describe how you created it.

Answer: The purpose of this exercise is not to write the paragraph, but rather to identify the process involved in creating it.

Often, the hardest thing about writing is to start. Inexperienced writers often develop a bad habit of self-editing while initially putting words to paper. However, this habit can inhibit the creative force within the writer.

I notice that when clients try to develop copy, or even just talking points, for their Web site, it seems that they first need to give themselves permission to write. Most people have heard of math anxiety. There seems to be a writing component to this as well. Often, this is what the writing/editing team is dealing with when trying to procure copy from a client.

When trying to motivate writers, I often tease them that it's best to adopt Nike's "Just Do It" philosophy. First, just get the words and ideas down on paper and worry about the editing later.

It helps the writer first to define what it is that he or she wants to address in the piece and then decide which specific points to cover. After this is accomplished, writing the first draft is much easier. There's an outline to follow.

It's best to have a team member edit the piece for clarity, spelling, grammar, and content. (As discussed in Chapter 8, writing for the Web is different from writing for other mediums. Review that chapter and the appropriate links to helpful Web sites, if necessary.) Then the writer can add depth to the piece by incorporating the editor's suggestions into a final draft.

The following link is very helpful to understanding the writing process: The Writer's Toolbox—http://dlc.tri-c.cc.oh.us/wb/write/docs/process.htm.

9.1.2 ANSWERS

a) Draw a company logo for your brand new (fictional) Web firm. Describe how you created it.

Answer: I've worked with several great graphic designers through the years, and given that graphic design seems to be my weakest Web talent, I look to graphic designers with a bit of awe.

Somewhere along the way, a lot of us stop drawing, although we start out with the desire to create images. My house is littered with drawings that my elementary school-age sons create. The drawings hang on bulletin boards, on the refrigerator, and all over my office. There's no self-consciousness in their attempts at drawing. My sons think that their dinosaurs are the best, as I certainly do. However, I know the day may come when the supplies of crayons, construction paper, and watercolors may need to be replaced less often.

Even kids, who have trouble with fine motor skills, can now use graphic programs on the computer, which allow them to unleash the pictures in their heads without struggling with the grip of a crayon.

As people get older, they seem to become more self-conscious about their artwork and stop developing this talent. A lot of us decide, myself included, that we just can't draw—that we're not artistic—and hide any attempts with the caution that we hid our teenage journals.

Therefore, I always ask the graphic designers I work with how they come up with their ideas. It may be that I need only look to my two sons, who have given themselves permission to draw without regard for other people's opinions. As with writing, this seems to be the first step.

The consensus among designers that I've interviewed seems to be that they start with a picture in their head. Call it intuition or perception. Then they brainstorm with the client and with other team members to create their next visualization. Designers can then build prototypes for others to see so that there is a baseline for comments, allowing the designer to begin the refining the final product.

9.1.3 ANSWERS

a) If you wanted to show prospective customers how your Web firm can produce cutting-edge programs, how would you accomplish this? Describe the process by which you determined the technical requirements.

Answer: While creative people need to listen to their hearts and seize upon their intuition, programmers come at their tasks from an entirely different perspective. Their world is black and white, as opposed to the 256 RGB palette that the Web has to offer graphic designers. As far as programmers are concerned, the Web site programming is either going to work or it isn't—end of story.

A typical conflict between a graphic designer and a programmer may be the use of a complex animation. That animation might be the best thing the graphic designer has ever created, and it might run perfectly well on his or her local machine. However, the programmer isn't going to care for its artistic value. He or she is going to worry about how it loads over the Web, when many users are still using a 28.8-baud connection. Some graphic designers who are new to the Web often have trouble with creating graphics that are optimized for this medium.

Therefore, the programmer is going to be interested in defining the technical requirements and risk analysis up front. Is that 90,000-record database going to work well on a middleware, such as MySQL, or does the client need to break down and get Oracle licensing? Can the requirements be completed on time? Many new software tools promise a quick and dirty approach and few of them actually deliver.

As my primary training was in electrical engineering, I tend to take conservative, almost skeptical approaches to my Web sites. While other firms espouse their cutting-edge processes, I'm interested in providing the client with tried and true methods, which bring the Web site to implementation on time and on budget and, most important, working correctly. I'm focused on using cross-platform technologies, and while I may be beta testing XML and some of the newer languages, I wouldn't discuss them with a client until those environments are completely stable.

9.1.4 ANSWERS

a) If you were to market your new firm's Web site, how would you do so? Then detail the process through which you determined the marketing requirements.

Answer: Marketing is one of the most important pieces of Web site development. The marketing team is often dealing with a client who feels that the Web now puts him on a level playing field with his largest competitors. Making that clients understand that the amount of dollars budgeted to market the Web site will have a lot to do with its success can be touchy but not impossible. In my firm, we always state that a Web site complements an overall marketing plan. If it's to be a standalone venture, then other forms of advertising will need to support it.

What about branding? The marketing team must work closely with the creative team to be sure that company logos and tag lines are consistent throughout the site, reiterating the client's message. This reinforces the concept that most people must see an advertisement seven times before it finally sinks in. It also might explain the new marketing gimmick on television, in which one commercial is repeated consecutively and often during a specific time slot.

The marketing team must determine which are the best ways to get that message out there about this new Web site, be it direct mail, targeted e-mails, banner advertising, links from other sites, radio, and/or television advertising. There are also the obvious, organic ways for a business to get the Web site address out to prospective customers. Items like business cards, brochures, and letterhead can become platforms for announcing the existence of the Web site.

The marketing team is concerned with how we as human beings react subliminally to messages. What's a turnoff? What piques our interest? Have you ever seen a billboard with just a few words on it and wondered what it meant. The billboard grabs your curiosity as you drive by for a few weeks. Then the billboard is redone with the appropriate contact information. This certainly grabs interest.

We've all seen teasers that may say, "It's Coming!" and nothing else. "Well," we say, "what's coming?" Then, in two weeks, we might see, "In three weeks, it'll be here!" "Well," we think, "what the heck will be here? I want to know!" Several messages later, we're involved. When the final announcement comes out that "Joseph and the Amazing Technicolor Dreamcoat" is being staged at our local elementary school, it's effective—much more effective than if the promoters had initially just put up a flier that said, "Acme Elementary School presents Joseph and the Amazing Technicolor Dreamcoat." At this point, my kids are counting the days and giving me daily reminders. We'll be going, because we're invested.

The marketing team has to psychoanalyze the target audience and determine how to pique their interest. Meeting with the company's marketing director and understanding how this business entity has been marketed in the past can help give the Web firm a jump start.

9.1.5 ANSWERS

a)   Describe strategies through which you would incorporate these writing, artistic, engineering, and marketing processes.

Answer: As you can now see, there are many agendas among team members in a Web site project. How does it all fit together?

It's simple. Each member has to respect the other's realm of expertise. If the engineering department says that the super-cool animation that the creative department has developed will slow down the site, the departments need to work together to come up with elements that will satisfy each constituency.

If marketing feels that creative hasn't reinforced the company's branding enough within the site, there needs to be teamwork to solve the problem. If creative feels there isn't enough "eye candy" to grab the user's attention, the other departments need to respect this.

Someone has to have the last say in all of this. It's usually the project manager. This is why it's important for the project manager to be familiar with the challenges each member is facing. This is not an easy process, but with a little respect and some savvy conflict resolution on the part of the project manager, it works. More on team building and conflict resolution will be discussed in the next lab.

LAB 9.1 SELF-REVIEW QUESTIONS

1) The creative and technical teams can have differing objectives which the project manager must help to coordinate.
   a) _____ True
   b) _____ False

2) By understanding the various processes involved with creating a Web site, the project manager can help the project team to create the site faster.
   a) _____ True
   b) _____ False

LAB 9.2

TEAM DYNAMICS

LAB OBJECTIVES

After this lab, you will be able to

- Strategize for Conflict Resolution
- Facilitate Positive Communication within the Team
- Build Team Enthusiasm for a Project

Anyone who has ever been part of a poorly functioning company will attest to how unresolved conflicts affect productivity. Senior-level team members who are impatient with mentoring more inexperienced members can generate resentment, especially if they are responsible for challenging the junior-level members with new tasks.

As a junior-level team member, I was very lucky to work in both the best and the worst of these environments. My best experience was working in a large corporation at a time when a great deal of excitement was building around its products. There were two junior-level analysts, myself included, assigned to a senior-level analyst, who was a demanding but excellent teacher who truly cared. The relationship I had with the other junior-level analyst was based on mutual respect, and we were careful to keep things light. Mistakes could be made, because we were learning, but both of us were determined to help the other. I can't ever remember any undercurrent of hostility or flexing of egos.

Having just come from an environment in which I had difficulty gaining support from other junior-level members and finding a mentor among the senior staff, I breathed a sigh of relief in my new position. I also had a benchmark by which I could appreciate it, which probably improved my willingness to have things go well. Many years later, I still regard that working environment as being one of the most pleasant I have had. As a result, I have tried to promote a positive environment within my own firm, an environment in which each individual feels valued and his or her skills are fostered. In doing so, I have thought a great deal about communication and how easily it can break down. Often, I have found that if people only know each other on the level of their skill sets, as opposed to having a more three-dimensional relationship, it's easy to be uncharitable should a misunderstanding occur. Establishing a good rapport among team members is key to running a well-functioning project.

Santech Corporation, a manufacturing firm located in Fort Worth, Texas, reached a point where it had to take a hard look at how work was being performed and decided to adopt, in some areas, self-supervised teams, very similar to how most software development firms operate. Santech had found that when there were supervisors on the team, individual team members did not take the initiative to accept responsibility. Rather, the supervisor maintained vertical pressure downward and became the fall-guy when things went wrong, as opposed to the group sharing and being invested in the outcome. The supervisor took on the role of project manager and became the "go-to" person when problems arose. By implementing a self-supervised approach, all team members shared in the failure or success of a project. All team members were made accountable, instead of just the supervisor.

At Santech, the teams provided horizontal peer pressure to ensure completion of project tasks. If one member was not performing, another team member might speak to him or her and then speak to the project manager if there was no improvement. This shared leadership clearly identified bottom performers through peer review.

Once the implementation of this process was through, the executives at Santech said, "Moving equipment is easy. Moving the minds of people is difficult." This is just what the project manager is responsible for—moving the minds of the team and the client, communicating the common goals, so that team members can hold themselves accountable for meeting those goals.

As discussed in Chapter Eight, major deadlines and tasks can be defined so that the project can move forward in a logical manner. Teams break down when individuals are unclear about expectations. By being task oriented during conflicts, instead of allowing disagreements to deteriorate to a personal level, each team member becomes aware of the big picture.

LAB 9.2 EXERCISES

**LAB
9.2**

9.2.1 STRATEGIZE FOR CONFLICT RESOLUTION

Offer three techniques for helping two team members resolve a conflict over a project task, with the goal of an eventual good rapport among them.

_____

_____

_____

_____

_____

_____

_____

_____

_____

_____

_____

_____

_____

_____

_____

_____

_____

_____

_____

9.2.2 FACILITATE POSITIVE COMMUNICATION WITHIN THE TEAM

Describe three tools you would use to facilitate positive communication during the building of a project. Your goal is to promote clear, objective interaction among team members.

LAB
9.2

_____

_____

_____

_____

_____

_____

_____

_____

_____

_____

_____

_____

_____

_____

_____

_____

_____

9.2.3   BUILD TEAM ENTHUSIASM FOR A PROJECT

Describe three techniques you would use to initiate team enthusiasm for a project and keep it flowing through until implementation.

LAB
9.2

_____

_____

_____

_____

_____

_____

_____

_____

_____

_____

_____

_____

_____

_____

_____

_____

LAB 9.2 EXERCISE ANSWERS

9.2.1 ANSWERS

a) Offer three techniques for helping two team members resolve a conflict over a project task, with the goal of an eventual good rapport among them.

Answer: A running joke in my firm is that I think all problems can be solved by going out to one of our clients' restaurants for a glass of white zinfandel and a piece of Chaos pie. I am blessed to have an office manager who reads me well and knows when it's time to bail out of the office with me for an hour or two, so we can come back with a new perspective.

Keeping the atmosphere light, while making team members aware of the project demands, can be a delicate balance. Communication is key.

There are several types of project meetings that are helpful to keeping everyone informed and thus heading off conflicts before they arise. The first step toward conflict resolution between individuals is the effective use of meetings.

__The Project Status Meeting:__ At this meeting, each team member is allowed ten minutes to report on his or her area of the project. There should be no brainstorming at this point. The focus of this meeting is to bring everyone up to speed on the project's progress and identify problem areas that need attention.

The project manager needs to be focused on schedule and budget and aware of how client approvals are progressing.

The project manager should develop a formal agenda, which is followed to the letter. No one is allowed to interrupt the flow of the speaker's conversation until that individual is finished. Each topic warrants a full ten minutes.

The agenda is used as a working tool. Each issue should have a resolution recorded, an action item attached (with the person responsible for resolving it), or a note to continue the discussion in a brainstorming meeting or at the next status meeting, when more information has been gathered.

This type of meeting has the strictest format. However, it should happen at least weekly, so that all team members are aware of what's happening. While this kind of disciplined meeting may seem counter productive to a relaxed and productive office atmosphere, it actually informs all team members, without some of the stronger personalities on the team dominating the meeting.

__Brainstorming Meetings:__ When someone goes over their allotted ten minutes in a status meeting, I often say, "Okay, this is now brainstorming, and it belongs outside this particular meeting." The reason is that while two or three team members are hashing out a particular issue, the rest of the team, who is not involved in the issue, is falling asleep. This is a waste of their time, and it is nonproductive.

A brainstorming meeting is where the involved constituencies can get together and discuss the issues at hand in a free-form structure. The difference is, if this is a creative issue, only creative team members are at this meeting, without holding the technical team hostage.

As with the status meeting, each member should be able to speak without being interrupted. Still, no one member should be allowed to dominate the meeting. All members need to be heard from. How does one facilitate this kind of exchange? There are a few simple techniques:

- *Specifically ask for each person's opinion on the issue.*
- *Conduct a vote, once everyone has been heard.*

I find that most conflicts between individuals take place when one or the other feels that he or she hasn't been heard. One team member may be very vocal and dominant. The other team member may have valid ideas but is not being provided the format in which to voice them. The person is being steamrolled by a stronger personality and doesn't appreciate it. Peer meetings in which everyone is held accountable for fair team behavior can circumvent a lot of this. Action items are identified and assigned equally, and everyone is given a chance to speak. Most conflicts have to do with individuals feeling that their empowerment is being reduced because of another individual, which builds resentment. These kinds of meetings keep everyone in check.

Perhaps a way to improve the relationship between two team members is to send them off to lunch together with the distinct purpose of coming up with a fair set of ground rules for their working relationship. Ask them to identify to each other what is going wrong and to come up with solutions for how to circumvent the problems.

Make the individuals aware that it has come to your attention that things aren't going smoothly and that you would like them to settle their differences. There should be a sense of urgency about getting the air cleared. Part of their job responsibility is now to find a way to work effectively with this other person. By leaving it to the two people in question, neither one feels that he or she is being treated as anything less than a responsible adult. Let them come up with the ground rules for their relationship. However, make them aware that it is their responsibility to do so and that there will be consequences if this conflict is not resolved.

When teams are working closely together, backbiting can't be allowed. One of the worst things that a project manager can do is to get in the middle of a conflict. Inevitably, one side will feel that the project manager is playing favorites or taking up a personal cause, when neither case is true. A dear friend once advised me to "take the high road." By staying neutral and just offering tools to facilitate a meeting of the minds between the combatants, the project manager will hopefully engender the best results.

A third way to deal with conflict is to fire one or both of the team members. Obviously, this isn't the preferred way to deal with the problem. However, I was witness to a situation in which the divisiveness between two executives was so great that it filtered down to the most junior-level employees, and it effected productivity every day. This is unacceptable in any firm and can affect everyone. In a professional atmosphere, every team member should have the opportunity to become empowered and contribute.

However, if conflict has become too embedded in a firm, other people get pulled into it and categorized according to what side they are affiliated with, whether they know it or not. It's poison. If the conflict is that intense, it's best to start fresh with new people.

9.2.2 ANSWERS

a) Describe three tools you would use to facilitate positive communication during the building of a project. Your goal is to promote clear, objective interaction among team members.

Answer: The best way to get all team members up to speed quickly is to establish rules. Protocols, such as deciding how decisions are going to be made and how everyone will communicate with each other, and establishing initial deadlines give team members the glue to keep moving in the same direction.

A second way to facilitate communication between team members is the creation of a project site. In Secrets of Successful Web Sites, David Siegal gives a great example of how a project site can allow both clients and team members working in remote locations to stay on top of the latest developments. Check out http://www. secretsites.com for a fine example of a working project site.

The third method is to run meetings like those discussed in Exercise 9.2.1. Regular and efficient communication keeps all team members informed.

Thomasina Borkman, an instructor at George Mason University, wrote a wonderful case study regarding two poorly functioning teams. This paper was based on her Small Groups Dynamics class. It is with her permission that excerpts are included here.

Case Study of Two Poorly Functioning Teams*

Overall, both teams completed their assignments on time but at great personal cost to some members because other members could not be counted on to do their work in a timely manner, among other factors. I characterize both teams as poorly functioning. A number of factors are involved in the lack of effective functioning of the team.

Team A

A subgroup of four of the seven members of Team A consistently worked on the team project throughout the course of the semester. The other three members appeared briefly in the beginning and then dropped out for shorter/longer periods in the middle. One of these three members assumed an ambiguous leadership role at the beginning

*Thomasina Borkman, virtualschool.edu/98c/soci305/soci305Thomasina.html. December 17,1996, Taming the Electronic Frontier, George Mason University Distributed Learning Community and Virtual School.

of the course, then dropped it, which was confusing to other members. His idea for the project was accepted reluctantly after several other project ideas had been debated. He then became unavailable to guide the development of his project idea. He will be named All Talk (little action) in this paper, which is how his teammates characterize him.

Leadership

Were there too few leaders, too many leaders, or a lack of legitimate leaders (whose authority as leaders was agreed upon by the members)? Interviews revealed that one had the opinion that there were too many leaders, others that leadership was problematic, or team members had different perceptions about who were legitimate leaders of the group. When members of a group have such different perceptions of what is going on, it indicates a problematic area and a lack of consensus. In well-functioning groups, members agree for the most part on what are the authority, role, and communication structures of the group and how they operate.

At a face-to-face (f2f) meeting early in the semester that was not attended by everyone, consensus was reached among attendees that two women, the Caretaker (who telephoned people about activities and urged them to keep participating), and the Organizer (who kept the group moving forward with its project), would be the leaders. Nonattendees did not necessarily know about this consensus of leadership and one isolate never did realize two women had been "elected" to be leaders.

All Talk's idea for the project was reluctantly accepted after several other ideas were discussed, and one idea at least discarded. The Functioning Subgroup (see sociogram discussion below) expected All Talk to take the initiative in guiding the development of the project since it was his idea and others had no clear idea of his vision and how to implement it. He then disappeared and did not perform a leadership role of guidance, which became very frustrating to the Subgroup.

Communication

The members had different perceptions about whether or not the instructor encouraged teams to interact only on line or whether or not he encouraged or sanctioned f2f meetings. The female nerd had a difficult schedule and had selected the course partly because she would not have to show up on campus; she did not regard f2f meetings important until late in the course, when so much nonaction, conflict, and problematic group functioning changed her mind. She did meet at least once f2f. However, she kept in touch with the group otherwise. She complained that people who did not attend f2f meetings were not notified on the Discussion Tool (the discussion tool was a Web based bulletin board provided by the Virtual School) as to decisions taken at meetings.

The idea of using the Discussion Tool as the primary means of communicating group decisions was discussed and agreed upon by some members. An assumption was made that the other members agreed to this decision and would abide by it. But they did not, and the Discussion Tool was only sporadically used as a major means of communicating group decisions. Decisions taken at f2f meetings with only a few members present were not reported on the Discussion Tool to update missing members.

All Talk appears to have almost unilaterally decided to have f2f meetings at his house near campus without consulting members about preferences for where to meet, how often to meet, etc. A number of times f2f meetings were scheduled at his house at the beginning of the semester, but people were not notified in time, or they could not come and no accommodations were made to their schedule, or they did not notify anyone they were not coming to the meeting. A lot of chaos! In one case Organizer female showed up at All Talk's house for a scheduled meeting and even he was not there! Part of the chaos stemmed from not following through on the agreement to use the Discussion Tool as the primary means of communication to the entire team.

The experience of this team with inadequate and missed communication illustrates that even if a team develops a norm to use the Discussion Tool as primary team communication, if they don't in fact use it for team communication, they might as well not have the norm. This appears to be the situation with this group.

The Sociogram

A sociogram was made of the team which reveals who liked to work with whom. Each person is asked "Who are the three team members you most liked to work with?" A diagram is made from the answers. Choices are indicated with an arrow. From the diagram you can identify if there are isolates (who are chosen by no one), stars (chosen by most members), and subgroups (with reciprocal choices).

The findings of the sociogram are an indication that the qualitative comments during the interviews are consistent. The sociogram replicates what people expressed about each other in the interviews. The sociogram appears below.

The team has three isolates and one subgroup of four. One isolate was not interviewed so his choices were not known. Pseudonyms were given team members based primarily on the role they played in

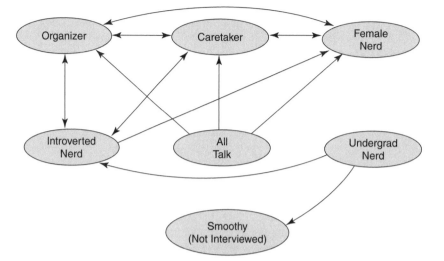

the group. All Talk, Undergrad Nerd, and Smoothy were the three isolates, all male. The four in the subgroup were Caretaker, Organizer, Female Nerd, and Introverted Nerd.

When the interviews are examined, the perceptions and information from the four members of the subgroup are more likely to be similar to each other than are the perceptions and information from the isolates. Most probably, the subgroup members discussed various issues among themselves, coming to some informal consensus on the way they perceived the situation. One or more isolates were likely to have quite different interpretations of events or their meaning (such as who were the leaders).

Conflict and the Too Nice Syndrome

According to Tuckman's five stages of group development, conflict occurs as the second stage, after the orientation phase, in ordinary groups. In my experience with undergraduate groups in Sociology 305, Sociology of Small Groups, they are very likely to skip the conflict stage as a second stage. If they go through that stage in any noticeable way or admit to going through it, it is usually right at the end, when they are performing with looming deadlines to complete their projects. Often then the conflict is ugly and contentious, with name calling and hurt feelings.

Team A appeared to experience some conflict almost from the beginning, but it was not dealt with up front and honestly or strongly confronted until the last week or two of class. Part of this seems to be due to what I will call the Too Nice Syndrome.

Too Nice Syndrome

The Too Nice Syndrome (hereafter TooNice) I have observed in my small groups classes year after year. People are so concerned about "not hurting someone's feelings." They are "so nice" and only indirect in negatively sanctioning people who do not do their part. In the process of being TooNice, they endure extensive anxiety, anguish, and overwork all in the name of not hurting someone's feelings. Instead of being firm while respectful by holding people to the agreed norms and performance/attendance standards as they go along, they avoid any direct discussion or confrontation of conflict. Sometimes it explodes at the end erupts into ugly and angry verbal conflict, which results in hurt feelings and negative consequences for the group as a whole.

In Team A the three isolates had not been doing their part when the situation became critical more than a week before the deadline. Part of the group grade depended on everyone completing their individual computer tasks assigned during the first five weeks. The leaders phoned Brad, the instructor, about what were their rights . . . could they kick people out of the group. Brad apparently suggested they e-mail the offending parties, warning them that if they failed to complete their tasks and failed to show up for the mandatory Friday meeting, they would be kicked out. The Organizer also posted this message on the Discussion Tool, Monday Oct. 25.

On Friday and again on Saturday the three isolates showed up at one time or another. The Undergrad Nerd appeared for an hour or less on Friday, making an appearance so that the TooNice subgroup thought that they could not terminate him even though they thought he was obeying "the letter but not the spirit of the law."

An apparently nasty and very upsetting verbal conflict occurred Friday and Saturday between most of the subgroup and All Talk during the f2f meetings and over the phone. The versions of what happened differ considerably from the subgroup and from All Talk. All Talk thought that the quality of the digital product was poor and could quite easily be remedied; he thought the group had plenty of time to fix the product and post it to Brad. Undergrad Nerd agreed with this assessment and was willing to help do the programming job to remedy the product, which would take only an hour, according to him. The subgroup who had worked so hard to finish the product and with so much frustration because the three isolates had dropped out at the crucial time were determined to hold firm to the deadline of Friday. Some interpreted All Talk's conversation to be discrediting the work of the subgroup members, which made them very angry. They did not want to change the group's deadline and held firm. The Organizer and other subgroup members were supportive of each other in being tough against All Talk, repeatedly saying no, they were not changing the product or slipping the deadline.

LAB 9.2

The subgroup members appeared to be left from these encounters with actual fear of All Talk because of his seeming irrationality and perseverance of trying to change the product at the last minute. All Talk had the job of making the Team Home Page, but the subgroup no longer trusted him to do his work by the last week and they made a dummy copy of the team home page. Female Nerd stayed up all night Monday night before the Tuesday deadline to complete and post it, missing work the next day due to exhaustion. The distrust of All Talk was massive after the ugly conflict. Some of the subgroup actually regard him as violent and threatening to their personal safety. All Talk did make a Team Home Page, but it was ignored by the subgroup.

Lack of Commitment

In the interviews the subgroup and All Talk alike attributed much of the team's poor functioning to a lack of commitment among the members. Each had different people in mind. The three isolates did not complete their commitments in a timely fashion, although all three did by the last week, after strong negative sanctioning. The team had not communicated adequately in the beginning or throughout with everyone to know what was each individual's situation. Caretaker apparently telephoned and e-mailed Smoothy and Undergraduate Nerd regularly to keep them informed of the team's progress but she seemed unaware that Undergraduate Nerd had been sick with Hepatitis A, which was described in his biography.

Would the situation have been less stressful for the subgroup if they had not expected consistent attendance (showing up) and effort from everyone? If disappearing members had communicated upfront that "I will be unavailable to do my share the next two weeks," or the equivalent, would that have eased the situation? Was it lack of commitment or inability to function consistently throughout combined with poor communication skills and not notifying the team that produced the accusation of "lack of commitment"?

Awareness of Group Dynamics

At least one member of Team A was very aware of communication problems, leadership problems, and the problem personality All Talk by halfway or so through the semester. She spoke privately to me in class and over e-mail, concerned about her group. In the interviews, other team members did not reveal any explicit awareness of problems in group dynamics on their team.

Team B

Team B was slow to get started, with several key members describing the team as "laid back." After three weeks few messages had been posted on the Discussion Tool, and these messages consisted of people reporting that they just got their computer set up or a seventh person in the team dropped the course. Apparently after a month or so of "laid back" inaction, one member proposed a f2f meeting at the university at which a handful showed up. The organizer had recent surgery and was not too mobile; he suggested meeting at his house which was near the university and convenient to everyone. At the second meeting, all six showed up for the first and last time. The team met probably 8–10 times f2f and used the Discussion Tool very little. All members appeared willing to contribute their share in the beginning. The Technical Leader was slow in the beginning to contribute and had to be firmly told that his contribution was necessary. The two that became the dropouts appeared to be willing to participate, but in the performing stage toward the end of the class neither contributed. On the last available evening before the deadline, with their group grade threatened due to the lack of contribution of two people, a mandatory meeting was called and the decision was made to drop both members from the group. One, referred to as Overwhelmed, agreed to voluntarily withdraw. The second one, Unavailable, no one knows her reaction to this. She claims that she was barely informed of the existence of the mandatory meeting and thinks she should have been involved in deciding whether or not and when and where to hold such a meeting.

Leadership

The organizer assumed the leadership position without much discussion or consensus building, but most team members were appreciative that he assumed this role. The person labeled Unavailable was not too happy that the leadership was assumed rather than discussed and mutually agreed upon, but she never said anything to anyone. Toward the end, when the intensive work on the project had to be done, the most technically proficient, who had been a slow starter, took charge technically and provided leadership in the technical aspects of the project and building the Team Home Page. Two leaders thus emerged during the course of the semester . . . the Organizer and the Technical Leader.

Norms and Communication

Were norms established of what communication tools to use to transmit group decisions, of the division of labor of tasks, of expectations about attending meetings and contributing, and so forth? Team members disagreed about whether or not norms had been agreed upon. Some said yes, we agreed upon what we were going to do, but few followed the norms. Others thought no clear expectations for communicating, division of labor, or participating had been established by the team. One leader sarcastically said, yes, we agreed on norms such as: It is okay to miss meetings? It is okay not to communicate with anyone in the group for weeks?

The Sociogram

A sociogram was made of the team that reveals who liked to work with whom using the same procedure described in the section on Team A. Team A also had a subgroup of four people, the two leaders and the Procrastinator (who eventually did his work), and Did What Told, who faithfully did what he was told but not any more than that. The two members who were dropped from the team are isolates who were not chosen by anyone (a couple of people said they really did not know Unavailable as she had been around so little). However, a couple of people in the subgroup indicated that they personally like Overwhelmed and found him agreeable at meetings but he just did not deliver at the end.

As with Team A, when the interviews were examined, the perceptions and information from the four subgroup members were more similar and consistent with each other than with the two isolates, which is an indirect way of indicating consensus.

Awareness of Group Dynamics

Two members of the group explicitly discussed what they thought were problematic with their group dynamics. Procrastinator attributed the group's problems to the equivalent of what I call the Too-Nice Syndrome. He was very aware of the social context of the course and how students do not easily assume an authority role over their fellow students in a class context. He thought that the consequences of poor performance are not that serious in a class group in comparison with groups on the job where your paycheck and livelihood may be dependent on achieving group goals.

Unavailable thought that the group would have functioned more effectively if team building and consensus had been tried instead of Organizer rather arbitrarily assuming the leadership position the part of Organizer or arbitrarily setting the date and time of the mandatory meeting without consulting anyone. She thought that it was a failure on her part to keep quiet about these group dynamic issues and not to bring them up to the team as a whole.

Conflict and the Too Nice Syndrome

Conflict appears to be defined by Team B members as expressed hostility, anger, or fighting. When asked about conflict in the group, several subgroup members claimed there was none. In the face of nonperforming members, they jumped in and did what was neces-

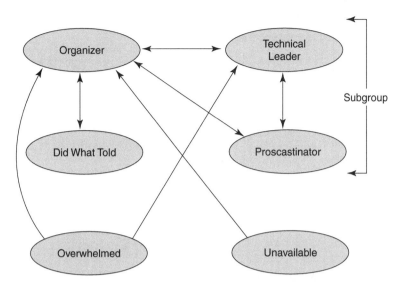

sary to get the job done without resentment or anger. Other subgroup members would describe these same people as angry and frustrated. Procrastinator talked at length about the subgroup members being too comfortable and polite and the difficulty in getting tough with nonperforming members.

Unlike Team A, which had several angry, contentious, and very upsetting verbal bouts with one member in front of the team during the last days of the project, Team B avoided active expressed conflict.

During the last class, each team made a presentation to the whole class and to the instructor. The Organizer gave the presentation for Team B. When asked if they agreed with the way he described their team, several subgroup members and one isolate thought that he had been too negative about the team, that in fact the subgroup and Overwhelmed had worked well together for most of the semester and were very compatible. Most team members have had quite a bit of experience working in groups both in school and at work.

Payoffs to Individuals

Although two of six members were dropped from the team at the last possible minute, the subgroup members seemed to have been a little frustrated but not very upset with the turn of events. The Technical Leader thinks that the product was not as high quality as it could have been if the noncontributors were known about earlier and the others had more time to perfect the product. The Procrastinator thought the product's quality suffered at the end. Unlike Team A, members were not left with some very negative feelings as a result of the conflict at the end of the course. Several Team B members did more than their share of work but regarded that as okay and similar to what they have to do in work groups.

The subgroup members and even Overwhelmed expressed receiving a lot and learning a lot from the course. When asked how they would rank themselves now in terms of computer experience, several explicitly talked about increased Internet literacy, but not more knowledge of programming. They ranked themselves higher than at the beginning of the course by 1.5 to 3 rankings (that is, from 3 to 4.5 or from 3 to 6 on a 0–9 scale).

Conclusion

Several items I want to highlight:

- The course requirements are perceived to be extremely demanding in terms of time and difficulty by a number of team members. At least one or more members dropped out because the time and difficulty of weekly tasks, project tasks, and their individual tasks were overwhelming to them.

- Multiple factors "caused" the poor functioning of these groups in my opinion. In Team A, the dysfunctions were not solely the result of one problem person, All Talk, although he was a challenge to anyone/everyone.

- People made assumptions that I think were unwarranted: If something is posted on the Discussion Tool that it was (a) read by everyone, and (b) accepted by them unless they specifically protested. If a general warning about failure to attend/perform your work is posted on the Discussion Tool, then the people for whom it is intended will (a) read it and (b) take it seriously as applying to them.

- The teams probably need more structure in the beginning in order to help them identify people who are not carrying their weight so that they can sanction them. A deadline, perhaps 2/3 of the way through the course, for when the 5 individual tasks have to be completed could be useful so that the team would know who was and who was not participating.

- Teams should be required to do a "contract" that is developed, agreed upon, and signed by all persons as binding about one third of the way through the course. A deadline should accompany the contract: perhaps give them about 2 weeks to negotiate it and achieve consensus. The "contract" should specify their norms and organizational plan, and division of labor expectations about attendance and participation, expectations for people who travel a lot or have periods of intensive work/family obligations, and negative sanctions for nonperformance, including conditions under which members are terminated.

- Conflict can be a serious problem in these groups; perhaps some specialized help in conflict recognition and resolution might be sought and taught to all the groups.

- A consultant who is not an authority could be made available to the group for help with problems of group dysfunction in order to catch some problems earlier. Team members hesitated to discuss their problems with the instructor Brad Cox in order not to "look bad" to the person evaluating them. I, as informal co-teacher with no legitimate authority, was a more neutral person with whom they could discuss their problematic group dynamics.

9.2.3 ANSWERS

a) Describe three techniques you would use to initiate team enthusiasm for a project and keep it flowing through until implementation.

Answer: There are several ways to keep enthusiasm flowing throughout a project. It's realistic that every project is going to have its highs and lows. Subcontractors can disappear, clients can become uncooperative, and the demands of the project can make it feel like it never will end.

However, by promoting team morale and encouraging the team members to be supportive of each other, these are storms that can be weathered. Everyone has heard about team building. Corporations send employees off to play laser tag, or go whitewater rafting. Believe it or not, they even take the direct approach and send employees to team-building seminars.

Project kick-off parties, celebrations when certain benchmarks are reached, building in bonuses for team members if the project comes in on budget and on schedule, and an atmosphere that daily empowers team members builds team enthusiasm. The daily atmosphere has always made the biggest difference to me, both as a team member and a team leader.

LAB 9.2 SELF-REVIEW QUESTIONS

1) A project manager should be aware of any and all conflicts within the team.
   a) _____ True
   b) _____ False

2) Conflicts within the team always slow down the process of building a Web site.
   a) _____ True
   b) _____ False

C H A P T E R   9

TEST YOUR THINKING

The projects in this section use the skills you've acquired in this chapter. The answers to these projects are available to instructors only through a Prentice Hall sales representative and are intended to be used in classroom discussion and assessment.

1) Describe the impact a dysfunctional project team might have on project. Comment on communication and production issues. How might you troubleshoot these issues if you were project manager?

2) Which process do you find most comfortable for you (writing, artistic, marketing, and technical) and which most difficult? How do you think this could impact on your role as a project manager?

C H A P T E R   1 0

PROJECT BIDS, CONTRACTS, AND SPECIFICATIONS

 "You never know anyone's true character until it comes time to for that individual to part with a dollar bill."

—Anonymous

CHAPTER OBJECTIVES

In this chapter, you will learn about

Sometimes, the game is over before it even starts.

I can think of several projects that my firm ended up completing at a loss because I bid the project badly. Luckily, I'm the owner. But, if I was working for someone else, under these conditions, I could see my tenure as their project manager coming to an abrupt close. Of course, I've also heard it said that it's better for the owner not to be bidding on projects, that the owner is too close to the outcome. However, since many web firms begin as one single developer pounding out code from a home PC, I can not see how this situation can be avoided.

My feel for bidding projects comes strictly from experience. Honestly, I used to abhor the process. It made me so anxious because I wanted to close the deal and get the work. Now, I can truly say that I find this process one of the most enjoyable tasks that I have. I love going into new companies and meeting new people. It's great to have the luxury to size up the project and say, "Yes, we'll pursue it," or "No, it doesn't look like a good fit," based on whether I feel that we can adequately meet the client expectations while remaining profitable.

Now, there are some projects that we decide to take on and strictly cover costs because of their portfolio value and non-profit status. This was the case with Battleship cove.com. We took this project on because frankly, I really wanted to do it. I had a family connection to it. My grandfather and uncle had worked on the Battleship Massachusetts, which is now berthed in Battleship Cove, along with the Joseph P. Kennedy II, the Lionfish, and the Russian ship, the Hiddensee. My father, as a young boy, had seen the Battleship launched from the Quincy Shipyard in 1937. Given that my parents were themselves raised in Quincy and in turn, raised my brothers and I there, I felt a strong connection with Quincy shipbuilding history. This was a client, albeit a very unusual one, which I already knew well and was intrigued to learn more.

After we contracted with Battleship Cove, I roamed all over the "Big Mamie" with my sons and nephew and realized that this was the fourth generation of Morses (Morse being my maiden name) to appreciate the old girl, and the third generation to do work for her. I was truly excited about bringing the Battleship Massachusetts and her sister ships into cyberspace with the functionality I knew our firm could provide. Not only was the project high profile, but the people down at Battleship Cove in Fall River, Massachusetts, were wonderful to deal with, making it easy to commit to their project.

Once in a while, a Web firm can do a Web site for portfolio value and strategically, for the long term, it turns out to be an excellent choice. Me, I was just really honored and thrilled to do Battleshipcove.com.

The Internet itself has often been described as a new frontier or, "The Wild West," strictly because of its unregulated nature. Developing on the Web brings its own set of issues. Picture your grandparents watching television for the first time. Something objectionable is shown, and they feel damaged. Who would they feel is responsible? Perhaps it was the network or the television station? Maybe it was the actors? Maybe it's the guy who sold them the television? They don't know. It's a new medium.

So, now, picture the scenario where someone reads something objectionable on a Web site. They feel that it is damaging to them personally and decide to pursue litigation. Who do they name in the lawsuit? If the litigating party does not know the Web terribly well, there's a good chance the party will name the company who owns the Web site, the Web firm that designed it, and any other entity attached to it—perhaps the hosting company.

Is my Web firm responsible for something that a client company chose to put on its Web site? No, I'm not. But, does the litigating party know this? In the time it takes for me to explain this to them in a courtroom setting, I can be out attorney's fees and days of work. I need to have a contract that will stand up in court, which will not only protect my client, but most importantly, will protect me. My contract must stipulate that I will be held harmless should my client come under prosecution and that my client agrees to defend me.

This is only one example of why contracts are crucial and why it's important for a Web firm to invest in one and **use** it. In this chapter, we'll explore many other applications of such a contract.

Project specifications are an agreement between the client and the Web firm as to how and when the project will be built. This sounds similar to a project proposal. However, a proposal is a short document detailing the scope of work. A project spec is also known as the "project bible." The specification is going to be fully executed by all participating contractors and subs and needs to be as detailed as possible, as this is the tool that keeps clients from asking for work that they are not entitled to under the contract. The specification is written directly after work orders and contracts are signed. The client has a chance to review the specification, and all parties must sign it. Very few Web firms have the resources to write project specifications unless they are already under contract. Therefore, this is just another check and balance along the line to keep the road clear for production.

In this chapter, you will read several project specifications and analyze their significance.

LAB 10.1

PROJECT BIDS

LAB OBJECTIVES

After this lab, you will be able to

- Qualify the Client
- Create a Client Questionnaire
- Determine a Client's Organization
- Write a Project Proposal
- Understand Various Types of Bids

After a Web firm has built up a decent reputation and a good portfolio of sites to show potential clients, the number of inquiries regarding work can grow exponentially. As the owner of a Web firm and its primary project manager, I spend just as much time sorting out which projects I feel my company should go forward with and responding to inquiries as I do participating in the building of the sites.

Doing my homework up front can save my company as much money as possible in the following ways:

- I weed out potential clients who are not prepared to follow through with contracting with us but are using us as "free consultants" for their projects. These types of situations can waste a great deal of the firm's time.

- I determine the project requirements as closely as possible. Down the line, poor communication can lead to lost billable working hours—ones that programmers, graphic designers, and editors need to be compensated for by the firm, but the client will not be responsible for and should not be.

- I feel out the client in their environment. This allows me to evaluate their organization level and how their team operates. If the client seems disorganized, they will ultimately require more time and hand holding by the Web firm. I don't necessarily have a problem with this, but when I'm determining how much I'm going to bid for doing a Web site, I will add a "fudge factor," which always ends up covering the extra hours it takes to manage this type of client.

- I evaluate whether this client is comfortable with making a commitment to the Web site by requiring a substantial amount of money up front. Unfortunately, the days when business can be done on a handshake are gone. I don't let the discussions go on for too long before I come up with a bid for the project and require money to continue discussing it. I've noticed that potential clients do not make a psychological commitment to these types of projects until a check is written—and yet, they will take hours of a firm's time discussing it and may go somewhere else in the end. My job is to ask people to "put their money where their mouth is" and decide when the appropriate time is to do so.

- Based on all of these factors—client organization, project requirements, and client commitment—I make the decision as to whether I will flat bid a project or charge an hourly rate. Flat bidding commits me to the project from start to finish. An hourly rate gives more flexibility and a better opportunity to exit from the project should things not be going well.

- When all is said and done, I look at the viability of the project. I have to feel that this venture could be a successful Web application before my firm gets involved. Regardless of the money involved, I feel that ethically I cannot participate in building a project that is ill fated from the start. The client will be unhappy and my firm's reputation could suffer. In the long run, taking on this sort of project is more costly to the Web firm.

Bidding projects is something that grows much easier with experience. One gets used to sizing up clients, requirements, and internal Web firm situations that make a certain project easier to handle than another. You should know how much your graphic designer, programmers, and support staff costs per hour. Also, don't forget the firm itself. Every firm must make so much an hour to support rent, telephone costs, equipment costs, advertising costs, and administrative costs. Software costs money, as well as the paper that goes in the copier. The project manager needs to be aware of what the firm itself costs per hour to operate. This is all determined by overhead.

My firm has operated out of my home for several years. Eventually, this may need to change, and growth is requiring us to look harder at that decision. However, I have always felt that this was an incredible plus because I could offer highly competitive bids and remain very profitable because of our lack of overhead. Most of the highly talented people working for me can work remotely at their homes, although they are all local and available for staff meetings and project meetings. It has been the best of all worlds to work with talented and motivated professionals who can produce excellent work out of their home offices. I do not need to ask clients to pay for my marble office foyer. In a sense, during the life of my company, clients have only had to pay for labor costs incurred on their own Web site, my own personal equipment, and one administrative person who comes in, pays bills, files, does errands, and facilitates customer service a few days a week.

However, there are many successful Web firm models that remain profitable and operate within an office environment to facilitate more projects at one time. A firm like this may also be able to bid highly competitively because of the sheer volume of work that is being done. An experienced staff reacting directly after a client's phone call is able to cut down on the unnecessary costs for the firm, which can be found particularly in design work when a graphic designer is going in one direction and needs to stop because the client wants something else. This is a commonplace scenario, and no matter how good a project manager is, there will always be a certain amount of effort duplication that can't be controlled.

So, keeping in mind the firm's hourly overhead, the project manager must consider that the firm's graphic designer costs $30/hour. The hardcore programmer, who does the databases and scripts that enable e-commerce functionality, costs $50/hour. The HTML intern may cost $10 an hour. However, someone who costs $30/hour, be it a senior HTML writer or the project manager, is going to need to review the intern's work before it goes out. When the project manager evaluates the project requirements and compares them to other similar projects, he or she roughly knows how many hours are involved and what that is going to cost the client.

Beyond covering costs and evaluating any pitfalls that will stem from a particular client-firm relationship, I always advise new Webmasters to charge enough to be respected. If the client feels they contracted you extremely cheaply, they may begin to wonder why you were so inexpensive in comparison to everyone else, and your time isn't valued as highly by the client as it should be. Strange, but true. On the other hand, the Web firm also needs to charge fairly. If there's a new Windows NT programmer on board and management knows there's a learning curve involved, the firm bears the burden of the learning curve, not the client. Some new fledgling Web firms charge outrageous amounts for shoddy work, just because the perception is that a Web site should cost a lot of money and they see that the client isn't necessarily Web savvy. Buyer beware! I usually end up taking care of these clients, once they realize what has happened. From my perspective, client-firm relationships are easy because all one has to do is treat the client fairly and they are appreciative of the services they have received.

LAB 10.1 EXERCISES

10.1.1 QUALIFY THE CLIENT

a) A small business has called your firm about a Web site. They have been in business for ten years and feel that it is time for a Web presence. They do not know exactly what they want to do on the Web, except that their competitors are there, and that fact is making them nervous.

What would you do to qualify this client? What do you want to know about the company? How long will you discuss this project before you ask for some sort of commitment? What kinds of requirements would you ask for from the client to address any production concerns?

_____

_____

_____

_____

_____

_____

_____

_____

LAB
10.1

b) A group of entrepreneurs, who would be involved in facilitating a new business venture part time at first, approach your Web firm regarding a viable Web site project. You know that they would be paying for this project out of their own pockets. What are your concerns? What questions would you ask them? What type of structure would you set up to circumvent any of the potential problems you have identified?

_____

_____

_____

_____

_____

_____

_____

_____

_____

_____

_____

_____

_____

_____

_____

_____

_____

_____

_____

_____

_____

c) A large, multi-billion-dollar corporation asks you to submit a bid regarding a large body of work. This could easily tie your firm up for six months. What are the pitfalls of such an arrangement? What are the benefits?

_____

_____

_____

_____

_____

_____

_____

_____

_____

_____

_____

_____

_____

_____

_____

_____

_____

_____

_____

_____

10.1.2   CREATE A CLIENT QUESTIONNAIRE

a) Compose a questionnaire for the client in Lab 10.1.1a.

_____

_____

_____

_____

_____

_____

_____

_____

_____

_____

_____

_____

_____

_____

_____

_____

_____

_____

_____

_____

_____

_____

_____

b) Compose a questionnaire for the client in Lab 10.1.1b.

_____

_____

_____

_____

_____

_____

_____

_____

_____

_____

_____

_____

_____

_____

_____

_____

_____

_____

_____

_____

_____

_____

c) Compose a questionnaire for the client in Lab 10.1.1c.

_____

_____

_____

_____

_____

_____

_____

_____

_____

_____

_____

_____

_____

_____

_____

_____

_____

_____

_____

_____

_____

_____

_____

10.1.3   DETERMINE A CLIENT'S ORGANIZATION

a) An owner-operated business contacts you regarding a Web site. Upon meeting with the owner, a few employees make several self-deprecating remarks about ill-fated attempts at other types of projects. The firm has only recently been funded and has been in operation six months. What are your concerns in this situation regarding the firm's ability to meet deadlines and keep the project moving?

_____

_____

_____

_____

_____

_____

_____

_____

_____

_____

_____

_____

_____

_____

_____

_____

_____

_____

_____

_____

_____

_____

_____

b) A large corporation contacts you regarding a Web site. There seem to be a great many people on the project team with differing opinions. The corporation is motivated to move forward on the project as the home office in London is now requiring all of the subsidiaries to be on-line. They are quite open about their budget and the fact that they are interviewing several Web firms. What are your concerns in working with this group?

_____

_____

_____

10.1.4 WRITE A PROJECT PROFILE

a) Say you've decided to move forward with the clients described in Lab 10.1.3b. You would like to document your discussions regarding site hierarchy, functionality, deadlines, site graphical and written presentation, and any other requirements that the potential client may have mentioned. What purpose could this document serve?

_____

_____

_____

_____

_____

_____

_____

_____

_____

_____

_____

_____

_____

_____

_____

_____

_____

_____

_____

_____

_____

_____

_____

_____

b) For the project mentioned in Lab 10.1.4a, write a one-page project profile. You may create your own set of requirements, reflecting a fictitious business plan.

_____

_____

_____

_____

_____

_____

_____

_____

_____

_____

_____

_____

_____

_____

_____

**LAB
10.1**

_____

_____

_____

_____

_____

_____

10.1.5 DETERMINE A FLAT VERSUS TIME/MATERIALS BID

a) Admittedly, 90% of new Web site builds are bid on a flat bid basis (the project manager determines the total project cost, the tasks covered by the bid, and the schedule of deliverables), and most clients are more comfortable with this. However, can you think of a scenario in which it is better for all parties to bid Web development based on an hourly rate?

_____

_____

_____

_____

_____

_____

_____

_____

_____

_____

b) If you are unsure of some of the project requirement modules, but the client wants to get moving right away, what are some options that could be available to you in bidding the project?

_____

_____

_____

_____

_____

_____

_____

_____

_____

_____

_____

_____

_____

_____

LAB 10.1 EXERCISE ANSWERS

This section gives you some suggested answers to the questions in Lab 10.1 with discussion related to those answers. Please post any alternative answers to these questions at the companion Web site for this book, located at http://www.phptr.com/phptrinteractive.

10.1.1 ANSWERS

a) A small business has called your firm about a Web site. They have been in business for ten years and feel that it is time for a Web presence. They do not know exactly what they want to do on the Web, except that their competitors are there, and that fact is making them nervous.

What would you do to qualify this client? What do you want to know about the company? How long will you discuss this project before you ask for some sort of commitment? What types of requirements would you ask for from the client to address any production concerns?

Answer: My first concern is that this in fact may be a potential client who has not made up their mind regarding whether they truly want a Web site. Their goals are not specific. It could be that the owner just saw his competitor's truck go by with a URL painted on it, and this is now the topic of the morning. I'm concerned that this client is calling to pick my brain for the finer points and then pursue having a high school kid build the site. They may not really understand the Web and how a professional presence may really enhance their company's marketing message.

I start off by citing a few case studies of industry-related firms, which have done well on the Web and assess the client response. If it's vague, I offer to fax a generic questionnaire to help the company to further define its Web project, suggest that they fill it out, and contact me should they wish to move forward or have any questions. If the client truly is interested, the conversation progresses from there to when I would be available to sit down and discuss it. Before I make the appointment, however, I do make sure that the client is aware of my rates and that if we come out, we're expecting that the company is ready to move and contract with us, not to build right away, but to reserve time in our programming schedule. This puts structure into the project right away. If all goes well, the potential client knows that we would be expecting to firm things up while at the meeting. We encourage potential clients to check out our portfolio ahead of meeting. Thus, when a price is quoted for particular project, our credibility is already set.

Before I meet with this potential client, I want to be sure that they have done their homework, know my firm, know our work, and know the rates so that when we sit down and meet, there should be no resistance to contracting. This cuts down on the "We'll get back to you" scenario. I find that if there isn't a good reason why a deposit check can't be cut immediately or within the week, chances are that I've wasted my time. Deposit checks are a good litmus test, because I often find that at these meetings, if there isn't serious intent, potential clients ask me to do research for them or do other kinds of freebies, under the guise that they are considering us for their Web site. I make it clear at this point that it sounds like what they really need is consulting, and my firm does that as well, and inform them of our rate for that type of work.

The point is, the only thing that I have to sell is time. My firm does very good work with its time. But I can't allow my own time as a project manager to be wasted prospecting with companies that either aren't serious or want to play games, getting free consultative work under the guise of contracting us for a Web site. Most of the time, people don't even realize that they're doing this. It's not a conscious agenda item with them to bring us in, pick our brains, and send us packing. It's just that they're not committed to the idea or quite organized yet, and the savvy project manager knows how much time to spend with this situation.

Even if we decide to move forward, I always require a signed work order, deposit check, and a commitment to get any and all deliverables to me by a certain date. Also, the bid that is given reflects the extra amount of consulting, which might be necessary to facilitate the project.

b)   A group of entrepreneurs, who would be involved in facilitating a new business venture part time at first, approach your Web firm regarding a viable Web site project. You know that they would be paying for this project out of their own pockets. What are your concerns? What questions would you ask them? What type of structure would you set up to circumvent any of the potential problems you have identified?

Answer: To be perfectly blunt, in this scenario, I would worry about getting paid. So my questions would be along the lines of where they were in their business plan. Had some significant money and time already been invested in setting up this new venture? Would it be difficult for them to walk away from it now?

You can get the answers to these questions easily just by listening. Usually, entrepreneurs are more than happy to tell you all about their plans and what they've done so far. Often, I'm asked to keep these details confidential, and I am more than happy to. I get caught up in their excitement too! However, should a partner drop out or someone lose interest or the Web component not be quite as hot as they initially thought, the Web firm could be inadvertently stuck holding the bag.

However, if I'm confident that serious commitment has been shown already, a corporation formed, and other expenses undertaken, and that it involves a relatively short Web build—two to three weeks—I often find that it's a very joyful experience to work with this type of client. Most Web developers are entrepreneurs too, and there's enthusiasm to spare!

c)   A large multi-billion-dollar corporation asks you to submit a bid regarding a large body of work. This could easily tie your firm up for six months. What are the pitfalls of such an arrangement? What are the benefits?

Answer: This is a prospect that can set many a project manager's mouth watering. If all goes well, for six months, the firm is busy. More time can be spent working on the project as opposed to prospecting new projects. Therefore, nonbillable hours, during this time, can be kept to a minimum.

However, I've also known these situations to be rather nightmarish. Large companies often work on a P.O. system (purchase order) and may not be terribly fast about paying. I know of a scenario where a firm contracted for a year and was never paid during that time. Finally, they had to take a percentage of what was originally owed.

Pitfalls can include the following:

- *The expectation that payment will be at the corporation's convenience, not as requested on the developer's terms.*
- *The Web firm being stuck in an unprofitable project because of client management issues.*
- *The working relationship between the client and the Web firm can deteriorate. Six months is a long time to be committed to an untenable situation.*

Benefits can include

- *Less nonbillable hours for the Web firm.*
- *A successful project for a large corporation can put a Web firm into a whole different category when bidding for other prestigious projects. A good track record puts the Web firm a step ahead.*
- *If this is a good client relationship, it's a super experience for everyone involved. The client will be coming back for updates and enhancements, and the site could work into a good source of steady work.*

10.1.2 ANSWERS

a) Compose a questionnaire for the client in Lab 10.1.1a.

Answer: I would be interested in having answers to all of the questions mentioned in Lab 10.1.2 for all three clients. However, I will list the questions that I would primarily be interested in for each client.

With this client, I'm assessing their seriousness in taking on the Web project and following through, so I am particularly interested in answers to the following questions:

- *What is your mission statement for the site?*
- *Who would you want to reach with your Web site?*
- *Describe your industry. Do you already see a niche for it on the Web?*
- *What are your company's present marketing efforts?*
- *By which measurements and over what time period would you expect your Web site to be successful?*
- *What is your Web site budget?*
- *What kind of functionality should be included on the site?*
- *Are there resources within the company at this time to focus on the Web site and supply approvals?*
- *What is your experience with the Web?*

b) Compose a questionnaire for the client in Lab 10.1.1b.

Answer: With this client, I'm assessing the viability of their business venture and their commitment to it, so I am particularly interested in answers to the following questions:

- *What is your mission statement for the site?*
- *What other marketing efforts do you plan to undertake?*
- *When do you need to break even?*
- *What is your Web site budget?*
- *What other kinds of plans are there for the business and how far along are you in adopting them?*

c) Compose a questionnaire for the client in Lab 10.1.1c.

Answer: With this client, I'm assessing the organization level of the team that I would be working with and if we can work well together over the next six months.

- *What is the mission statement for the site?*
- *Who on the project team will have the last say and give approvals?*
- *What are the long-term plans for the site?*

- *What is our exit plan should things not work out?*
- *How often will the firm be paid?*
- *Can we set up a schedule of project meetings and adhere to them?*
- *How will the approval process work?*

10.1.3 ANSWERS

a) An owner-operated business contacts you regarding a Web site. Upon meeting with the owner, a few employees make several self-deprecating remarks about ill-fated attempts at other types of projects. The firm has only recently been funded and has been in operation six months. What are your concerns in this situation regarding the firm's ability to meet deadlines and keep the project moving?

Answer: Obviously, this firm is in a state of organizational flux. It will be difficult to get deliverables from them and obtain approvals for work completed. It's not their fault. It's just the nature of a start-up company. Everyone is settling in, and the foundation is being built. There may not yet be a clear line of authority or hierarchy within the company. They are just pushing product out the door and trying to pay their creditors.

I would have no problem getting involved on something short term. The client should pick one person who has final approval on the Web site. That person has to stick to the deadlines or go to the bottom of the production schedule. Also, the person with final approval would need to be available by phone during the Web site build to make decisions.

b) A large corporation contacts you regarding a Web site. There seem to be a great many people on the project team with differing opinions. The corporation is quite motivated to move forward on the project as the home office in London is now requiring all of the subsidiaries to be on-line. They are quite open about their budget and the fact that they are interviewing several Web firms. What are your concerns in working with this group?

Answer: This is a recipe for failure, unless it's managed correctly. Although I believe very strongly in a team approach, when it's on the client side rarely have I seen it benefit a project. One person has to have the final decision.

I find that client teams tend to slow down a project considerably. It's like having too many cooks in the kitchen. Decision making can have a tendency to bog down with too many different opinions and ownership issues. A team approach, where one person makes the final decision and the team commits to making project deadlines, can work well. Otherwise, everyone's hands are tied, and the project moves very slowly.

I would bid high for this reason, knowing that this will be a problem. Also, if the client is interviewing several firms, I would like to know who they are. I also would like to know if my firm is being invited to bid because the company is interested in my Web firm's work and has seen it, or if we're bidding because they need to meet an internal quota of project bids before the money can be approved. This would have a great deal to do with the effort I would put into a proposal and/or presentation.

10.1.4 ANSWERS

a) Say you've decided to move forward with the clients described in Lab 10.1.3b. You would like to document your discussions regarding site hierarchy, functionality, deadlines, site graphical and written presentation, and any other requirements that the potential client may have mentioned. What purpose could this document serve?

Answer: If the project is complex, it's always a very good idea to include a one-page outline to be signed by the client along with a work order at the time of contracting. This way, the client knows exactly what services are being covered under the work order and has the opportunity to dispute any inaccuracies. It's much easier to rebid a project than it is to get into a design phase and find that the client is expecting much more than was covered by the initial agreement. The firm would then be put in the position of renegotiating everything after money has changed hands, and this can strain the relationship between the firm and the client as well as slow down the project immeasurably.

In a sense, the project manager is akin to a lawyer hammering out an agreement between two parties. A successful agreement provides a win-win situation for both the Web firm and the client. It facilitates the building of a project, which satisfies the client and pays the Web firm. If the client is happy, there will be repeat and referral business. As a result, there is a great deal riding on the clarity with which the bid is presented to the client.

b) For the project mentioned in Lab 10.1.4a, write a one-page project profile. You may create your own set of requirements, reflecting a fictitious business plan.

Answer: This is a project profile for ABC partners, located at 222 Acme Avenue, Anytown, USA 00000.

ABC partners has contacted DEF Web firm to build a Web presence for their company that encompasses the following:

- *Custom graphics—high-end graphics for navigation and overall look and feel of the site. The client agrees to supply DEF with any logos and inform us of any particular requirements regarding color. Should ABC Partners already have a rough design in mind, they agree to work with DEF to storyboard this concept before the graphic designer goes to work.*

The client will be presented with three look and feel concepts completed by the graphic artist. ABC Partners will then work with DEF's graphic artist from these composites to refine the graphical presentation of the Web site.

- *Eight static HTML pages that contain information regarding the company, its services, and contact information. ABC Partners agrees to compile this information internally and send to DEF before the start date.*

- *One searchable database, which contains information the client plans to present to users. Client agrees to help DEF to finalize all of the fields required in the database before programming begins.*

- *Upload to server and registration with seven major search engines.*

Total cost: $4000–$4500

Estimated Delivery Date: 2–4 weeks from start date

10.1.5 ANSWERS

a) Admittedly, 90% of new Web site builds are bid on a flat bid basis (the project manager determines the total project cost, the tasks covered by the bid, and the schedule of deliverables), and most clients are more comfortable with this. However, can you think of a scenario in which it is better for all parties to bid Web development based on an hourly rate?

Answer: In the scenario described in Lab 10.1.3b, I would be tempted to bid based on an hourly rate. It's obvious that there isn't a great deal of organization yet toward developing the site. The large corporation has deep pockets, so there most likely isn't the possibility of stressing the client financially, and one is only asking to be paid for the hours spent on the corporation's project. Chances are that, given this situation (too many chiefs and not enough indians), decisions are going to be made and remade, causing the Web firm to redo work already completed.

If there is a pleasant surprise, and the corporation's team does work effectively, then it will reap the benefits of less outlay for the site. However, should this not be the case, the financial burden will not fall upon the Web firm.

I often work at a flat hourly fee on any maintenance projects for existing clients. By then, a trusting relationship is already established. There is a track record of payment and delivery already in place. The client trusts that I will not overcharge, and I trust that within thirty days the client will pay my bill.

b) If you are unsure of some of the project requirement modules, but the client wants to get moving right away, what are some options that could be available to you in bidding the project?

- Bid a combination of a flat fee for those programming modules that are defined and an hourly fee for those modules that are still being analyzed.

- Bid a range. If the impact of the unclear requirement is relatively small, the Web firm can bid between A and B dollars for the site. I often will do this anyway. That way, if the client is cost conscious, they will also be conscious of defining things as well as possible up front to get the lower price.

- Bid the project in phases. If the programming isn't firmly defined, but the client can get ready to move on the graphics, then bid the graphics. Vice versa, bid the programming first, if there is still uncertainty regarding the graphical presentation of the site. Usually by the time one of these phases is complete, the client has moved to the definition phase of the previously underdefined task.

LAB 10.1 SELF-REVIEW QUESTIONS

In order to test your progress, you should be able to answer the following questions:

1) (True/False) Which project(s) seems fairly safe to flat bid?
   a) _____ Potential client presents highly defined specifications, although the business is a start-up and seems a bit disorganized
   b) _____ Established business is a little vague on its Web site requirements but is having consulting work done ahead of time to firm up the details.
   c) _____ Large corporate entity has put together a project team with an unspecific chain of command to work with an outside Web firm to build a Web site.

2) (True/False) When bidding a project, a project manager is like a
   a) _____ Real estate broker
   b) _____ Internet consultant
   c) _____ Lawyer

L A B   1 0 . 2

CONTRACTS

LAB OBJECTIVES

After this lab, you will be able to

- Identify Possible Project Pitfalls
- Create a Work Order
- Evaluate a Sample Contract

In a capitalist society, most of us are firmly attached to our possessions. The prospect of losing one's home and/or savings in a dispute with a client can be extremely daunting. Most likely, if you work for someone else, you are insulated against this type of litigation, which might threaten your personal assets. However, as a self-employed contractor, you have to take steps to protect yourself, one of which is the regular use of a programming services agreement or contract.

This lab is not meant to replace a well-timed visit to a lawyer who specializes in contract law and understands the Internet. Rather, it explains how the contract fits into the project management process. If used correctly, a contract is yet another tool that protects not only the Web firm but the client as well. It further defines the relationship and what is expected, given several project outcomes. All avenues should be explored, even the one that no one likes thinking about while enthusiastic about a project kick-off: the possibility that one or both parties wants to terminate the agreement.

Contracts should be reviewed regularly and updated to reflect changes in the industry. In the coming years, the U.S. government will be looking much harder at Internet law. Newt Gingrich, Former Speaker of the House, speaking at a recent Internet Commerce Expo in Boston, said that the challenge with effectively regulating the Web is that Web entrepreneurs are extremely busy. The Web is literally exploding around them, and keeping up with industry and technical advances is more than a full-time job. These entrepreneurs may not yet understand how crucial it is to educate government officials with regard to effective implementation of Internet law. It's the common debacle where those that are talking aren't necessarily in the know, and those that are in the know are too busy to talk. However, the way this law is eventually handed down will affect everyone in the industry.

Intellectual property and copyright are other considerations for the client. Often, the client will ask the Web firm questions with regard to these issues. What kind of liability might the Web firm assume if it inadvertently consults on these issues? The Web firm is not a law firm. It's always better to refer the client to a lawyer when questions such as these arise or punctuate a response with, "We're not lawyers, so you'll need to consult one. This is only our understanding of the issue."

Contracts help to define what the Web firm is and is not responsible for. They identify liability in case the client is sued and the Web firm is also named in that lawsuit. Also, contracts define terms of use. The source code written by the Web firm is reserved for the client's use; if it is resold to another entity without the Web firm's permission, the Web firm could be due restitution. Therefore, the terms of use or licensing of the source code must be clarified within the contract.

LAB 10.2 EXERCISES

10.2.1 IDENTIFY PROJECT PITFALLS

a) A company that specializes in adult entertainment wishes to contract with your firm to build a Web site that would incorporate X-rated material. Regardless of how you feel about free speech on the Internet, if the owner of your firm is considering the project, what questions should you as project manager pose to legal counsel regarding your firm's liability?

_____

_____

_____

_____

**LAB
10.2**

b) Several entrepreneurs plan a Web site that would offer advising as well as brokerage services. What questions would you ask legal counsel?

**LAB
10.2**

_____

_____

_____

_____

_____

_____

c) Your firm considers bidding on a site in which visitors are allowed to gamble. What kinds of questions might you have regarding liability?

_____

_____

_____

_____

_____

_____

_____

_____

_____

_____

_____

_____

_____

_____

10.2.2   CREATE A WORK ORDER

a) A work order, similar to those used in the construction industry, is a preliminary agreement between the client and the Web firm that states what services have been ordered by the client, how much they will cost, when they will be performed, and any disclaimers or guarantees. It is a piece of paper that essentially says, "You are ordering these services, and you are going to be billed this much." Draft a sample work order. What items would you have in it?

_____

_____

_____

_____

_____

_____

_____

_____

_____

_____

b) How advantageous is a work order when the prospective client is discussing the reservation of development time with your firm?

_____

_____

_____

_____

_____

_____

_____

_____

_____

_____

10.2.3 EVALUATE A SAMPLE CONTRACT

The following is a standard programming services contract between a Web firm and its client.

This PROGRAMMING SERVICES AGREEMENT ("Agreement") is made and entered into this_____day of_____, _____, by and between_____, with an address of ("Client"), and Acme Web Development, with an address of_____ ("Developer").

1. Definitions. For purposes of this Agreement, the following capitalized terms shall have the meaning ascribed to them below:

Code shall mean computer programming code. Unless otherwise specified, Code shall include such computer programming code in both object code and source code forms.

Confidential information shall mean Work Product and any other information that Client indicates to be confidential and Developer acquires (as a result of disclosure by Client, access to Client facilities, analysis of Client's products or enhancements, or otherwise) in connection with the Services. However, Confidential Information does not include information that rightly becomes public or that Developer independently develops or acquires without reliance on other Confidential Information produced or acquired by Developer.

Services shall mean programming and development services relating to existing and planned products and enhancements of Client or Client's customers, whether heretofore or hereafter provided by Developer.

Work Product shall mean all Code and other media, materials, or other objects produced as a result of the Services or delivered by Developer in the course of providing the Services.

2. Scope of Services; Compensation. All Services provided by Developer shall be subject to this Agreement unless otherwise agreed upon by both parties in writing. All Services shall be performed in a workmanlike and professional manner. Services are to be described more specifically in Work Orders, which shall be set forth in writing, shall be signed by both parties and, once signed, shall be made a part of this Agreement.

The parties are and shall be independent contractors to one another, and nothing shall be deemed to cause this Agreement to create an agency, partnership, or joint venture between the parties. Nothing in this Agreement shall be interpreted as creating or establishing an employer/employee relationship between Client and either Developer or any employee or agent of Developer.

The terms for compensation of Developer shall be agreed upon by both parties in writing in such Work Orders. Client shall be responsible for reimbursement of expenses incurred by Developer as stated in such Work Orders. On any bill (interim or final) remaining unpaid for a period of ninety (90) days, a service charge of one and one-half (1.5%) percent per month will be charged from the date the bill is rendered. This represents an annual rate of eighteen (18%) percent. In the event Client fails to pay any bill or expense reimbursement beyond ninety (90) days, then Developer may declare the entire unpaid amount immediately due and payable ("default"). In the event of default Client agrees to pay all reasonable costs of collection, including reasonable attorneys' fees and Court costs, to the extent allowed by law.

3. Confidential Information. Developer shall receive and hold all Confidential Information in trust and confidence for Client. Developer may not use any Confidential Information except as authorized by Client and for the benefit of Client. Developer may disclose Confidential Information only to those employees who have a "need to know" in order to help Developer perform Services and who are legally bound to maintain confidentiality of the Confidential Information. Developer shall be responsible for safekeeping of all materials and media containing Confidential Information and shall account for such materials and media at Client's request. Upon completion or termination of all or any relevant Services, Developer shall deliver to Client or destroy (as requested by Client) all materials and media containing Confidential Information (including all copies and extracts thereof). Developer shall certify its compliance with such obligation at Client's request. These confidentiality obligations shall remain in effect until five (5) years after any relevant Services are completed or terminated and Developer has delivered to Client or destroyed materials and media containing Confidential Information associated with Services.

4. Rights in Work Product. All Work Product shall be deemed to be works made for hire and shall belong exclusively to Client and its designees. Developer grants to Client an irrevocable, nonexclusive, worldwide, royalty-free right and license to use, execute, reproduce, display, perform, and distribute (internally and externally) copies of, and prepare derivative works based upon, such Work Product.

5. General Provisions. Developer shall not be liable to Client for any failure or delay caused by events beyond Developer's control, including, without limitation, Client's failure to furnish necessary informa-

tion, sabotage, failure or delays in transportation or communication, failures or substitutions of equipment, accidents, materials, or equipment or technical failures.

Client shall defend, indemnify, and hold harmless Developer from and against all claims, liability, losses, damages, and expenses (including attorneys' fees and court costs) arising from or in connection with the use or application of Developer's work by Client or any direct or indirect purchaser or licensee of Client.

It is assumed, and Developer strongly recommends, that any and all materials, media, or Confidential Information provided by Client to Developer in order to perform Services will be in duplicate form and not the originals. Developer shall not be liable to Client for any loss or damage to any and all such materials, media, or Confidential Information, whether in duplicate or original, that are provided to Developer from Client in order to perform Services.

This Agreement supersedes all other communications, understandings, and agreements relating to the subject matter hereof, and may be amended only in writing. This Agreement shall be governed by the laws of the Commonwealth of Massachusetts as they pertain to contracts executed under seat delivered and performed in that State.

IN WITNESS WHEREOF, this Agreement has been executed under seal and delivered by authorized representatives of both parties as of the date first indicated above.

Acme Web Design

...............................(client)

By:........................... By:........................

Title: .... Title:....................

a) In the preceding contract, which points do you feel are identified well as they apply to the Web and Web site development?

_____

_____

_____

_____

b) What areas do you feel are vague, given your knowledge of the Web industry?

_____

_____

_____

_____

_____

_____

_____

_____

_____

_____

_____

_____

_____

_____

_____

_____

_____

_____

_____

_____

_____

_____

_____

_____

_____

_____

LAB 10.2 EXERCISE ANSWERS

This section gives you some suggested answers to the questions in Lab 10.2 with discussion related to those answers. Please post any alternative answers to these questions at the companion Web site for this book, located at http://www.phptr.com/phptrinteractive.

10.2.1 ANSWERS

a) A company that specializes in adult entertainment wishes to contract with your firm to build a Web site that would incorporate X-rated materials. Regardless of how you feel about free speech on the Internet, if the owner of your firm is considering the project, what questions should you as project manager pose to legal counsel regarding your firm's liability?

Answer: First, after begging my superior to put me on a different project and then tendering my resume elsewhere, I would be highly concerned about liability with this site. It would be necessary to research the following with Internet lawyers:

- *What is the current legislation regarding the distribution of adult media? How does this legislation apply to the Web?*
- *Which disclaimers need to be present on the Web site?*
- *If it is permitted to build and maintain a Web site containing adult materials, is it possible to develop an ironclad contract that fully protects the Web firm against lawsuits?*

b) Several entrepreneurs plan a Web site that would offer financial advising as well as brokerage services. What questions would you ask legal counsel?

Answer: There are many Web sites owned and maintained by financial planners, accountants, and stock brokers. Some of these offer stock picks, others just outline services offered. Sites like e-trade allow e-commerce-enabled stock trading, allowing investors to day trade. At this writing, day trading is just beginning to impact the stock market. It will be fascinating to see what happens in the financial industry, given the easy access investors now have to managing their own investment assets.

However, as more people take advantage of Web financial services, more misunderstandings and opportunities for transaction failure can occur. Several questions, including the following, come to mind:

- *If there is a technical failure that results in a poor trade for a site user, what is the liability for the Web firm should the user seek restitution?*

- *Is there any way to insulate the Web firm against losses caused by technical glitches?*

- *If there is a technical problem that resides with the hosting company, as opposed to the programming performed by the Web firm, how will fault be determined? Can an independent consulting firm assess fault? (Often, it cannot be apparent to all, except to those directly involved with the technology, where the failure occurred.)*

- *Is it standard procedure to ask the client to assume all responsibility for defense expenses, even if there is a technical problem?*

- *How can the Web firm be insulated against faulty investment advice given on the site?*

c)   Your firm considers bidding on a site in which visitors are allowed to gamble. What kinds of questions might you have regarding liability?

Answer:

- *What is the current legislation regarding gambling on the Internet?*

- *If the client questions the results of a bet, how can the possibility of a technical glitch be evaluated independently? Who takes on the cost?*

- *How can the Web firm be completely insulated from user and client claims?*

10.2.2   ANSWERS

a)   A work order, similar to those used in the construction industry, is a preliminary agreement between the client and the Web firm that states what services have been ordered by the client, how much they will cost, when they will be performed, and any disclaimers or guarantees. It is a piece of paper that essentially says, "You are ordering these services, and you are going to be billed this much." Draft a sample work order. What items would you have in it?

Answer: The following is the work order I have used in the past. This document is developed internally, stating pricing and guarantees. It is used in combination with a programming services contract.

Work Order Example

Starter Package	$300	____
Business Package	$600	____
Deluxe Package	$1000	____
Additional Page	$100	____
CGI/JavaScript programming	$100/hour	____
Guest Book	$200	____
Auto Responder	$200	____
Bulletin Board	$200	____
Chat Room	$200	____
Submit to 7 Major Search Engines Free with Web Site Build		
Internet Consulting	$100/hour	____
Web Site Maintenance	$40/hour	____
Writing/Editing Services	$40/hour	____
Graphic Design	$40/hour	____
	ESTIMATE	____
	DELIVERY DATE	____

• Acme Web Design guarantees its work. If a site fails due to a programming issue, we will guarantee a prompt "fix" within one to three business days.

• Acme Web Design cannot guarantee server performance, as this is a separate business relationship.

• Acme Web Design cannot guarantee how a site will be listed or ranked on the search engines, as this is a separate business relationship.

• Acme Web Design cannot guarantee dollar volume or number of hits.

• Client agrees to supply Acme Web Design with any written or digitized materials by_____.

If Acme Web Design does not receive these materials by the above date, the client understands that the completion of the Web site may need to be rescheduled according to the current production schedule and an updated work order signed.

• Standard billing procedure is remittance of half the project estimate when the work is ordered and the other half due before Web site upload. Acme Web Design reserves the right to interim bill.

- A separate work order will be completed for all upgrades and appropriate deposit remitted, should more features be added during the Web site build that are not covered by this work order. Additional work may require the Web site completion date to be revised. Acme Web Design has been contracted to build_____'s site between_____and_____. The client will make a representative available during this time to approve work completed.

_____   _____

Acme Web Design Representative   Client Representative

b)   How advantageous is this document when a prospective client is discussing the reservation of development time with your firm?

Answer: I see a work order as being a transition document. With a client, it states that the relationship is now transitioning from a selling phase to a payment for services completed phase, which may include consulting. We use the work order to subtly ask the client for a deposit on the time we're scheduling for that company's development work.

Truly, the work order serves as a psychological dividing line between, "Yes, we can do your project. These are the services my company offers," and "Yes, we are doing your project. Let's discuss the business arrangements." Often, if I feel an initial meeting is taking too long, and I want to see if the prospective client is really serious, I take out a work order. I begin to estimate the work that has been discussed. This causes the prospective client to focus on what is needed, as opposed to brainstorming ideas. From there, it moves the conversation into, "We have development time open on this date; we could schedule you then." Finally, the work order drives the exchange to, "Roughly, I think it's going to cost x amount of dollars. In order to reserve the time, we'll need a deposit of such and such." This easily brings the meeting to some sort of completion. I've given my time. I've listened, but I'm not going to hamstring my company by spending the entire morning brainstorming over a Web site that we are not yet contracted to consult on and/or to build. I have also taken control of the situation, which may, in effect, add to the prospective client's faith in me and break down resistance to moving forward. It's called "closing the deal." I find the work order is a great tool to accomplish this.

A good work order makes the client feel more confident as well. In it, hopefully, the Web firm is formally stating its commitment to the client in time, estimated dollars, and guarantees. It should be clear and explain what is within and not within the power of the Web firm to effect. Things like search engine ranking and hosting, unless the firm is being paid specifically for search engine positioning and for hosting, are sepa-

rate business relationships. The Web firm can support its client in these areas, but cannot take responsibility for something outside its direct control.

The work order provides structure, specifying a date at which all collateral materials should be received by the Web firm in order for work to move forward, and it gives the firm a scheduling option, if materials do not come in on time. Plus, it should specify payment terms. When will payment be expected? Will it be billed? Will it be directly upon receipt of services? Will payment be required over several installments? Again, clarity up front can diffuse many disagreements.

10.2.3 ANSWERS

a) Above you will find a standard programming services contract. Which points do you feel are identified well as they apply to the Web and Web site development?

Answer: The following points seem to be identified well as they apply to the Web site development process:

- *The definition of terms up front is an excellent feature of this contract (ie, Code, Confidential Information, Services, and Work Product).*

- *This contract allows for the work order to become part of the agreement, thus allowing for quick customization for each project.*

- *The contract specifies that all parties are independent of each other, and not connected to one another in anything other than in a contracting arrangement.*

- *The terms of compensation legally allows the developer to begin assessing late fees for any overdue payment. Should the payment be in default, the client must pay additionally the costs of collecting the payment and/or court fees.*

- *A confidentiality agreement allows for protection of the client's privacy. This is an assurance that information pertinent to the project will not be disclosed to outside parties without the client's prior permission.*

- *This contract specifies clearly that the client has complete right to all work performed by the firm and may redistribute this work as it sees fit.*

- *The development firm is not liable to the client for any circumstances, resulting in Web site failure, beyond its control.*

- *A very important clause is the requirement on the part of the client to defend and hold the contractor harmless in any lawsuits leveled by outside entities as a result of the Web site.*

- *Another clause indemnifies the contractor against loss of materials and suggests that the client make duplicates of any materials provided to the development firm.*

b) What areas do you feel are vague, given your knowledge of the Web industry?

Answer:

- *The agreement does not specify how the parties will part ways should the business arrangement become unsatisfactory. Questions like who owns which materials at each point in the process are unanswered.*
- *The contract does not specify how it will be determined that certain events are beyond that of the developer's control. Would an independent consulting firm be hired? Who takes on the cost?*

LAB 10.2 SELF-REVIEW QUESTIONS

In order to test your progress, you should be able to answer the following questions.

1) Which project seems to hold the most liability for the Web firm?
   a) _____ An on-line banking Web site
   b) _____ A Web site which offers financial/stock advice
   c) _____ An on-line book store

2) Which of the following items belongs in the initial work order?
   a) _____ Colors to be incorporated into the site
   b) _____ Schedule of payment
   c) _____ Identification of Web site hosting company

LAB 10.3

PROJECT
SPECIFICATIONS

LAB OBJECTIVES:

After this lab, you will be able to:

- Establish Web Site Hierarchy
- Write a Project Description
- Identify a Project Budget and Schedule

After the Web firm has been contracted to build a Web site, the best way to identify very specific content and functionality, and to allocate resources for the completion of these tasks is to write a project specification. This specification, in effect, becomes the "Project Bible," as it is one document used to solidify agreement between the client and the contractor on Web site specifics.

The following documents should be included in the project specification:

- Web Site Hierarchy (Other names include: Flow Chart and Information Architecture
- Detailed Project Description
- Budget and Schedule

It's much easier for the Web firm to catch differing project goals between client and contractor, while remaining profitable, by identifying them at the project specification stage than when work is completed and doesn't meet with the client's expectations.

You will also be introduced to a Web site that will be used throughout this book as a case study, DisabilityNews.net. Disability News is a clearinghouse for information related to mental health and disabilities. It is targeted toward mental health professionals, students and educators, families of disabled individuals, and people with disabilities.

The following is a project specification, written and compiled by Charlie Bleau, the Web Development Director for Disability News. In retrospect, Charlie emphasizes that not only was the project specification used to identify the project details, it was also used as a business plan for the entire Web site venture. Disability News was created under the direction of Greater Lynn Mental Heath and Rehabilitation, a leading non-profit organization supporting people with disabilities and their families in the Boston area. However, the best way to learn about this project and its objectives is to read the project specification:

DisabilityNews.net

SERVICE OVERVIEW:

Disabilitynews.net is a comprehensive on-line service for healthcare professionals, families, students, people with disabilities and advocates with a focus on the mental retardation and mental health fields. Disabilitynews.net is a division of Greater Lynn Mental Health & Retardation Association, Inc. (GLMHRA). The service will leverage GLMHRA's expertise with the dually diagnosed population, specifically the Robert D. Sovner Behavioral Health Resource Center in Danvers MA.

The key components of Disabilitynews.net web site will be:

> On-line Publishing Service
>
> On-line Communications Service (on-line chat)
>
> Training Service

The service will be Electronic Commerce enabled for on-line purchases and membership fees—the primary means for revenue. Additionally, advertising and sponsorships will be a secondary means for revenue.

Disabilitynews.net will be built in 2 Phases to ensure proper technical implementation. The following is a project description for the key components in each phase.

Phase 1: To be completed by July 15, 1999

GOALS:

Launch On-line Publishing Service

Launch Training Service

Market Survey to determine feasibility of Phase 2

On-line Publishing Service:

Users will have the opportunity to purchase journal articles and books on Disabilitynews.net, very similar to the services provided by Amazon.com and Harvard Business Review (hbr.org). Currently, Disabilitynews.net is in negotiations with Psych-Media for permission to publish the *Mental Health Aspects in Developmental Disabilities Journal*. If negotiations are successful, this will give Disabilitynews.net access to over 20 years of journal articles from the most reputable professionals from the dually diagnosed field. A fee structure will be negotiated with Psych-Media. Biographies and contact information for all authors will be provided.

Additionally, Disabilitynews.net will provide book sales via the site. We propose to partner with Amazon.com through their Associates Program. If our application is approved, visitors to Disabilitynews.net will have the opportunity to purchase books specific to their area of interest from the vast libraries of Amazon.com. In return, Disabilitynews.net will receive between a 5 and 15% royalty on all sales as a result from the link from Disabilitynews.net. Associates with Amazon.com are given the right to promote this relationship on their site and in any sales literature and advertising. There is no cost to become an Associate and Amazon.com coordinates fulfillment and shipping. It is our hope to eventually expand upon the book sales portion of the Publishing Service from other sources.

Other Resources will be provided to users such as: community services, support groups, government agencies, other contact information and links on the Web. This material will be searchable by geography or keywords.

The backbone of the On-line Publishing Service is a large database containing the title of articles, subjects, summaries, geographic regions, pricing and the actual articles. In addition, this database will have the added benefit of being tied into the Amazon.com database for book sales. The e-commerce portion of Disabilitynews.net will play a key role in the database. Once a user has successfully purchased an article through e-commerce, they will be able to download a copy of the journal article, in Adobe Acrobat (*.pdf) file format, onto their computer. This file will be readable in Adobe Acrobat Reader 3.0 or higher (a free shareware program). E-commerce for books purchased on Amazon.com will be handled by Amazon.com.

Launch Training Service:

Online registration and other information regarding the 2nd Annual Training Institute on Mental Health and Developmental Disabilities (sponsored by GLMHRA and the Sovner Center) will be available via Disabilitynews.net. We hope to involve other trade organizations in both the Training and Publishing Services to expand our service offerings.

Market Research:

The Sovner Center Research & Development Department will develop a comprehensive survey to determine the feasibility of launching the On-line Communications Service and to make adjustments in the services provided in the Phase 1 web site.

Phase 2: To be completed by October 1, 1999

GOALS:

>   Launch On-line Communications Service (Membership Services)
>
>   Evaluate successes of On-line Publishing Service—make adjustments

Launch On-line Communications Service:

An additional database will be created to manage the On-line Communications Service for Members. If Phase 2 is implemented, Disabilitynews.net will recruit Members via the existing Web site who are interested in gaining additional, fee based services from the Web site. Some examples include on-line discussion groups, on-line support groups, and 1:1 professional consultations. A key component of this service will be the ability to recruit "Professional Members." Professional Members will be doctors, therapists, licensed social workers, and other health care professionals interested in participating in Disabilitynews.net, either by being an on-line consultant or submitting a research paper or journal article to Disabilitynews.net.

Different levels of Membership will be provided at a certain fee paid via the e-commerce portion of Disabilitynew.net. Basic membership plans will include a distinct number of hours of "public chat." "Private chat" time (including 1:1 consultations) will be provided to members for an additional fee.

Other areas of interest, such as real estate and property renovations for people with disabilities, may be included based upon the feedback from the Phase 1 Market Survey.

MARKET SUMMARY:

Overall, the Internet and World Wide Web community has been expanding significantly since 1995. According to market research giants Forrester and International Data Corporation, the number of Internet users reached an estimated 100 Million North Americans by the end of 1998. By 2002, forecasters predict that 20 million Internet users will make on-line purchases totaling $400 billion (source: Hoffacker, Claudia; "The World Wide Mall," *The Manager,* Fall 1998: page 23). This number is expected to grow considerably over the next decade.

As the general demographics of Web users shift to representing the demographics of the general public (result of price decline of computers and Internet access), more opportunities will become available for more demographic groups. The current average user of the Web is a male 35 years old, college educated. 80% of Web users are men—but these numbers have been changing rapidly.

COMPETITION:

The following is an analysis of potential large competitors of Disabilitynews.net. Each of these Web sites offer similar services as are proposed by Disabilitynew.net.

Psychwatch.com—"The Online Site for Professionals in Psychiatry & Psychology"

Psychwatch provides a comprehensive list of resources specifically for professionals in the mental health field. Much of this information has been gathered through linkages with professionals and organizations participating in Psychwatch. Psychwatch provides the following services: training information, job postings, journal articles, listings of doctors, an on-line newsletter, and bulletin boards. The service is not fee based (other than Banner Advertising) and is free for users to access. Graphically the site is very basic and is formatted with frames for easy site navigation. Overall, a very effective site and providing useful information to its target audience of mental health care professionals. No e-commerce.

TheArc.org—The Arc of the United States

TheArc.org is a informational site for a general audience of people interested in mental retardation. The site provides a wide array of resources for free or for sale via the site (site is not e-commerce enabled). Examples include listings of books, government information, bulletin boards, a newsletter, and contact information for member chapters (The Arc is a national trade association). The site also has an affiliation with Barnes and Noble, so there is a means to purchase books on-line through the Barnes and Noble Web site. For a national trade association, the site is not very graphically appealing but it does provide access to a wide variety of information for users. The site provides straightforward navigation through the use of tables. The target audience is (1) human services/health care professionals, and (2) families and advocates.

Another model site, but not a direct competitor, is the HivInsite Web site sponsored by the University of California at hivinsite.ucsf.edu. This site provides an excellent outline for arranging resources for a particular disability. The site is well organized and is attractively presented given that it is a nonprofit site. It also shows a great example of utilizing sponsorships, should Disabilitynews.net decide to go this route also with site advertising.

POSITIONING:

Disabilitynews.net will be the preeminent resource for disability-related information and resources on the Web, both free and for-fee services. The Target Audience will be comprised of (1) health care professionals, (2) families and advocates, (3) people with disabilities, and (4) students and educators from higher education.

Disabilitynews.net will provide customers with the following:

Access to the latest, most current information and resources for disabilities (particularly developmental disabilities, psychiatric disabilities, and physical disabilities)

Convenient and timely access to information

Excellent customer service and response times

Expertise from the most reputable professionals

COMMUNICATIONS STRATEGY:

The Communications Strategy and Web design of Disabilitynews.net will reflect the needs and interests of our Target Audience of (1) health care professionals, (2) students and educators, (3) families and advocates of people with disabilities, and (4) people with disabilities.

A key component of the site will be its ability to present a unique offering of products and services customized for each target audience. This will also include the content and copywriting. Products and Services will be further refined with the analysis of the Market Surveys, which will be distributed to a sample of each Target Audience (currently in process).

The primary means of the Marketing and Communications strategy of Disabilitynews.net is the graphical presentation of the web site itself. It is important, not only for the site to be attractive, but also to have easy functionality and navigation for users. The site will provide a wide variety of information with many different categories and subcategories, so it is vital for it to present much more organized and straightforward for users.

LAB 10.3

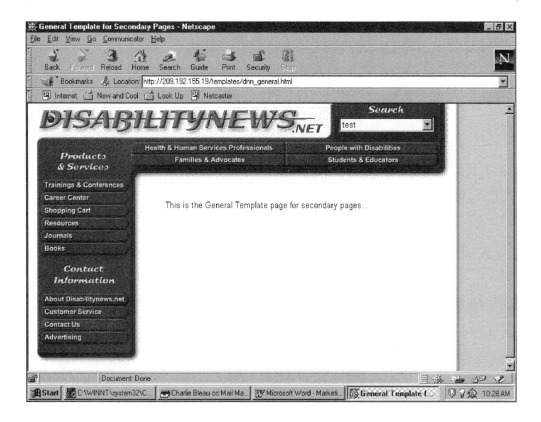

Task	Completion Date
Completion of Phase 1 Technical Development. Including: Database construction, embedding graphics, and site layout.	5/10/99
Commence Phase 1 Content Development. Including: Scanning, Indexing of articles for database, and Misc. materials for site.	5/10/99
Complete Preliminary Market Survey for AAMR Conference in New Orleans	5/17/99
AAMR (American Association for Mental Retardation) Annual Conference in New Orleans. Have all presentation materials for booth.	5/25–28/99
Beta Test Web site with adjustments based on preliminary survey and focus group feedback (use Target Audience sample)	7/1/99
Implement launch Public Relations	7/1/99
Official Launch Date of Phase 1 Web Site	7/15/99
Commence Phase 2 Development with inclusion of final Survey Data	8/1/99
Troubleshoot and make refinements	8/1–27/99
Post-Launch Direct Mailing to Target Audience promoting site	7/30/99
Commence Post-Launch Advertising Campaign	8/15/99
Commence Post-Launch Public Relations Campaign	8/30/99
Official Launch Date of Phase 2 Web Site	10/1/99
National Association for the Dually Diagnosed Annual Meeting at Niagara Falls, Ontario	11/10–13/99
TASH Conference in Chicago	12/99

Advertising Plan:

The core advertising will be done in a major roll-out campaign during the months of July and August 1999. The following media will be utilized:

Print Advertising: selected trade newsletters, magazines and journals. These include:

> Mental Health Aspects in Developmental Disabilities Journal
>
> American Association for Mental Retardation Newsletter
>
> YAI Newsletter
>
> American Association on Mental Retardation Newsletter
>
> TASH Newsletter

LAB 10.3

These selections will be ideal for building brand awareness for Disabilitynews.net with health care professionals.

On-line Advertising: banner advertising, affinity groups, and cross-marketing/banner exchanges will be utilized, including:

> Banner Advertising on health care–related and search engine Web sites. Specific sites to be determined.
>
> Banner Exchanges with Web sites marketing to same target audience(s). Examples may include AAMR, McLean Hospital, NADD, Healthcare Providers, and other health care/advocacy sites for people with disabilities.

Advertising in the above areas will allow Disabilitynews.net to reach each of the four Target Audience groups on the Web. Further research will be done to identify additional sites for on-line advertising.

A total of $4000 has been allocated in budget for the Phase 1 launch Advertising Plan. Therefore, cost-effective means for both print and on-line advertising will need to be identified.

3. Public Relations Plan:

Public Relations will be an ongoing process for Disabilitynews.net. A combination of trade shows, conferences, and traditional press placements will be utilized both to announce the launch and build ongoing awareness.

Areas will include

> Local/Regional Newspapers in Massachusetts
>
> State and National Trade Association literature
>
> National/International Health Care Magazines
>
> National/International Web/Internet publications

State/national University/college newsletters

Tradeshow/ Conference involvement will also be utilized to further build awareness and interest in the Disabilitynews.net service. Some preliminary locations identified, include:

MCHP Annual Meeting in Boston—Fall 1999

NADD Annual Meeting in Niagara Falls, Ontario—11/10-13/99

TASH Annual Meeting in Chicago—12/99

AAMR Annual Meeting in Washington—5/00

Additional Tradeshow/conference involvement will be identified as information becomes available.

Estimated Public Relations budget for Phase 1 Public Relations (tradeshows/conferences): $8,000

Other Promotion:

Direct Marketing: a comprehensive direct marketing campaign will be conducted to promote Disabilitynews.net to 1) Healthcare Professionals in Massachusetts and nationally, 2) Community Healthcare Providers both locally and nationally, 3) Selected educators in psychology and psychiatry nationally, 4) Special Education directors and teachers in Massachusetts.

This direct mailing will be sent to the above groups the end of July, beginning of August 1999. The mailing will most likely be a postcard or other cost-effective mailing piece to go out 3rd class bulk rate. Mailing lists will be acquired from both existing mailing lists and fee-based list services. The estimated number of units to be mailed will be between 15,000 and 20,000.

An additional direct mailing will be sent upon completion of the Phase 2 web site in November. We will define this campaign at a later date.

Total budget for Phase 1 Direct Marketing: $5000.

Sales Strategy:

A major component to the success of Disabilitynews.net will be the recruitment of advertisers and companies who are interested in selling their products and services on Disabilitynews.net. Based upon feedback received at the AAMR Conference in May, future involvement in trade shows as well as contacting potential participants in this service personally will be key to the future growth and success of Disabilitynews.net.

It is proposed that a position be made available that will solely focus on developing relationships, networking, and essentially "selling" Disabilitynews.net to other companies. Additionally, this position will be responsible for assisting in promoting the service at trade shows and conferences.

Once Phase 2 is underway, this Sales/Marketing Consultant will assist in coordinating the On-line Communications (Chat) service and recruit Professional Members.

PRICING PLAN:

The primary means of generating revenue through the Phase 1 Web site will be through the sale of Journal articles and other publications on-line.

An average article fee of $7 has been established for purposes of this marketing plan. For journal publishers, we will mark up journal articles by 100% for on-line sale—50% of the revenue to the publisher and 50% for Disabilitynew.net (currently in negotiation with Psych-Media). Buyers will purchase each article at a premium in exchange for receiving the article of their choice on demand (i.e., a convenience premium). Essentially, Disabilitynews.net will operate as a Value Added Reseller (VAR) in the distribution channel. Additionally, if approved, we would also receive royalties from being an Amazon.com Associate—as mentioned earlier.

E-commerce will be the primary means for processing all transactions.

The following is the proposed Pricing Plan for the Phase 2 web site:

Membership Fees: 4 membership packages have been established for Disabilitynews.net, all with different offerings:

Membership Plan 1 (Basic Plan): This includes 5 hours of Public Chat, access to additional resources, email monthly newsletter w/updates and other links not offered to non-members. Additionally, web site customization at login based upon past purchases, and areas of interest indicated in membership application. This membership plan has a 6 month duration. Planned cost: $50. Renewal cost: $40.

Membership Plan 2 (Family Plan): This includes 10 hours of Public Chat, access to additional resources, email monthly newsletter w/ updates and other links not offered to non-members. Additionally, web site customization at login based upon past purchases, and areas of interest indicated in membership application. This membership plan has a 1 year duration. Planned cost: $80. Renewal cost: $60.

Membership Plan 3 (Corporate Plan): This includes 30 hours of Public Chat, access to additional resources, email monthly newsletter w/ updates and other links not offered to non-members. Web site customization based upon type of business/organization with more

LAB
10.3

of a business emphasis in presentation. This membership plan has a 6 month duration. Planned cost: $200. Renewal cost: $200.

Membership Plan (Non-profit Plan): This limited membership allows access to additional resources, email monthly newsletter w/updates and other links not offered to non-members. No public chat and web site customization. In order to be eligible, non-profit must present a valid Federal Non-profit Identification code—need 24 hours for varification. This membership plan has an indefinite duration and does not cost anything for a valid non-profit organization.

2. Private Chat: Private Chat will be a unique service offered by Disabilitynew.net. Pricing for this is based upon a "sliding scale" depending on the number of participants—1 to 5 people and the credentials of the professional facilitating the Private Chat session. Each professional has been designated an average hourly rate for services. Individual rates may need to be established depending on the reputation and credentials of the professional.

RESOURCES:

Web Development Director—20 hrs/wk:

> Provide management oversight of the service during and after project development phases.
>
> Web development and Web site administration
>
> Manage contractors
>
> Scan existing journal articles
>
> Meet with CEO for approvals and input in project development

Senior Editor—8 hrs/wk:

> Manage the organization of editorial content, including content creation for Web site

Editor/R&D Consultant—4 hrs/wk:

> Assist in organizing editorial content
>
> Scan journal articles

Editor/R&D Consultant

> Recruit sponsors and other trade publications
>
> Provide editorial consultation
>
> Develop market survey and statistical analysis

Sales Consultant

> Network with providers, trade associations, and educational institutions to recruit advertising and product offerings
>
> Attendance and representation at conferences and trade shows

Marketing Consultant

> Network with providers, trade associations, and educational institutions to recruit advertising and product offerings

> Coordinate Professional Membership and On-line Communications Service

The site should be very functional, yet it needs to be eye-catching for the target audience. Please refer to Attachment 3 for a hard copy of the HIV/Aids Web site sponsored by the University of California at San Francisco. This Web site is very functional yet has a professional, eye-catching representation. Additionally, the HIV/Aids Web site has some similarities to the proposed DisabilityNews web site—i.e., the way information is organized and presented.

Graphics to be created include

> Large Logo bar for home page

> Small Logo bar for subsequent pages with page identifier

> Navigational Bar (to be used on all pages)

> Buttons/bullets and horizontal separators

> Background graphic

Additional graphics may be needed as the project progresses.

After development of a "demo site" depicting the overall theme and presentation of the Web site, input will be requested from a cross section of the users of the Web site.

Based on this feedback as well as internal feedback from GLMHRA and other contractors, creative work on DisabilityNews will be finalized.

Content Development

All content relating to the marketing and purpose of DisabilityNews will need to be developed from scratch. In other words, content on the home page and other pages will need to be written—most likely the Web Developer.

Clinical content and papers will need to be organized by someone designated as "Editor." This person will have the responsibility of locating information, and getting any necessary permission waivers, to be reprinted on DisabilityNews. Administrative supports may be needed to retype information in hard-copy format. Additionally, the Editor will be responsible for locating directories and other information sources to be included in the "Links" section.

All papers and resources will then need to be integrated into a comprehensive back-end database—Based on "type of disability" as a search criteria. Additionally, the database will need to be searchable by geographic location, specific words and phrases, title of papers, etc. An RFP will be sent to various database contractors detailing this information and asking for a bid on the project.

Information presented on the web site and in the database will need to be updated regularly. It is suggested that the database contractor develop an easily accessible, password protected access area where information can be updated on the database on a regular basis.

Technical Development

DisabilityNews will be built utilizing HTML, Perl, back-end database (type to be determined by database contractor), and JavaScript.

The web server will be a virtual host with a local Internet Service Provider. The server will need to be an UNIX and/or NT platform supporting Perl scripting, a back-end database, Front Page Server Extensions and Microsoft Site Server Commerce Edition (needs WinNT).

The hosting company will provide comprehensive e-commerce capabilities through Microsoft Site Server Commerce. Will establish a new account for DisabilityNews with them.

The "Chat Room" will be built using currently available off-the-shelf software—any necessary software licensing will be purchased.

Further information about Technical requirements will be finalized based on input from Database Contractor.

Site Map/Navigation

Please see Attachment 5 for an outline of the proposed Site Map.

Section 1: Home Page:

Current News and information from Professional Members—specifically highlighted and promoted

Other news and information printed w/permission from major news sources

Links to: 1) Resources (searchable by disability, author, other keyword); and 2) Membership Registration.

Section 2: Resources

Public

Database searchable by disability, author, or other keyword

Links to available papers, links and other resources pertaining to specific disability. User can purchase papers/pubs individually—the e-commerce software will provide a "Shopping Cart" option.

Private/Members-only (username and password protected)

If user clicks on one of the following "members-only" links, user will be prompted to become a member . . . will link to "Membership Registration"

Training and Conference Info (specific to disability)

Public Chat section (specific to disability/guest speaker??)

Private Chat section—set up an appointment with physician, clinician or other professional in the field relating to the specific disability.

Directory of Professional Members

Other Resources and Links to Service Providers

Section 3: Membership Registration

Offers Membership options with separate pages for General Members and Professional Members.

New members will need to fill out a form with 2 payment options—by mail or via e-commerce. General membership options will be available for different "a la carte" items (i.e., 2 hours of chat, 4 hours of chat plus a free training, etc.)

Once members have submitted payment option, will then receive an email back with registration confirmation. Professional Members will be provided with an email address for them to send in papers or other information they would like posted on DisabilityNews.

Maintenance Schedule (i.e., Service & Support)

The Web Development Director will maintain DisabilityNews daily. The Editor will provide new information to be posted on a weekly basis (or as new information comes in).

Milestones (how will we measure success?)

Success of the DisabilityNews proposal will be based upon the following criteria:

> Successful coordination of all necessary resources needed to complete this project (as outlined in this Business Plan)

> Successful completion of project on schedule

> Successful use of Beta testing of web site—receive input from a cross-section of the various user groups.

> Successful launch of web site and necessary post-launch marketing activities

> Successful acquisition of both general members and professional members. Will evaluate effectiveness 6 months after launch.

The success of this project depends heavily on the ability to recruit Professional Members for DisabilityNews. Professional Members will provide their papers and research to be displayed on DisabilityNews. Because we won't have the linkages with Professional Members outside of GLMHRA and the Sovner Center, heavy marketing and recruitment with these professionals from across the country needs to be undertaken before and after the launch of the web site. Hopefully, the success of DisabilityNews will promote the site itself in professional and academic circles. Only time will tell if this assumption is overly optimistic—it will be evaluated on an ongoing basis during and after launch.

LAB 10.3 EXERCISES

10.3.1 ESTABLISH WEB SITE HIERARCHY

a) If you were to ask a graphic designer to develop buttons to define main areas, what would they be?

_____

_____

_____

_____

_____

_____

_____

_____

_____

_____

_____

_____

_____

b) Create a flow chart for events described in the project specification for Disabilitynews.net.

10.3.2 WRITE A PROJECT DESCRIPTION

a) Which topics do you feel need to be covered in a project specification? Are there any points here that you feel need to be covered in more detail? What do you feel is detailed particularly well in this specification?

_____

_____

_____

_____

_____

_____

_____

_____

_____

_____

_____

_____

_____

b) Write a sample project description for your favorite Web site.

_____

_____

_____

LAB
10.3

_____

_____

_____

_____

_____

_____

_____

_____

_____

_____

_____

_____

_____

_____

10.3.3 IDENTIFY A PROJECT BUDGET AND SCHEDULE

a) The budget is intentionally missing from the project specification for Disabilitynews.net. However, there is a defined schedule. Research salaries on the Web (don't forget database development) for the resources listed in Disabilitynews.net's project specification. Plan on an additional administrative cost of $500/week to cover administrative and office expenses. Then estimate the cost of this project.

_____

_____

_____

_____

b) Develop a schedule for your favorite Web site (use the project description from Lab 10.3.2b).

_____

_____

_____

_____

_____

LAB 10.3 EXERCISE ANSWERS

This section gives you some suggested answers to the questions in Lab 10.3 with discussion related to those answers. Please post any alternative answers to these questions at the companion Web site for this book, located at http://www.phptr.com/phptrinteractive.

10.3.1 ANSWERS

a) If you were to ask a graphic designer to develop buttons to define main areas, what would they be?

Answer: Check out http://www.disabilitynews.net and see how close your vision came to the final product.

b) Create a flow chart for the events described in the project specification for Disabilitynews.net.

Answer: Again, visit http://www.disabilitynews.net and see how close your vision came to the final product.

10.3.2 ANSWERS

a) Which topics do you feel need to be covered in a project specification? Are there any points here that you feel need to be covered in more detail? What do you feel is detailed particularly well in this project specification?

Answer: When it comes to a project spec, I want to see plans for analysis, design, coding, testing, implementation, and marketing.

A few years ago, having only been working for myself a short time, I took on a subcontracting project for a local Web marketing company to build part of a Web site. The client had a very sound business plan, and he was well prepared with financial resources to back up the project. He made a significant investment in this project and made himself available for the project team.

Unfortunately, a project specification was never drafted between the client and the Web firm. Thus, the client had developed certain expectations, which were at odds with the scope of work expected by the project team. The project manager was at wit's end trying to balance these expectations against the requirements of the subcontractors, leaving everyone with this open-ended project that had no end in sight. Given this scenario, there was no way the project manager or the project could succeed.

The disgruntled and disappointed client ended up going to another Web firm, and the subcontractors were left with such a bad taste in their mouths that it was highly unlikely that they would take on additional projects through this firm.

Taking two weeks to develop a well-defined project specification would have most likely ensured this project's success. The client would have had realistic expectations. The subcontractors, who flat bid the project, would have had a defined scope of work. Most important, the Web firm would have made a good profit on this project, solidified relations with subcontractors, and probably garnered a great deal of business based on this Web site. It was obvious to me, as one of the subcontractors, that the Web firm had devoted a great deal of effort to managing this Web site and in the end lost time and money. It was very unfortunate for everyone involved.

The project specification for DisabilityNews.net covers the marketing aspect of the site particularly well. Plans for marketing a Web site are just as important as the build, if it's to be a high-profile entity on the Web. Charlie Bleau, the author of the project specification for DisabilityNews.net, having a very strong marketing background, outlines a logical flow of events.

b)   Write a project specification for your favorite Web site.

Answer: My favorite Web site is usually the one that I'm currently involved with building. I guess that's what makes Web architecture more than just a occupation for me.

This specification is one that I wrote quite some time ago and use as an example for the students in my Web Project Management class. This spec definitely falls short on discussing the detailed scheduling and marketing plans covered by Charlie's project spec. However, it does have a good technical summary, clearly defining the Web site's functionality. Thus, I do believe it to be a more than accurate description of the scope of work. (The names of both the Web firm and the personnel firm have been changed to protect the confidentiality of both firms.)

Acme Personnel, Inc. 888 Internet Avenue, Anytown, MA 00000

Phone: xxx.xxx.xxxx Fax: xxx.xxx.xxxx Email: ack@acme.com

Project Mission Statement: To establish Acme Personnel, a permanent placement firm with a Web presence that attracts both hiring companies and qualified applicants. Acme Personnel specializes in permanent placement for software professionals with local high-tech companies. Providing clients with the assurance that the firm is searching on their behalf to place the right person today in the right position, Acme Personnel helps companies better serve their customers in the future and software professionals reach their career goals.

Site Overview: Acme Personnel will provide a facility for its contracted companies to post job opportunities on its site. An additional feature will present job seekers' resumes. Marketing information about Acme Personnel will be included, as well as a possible page that offers links to on-line education, town information, and day-care facilities.

Audience: Human Resources managers from local software companies and upwardly mobile software engineers.

Creative Development: Cyber Warrior Web Design will begin addressing Acme's need for an effective graphical presentation by developing a logo, a button (which will be embedded with text for the various sections of the site), and a background.

Acme Personnel specializes in placing software professionals. Thus, a professional look and feel, which might appeal to this segment of job seekers, would be appropriate. Computer industry related images and an enthusiastic upwardly mobile message should be incorporated into the site. The site, telco.com, was mentioned as having a desirable look and feel.

Cyber Warriors will develop three sets of buttons, logos, and backgrounds and present them to Acme by August 5.

After developing the overall look and feel of the site, Cyber Warrior Web Design will consult with Acme to develop secondary graphics, which enforce the message in the various sections of the site. Graphics should be used judiciously, having a distinct purpose, as they slow page-loading time. All graphics will be saved in a low-resolution format.

Content Development: Cyber Warrior Web Design will consult with Acme Personnel to either repurpose existing content or to develop

**LAB
10.3**

new material expressly for the Web site. Possible suggestions include helpful hints to job seekers, links to information regarding relocation and education, marketing information about Acme Personnel, and forms that both job seekers and hiring companies can submit for review containing resumes and job postings, allowing Acme to review this information for possible inclusion into its database.

Two database tables (their functionality will be detailed under Technical Development) will present resume and job posting information. These databases will be searchable by position, skills, geography, and salary requirements. The resumes should reside in an area that is password protected, so that only authorized companies can access this information. The job postings can be publicly accessible.

An administrative back room will be built (see Technical Development). This area will be password protected and will allow Acme to add, modify, and delete job posting and job-seeker information, as well as searching under specified categories.

Technical Development

This site will be built utilizing HTML, Perl, a mySQL database back-end, and possibly Java and JavaScript. Server requirements include UNIX platform, Perl 5.0, mySQL. Front Page extentions are *not* necessary. Plans at this time are to install the site on the server owned by We Host 'Em, a local hosting company. Another future option includes Host.Net, located in Anytown, MA.

A UNIX platform provides for greater functionality and security than the NT platform and is the appropriate choice for a site of this type. HTML will be used to code the standard Web pages. Perl will be utilized in conjunction with the mySQL database back-end to build the Acme database and for CGI interactive functions. JavaScript and Java applets may be used to create a more interactive graphical presentation.

This site will be best viewed in Netscape Navigator 2.0 and Internet Explorer 3.0 and above.

Database Functionality

Two database tables will track job-seeker and job-posting information. Both tables will need to be searchable with with an AND interface (i.e., Position AND Salary Requirements) or by a singular criterion (i.e., Geography). Links will be provided to more detailed resume and complete job posting information. These files will be uploaded to the server as text files and coded with a number that mirrors the Access database numbers assigned interoffice.

A separate database table will track authorized company names with their user names and passwords.

Job Seeker Table

This table will be password protected. Distinct user names and passwords will be assigned to authorized companies, allowing them to view its contents.

TABLE RESUME FIELDS

id, name, contact_person, current-company, skills, salary, location-desired, desired_position

The id number will link to a separate file, "id.html", which will be a text file containing the candidate's text-based resume. Administrators at Acme will need to blank out the name and current company information from the resumes before uploading them.

Name will be a "hidden" field not shown to the user. This will be included as an administrative back-up alternative, in case the interoffice numbering scheme fails due to misfiling, etc.

This table will be searchable by skills, salary, location-desired, and desired-position by the user. It will be searchable by name, id, skills, salary, location-desired, and desired-position through the administrative back room.

"Hits" that bring up candidates who currently work at the company that is searching the database will be dropped and not shown.

Job Posting Table

TABLE JOB FIELDS

id, company, contact_person, skills, salary, geographical-location, position, date

The id number will link to a separate file, "id.html", which will be a text file containing the company's detailed text based job posting. Administrators at Acme will need to blank out company information from the job postings before uploading them.

Company will be a "hidden" field not shown to the user. This will be included as an administrative back-up alternative, in case the interoffice numbering scheme fails due to misfiling, etc.

This table will be searchable by skills, salary, geographical—location, and position by the user. It will be searchable by company, id, skills, salary, geographical_location, and position through the administrative back room.

Records should be automatically deleted from the system after residing there for over thirty days.

User Name/Password Table

TABLE USER FIELDS

user_name, password, company

This table will be searchable by user_name and company.

An administrative back room will be created for all tables with an add, modify, delete, and the aforementioned searching capability.

Forms

Two forms will reside on the site that allow the user to input either job-seeker or job-posting information. This information will be e-mailed to Acme Personnel, giving Acme the option to follow-up with the prospective candidate or company.

The candidate form will first present questions regarding desired position, current role, skills, current company, and then contact information. Name, address, city, state, zip, day-time phone, evening phone, and e-mail will be required fields.

The job posting form will include company name, contact name, address, city, state, zip, phone, position, skills required, and salary range.

Training Requirements:

There will be an extremely simple user interface used to maintain the database. Still, Cyber Warriors will provide two hours of on-site training. This should be adequate to bring staffers up to speed.

Marketing and Launch Plans:

Acme Personnel should plan to include the URL address, www. acmepersonnel.com, in any marketing materials, advertising, and/or business cards.

The site will be submitted to the major search engines, Excite, Webcrawler, Infoseek, Lycos, Hot Bot, Open Text, and Alta Vista, as well as the Yahoo directory. Keywords will be devised that include all of the categories under which this site should be listed, as well as names of possible industry competitors. Some search engines take up to 4–6 weeks to update.

Optional additional marketing work can be done after the site is operational 5–6 weeks. Research will be done to determine where the site resides in the search engines, and it will be determined whether further marketing strategies should be implemented and whether these strategies would be cost effective.

Authorized Cyber Warriors Representative

Authorized Acme Personnel Representative

10.3.3 ANSWERS

a) The budget is intentionally missing from the project specification for Disabilitynews .net. However, there is a defined schedule. Research salaries on the Web (don't forget database development) for the resources listed in Disabilitynews.net's project specification. Plan on an additional administrative cost of $500/week to cover administrative and office expenses. Then estimate the cost of this project.

Answer: Phase One of this project lasts approximately 10 weeks from analysis to implementation. The marketing phase then begins and takes place intensely over a three month period. The site will need to be continually marketed. However, this initial period is the most intense, as the success of various marketing initiatives is analyzed. Phase Two will last roughly eight weeks.

Administrative costs (1/2 time) over 18 weeks:	*$4500*
Database Programmer—80 hours @ $75/hour:	*$6000*
Graphic Design—60 hours @ $40/hour	*$2400*
Project Manager (1/2 time) over 18 weeks:	*$9000*
Content Editors and Providers—80 hours @ $40/hour	*$2400*
Marketing Analyst—40 @ $40/hour	*$1600*
Cost of Domain Name	*$70*
Hosting and Setup fees over 18 weeks *e-commerce hosting $100/mo avg.*	*$500*
Cost of Marketing Initiatives to be determined by Marketing Analyst	
TOTAL PROJECT ESTIMATE (w/o Marketing)	*$26,470*

b) Develop a schedule for your favorite Web site (use the project description from Lab 10.3.2b).

Answer:

Project analysis	*1.5 weeks*
Graphic design (taking place as database is being built)	*2 weeks*
Database and HTML programming	*2 weeks*
Embedding graphics into site	*.5 week*
Testing	*1 week*
Initial population of database	*1 week*
TOTAL PROJECT LENGTH	*6 weeks*

**LAB
10.3**

LAB 10.3 SELF-REVIEW QUESTIONS

In order to test your progress, you should be able to answer the following questions:

1) (True/False) A project specification
   a) _____ can double as a business plan
   b) _____ defines the scope of work
   c) _____ defines the billing schedule

2) (True/False) A significant hidden cost that many project managers can tend to forget about is
   a) _____ Bringing the clients out to lunch
   b) _____ Administrative costs
   c) _____ Their own salary (project management costs)

C H A P T E R   1 0

TEST YOUR THINKING

The projects in this section use the skills you've acquired in this chapter. The answers to these projects are available to instructors only through a Prentice Hall sales representative and are intended to be used in classroom discussion and assessment.

1)　Determine your own bidding personality. Do you think that you'd have a tendency to overbid or underbid Web projects? Why? You can do this by locating a Web site with which you are aware of the budget (use the Disability News site if there is no other). Knowing what you do now, how would you have bid that Web site? It's important for you to understand what your tendencies are so that you can automatically adjust them to make the sale or make the project more profitable for the firm.

2)　Many Web firms start out with sole-proprietor status. Later, they incorporate. What are the reasons that most businesses incorporate? What shift in project requirements might cause a Web firm to incorporate?

3)　Describe a Web project in which a full-blown project specification might not be cost-effective to develop. If a project specification was not written, how would you assure that the client's expectations and the project team's vision were in agreement?

C H A P T E R   1 1

CREATIVE DEVELOPMENT

"If you can't define 'Done', don't do it."

CHAPTER OBJECTIVES:

In this chapter, you will learn about

✔ Content Identification   Page 456
✔ Graphic Design   Page 471
✔ Writing and Editing   Page 488

One area that requires the most client management is content development. Most Web developers find building databases and interactive CGI programs preferable to designing graphics and presenting copy, because the requirements are relatively clear—the program either works or it doesn't.

The success of a graphic design, writing, editing, and/or lay out initiative is so subjective to what hits a client's fancy that it can be more difficult for a Web firm to succeed and be profitable in this area.

As much as possible, we try to make the client responsible for our creative initiatives and document any and all conversations regarding this subject. That way, if the client has asked us to develop using a blue background and red logo, and we have completed this task, the firm has this documentation to fall back on if the client does an about-face and demands red background with a blue logo.

To a client, I'm sure this doesn't sound like a big request. However, to the Web firm, which must pay a good graphic artist $40 an hour, it's a big deal. When I first began to build sites, I would go through the local fast food drive-thru and wonder if the person serving me my hamburger was doing better per hour than I was. This is because 90% of Web sites are flat bid up front. If there's no documentation to support that the client veered from their original direction, the project manager has a hard time billing any additional hours to the client.

Another area that makes content development difficult is a scenario in which the client keeps changing their copy. Many clients see changing Web documents as being as easy as making a change in the word processing program. True, if the changes don't impact on the site hierarchy or radically change an entire page, it does not entail a morning of an HTML developer's time. However, if there's some fairly complicating formatting on the page, which needs modification after being built to a client's earlier expectations, this causes a time overrun. In the Web development business, time is money. If the Web firm graciously makes these changes with the idea that the client will not yet again change their mind, often the client will do just that, expecting the Web firm to turn tail yet again and make changes on the fly. In a project specification, the project manager can stipulate that after two to three exchanges between the client and the firm with regard to the Web site copy, the content will be locked. Any additional changes will need to be implemented at the end of the project.

The success of how everything goes really hangs on how honest and up front project managers are with their clients. I often use the same analogy that I used in Chapter 8 with my clients, and it works out extremely well: If we've painted the living room yellow, please don't expect me to get excited about painting it pink for free.

As a business grows, so do your choices when it comes to keeping long-term clientele. I have clients that I'd walk through fire for. I feel a very strong sense of loyalty to them, and I'm very grateful to have a working association with them because not only are they good businesspeople, they are good people, period. When they call my firm, they know what they want. And if they do not, they understand that we are going to put together mock-ups, and our time needs to be covered. It can't be an open-ended sort of deal where we work until we make something the client likes. They know that I'm sincere about wanting them to be 100% satisfied, but they know that this is my living, and I can't afford to work for free, so they respect our need for a defined scope of work. Fortunately, as time has gone on, I've had the luxury to drop those clients who do not value my firm's time. No one likes to turn someone away. I certainly do not. But, after a pattern exists—the person is difficult to deal with, the person keeps changing their mind, and/or it's then difficult to collect payment—there's no reason to keep these clients on, as they are highly unprofitable.

Again, these are all client management issues that seem to become stumbling blocks more in the content development stage than any other, once a contract is signed.

In mentioning the pitfalls and typical scenarios encountered during this phase of Web site development, I'm really just urging project managers to be as clear as possible with the client. Never take something on faith, but rather ask the question before work progresses. Therefore, if work is being done according to a client's instruction and it is later rejected for reasons other than the quality of the work (e.g., a change in direction), the Web firm does not have to take on the financial burden of this change.

Most people who go into Web developing as a career truly enjoy the creative aspects of it. As a former software analyst, I found the use of graphics and written copy quite liberating. Suddenly, the Web site becomes a sculpture, and the computer is a chisel. As long as the lines of communication remain clear, this can also be a very rewarding phase as the client sees their vision take shape. Often, it's the successful completion of creative tasks that really cements the relationship between client and developer, helping to seal the client's faith in the Web firm's ability to perform other noncreative tasks.

LAB 11.1

CONTENT IDENTIFICATION

LAB OBJECTIVES:

After this lab, you will be able to

- Conduct a Client Creative Interview
- Establish Branding
- Identify the Main Ideas
- Storyboard the Web Site

In Chapter 10, we discussed putting together client questionnaires, assessing their goals for the Web site. In the content development phase, we must identify specifically how the Web site will help the client to attain these goals through written copy and graphical presentation.

David Siegel's wonderful book, *Secrets of Successful Web Sites,* suggests sending the client on a field trip, asking them to rate sites based on appearance, content, and functionality. This is a great way to get a feel for what the client is attracted to and sees as a priority. Do they want multimedia presentations, using technologies such as Macromedia Flash (an application that incorporates sound and graphic animation seamlessly) to impress their customers? Or would the client rather present a site that makes information very easy to get to, so visitors will have an immediate feel for the navigation scheme and can immediately get where they want to go?

Consistency throughout the site—reinforcing the client's logo or "branding"—is also important. One often hears the estimate in the advertising industry that individuals need to see a message seven times before it really begins to make an impression on them. We like to keep repeating a client's logo not just because we want to be sure that the visitor knows that he or she is still within that client's Web site but because it helps to reinforce the logo or the brand name in the visitor's mind. That way, if through cross promotion the visitor sees print, television, or advertising on other Web sites, the chances for instant brand recognition increase. Consumers tend to feel more comfortable about opening their wallets for a "familiar face."

As the client is identifying their goals for building a Web site, the creative team can also help the client to consider the main messages being communicated. If the firm is selling computers, do we want to key on the fact that this firm is particularly good with customer service, can access any and all parts, whether discontinued or currently in production, or offers the best prices anywhere? Perhaps it's a combination of all of these messages that is important. The creative direction and the functionality will all support these ideas.

If a financial advisor wishes to build a site focusing on a particular sort of mutual fund, is it better to project the image of being an old, well-established firm that has been around for a thousand years, or should the image be highly edgy and contemporary? While an edgy, more casual image might work very well for a Web firm, consumers want to see stability when initiating investment activities. So the message goes beyond what is written on the screen to the subliminal impressions a visitor may have while at the Web site.

Hopefully, in the process of identifying main ideas, a story will emerge. Drawing on the hierarchy developed during the project specification stage and incorporating the creative team's (including the client) creative ideas, one can "storyboard" the site. Often, very savvy clients have already done this. They come with designs written on graph paper or even napkins, and it's all extremely helpful. Even if a client can use squares or circles to block things out on a piece of paper, it's a fantastic start. From there, the creative team can refine the design and effectively storyboard the site.

LAB 11.1 EXERCISES

11.1.1 CONDUCT A CLIENT CREATIVE INTERVIEW

a) Your client owns a venerable old bookstore, which has been a fixture in its community for over seventy-five years. The people who run it now understand the value of offering goods and services over the Web. They are not trying to compete with amazon.com but want to emphasize the store's ability to provide highly personalized attention and perhaps create a much different look and feel from Amazon. What types of questions would you ask of this client? In order to distinguish itself from Amazon, what might this bookstore do in terms of Web site content?

_____

_____

_____

_____

_____

_____

_____

_____

_____

_____

_____

_____

_____

_____

_____

_____

_____

_____

_____

_____

_____

_____

_____

_____

_____

_____

_____

_____

b) A small Mom and Pop computer store wishes to project a bigger, more corporate image on the Web in hopes of attracting corporate customers. What kinds of questions would you ask them? What might you advise them to do?

_____

_____

_____

_____

_____

_____

_____

_____

_____

_____

_____

_____

_____

_____

_____

_____

_____

_____

_____

_____

_____

_____

11.1.2 ESTABLISH BRANDING

a) Give three examples of how branding can be implemented on a site. Which do you think is best? Why?

_____

_____

_____

_____

_____

_____

_____

_____

_____

_____

_____

_____

_____

_____

_____

_____

_____

_____

_____

_____

_____

_____

b) How would you establish branding on the bookstore Web site mentioned above in 11.1.1a?

_____

_____

_____

_____

_____

_____

_____

_____

_____

11.1.3   IDENTIFY THE MAIN IDEAS

a) What sort of strategies might you use to encourage a client to identify the main ideas they wish to convey in their Web site, both the evident ideas and the ideas a visitor would pick up in a subliminal fashion?

b) Give three examples each of the direct communication of a message versus a subliminal message.

_____

_____

_____

_____

_____

_____

_____

_____

_____

_____

11.1.4   STORYBOARD THE WEB SITE

a) How would storyboarding the bookstore Web site (11.1.1.a), with the client better facilitate the creative development of it?

_____

_____

_____

_____

_____

_____

_____

_____

_____

_____

_____

_____

_____

_____

_____

_____

_____

_____

_____

_____

_____

_____

b) Storyboard your vision of the bookstore Web site.

_____

_____

_____

_____

_____

_____

_____

_____

_____

_____

_____

_____

_____

_____

_____

_____

_____

_____

_____

_____

_____

LAB 11.1 EXERCISE ANSWERS

This section gives you some suggested answers to the questions in Lab 11.1. with discussion related to those answers. Please post any alternative answers to these questions at the companion Web site for this book, located at http://www.phptr.com/phptrinteractive.

11.1.1 ANSWERS

a) Your client owns a venerable old bookstore, which has been a fixture in its community for over seventy-five years. The people who run it now understand the value of offering goods and services over the Web. They are not trying to compete with amazon.com but want to emphasize the store's ability to provide highly personalized attention, and perhaps create a much different look and feel from Amazon. What types of questions would you ask of this client? In order to distinguish itself from Amazon, what might this bookstore do in terms of Web site content?

Answer:

- *Who does the client want to use its Web site?*
- *Is the client targeting people who come into the store and providing them with an on-line alternative?*

- *Is the client trying to attract new customers?*
- *How does the client see their bookstore as being different from Amazon?*
- *Is the client comfortable with putting together a graphical representation of a well-established old bookstore, complete with all of the subliminal messages to support this? Or, are they interested in another direction?*
- *What makes this bookstore different from other bookstores?*
- *Would the client be comfortable with featuring long-time employees on the site, who might specialize in a certain area, and allowing them to make recommendations?*
- *Are there any logos or graphics identified with this bookstore that the client would like to adapt for the Web?*

b) A small Mom and Pop computer store wishes to project a bigger, more corporate image on the Web in hopes of attracting corporate customers. What kinds of questions would you ask them? What might you advise them to do?

Answer:

- *To add credibility, what kinds of informational resources are available to them? Would they feel comfortable writing white papers and press releases and including them on their Web site, just as a large corporate entity might do?*
- *Of the Web sites maintained by large corporations in this industry, which does the client feel are most effective from a graphic and content perspective?*
- *What themes do they wish to emphasize? An example might be "Large enough to have a wide inventory, small enough to know you." Or perhaps they wish to make no reference to smaller size at all. "We are a big Corporate Entity—TRUST US!"*
- *What sort of navigation will best present the products? Which products do they wish to push?*
- *If the visitor has ten seconds to get to know this company, what would the client wish the message to be?*

11.1.2 ANSWERS

a) Give three examples of how branding can be implemented on a site. Which do you think is best? Why?

Answer: Three ways to establish branding on a Web site include

- *Domain name*
- *Regular use of logo embedded with the navigation*
- *Use of logo as a watermark*

I like to establish branding using the logo embedded in the navigation scheme. Unless the company is well known, the domain name can be used to establish better ranking with the search engines by incorporating important keywords that the company would want to be found under. Also, using the logo as part of a water mark can obscure the text. While these two methods help to establish branding, they take away from communicating other important messages.

Using a navigation bar that incorporates the company's logo consistently throughout the site firmly roots the artwork in the visitor's mind without threatening other useful features of the Web site.

b) How would you establish branding on the bookstore Web site mentioned in 11.1.1a?.

Answer: First, I'd use the method of firmly tying the logo to the navigation scheme. Then I would be sure to include the logo in any banner or tile advertising done on other Web sites. Any ordering text-based ordering confirmations should also include the name of the bookstore. If the user has elected to receive HTML based e-mails, the logo can be sent as part of the e-mail.

Also, offer license plates on the site. A license plate is a small graphic that the visitor can download and place on their own Web site, similar to "Best Viewed with Internet Explorer 5.0" or "Netscape Now!". It might be fun to offer a license plate with messages like "I get the best books at the Book Nook," "Book Nook Groupie," or "I belong to THE World Wide Web book group!" Let people link to these graphics via the bookstore's site and make it easy to provide the link back to the site.

11.1.3 ANSWERS

a) What sort of strategies might you use to encourage a client to identify the main ideas they wish to convey in their Web site, both the evident ideas and the ideas a visitor would pick up in a subliminal fashion?

Answer: The following questions might be useful:

- *Picture having thirty seconds to introduce your company; what do you want the potential customer to know?*
- *Do you like a casual, edgy, classic, conservative, or contemporary image?*
- *Are you interested in attracting impulse buyers or long-time clientele?*
- *You have ten keywords to use to organize your company's information. What would they be?*

b) Give three examples each of the direct communication of a message versus a subliminal message.

Answer: The following are examples:

- *Direct Message—Placing text in the company profile page about how a financial services firm has over forty years of experience, touting the various positions held by members of the firm.*

  Subliminal Message—The use of very classic graphics and fonts, which speak of upscale conservatism.

- *Direct Message—Including text on the main page about how a bookstore was founded based on the owner's love of books and wish to share this with others. The business has grown due to the devotion of its customers, because the owners know their customers' tastes and wish to cater to them.*

  Subliminal Message—Pictures of "customers" reading and enjoying a cup of tea around a fireplace, or a book discussion group talking with an employee at the store. Perhaps pictures of a famous author doing a book signing at the store surrounded by many happy faces.

- *Direct Message—Our hardware store is service oriented, not like the large corporations. We will hunt down the most obscure tool because it's our specialty.*

  Subliminal Message—Pictures of hardware store employees speaking with happy customers. Pictures of odd tools. A graphical image that is reminiscent of fonts and logos one might find in an old-time hardware store.

11.1.4 ANSWERS

a) How would storyboarding the bookstore Web site (11.1.1a), with the client better facilitate the creative development of it?

Answer: If the client is fairly reasonable to work with and doesn't go off on tangents, storyboarding is a good tool, like the project spec, to pin the client down to an exact model. This is best accomplished at a meeting with the Web developer. Whichever way vagueness can be eradicated from project requirements, it will only help the process.

True, there are times when you get a client who just can't seem to make a decision. I sometimes find myself pushing this client along and taking them out of the creative decision-making process as much as possible, just so that we can complete the project to the best of our ability. I've been known to make comments like, "Our graphic designer knows the message you are ultimately trying to communicate, and he also knows the Web. Don't worry about it." And sometimes that comment works!

However, if the client not only can't make a decision but also prefers that we do not either, I sit them down with a pad of graph paper. I explain the storyboarding process and tell them that I need that storyboard completed by the end of the week. If it's not completed by the end of the week, we will have to bump the site out of its place in the production schedule, and we will have to reschedule at our convenience. We will not perform work until the client can settle on a vision.

LAB
11.1

b) Storyboard your vision of the bookstore Web site.

Answer: The following is a rough front page representing my vision, with the navigation on the side.

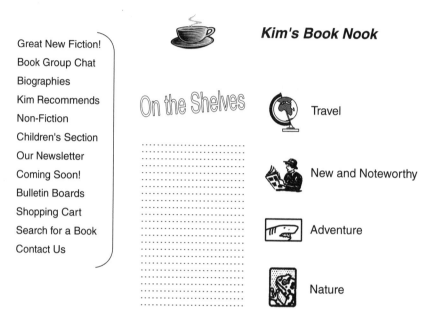

Kim's Book Nook

Great New Fiction!
Book Group Chat
Biographies
Kim Recommends
Non-Fiction
Children's Section
Our Newsletter
Coming Soon!
Bulletin Boards
Shopping Cart
Search for a Book
Contact Us

On the Shelves

Travel

New and Noteworthy

Adventure

Nature

LAB 11.1 SELF-REVIEW QUESTIONS

In order to test your progress, you should be able to answer the following questions:

1) (True/False) Creative development can be difficult because
   a) _____ Clients' requirements can be vague due to the subjective nature of evaluating artwork.
   b) _____ Subliminal messages are so difficult to convey on the Web.
   c) _____ Most graphic designers want to create Web sites their own way.

2) (True/False) When there is a difference in opinion about whether a certain creative direction was authorized by the client, the project manager can refer to the
   a) _____ Creative interview
   b) _____ Web site storyboard
   c) _____ Graphic artist

L A B   1 1 . 2

GRAPHIC DESIGN

LAB OBJECTIVES:

After this lab, you will be able to

- Write a Creative Brief
- Invite Feedback
- Identify Site Look and Feel
- Create Finalized Graphics

Often a Web firm comes into a project in which the client really doesn't know what he wants. All he knows is that he wants a cutting-edge Web site up by a certain date. The client wants the site to be individual, communicate his message, perform the functionality, and represent him well. However, this person may not have a picture of this in his head. Some will be led. Others want the firm to keep presenting ideas until they see something they like. Unfortunately, this can work against both parties.

Creative can be one of the most difficult processes to get the client through. Even if the programming involved with a Web site is much more involved than the graphics, it is not what the client sees. The programming contributes to but does not directly communicate the client's message.

If you ever go shopping with a friend, you might find that you both like jeans and T-shirts. But when you pick out the look that works for you, it may be a baggy pair of jeans and a big red 100% cotton T-shirt, with a pocket on the left. Your pal likes a smooth fit and a straight leg cut. She wants a pink V-neck T-shirt that she can wear under her white cashmere sweater. You both like jeans and T-shirts, but the style is very different. How one company views a certain concept does not always add up to how another will view it. Almost every Web build I have been involved with has had the creative effort initially described as requiring a clean, cutting edge, and professional look. In the end, these characteristics meant many different things to the people involved.

Creative development is almost like buying clothes for someone who will keep sending you back until you buy them exactly what they want. You have to try to picture what is in someone else's head, understand their tastes, and act accordingly. Informing the client up front that there will be so many composites and so many revisions might help. However, that can be intimidating to the client. Some firms will display their portfolio and charge an up-front cost just to develop composites. If the client likes them, then perhaps with some revision, they will design the Web site. However, if the client does not like the comps, he is welcome to pay for another set of composites through this firm or to shop at another Web firm. This makes a great deal of sense, businesswise, in limiting the exposure the firm has to doing wasted work. Still, I can think of several projects that I was able to bring to a profitable end that would not have been finished that way. So much depends on the client involved and how much risk the Web firm wishes to assume.

Sometimes a client will become stuck on a particular issue. The project manager knows that it would be much easier to solve the problem than to argue about it. But for whatever reason, the problem cannot be solved. If the client has a very vague idea of what he wants the Web site to look like but just cannot describe what he wants, the project manager can offer suggestions but cannot make the client decide. You can well understand the client's dilemma, but that dilemma is a project killer. Having been through enough projects, the project manager can recognize the dynamic, is aware of how this can stop forward movement, and how thoughtful communication might keep things on track. In the long run, it won't benefit the client to have the project go incomplete. This is where the project manager needs to take an assertive role and make the client aware of the schedule, the financial obligations involved with bringing in another graphic firm to present more ideas, and try to ease him into something that he likes. Web sites can change the face they put forth several times in a year. If there are elements that don't make it into Phase One, there's always Phase Two. However, the point is to get the Web site up and get it working to benefit the client. If the Web site is making money for the client, he might even forgive you for pushing him along during Phase One.

A creative brief will take the information derived through storyboarding and client interviews and discuss the creative initiative for the Web site. Target audience, client preferred sites, and sample creative directions should be included. This is yet another tool that can be used to help define the project. However, the creative brief does not just encompass graphics, it covers the written copy to be embedded into the Web site. A marketing firm whose Web site I absolutely love, called The Big House (www.bighouse.bc.ca) clues clients into their process. They look for answers to the following questions:

- What is the project meant to accomplish?
- How will we know that we have accomplished our goal?
- What is the main idea that must be communicated?
- If the consumer can only take one idea away from the Web site, what must it be?
- How does your product stack up against the competition?
- Tell us why your firm is unique, best, or first at.
- What marketing tools are most effective for your company? Among your competitors?
- What's in it for the customer? Prove it.
- What is your brand personality? Examples: Professional, exciting, irreverent, humorous, outrageous, etc.
- Sometimes referred to as the "target consumer," this group can be described by age, profession, geographic location, or attitude.
- How do we want our viewer to react? What would be the ideal response?
- What are the mandatory items that need to go into the site?
- Define a budget amount so a range of solutions can be considered. What is the roll-out sequence? When must the program be finished?
- Background detail, other important considerations, notes on the competition, potential problems, format restrictions, etc.

LAB 11.2 EXERCISES

11.2.1 WRITE A CREATIVE BRIEF

a) Interview a friend or relative who owns his or her own business. What are his or her answers to the The Big House's questions?

_____

_____

_____

_____

_____

_____

b) Write a creative brief for the prospective client described in 11.2.1a.

_____

_____

_____

_____

_____

_____

_____

_____

_____

_____

_____

_____

_____

_____

_____

_____

11.2.2   INVITE FEEDBACK

a) How would you best present a creative brief to the client?

b) How would you respond to the feedback given in such a way that moves the project forward?

_____

_____

_____

_____

_____

_____

11.2.3 IDENTIFY SITE LOOK AND FEEL

a) How would you best walk the client through identifying a look and feel for the Web site?

_____

_____

_____

_____

_____

_____

_____

_____

_____

_____

_____

_____

_____

b) How would you respond to the feedback given by the client in such a way that moves the project forward?

_____

_____

_____

_____

_____

_____

_____

_____

_____

_____

11.2.4 CREATE FINALIZED GRAPHICS

a) What project tasks need to be completed before finalized graphics can be created?

_____

_____

_____

_____

_____

_____

_____

_____

_____

_____

_____

_____

_____

_____

_____

_____

_____

_____

_____

_____

_____

_____

_____

b) What kinds of issues, inherent to Web technology, must the graphic designer consider when creating the finalized graphics?

_____

_____

_____

_____

_____

_____

_____

_____

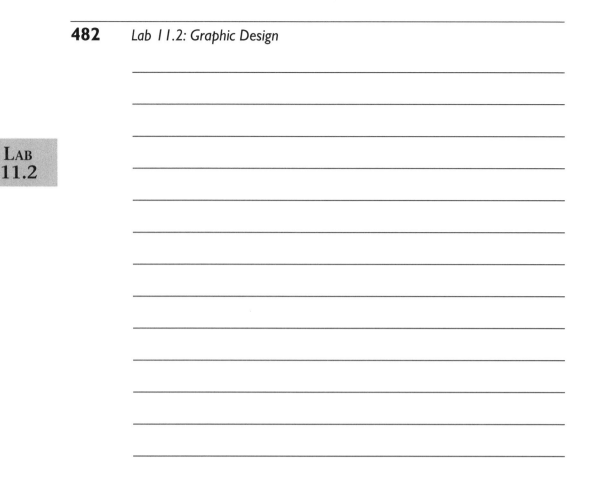

LAB 11.2 EXERCISE ANSWERS

This section gives you some suggested answers to the questions in Lab 11.2 with discussion related to those answers. Please post any alternative answers to these questions at the companion Web site for this book, located at http://www.phptr.com/phptrinteractive.

11.2.1 ANSWERS

a) Interview a friend or relative who owns his or her own business. What are his or her answers to The Big House's questions?

Answer: The project manager is almost always dealing with the principal management of the client company. This is a wonderful opportunity to learn about other industries and understand the challenges that they face so the Web site can overcome these issues. It's only through truly caring about communicating this company's message that the Web site will be successful. Therefore, it's a good idea to get to know the people running the company. The Web site begins to have a face on it as you become more invested in the client's success. If you are not becoming invested, then do the client a favor and refer them to another firm or to another project manager.

By asking these questions, you will be able to extract most of the primary and secondary marketing messages. You will also get to know your client better.

b) Write a creative brief for the prospective client described in 11.2.1a.

Answer: The following is a sample creative brief. This one is vague. You will want your brief to address the issues discussed and answer the questions posed by The Big House.

Acme Communications Creative Brief

Project Mission Statement

To establish Acme Communications.com, a telecommunications, Web design, and Internet access provider, as the total communications solution. This Web site is being used not only to attract consumers but also agents interested in selling Acme Communications' products and services, as well as investors. The Web site must generate excitement about the Acme Communications solution and establish credibility with all constituencies.

Site Overview

In order to make Acme Communications.com a fully functional informational and transaction-producing conduit, the following areas will need to be addressed:

- A snappy informational area used to attract new customers. This area must inspire confidence in Acme Communications' services, motivating users to manage and present their businesses in the same exciting way through Acme Communications.

- A simple, e-commerce enabled facility that will allow customers to view Acme Communications' catalog, sign up for goods and services on-line, and submit a credit application.

- A secure area that can be used by sales representatives to input and track customer orders.

- An informational area used to attract vendors and agents. Again, the credibility of Acme Communications' business objective must be emphasized, motivating individuals to adopt Acme Communications as a viable, profit-generating sales program.

Audience

Acme Communications should attract decision makers for businesses of all sizes. Specific products will be targeted to small, midsize, and large entities. Acme Communications should also attract job seekers in search of a credible product to agent. Also, Acme Communications should attract investors based on its innovative approach to the communications market.

Creative Development

Web Kahunas will begin addressing Acme Communications' need for an effective graphical presentation by developing three to five composites for review.

Acme Communications specializes in communications. Thus, a professional look and feel must be created, which might appeal to business owners who wish to establish their own cyberpresence. Communications and corporate environment images should be incorporated into the site. The following sites, 2323.com, 5656.com, and 7878.com, were mentioned as having a desirable look and feel.

Acme Communications has indicated a inclination toward a photo collage, which will incorporate communications and business images, along with subtle images like money, etc.

Web Kahunas will develop at least three composites and present them to Acme Communications by (insert date here).

After developing the overall look and feel of the site, Web Kahunas will consult with Acme Communications to develop secondary graphics that enforce the message in the various sections of the site. Graphics should be used judiciously, having a distinct purpose, as they slow page-loading time. All graphics will be saved in a low-resolution format.

Content Development

Web Kahunas will consult with Acme Communications as copy for all of the products and services will need to be supplied by (insert date here) in order to incorporate this information into the Acme Communications Web site. Other required information will include investor, initial promotion, and agent copy.

11.2.2 ANSWERS

a) How would you best present this material to the client?

Answer: A lot depends on the client's style. If you notice that this individual wastes a lot of time in face-to-face meetings, turning them into brainstorming meetings that never go anywhere, you might like to limit your exposure to these situations. However, if this isn't the case and you aren't working with the client remotely, nothing beats meeting with the client face to face. The client can see your facial expressions, leaving little room for misinterpretation. If you go to see the client, professionally dressed, well organized, and well prepared, it adds the appropriate credibility to the material that you are presenting. You have put effort into analysis. You should take the effort to present it correctly. Otherwise, it becomes too easy for the client to misinterpret the amount of effort you are putting into their project.

If it's possible, fax specifications, status reports, and other project-related materials to the client the day before the meeting, giving him or her time to review them for the meeting.

b) How would you respond to the feedback given in such a way that moves the project forward?

Answer: At this point, quite honestly, the firm has nothing invested in graphics or composites. You are only dealing with theory. Unless client feedback requires something that is technically impossible or is going to destroy the graphics budget, you should be open to incorporating any and all feedback from the client.

Remember, it is also important to stay on schedule. Emphasize that this is the time where the client should bring all creative issues to the fore. If this issue keeps getting revisited, it will delay production. So urge the client to organize himself or herself.

11.2.3 ANSWERS

a) How would you best walk the client through identifying a look and feel for the Web site?

Answer: By this point, you have already storyboarded and finalized the site hierarchy. Now the client needs to see something tangible. It's time to present the client with three to five composites that incorporate the creative objectives that have been communicated to the Web firm.

The composites are just ideas. You should not cut up the images so that they load quickly or incorporate JavaScript rollovers at this point. The client just needs to see how the page layout might look. He needs to get an idea for color and navigation. Once there are some composites to work from, the creative direction can be refined several times so that finalized graphics can be built on the last refined composite.

Again, sometimes clients get caught up in wanting to do everything at once. It's always a good idea to remind the client that different concepts can be implemented in the future. In fact, it's important for a high-profile Web site to present a fresh design every few months as part of an overall push to keep interest alive.

b) How would you respond to the feedback given by the client in such a way that moves the project forward?

Answer: The key to good composite work is following the client's instructions exactly but putting as little work into each one as possible. Many clients like to see a lot of dif-

ferent ideas so that they can have a good variety of things to choose from. From there, a graphic designer can refine according to the client's instructions. However, if a graphic designer puts ten hours into one composite and the client rejects it, the firm has lost between $300 and $400 in wages, a day in the graphic production schedule, a little client goodwill, and an opportunity to give the client more choices.

So when soliciting feedback from the client, think about whether the client has been given enough ideas, incorporating his instructions. If this is true, then it's fair to ask the client to work within the framework he has been given. Some clients might ask for comp after comp, until the project becomes unprofitable or the schedule is compromised. If the firm is running into an unreasonable situation, it must evaluate whether it can continue with the project.

Unfortunately, defining the creative really is the litmus test as to whether the client/firm fit is a good one.

11.2.4 ANSWERS

a) What project tasks need to be completed before finalized graphics can be created?

Answers: Make sure that the hierarchy is completely finalized. The graphic artist will need this to design the front page, navigation, and back page templates. Sometimes what seems like a simple change to a client can throw off the finalized design. So it's best to make sure that the hierarchy is completely finalized before the graphic designer(s) set to work on the last set of graphics.

Some graphic designers would like to see content so that they can design page layout around it. However, it is my experience that content is likely to have modifications several times during the process of the Web build. Sometimes the client needs time to pull it together. It makes me nervous to design around content until near the very end of the project. Then the project manager can implement plans for secondary graphics once the content freezes.

b) What kinds of issues, inherent to Web technology, must the graphic designer consider when creating the finalized graphics?

Answers: LOAD TIME! LOAD TIME! LOAD TIME!

Your graphic designer can make the most beautiful eye candy seen on a local Web browser. However, if it takes forever to download on a 28.8 connection, it's no good. The graphic designer needs to optimize to 256 colors at most in RGB (red, green, blue) format and cut the images up into small files. Even if there is a big image that resides on the front page, it can be cut up into several images and hung together in a table with zero cell spacing and zero cell padding.

Also, mission-critical graphical features that exhibit non-cross-platform multimedia have to have a cross-platform alternative. It doesn't matter how wonderfully the comet whoosh is timed to the comet flying across the screen if only 5% of the Web community can see it.

LAB 11.2 SELF-REVIEW QUESTIONS

In order to test your progress, you should be able to answer the following questions:

1) (True/False) A creative spec addresses the following issues:
   a) _____ Written copy for the Web site
   b) _____ Web site marketing messages
   c) _____ Client's concerns about moving the project forward

2) (True/False) If you are working remotely and cannot meet with the client face to face, which of the following is the best option for communicating with the client?
   a) _____ E-mail
   b) _____ Bulletin board on the project tracking site
   c) _____ Regularly scheduled conference calls

3) The following multimedia features are cross-platform:
   a) _____ Flash
   b) _____ Shockwave
   c) _____ Quick-time movies

L A B   1 1 . 3

WRITING AND EDITING

LAB OBJECTIVES:

After this lab, you will be able to

- Oversee Writing
- Oversee Editing
- Oversee Proofing

Writing for the Web on the top level is similar to writing ads for print, radio, or television. The point needs to be made quickly and pique interest on the top level; then additional longer content can reside on the site as the user drills down into deeper levels. There, the luxury exists to include longer, detailed content. In fact, by this point, the user is looking for it.

Users have a very short attention span. However, once they are hooked, the content has to answer their questions. This is where advertising a business on the Web allows for greater flexibility than radio, television, or print. Users can take their time going through site information, bookmark the site, and come back when they want to, without the limits of time or print space.

When planning content for a Web site, ask the client what they need the user to know in the first ten seconds, then the first thirty seconds. This is the information that should be on the front page. After that, keep in mind that content should be split up and edited in such a way that the user only has to scroll once to get to the end of a Web page. Ease of navigation increases the usefulness of a Web site. Therefore, content should be planned in such a way that it can be easily located and easily read. Too much scrolling causes vertigo.

In the beginning, before Web editors had spell checkers, a Web user could find many spelling and grammatical mistakes. One way to make your client look unprofessional is to allow a misspelling on their Web site. Nowadays, with better spell check tools, there's certainly less need for proofreading. However, the project manager should always have someone proof the site, before it goes live, just in case. After all, the spell checker on a Web editor is no smarter than the spell checker on a word processing program—see and sea can both pass!

Let's take a look at how we can best manage embedding written content into the Web site.

LAB 11.3 EXERCISES

11.3.1 OVERSEE WRITING

a) Who should write content for the Web site?

_____

_____

_____

_____

_____

_____

_____

_____

_____

_____

_____

_____

**LAB
11.3**

_____

_____

_____

_____

_____

_____

_____

_____

_____

_____

_____

_____

b) What is meant by a "content freeze"? Why would you implement it?

_____

_____

_____

_____

_____

_____

_____

_____

_____

_____

_____

_____

_____

_____

_____

_____

_____

_____

_____

_____

_____

11.3.2 OVERSEE EDITING

a) Which sites might you use as style guides for writing on the Web?

_____

_____

_____

_____

_____

**LAB
11.3**

_____

_____

_____

_____

_____

_____

_____

_____

_____

_____

_____

_____

_____

_____

_____

_____

_____

_____

_____

b) Name two writing tips that are mentioned in the style guides that have not been addressed in this lab.

_____

_____

_____

_____

_____

_____

_____

_____

_____

_____

_____

_____

_____

_____

_____

_____

_____

_____

_____

_____

11.3.3 OVERSEE PROOFING

a) Which skill sets might come in handy for a Web site proofer?

_____

_____

_____

b) Which member of the firm might you ask to proof the Web site?

_____

_____

_____

_____

_____

_____

_____

_____

_____

_____

_____

_____

_____

_____

_____

_____

_____

_____

_____

_____

_____

LAB 11.3 EXERCISE ANSWERS

This section gives you some suggested answers to the questions in Lab 11.3 with discussion related to those answers. Please post any alternative answers to these questions at the companion Web site for this book, located at http://www.phptr.com/phptrinteractive.

11.3.1 ANSWERS

a) Who should write content for the Web site?

Answer: One of the difficulties in doing graphic design for a client is that one has to try to interpret a vision that the client has in mind and translate it to the screen. Clients are generally not going to supply the Web firm with Web-ready graphics and a template for the Web site. A lot of money can be spent in trying to define this vision.

In the case of written copy, though, it's best to depend on the client for this deliverable. The client can best produce the messages that are needed to convey in the Web site. The Web firm can consult regarding the best way to communicate these messages.

I'm always a little leery of a contract in which the client does not want to donate the time necessary to write the content, with some editing help from the Web firm.

b) What is meant by a "content freeze"? Why would you implement it?

Answer: A content freeze is a deadline when all written copy must be finalized. A project manger needs to implement this as the copy is going to the HTML programmers for embedding into the Web site. If the client continues to change copy too many times after text is embedded into the Web site, it becomes expensive to change because the change involves an HTML programmer.

11.3.2 ANSWERS

a) Which sites might you use as style guides for writing on the Web?

Answer:

Sun Microsystems: Writing on the Web

`http://www.sun.com/980713/webwriting/`

W3C Style Guide for Online Hypertext

`http://www.w3.org/Provider/Style/Overview.html`

The Web Developer's Virtual Library: Writing for the Web

`http://wdvl.com/Internet/Writing/`

There are many others, but these links are a great place to start.

**LAB
11.3**

b) Name two writing tips that are mentioned in the style guides but have not been addressed in this Lab.

Answer: Jakob Nielson, in his Alertbox article located at http://www.useit.com/alertbox/9710a.html, identifies the following points:

Text needs to be scannable. Users don't read. They scan. Therefore, Web sites should have

- *Highlighted keywords.*
- *Meaningful subheadings to break up ideas.*
- *Bulleted lists, as opposed to paragraphs, which go on and on.*
- *Paragraphs that deal only with one idea.*
- *An inverted pyramid style, giving the conclusion first.*
- *Credibility shown through the use of links to other Web sites that substantiate the information presented.*
- *Straight information. Do not use slick or boastful marketing. The Web is low key.*

11.3.3 ANSWERS

a) Which skill sets might come in handy for a Web site proofer?

Answer:

- *Thorough understanding of how to use the Web*
- *Excellent command of written language*
- *Strict attention to detail*
- *No previous involvement in the production of the Web site*
- *Ability to work quickly, as proofing typically takes place near the end of the production schedule, and often the deadline is looming*

b) Which member of the firm might you ask to proof the Web site?

Answer: We have a legal secretary on staff who is accustomed to proofing legal documents. She usually does not participate in any of the production phases involved with the Web site. Rather, she handles more of the administrative functions of the firm. Because she can look at a Web site with a fresh perspective and will see things that those of us who have been looking at it every day can become blind to, she is able to identify problems very quickly.

LAB 11.3 SELF-REVIEW QUESTIONS

In order to test your progress, you should be able to answer the following questions:

1)   (True/False) The following writing techniques can work well on the Web:
   a) _____ Exciting advertising and promotional messages
   b) _____ Friendly, casual tone
   c) _____ Use of headlines

2)   (True/False) The Web firm should involve itself in
   a) _____ Writing content
   b) _____ Editing content
   c) _____ Proofing content

C H A P T E R   1 1

TEST YOUR THINKING

The projects in this section use the skills you've acquired in this chapter. The answers to these projects are available to instructors only through a Prentice Hall sales representative and are intended to be used in classroom discussion and assessment.

1) If your client does need help writing the Web site, how should your firm respond?

2) How might you respond to a client who is constantly changing text and is unaware of the havoc this is causing for the production team?

C H A P T E R   1 2

TECHNICAL DEVELOPMENT

 "A pioneer is the guy lying in the mud with an arrow in his back."

—Unknown

CHAPTER OBJECTIVES:

In this chapter, you will learn about

✔ Hardware/Software Requirements   Page 504
✔ Technical Brief   Page 522
✔ Programming and Testing   Page 542

You might feel that the quote chosen for this chapter seems a bit odd, given that many Web developers see themselves on the cutting edge of technology. E-commerce is no longer a sexy buzzword but is rather a conduit for social and economic change. As a result, more people sign up for dial-up accounts to buy their groceries and do their banking every day. These users are investing in high-speed modems and installing the latest browsers, giving Web developers more flexibility to build applications using newer multimedia capabilities.

However, three years ago, how many users would have easy access to sites running Flash and Shockwave applications? Not many. Shockwave required the user to visit the Macromedia site to obtain a plug-in for the browser. How many people could one realistically expect to reach using this application? If there's an interruption in the distribution of said message, most likely the message isn't going to be delivered to anyone but the most determined visitor.

Nowadays, more Web sites are coded using Flash, Shockwave, Real Audio, and Real Video capabilities. All of these tools can be used to send a message to a large audience, because the audience has come up to speed. The latest Microsoft and Netscape browsers intrinsically support many of these newer tools without requiring the user to get a plug-in.

Web developers, who expected to deliver their clients' messages to the world at large using one of the aforementioned tools in 1996, without providing an easy alternative distribution channel, were truly pioneers.

I don't have to make the first wave. I'd rather make it to Oregon. Most of the time, I'm on a limited budget and don't have too many oxen to lose along the way. I have always preferred to take my time reading the map, arriving later, and thus stepping over the bodies in the mud.

While e-commerce is not news to many Web developers, it is only recently that Web firms are getting called to deliver these types of Web sites on a highly consistent basis. My firm had the capability two years ago to build e-commerce Web sites, but I often wondered why we didn't have more requests to build them. Now, just about every Web site that we contract is e-commerce enabled. Yes, the technology was sound and in place two years ago, but the premise had not reached the public imagination as a viable business plan until recently. Sometimes it isn't even a matter of whether the public is technically ready for an idea but whether it is psychologically ready.

A realistic example may be Disabilitynews.net. When Disabilitynews.net was first on the drawing board, the project manager had to assess exactly who his audience might be. The Web site needed to be viewable by health care professionals, families, and people with disabilities.

Disabilitynews.net wanted to provide an ability to purchase journal articles and related books through its Web site. A few years ago, there might not have been enough families or physicians online to support such a specialized e-commerce endeavor. Now demographics show that there would be enough audience members to support Disabilitynews.net's e-commerce effort.

Using another example from Disabilitynews.net, we determined that to serve the visually disabled audience, frames could not be used. The most common Web browser tool used by vision-impaired people reads the text aloud to the user. However, it could not yet deal with frames effectively, and all of the images had to have alternative tags, so that the browser could read a description from any pictures used in the Web site. All of this may not seem like a big deal, but if a vision-impaired user came upon Disabilitynews.net and is not accommodated, this experience would directly impact upon the message Disabilitynews.net wishes to convey. Its main goal of being an informational clearinghouse and community-building mechanism for people with disabilities, their families, and health care providers would not be met. It would have already locked one constituency out of the community. A little thoughtful planning while putting together a technical brief avoids this.

In the excitement of making a Web site and working with new media, it is easy for people's expectations to get off track. The project manager must work with the client company to educate them about making sound choices for the technology at hand rather than developing fancy bells and whistles, which bog the message down because of their inability to deliver en masse. In the case of Disabilitynews.net, the use of a fairly common Web site device—frames—would undermine its message. The project manager was able to foresee this before it became a problem.

As developers, we can envision the day when we can punch in the name of an old 1960s television series, name the exact episode that we want to view, and have that show delivered right to our computer screen on demand. Right now, only video clips lasting a minute or two are working well over the Web. Any clip longer than that requires a cable modem, T1, ISDN, or DSL connection to work efficiently. In magazines and on television, mention is made of Internet teleconferencing as though it's a widespread phenomenon. Still, how many users actually have the cameras hooked up to their computers? These are all applications of the Web that seem viable today, but are we really there yet? In most cases, no.

The smart Web firm must underpromise and overdeliver, making the best use of tried and true methods to successfully develop a client company's Web vision.

LAB   12.1

HARDWARE/SOFTWARE REQUIREMENTS

> ## LAB OBJECTIVES:
>
> After this lab, you will be able to
>
> * Identify Server Requirements
> * Identify Connection Requirements
> * Identify Operating System
> * Identify Middleware Requirements
> * Identify User Requirements

I often open my Web Project Management class at Merrimack College in North Andover, Massachusetts, with two statements. The first statement you are already familiar with. It opens Chapter 8 of this book, and I hung it on the wall of my dorm room when I was a young engineering student: "The road is not always to the swift, but to those who keep on running." The other is purely personal reflection:

"I have made mistakes. I am not proud. I will share. However, I will disavow any knowledge of said mistakes, you as my student, and my involvement at Merrimack College, should anything be discussed beyond the walls of this room. This presentation will self-destruct in ten seconds."

Like most people, I probably have learned more from my mistakes than my successes. One of my more important nonsuccessful experiences involved a database that my company built for a large computer distributor in our area. I was very anxious to impress my new clients with a highly functional Web site. So the software architecture of this particular site flowed freely, and I enthusiastically coded SQL statements in my sleep. I didn't worry too much about my coding hours as I was interested in adding this to a list of portfolio sites for my company. However, as much as I was solid with the software requirements, I didn't spend enough time finding out about a more foreign concept called the "RAID System." (RAID stands for redundant array of independent disks.)

My education began one spring morning when I tried to connect to the site, and I kept getting errors. When I called the server administrator, I was told that the hard drive on the server had crashed. The machine was being worked on. However, all of the sites on that server were down. I accepted that. After all, computers went down—end of story. However, when the down time stretched into the afternoon and into the next day, and my clients were wondering where their Web site was, it was a panic!

When my associate and I had gone in to pitch the Web site, we had suggested hosting the site off site, even though our clients built servers and had them readily available to use to host a site in house. I explained that while subcontracting on another Web site, I had previous experience coding on a particular server. It was all set up with the software configuration that I wanted and would make for rapid deployment of the Web site. My clients graciously went along with me.

When the server hiccuped, I found out more than I ever wanted to know about server hardware configurations, RAID systems, and connectivity.

For my clients, this was a big issue. After all, they built and sold servers. Their clients would find it odd that their Web site was *ever* down, slow, or not functioning perfectly. It would be a poor reflection upon them. They had gone along with my idea of hosting it outside, but I could tell that this option was not their first choice.

Apparently, my server choice did not have a RAID system in place. Thus, when the hard drive crashed, the server administrators could not recover quickly, reducing the amount of necessary, if any, down time.

As a programmer, I was crushed that my hard work was not visible for my clients to see. As a project manager, I kicked myself hard. Why didn't I know about this? Already too many hours to count were invested in this Web site, hours that could not be billed, and, what was much more upsetting, I let an important client down. They were right to insist that the Web site not remain on this server. However, it would mean that the client would have to assume the burden of building, configuring, and co-locating a box that could handle the code that I had already developed. I figured that I was history with them.

Luckily, the people involved at the client side were extremely forgiving. They set up their own box, had the operating system and middleware configured, and co-located it with an ISP. I made the modifications necessary to allow the UNIX-based database to run on the new server, gratis, and thanked heaven that I had run into nice people. They remain good clients to this day, and I happen to buy all of my computers from them— not because they're clients, but because in dealing with them, I know that they'll stand behind what they sell.

This is a dark project management story with a silver lining. If I make a mistake, I do try to "keep on running," as the saying goes, keep at the project until it finishes successfully. However, a project manager can never expect that a client is going to help solve any technical difficulty. Thus, if one's expertise is in coding, one must come up to speed quickly in understanding the hardware side and vice versa. One hinges tightly upon the other, as I found out.

LAB 12.1 EXERCISES

12.1.1 IDENTIFY SERVER REQUIREMENTS

a) Define a RAID system. What are the benefits of having such a system in place on a server?

_____

_____

_____

_____

_____

_____

_____

_____

b) Determine the hardware configuration for an up-to-date robust server.

_____

_____

_____

_____

_____

_____

_____

_____

_____

_____

_____

_____

_____

_____

_____

_____

_____

_____

_____

_____

12.1.2   *IDENTIFY CONNECTIVITY REQUIREMENTS*

a) What is referred to as a "pipeline" or "pipe" to the Internet? Give examples of several acceptable pipeline configurations.

_____

_____

_____

_____

_____

_____

_____

_____

_____

_____

_____

_____

_____

_____

_____

_____

_____

_____

_____

b) Describe how connectivity redundancy effects server performance.

12.1.3 IDENTIFY OPERATING SYSTEM

a) You are building an online store. Describe the benefits of using an NT platform as a foundation for development.

_____

_____

_____

_____

_____

_____

b) As in 12.1.3a, describe the benefits of using a UNIX platform to build an online store.

_____

_____

_____

_____

_____

_____

_____

_____

_____

_____

_____

_____

_____

_____

12.1.4   IDENTIFY MIDDLEWARE REQUIREMENTS

a) Middleware is a software application that provides a coding environment for developing databases and online stores. Give several examples of NT-based online store middleware and its capabilities.

_____

_____

_____

_____

_____

_____

_____

_____

_____

_____

_____

_____

_____

_____

_____

_____

_____

_____

b) Give several examples of UNIX-based middleware and how it could be used in the development of an online store.

12.1.5 IDENTIFY USER REQUIREMENTS

a) You are developing an online store that company employees will access to purchase t-shirts, bags, and other promotional items with the company logo on it. Employees will access this Web site through the company intranet. How will this impact upon programming tools used to deliver content?

**LAB
12.1**

_____

_____

_____

_____

_____

_____

_____

b) What kinds of user requirements might impact upon the development of a law firm's static brochureware Web site?

_____

_____

_____

_____

_____

_____

_____

_____

_____

_____

_____

_____

_____

LAB 12.1 EXERCISE ANSWERS

This section gives you some suggested answers to the questions in Lab 12.1 with discussion related to those answers. Please post any alternative answers to these questions at the companion Web site for this book, located at http://www.phptr.com/phptrinteractive.

12.1.1 ANSWERS

a) Define a RAID system. What are the benefits of having such a system in place on a server?

Answer: The following information was found at PC Webopaedia—http://webopedia .internet.com—a super resource providing explanations for current technical terms.

A server's ability to deal with a software or hardware crash is called "fault tolerance." A RAID (redundant array of independent disks) System is one mechanism used to improve fault tolerance. RAID systems are designed to provide the following levels of protection:

Level 0: Data striping (blocks of each file are spread out across multiple disks) but no redundancy. This improves server performance, but doesn't enhance fault tolerance.

Level 1: Provides disk mirroring, which is the process by which two disks are kept up to date. Should the primary disk crash, the back up disk can be instantly activated, thus insuring there will be no interruption of service.

Level 3: Provides the same level of protection as Level 0 but reserves a disk for error correction data.

Level 5: Data striping at the byte level and stripe error correction information. Again, this provides better server performance and some level of fault tolerance.

When launching an online store and/or database with a RAID-enabled server, I would most prefer a server using RAID Level 1.

There are other more expensive options, such as server mirroring. Unlike RAID Level 1, where disks are mirrored, with server mirroring the entire server is duplicated by a back-up server, ready to come online should the primary one fail.

b) Determine the hardware configuration for an up-to-date robust Web server.

Answer: My main concerns would center around server processor speed, hard drive capacity, and RAM (random access memory).

As far as the hard drive goes, the project manager must ascertain that the server isn't running middleware, like SQL server, and hosting too many Web sites. This is going to slow the server down, just as if one has too many applications running on a PC. The requirements are going to vary from server to server. The server's hard drive compatibility for your Web site is in direct ratio to how it's being used. The question here is, "What else is on it?" Then make up your mind as to whether the server is overburdened.

Most current Web servers are running Dual Pentium 400-MHz processors or above. Recently, while looking into the purchase of an NT box to stage Web sites on, I received a specification that included Dual Pentium III 450-MHz processors. This is now pretty standard among new equipment. Of course, those of us with several old PCs in the basement know that these numbers are constantly changing.

Lack of RAM definitely can slow a server down, especially if it is running memory-heavy middleware. 512 MB or above can help to facilitate a robust database environment.

You must weigh the type of Web site being staged on a server, the number of hits that site may receive, and the weight of the graphics. Then you can evaluate whether the site needs to reside with a more robust host or can be uploaded without too much worry on just about any reasonable platform.

12.1.2 ANSWERS

a) What is referred to as a "pipeline" or "pipe" to the Internet? Give examples of several acceptable pipeline configurations.

Answer: The terms "pipe" or "pipeline" are usually used to refer to a server's connection to an Internet backbone provider, like UUNet or MCI.

A T1 line transfers data at a rate of 1554 Kbps, and a T3 line will move data at 44.7 Mbps.

Most ISP servers are connected to the Internet using a combination of T1 and T3 lines, as well as one or more Internet backbone providers. The reason behind this is redundancy. If one T1 line becomes inoperable or one backbone service provider goes down, there is another connection that can be used to route traffic. As a developer, depending on the size of the ISP, I would at least want to see two TI lines used to connect to two different Internet backbone providers.

Many medium-sized ISPs use two T3s, a TI, and several backbone providers.

b) Describe how connection redundancy can effect server performance.

Answer: If an ISP's pipeline includes only one TI or T3 line out to one backbone provider, should anything go wrong either with the line or the backbone provider, the ISP's server will be unable to process requests. Therefore, redundancy is key. Depending on the size of the ISP, the system administrator should determine whether the current server connectivity can handle all of the traffic effectively, should one component fail. The best configuration, albeit not the least expensive option, would include TI or T3 connections, preferably through several different systems (e.g., Bell Atlantic or Sprint), going to several different Internet backbone providers. This would better the chances of keeping any connectivity problems transparent to the user.

12.1.3 ANSWERS

a) You are building an online store. Describe the benefits of using an NT platform as a foundation for development.

Answer: If the client isn't too choosy about customization, the NT platform, using Microsoft programming wizards, provides a good foundation for rapid application development. The client can be trained to update his or her site using products like Microsoft Front Page and, if the site has been built using Microsoft Site Server Commerce Edition, has the ability to go in and change inventory on the fly. The development costs associated with an online store such as this, barring any huge customization of how the programming code functions, usually are lower when compared to developing a similar site using the UNIX platform.

b) As in 12.1.3a, describe the benefits of using a UNIX platform to build an online store.

Answer: UNIX allows developers direct access to code from the ground up. In an NT environment, I always feel that I'm programming through a veil, that I'm unable to access directly how programming code will function on the server. If you have ever built Web sites in Front Page versus writing straight HTML in a Web editor, you will understand what I mean. Using a straight Web editor, the developer can control exactly how the page will look, whereas Front Page sometimes controls the developer.

Therefore, after having used both platforms, I would much rather use a UNIX platform if the client requirements are very strict and differ substantially from what can be accomplished using the wizards in the Microsoft products.

Also, UNIX provides a more secure environment, which is especially important as a foundation for an online store. Unfortunately, there are still security glitches in even the most updated version of NT. Therefore, the client must weigh functionality versus flexibility versus security.

12.1.4 ANSWERS

a) Middleware is a software application that provides a coding environment for developing databases and online stores. Give several examples of NT-based online store middleware and its capabilities.

Answer: Middleware products used in the development of online stores on the NT platform include Microsoft Site Server Commerce Edition, SQL Server, and Oracle.

b) Give several examples of UNIX-based middleware and how it could be used in the development of an online store.

Answer: MySQL and Oracle can be used as database middleware for UNIX-based online stores. Granted, these middleware products do not support wizardlike rapid application development. Therefore, the use of them on UNIX is more labor intensive.

12.1.5 ANSWERS

a) You are developing an online store that company employees will access to purchase t-shirts, bags, and other promotional items with the company logo on it. Employees will access this Web site through the company intranet. How will this impact upon programming tools used to deliver content?

Answer: Developing applications on an intranet allows for a stable user environment. Most users will be accessing the intranet using similar software and hardware configurations. Thus, all the developer needs to determine is how the company's machines are configured and then build the application in such a way that it is cross-platform for those users.

For a Web site that is accessible to the public, a developer needs to build it in such a way that all browsers and connection speeds can be accomodated. Developing on an intranet does not require this type of cross-platform accessibility.

b) What kinds of user requirements might impact upon the development of a law firm's static brochureware Web site?

Answer: I would consider whether the lawyer dealt in personal injury law. If the firm did provide these types of services, the Web site should be accessible by visually impaired users. If the rest of the pages are static, our only concern would be providing alternate descriptions for the images and not using frames on the Web site.

LAB 12.1 SELF-REVIEW QUESTIONS

In order to test your progress, you should be able to answer the following questions:

1) (True/False) Developers should consider the following issues when deciding where to host a web site.
   a) _____ The hosting cost is competitive with other Web hosting companies offering the same services.
   b) _____ The Web hosting company is running the middleware and operating system necessary to fulfill the technical requirements of the contract.
   c) _____ The hosting company has redundant connections to the Internet.

2) (True/False) Client budget would affect the following:
   a) _____ Choice of operating system
   b) _____ Choice of server hardware configuration
   c) _____ Programming flexibility

LAB 12.2

TECHNICAL BRIEF

> ## LAB OBJECTIVES:
>
> After this lab, you will be able to:
>
> *   Write Programming Plan
> *   Write Test Plan
> *   Invite Client Feedback

A programming plan is an internal document used by the project team, based upon the described functionality in the project specification. One might not wish to confuse the client with highly detailed references to database middleware in the project specification, but these facts are important to all of the programmers working on the Web site. A programming plan can be drafted as an internal tool to fill the gaps between the project specification, which must be signed off and understood by the client, and the information necessary to convey to the programmers. For example, it may be necessary that the ASP programmers not use cookies to facilitate the operation of an online store because of incompatibility with earlier forms of Netscape browsers. The client needs to know that the Web site will be cross-platform; however, discussion of "cookies" may mean nothing to them besides confusion.

On another front, the programming plan is important because if any of the work has been subcontracted and does not meet the requirements, this is the document to which the contracting Web firm can refer, should the subcontractor be called upon to make corrections.

A testing plan is a formalized document that discusses the testing of the functionality of the Web site. People testing a Web site are charged with two objectives:

- Try to break it by using unexpected input, making sure that all error messages work as they should.
- Make sure that the site functions as expected.

So, when testing a search page that has the ability to search on several different parameters or only one, using an AND, LIKE, or OR criteria, some test criteria may be to test using numbers or the first letter of a matching word. It's best to use people who have not worked on the site and have very little knowledge of the way it is "supposed" to work. Otherwise, it's very easy to overlook problems due to a programmer's bias. It is similar to a writer trying to edit his or her own work. One cannot see the forest for the trees. The main programmers are often too close to the situation to test the site with a fresh perspective.

Once in a great while, the most difficult part of the programming process is inviting client feedback. This is where the project meets the cold light of day. As in the creative side, it is so important that the technical team work with the client to define "Done." No project can be run successfully without an end point in sight, with specific requirements to be fulfilled.

It's funny, because as I'm writing this book, I've run into several project management nightmares. I wish I could present case studies of circumstances that have happened to other people, but at least I have the ability to put these experiences into perspective and include my postproject nightmare reflections here.

Most of the problems that I run into have a very similar theme. The client's expectation does not match the contracting firm's view. In 90% of these cases, with a little discussion and brainstorming, both parties can come to a mutual agreement. The Web firm may need to give a little and the client may need to adjust a little. In 10% of these cases, the rejection of work does not have much to do with the work itself. The requirements have been met, everything is in place, but perhaps as a result of internal issues with the client, like inability to pay the final bill, they keep rejecting the work.

We found this to be true recently when a client company kept rejecting the programming end of the Web site, saying that there were problems every time we approached them for the final payment. When we notified them that the programming was completed, we never received negative feedback; it was only when we kept trying to present them with the final bill that all of a sudden there was a huge laundry list.

Rejection number one came when the client wanted pieces of their on-line store done with drop-down selections instead of the links that we provided. I considered that perhaps this was a stall tactic, but in thinking it over, I felt the best way to handle the situation was to charge the employee representing the client with "Defining Done." He sounded very clear, and he assured me that drop-down selections would finish the project. I wondered if somehow there had been a miscommunication, and in good faith, I decided to absorb the change, which was significant, costing another $1000 in programming hours. However, once this functionality was completed, we notified the client of completion, never heard from them, and then when the check was due, they complained that they didn't like how the drop-downs looked. In fact, not only did they not like how the drop-downs looked, but they had a lot of other issues with the site that had not been previously brought to our attention.

At this point, I was very angry, because I felt that the client was being uncooperative. As a Web firm owner/project manager, it's easy to become emotional because you know how nonproductive and costly this behavior can be. To make matters worse, this scenario was coming on the heels of another much smaller consulting project, in which the firm had been quite rudely stiffed. Just recently, a client had contracted for a day's consulting time and some graphic work. He had signed a contract and knew how much it would cost. Then, after he received consulting and development services, he told me that my time shouldn't be worth that much. My associates and I laughed about it afterward, knowing that he would certainly find out how mistaken he was with regard to Internet consulting/Web site development pricing. However, the levity at his expense did not take the sting out of his actions. Needless to say, when this next client payment issue arose so quickly on a much bigger account, I did not have a great deal of patience for it. Still, I was determined to keep a cool head. If I was upset and could not interface well with the client at certain points, I would defer to colleagues, who were not as emotionally invested.

We had completed all of the requirements, had documentation to back up all of our conversations with this company, and these folks just would not pay us, saying once again that they required changes. I backed off, saying that we would accept three-quarters of the final payment, the other one-quarter due upon completing a list of small cosmetic changes. However, I told the client representative that we would not even look at the punch list until this partial payment was received because we felt that there had been a breach of contract. Our contract requires that a client review creative and technical Web site initiatives completed on their behalf and provide feedback on a timely basis. This had not been happening to my satisfaction.

It took an entire day to reach this company. We walked them through the Web site and waded through a bevy of excuses as to why they couldn't talk to us. We listened to how the contact people had been out of the office and had not received our messages. As we continually barraged them with phone calls, their resolve began to weaken. At 4:45 P.M., I got the truth. The reason why we weren't being paid didn't have anything to do with us at all. The owner was wanted for violating a restraining order taken out against him by an old girlfriend. He was avoiding arrest on that particular day. However, these people representing him would have had us doing cartwheels under the guise that our work was not acceptable. I maintained my stance that we had asked them to define "Done" and we had delivered. Then I informed them that Web site would be coming down from the staging server by 5:00 P.M. that evening. They would be charged a $500 reimplementation fee should they want to put it back up, and if I still didn't receive payment within five business days, I would be filing a lawsuit against them for the outstanding balance. The young secretary finally cracked and told me what was going on.

Should it have gone that far? Absolutely not. There had been plenty of signs, which would have motivated a savvy project manager to cut losses and exit the project before any additional resources were used.

First, the client had shown all the signs of someone that would be difficult to work with. He seemed agitated in the first meeting and unable to focus. His broad statements that he could "get us so much business" put me off right away. Whenever anyone says this to me, it always raises a red flag. Usually they want us to cut them a deal, and I know, from experience, that this type of person will rarely deliver any viable business to our firm. It's a smoke screen. However, I felt the site seemed very straightforward, and we would be interacting with his employees, who seemed to be much more focused.

Next, it was sticky getting the deposit money from him. This is always an important sign. If someone graciously and promptly writes the first check, chances are they won't be terribly difficult about the last one. We had to keep after him for a week to get the deposit money to us.

Then, when we showed him the first iteration of the Web site, he never provided feedback. When we later asked for payment, he was so irrational on the phone that he let one of his employees explain why his boss was unsatisfied.

I was inclined to cut my losses and exit at this point. However, we did not have a formal project spec. He had shown us a Web site that he wanted his new site to function like, and I felt the requirements were clear. The client was in an extreme hurry to get a new site up and running as he felt that his old one was costing him money. I felt that he would be motivated to get the new site live and not hinder the process in any way. In fact, in the beginning of the project, his secretary called us daily, pressuring us to hurry. Therefore, we skipped some of the important documentation steps.

Given the fact that we did not have a formal project spec, which the client had signed off on, I felt obliged to try to fix any discrepancies that were identified in this conversation, although not without forcing the client to define "Done." When his definition still did not constitute "Done," I felt that something was definitely fishy.

Did I initially break every project management rule in this book? Yes. I didn't screen the client. I didn't prepare formalized specifications for the client to sign off on. Therefore, I got too far into the project too quickly, with too many expenses to back out easily. I allowed myself to be pressured and led. Having had plenty of experience with identifying and understanding client side project warning signs, I reacted to none of them.

I must say that 95% of our clients are delightful to deal with. I doubt there is a criminal record among them, and most behave with the utmost professionalism. We are extremely lucky in this sense. However, any business has to insulate itself against clients who are experiencing internal difficulties and expect the firm to bear the burden.

If this client had only been up front and had told us of their need to exit or postpone the project, we would have respectfully facilitated this eventuality. However, I felt that the client took an aggressive and damaging stance, like the bully in the playground, pushing us down before we could pick up the ball and run with it.

Did I learn from this experience? Absolutely. I learned that my business instincts could be trusted more often than not. Sometimes we just don't trust our inner voice. We try to tell ourselves that it isn't logical to base actions on "a bad feeling." I also changed our payment terms from half the project estimate due at contract signing and the other half due upon completion to half the project estimate due at contract signing and half due when the project is halfway complete. Most important, I set up a more structured project process. From that point on, every client would receive a client packet in the first two weeks of a project, before anyone touched a keyboard. No exceptions, no matter how much of a hurry they were in. Client packets include the following:

- *Work order.* An initial inventory of programming services requested, the estimated delivery date, and the terms of payment.
- *Programming services agreement.* The legal contract between the Web firm and the client company.

- *Schedule.* A detailed schedule of creative and technical deliverables. Clients should look to this schedule to determine when client review will be required.
- *Approval letters.* Client approval is required for all phases of project development. The following client signoffs are requested before the firm moves to the next phase of project development:

  1. *Receipt of project packet*—to acknowledge receipt and review of the client packet.
  2. *Project specification and site hierarchy approval*—to acknowledge approval of detailed project requirements as defined by the project specification and site hierarchy.
  3. *Composite approval*—to acknowledge which of three creative directions the client wishes to pursue, with any appropriate modifications, as defined in the project specification.
  4. *Graphic design approval*—to acknowledge approval of finalized graphic design.
  5. *Static page approval*—to acknowledge approval of static Web pages (Web pages that do not provide dynamic content).
  6. *Dynamic functionality approval*—to acknowledge approval of program functionality as defined in the project specification.
  7. *Receipt of training*—to acknowledge receipt of on-site training hours as defined in the project specification.

- *Stamped envelopes.* Provided for mailing approvals. However, in order facilitate rapid project deployment, clients can fax approvals, make copies for themselves, and mail the originals to the Web firm.
- *Acknowledgment of domain name and hosting arrangement.* Client will arrange for hosting and domain name acquisition at the beginning of the Web site project. This form supplies hosting company information, user name and password selection, domain name (or IP address), and the name of a technical contact at the hosting company. This arrangement must be completed

after the work order is signed and this acknowledgment forwarded to my company, Surf's Up Web Development, Inc.

- *Client questionnaire.* Copy of questionnaire completed previously before or during initial client interview.

- *Site hierarchy.* A flow chart of the proposed Web site architecture, as currently understood by the Web firm. The client is asked to review this hierarchy carefully, as graphics will be built based upon this design.

- *Project specification.* The project "bible," as the Web firm currently understands the client requirements. The client is asked to review this specification very carefully, as it is used as the foundation on which the Web site will be built.

- *List of client deliverables.* This is a list of deliverables (i.e., written copy for static Web pages, photos, etc.) that are needed from the client before the Web site goes into the graphic design or static Web page build phase.

We also now formally describe to the client, in writing, what our production process is, and we formalize client approvals before moving to the next phase. Therefore, long after graphic design is complete and the firm is working on the programming, graphic design cannot be revisited without compensation. We send the client the following letter:

When considering the production process used to build your Web site, please review the following phased approach: Client action items are in **bold** text.

Analysis

Request for quote submitted to Surf's Up Web development

Client questionnaire and interview completed with client company

Surf's Up project team reviews RFQ for viability and drafts a bid

Bid accepted by client company and contracts signed

First half of project estimate now due

Surf's Up drafts a detailed project specification and site hierarchy

Project packet is sent for review to client company

Receipt due

Client arranges for hosting, registers domain name, and applies for Verisign/merchant accounts (if the Web site is e-commerce enabled)

Verification of hosting/domain name now due

Client provides feedback on project specification and site hierarchy. New documents, reflecting any feedback, are drafted by Surf's Up and approved by the client company

Review and approval due

Design

Three graphic composites are drafted by Surf's Up and submitted to the client company for review.

Client picks one composite and provides feedback for any modifications.

Review and approval due

Web site graphic design is completed

Client reviews graphics, provides any feedback for modifications, and finalized graphics are built by Surf's Up and approved by client company.

Review and approval due

Last half of project estimate now due

Production

All deliverables on client deliverable list are now due

Static Web pages (pages that are not interactive) are completed, embedding client text and any secondary graphics

Client reviews these pages, provides any feedback for modifications, and finalized static Web pages built by Surf's Up and approved by client company

Review and approval due

Dynamic content (i.e., database and e-commerce driven Web pages) are completed

Client reviews this functionality and provides feedback for modifications. Finalized dynamic content is built by Surf's Up and approved by client company

Review and approval due

Implementation

Web site is tested and proofread by Surf's Up

Training hours are provided, as defined in the project specification, to the client company

Receipt due

Web site is set live and submitted to seven major search engines

LAB 12.2 EXERCISES

12.2.1 WRITE PROGRAMMING PLAN

a) Write a programming plan for the project you used in 10.3.2b.

_____

_____

_____

_____

_____

_____

_____

_____

_____

_____

_____

_____

_____

_____

_____

_____

_____

_____

_____

_____

_____

_____

_____

_____

_____

_____

_____

b) What kinds of issues did you address in the programming plan that you did not mention in the project specification?

_____

_____

_____

_____

_____

_____

_____

_____

_____

LAB 12.2

12.2.2 WRITE TEST PLAN

a) Write a test plan for the project used in 12.2.1.

_____

_____

_____

_____

_____

_____

_____

_____

_____

_____

_____

_____

_____

_____

_____

b) What kinds of errors would you hope this testing plan might identify?

_____

_____

_____

_____

_____

_____

_____

_____

_____

_____

_____

_____

_____

_____

_____

_____

_____

_____

_____

_____

_____

12.2.3 INVITE CLIENT FEEDBACK

a) Discuss how you would walk a client through a Web site, demonstrating the functionality.

_____

_____

_____

_____

_____

_____

_____

_____

_____

_____

_____

_____

_____

_____

_____

_____

_____

_____

_____

_____

_____

b) Which kinds of points must be documented in order to manage client feedback properly?

_____

_____

_____

_____

_____

_____

_____

_____

_____

_____

_____

_____

_____

_____

_____

_____

LAB 12.2 EXERCISE ANSWERS

This section gives you some suggested answers to the questions in Lab 12.2 with discussion related to those answers. Please post any alternative answers to these questions at the companion Web site for this book, located at http://www.phptr.com/phptrinteractive.

12.2.1 ANSWERS

a) Write a programming plan for the project you used in 10.3.2b.

Answer: The following was the technical description used in the project specification:

Technical Development:

This site will be built utilizing HTML, Perl, a mySQL database back end, and possibly Java and JavaScript. Server requirements include UNIX platform, Perl 5.0, mySQL.

Front Page extentions are *not* necessary. Plans at this time are to install the site on the server owned by We Host 'Em, a local hosting company. Another future option includes Host.Net, located in Any-town, MA.

A UNIX platform provides for greater functionality and security than the NT platform and is the appropriate choice for a site of this type. HTML will be used to code the standard Web pages. Perl will be utilized in conjunction with the mySQL database back end to build the Acme database and for CGI interactive functions. JavaScript and Java applets may be used to create a more interactive graphical presentation.

This site will be best viewed in Netscape Navigator 2.0 and Internet Explorer 3.0 and above.

Database Functionality

Two database tables will track job seeker and job posting information. Both tables will need to be searchable with an AND interface (i.e., Position AND Salary Requirements) or by a singular criteria (i.e., Geography). Links will be provided to more detailed resume and complete job posting information. These files will be uploaded to the server as text files and coded with a number that mirrors the Access database numbers assigned interoffice.

A separate database table will track authorized company names with their user names and passwords.

Job Seeker Table

This table will be password protected. Distinct user names and passwords will be assigned to authorized companies, allowing them to view its contents.

TABLE RESUME FIELDS

id, name, contact_person, current-company, skills, salary, location-desired, desired_position

The id number will link to a separate file, "id.html", which will be a text file containing the candidate's text based resume. Administrators at Acme will need to blank out the name and current company information from the resumes before uploading them.

Name will be a "hidden" field not shown to the user. This will be included as an administrative back-up alternative, in case the interoffice numbering scheme fails due to misfiling, etc.

This table will be searchable by skills, salary, location-desired, and desired-position by the user. It will be searchable by name, id, skills, salary, location-desired, and desired-position through the administrative back room.

"Hits", which bring up candidates who currently work at the company that is searching the database, will be dropped and not shown.

Job Posting Table

TABLE JOB FIELDS

id, company, contact_person, skills, salary, geographical-location, position, date

The id number will link to a separate file, "id.html", which will be a text file containing the company's detailed text based job posting. Administrators at Acme will need to blank out company information from the job postings before uploading them.

Company will be a "hidden" field not shown to the user. This will be included as an administrative back-up alternative, in case the interoffice numbering scheme fails due to misfiling, etc.

This table will be searchable by skills, salary, geographical—location and position by the user. It will be searchable by company, id, skills, salary, geographical_location, and position through the administrative back room.

Records should be automatically deleted from the system after residing there for over thirty days.

User Name/Password Table

TABLE USER FIELDS

user_name, password, company

This table will be searchable by user_name and company.

An administrative back room will be created for all tables with an add, modify, delete, and the aforementioned searching capability.

Forms

Two forms will reside on the site that allow the user to input either job seeker or job posting information. This information will be e-mailed to Acme Personnel, giving Acme the option to follow up with the prospective candidate or company.

The candidate form will first present questions regarding desired position, current role, skills, current company, and then contact information. Name, address, city, state, zip, daytime phone, evening phone, and e-mail will be required fields.

The job posting form will include company name, contact name, address, city, state, zip, phone, position, skills required, and salary range.

The programming plan must include a listing of programs used to drive this functionality, their modules, and any special technical considerations that might impact on the Web site's ability to provide cross-platform functionality.

A programming plan for one of the programs on this Web site might look like the following:

Acme Personnel Web Site Programming Plan—Seek.cgi

Based upon the requirements described in the project specification, this program allows the user to search the job posting database.

The search functionality must include AND/LIKE/BETWEEN/= conditions. A form must first be built, named seek.html, which includes a text field for skills, drop-down selections for geographical location, drop-down descriptions for types of positions, and two text fields for salary—named salary and salary 1.

Drop-down choices for the location field include North Shore, South Shore, 128 West, 495 North, Western Massachusetts, Greater Boston.

Drop-down choices for the position field include NT System Administrator, C++ Programmer, Web Developer, and Software Engineer.

Variables will be passed to the cgi search program, coded in Perl, using the cgi-lib.pl library.

First, the program must determine which fields have been used in the search criteria.

If several criteria are used, the automatic understanding of the program will be that each criteria will be included in the search parameters with an AND statement.

The other search statements, depending on the fields filled out and passed, include

Skills—LIKE function

Salary—Two fields will be input, facilitating a BETWEEN function

geographical-location—Drop-down input facilitates = function

position—Drop-down input facilitates = function

If there are search results, the user should be directed to an output page, seektrue.cgi, containing the information. If there are no search results, there should be a program, seekfalse.cgi, sending a message to the screen informing the user that there has been a null result, and giving the user a link back to the search page to try their search again.

Error messages should occur if

    Character strings are input into the salary fields

    There is no search criteria input

b)   What kinds of issues did you address in the programming plan that you did not mention in the project specification?

Answer: In this section of the programming plan, query structure was addressed, discussing which criteria would be attached to which field (i.e., Skills is a "LIKE", Salary is handled as a "BETWEEN", etc.). In addition, error conditions are addressed.

Perl coding will use the cgi-lib.pl library. This would not mean anything to the client. However, in order to maintain programming consistency, it is important to the programming team.

Programming code has to determine which fields are being used as search criteria. From there, a query statement can be constructed.

12.2.2 ANSWERS

a)   Write a test plan for the project used in 12.2.1.

Answer: The following conditions for seek.cgi should be tested:

    Search using each individual search criteria.

    Search using every combination of search criteria.

    Enter character strings in the salary fields.

    Enter no search criteria.

    Test "LIKE" functionality by entering the beginning letter of a true result.

    Verify search results containing correct output information.

b)   What kinds of errors would you hope this test plan might identify?

Answer: I would want the test plan to identify incorrect use of error messages and unreliable query results.

12.2.3 ANSWERS

a) Discuss how you would walk a client through a Web site, demonstrating the functionality.

Answer: The best way to walk a client through their Web site is through a face-to-face meeting. If this is not a possibility, it is best to speak with the client on the phone while the client is viewing sections of their Web site, as specified by the project manager.

If you are already into the technical phase of development, let us assume that graphics and site layout have already been approved. Therefore, if there is a database, test data should have been input ahead of time to illustrate the Web site's functionality. The project manager should have several scenarios to demonstrate to the client.

Then the project manager should walk the client through the administrative back room so that they may understand how information is input, modified, and deleted.

Lastly, invite the client to then click around the entire Web site, to assure them that all of the links are working correctly.

b) Which kinds of points must be documented in order to manage client feedback properly?

Answer: Clients are usually concerned with the method by which information may be requested and how that information is then output to the user. So detailed description of the front-end interface is key. Summary of this functionality must be included in the project specification and the more technically interpretive programming plan. The project specification is reviewed and approved by the client; therefore, any pertinent details that could be contested by the client must be included here.

LAB 12.2 SELF-REVIEW QUESTIONS

In order to test your progress, you should be able to answer the following questions:

1) (True/False) The following issues would be typically addressed in the programming plan rather than the project specification:
   a) _____ Sessions coded by ASP programmers might necessitate the use of cookies.
   b) _____ Perl 5.0 is the version of Perl used for the Web site.

2) (True/False) If a client contested the use of drop-down selections for their Web site, you would refer to which of the following documents?
   a) _____ Project specification
   b) _____ Creative brief
   c) _____ Programming plan
   d) _____ Test plan

L A B   1 2 . 3

PROGRAMMING AND TESTING

LAB OBJECTIVES:

After this lab, you will be able to

- Oversee Coding
- Oversee Testing

While a project manager need not be a programming guru, it is very helpful to understand what programming languages can accomplish certain objectives. In my Web shop, we use Perl, ASP, and VBScript, to do mission-critical operations and Java Script to deploy operations that enhance the graphics.

However, there are many Web programming languages and applications that can be used to bring a Web site to life.

The following article, "Characteristics of Web Programming Languages," is written by Steve Ford, David Wells, and Nancy Wells, of Object Services and Consulting, Inc.* While it does not cover some of the newer tools, like ASP and Flash (the article was written in 1996 and updated in 1997), Steve, David, and Nancy have put together an excellent resource for the project manager. We will research some of the newer programming tools later in this lab.

*Published on Object Services and Consulting, Inc's Web site www.objs.com/survey/lang.htm Characteristics

Characteristics of Web Programming Languages

Just as there is a diversity of programming languages available and suitable for conventional programming tasks, there is a diversity of languages available and suitable for Web programming. There is no reason to believe that any one language will completely monopolize the Web programming scene, although the varying availability and suitability of the current offerings is likely to favor some over others. Java is both available and generally suitable, but not all application developers are likely to prefer it over languages more similar to what they currently use, or, in the case of non-programmers, over higher level languages and tools. This is OK because there is no real reason why we must converge on a single programming language for the Web any more than we must converge on a single programming language in any other domain.

**LAB
12.3**

The Web does, however, place some specific constraints on our choices: the ability to deal with a variety of protocols and formats (e.g. graphics) and programming tasks; performance (both speed and size); safety; platform independence; protection of intellectual property; and the basic ability to deal with other Web tools and languages. These issues are not independent of one another. A choice which seemingly is optimal in one dimension may be sub-optimal or worse in another.

Formats and protocols. The wide variety of computing, display, and software platforms found among clients necessitates a strategy in which the client plays a major role in the decision about how to process and/or display retrieved information, or in which servers must be capable of driving these activities on all potential clients. Since the latter is not practical, a suite of Web protocols covering addressing conventions, presentation formats, and handling of foreign formats has been created to allow interoperability [Berners-Lee, CACM, Aug. 1994].

HTML (HyperText Markup Language) is the basic language understood by all WWW (World Wide Web) clients. Unmodified HTML can execute on a PC under Windows or OS/2, on a Mac, or on a Unix workstation. HTML is simple enough that nearly anyone can write an HTML document, and it seems almost everyone is doing so.

HTML was developed as part of the WWW at CERN by Tim Berners-Lee, who is now Director of the World Wide Web Consortium (W3C) at MIT's Laboratory for Computer Science. Refinement of HTML continues at W3C, with standardization via the Internet Engineering Task Force (IETF) of the Internet Society. HTML descended from SGML (Standard Generalized Markup Language), the ISO standard language for text. SGML is in widespread use by the US Government and the publishing industry for representing documents. HTML applies SGML principles to the WWW. As such, it implements a semantic subset of SGML with similar syntax.

HTML is a markup language rather than a complete programming language. An HTML document (program) is ASCII text with embedded instructions (markups) which affect the way the text is displayed. The basic model for HTML execution is to fetch a document by its name (e.g. URL), interpret the HTML and display the document, possibly fetching additional HTML documents in the process, and possibly leaving hot areas in the displayed document that, if selected by the user, can accept user input and/or cause additional HTML documents to be fetched by URL. HTML applications, or what we might consider the HTML equivalent of an application, consist of a collection of related Web pages managed by a single HTTP (HTTP is the tcp/ip protocol that defines the interaction of WWW clients and servers) server. This is an oversimplification, but the model is simple, and the language is simple, and that is one of its strengths.

As HTML moves through the standardization process, and is extended by various vendors, it loses some of its simplicity, but it remains a useful language. The Web programmer generally finds HTML lacking in only two areas: its performance in certain types of applications, and the ability to program certain common tasks.

The remainder of the paper: (a) discusses the issues involved in meeting the performance and expressibility goals while still providing safety, platform independence, and the ability to interact with a variety of formats, protocols, tools, and languages; (b) identifies design alternatives addressing these issues; and (c) discusses a variety of Web programming languages in this context.

Power. HTML is limited in its computational power. This is intentional in its design, as it prevents the execution of dangerous programs on the client machine. However, Web programmers, as they have become more sophisticated in their applications, have increasingly been hamstrung by these limits. Tasks unable to be coded in HTML must either be executed on the server in some other language, or on the client in a program in some other language downloaded from a server. Both solutions are awkward for the programmer, often produce a suboptimal segmentation of an application across program modules, both client and server, and reintroduce safety considerations.

Performance. Because of an HTML program's limited functionality, and the resulting shift of computational load to the server, certain types of applications perform poorly, especially in the context of clients connected to the Internet with rather low bandwidth dialup communications (<=28.8Kbps). The performance problems arise from two sources: (a) an application which is highly interactive requires frequently hitting the server across this low bandwidth line which can dramatically and, at times, unacceptably slow observed performance; and (b) requiring all computation to be done on the server increases the load on the server thereby reducing the observed performance of its clients.

Today, most users have pretty competent client machines which are capable of accepting a larger share of the computational load than HTML allows. For example, an Internet-based interactive game or simulation can be a frustrating experience for users with low speed connections, and can overwhelm the server that hosts it. If you were the developer of such a game, you'd be inclined to push more of the functionality to the client, but, since HTML limits the possibilities, another route to supporting computation on the client must be found. The developer might make an executable client program available to users, which would be invoked via the HTML browser, but users might only be willing to accept such programs if they trust the source (e.g. a major vendor), as such programs are a potential safety concern. Also, users don't want to be continuously download-ing client programs to be able to access Web pages, so this solution has real practical limitations considering the size and dynamism of the Web. If safe powerful high performance programs could be auto-matically downloaded to client platforms, in much the same way as HTML pages, the problem would be solved.

LAB 12.3

When code is to be executed on a client, there are two main consid-erations: what gets shipped and what gets executed. There are three main alternatives for each of these: source code, a partially compiled intermediate format (e.g. byte code), and binary code. Because com-pilation can take place on the client, what is shipped is not necessar-ily what is executed.

Byte code, according to measurements presented at the JavaOne conference can be 2–3× smaller than comparable binary code, so its transfer can be considerably faster; especially noticeable over low speed lines. Since transfer time is significant in the Web, this is a major advantage. Source code is also compact. Execution perfor-mance clearly favors binary code over byte code, and byte code over source code. In general, binary code executes 10–100 times faster than byte code. Most Java VM developers are developing JIT (Just In Time) compilers to get the benefits of byte code size and binary speed. Java byte codes are downloaded over the net and compiled to native binary on the local platform. The binary is then executed, and, possibly, cached for later executions.

It should be clear that any combination of these strategies could be used in the implementation of any particular Web programming language, and there is in fact wide variation among the systems actually surveyed.

Platform Independence Given the diversity of operating systems and hardware platforms currently in use on the Web, a great efficiency results from only dealing with a single form of an application. The success of HTML has proven this, and Java has seconded it. The ability to deliver a platform-independent application of great appeal to developers, who spend a large portion of their resources developing and maintaining versions of their products for the different hardware/software platform combinations. With Java, one set of sources and one byte compiled executable, can be maintained for all hw/sw platforms.

While platform independence has long been a goal of language developers, the need to squeeze every last ounce of performance from software has often made this impractical to maintain, at least at the level of executable code. However, in the Web this concern becomes less important because transfer time is now a significant component of performance and can dominate execution time.

Platform independence can be achieved by shipping either byte code or source code. One advantage of shipping byte code over source code is that a plethora of source languages would require the client machines to maintain many compilers and/or interpreters for the source languages, while fewer byte code formats would require fewer virtual machines.

Preserving intellectual property. Although not currently discussed much as an issue, the ability to download safe, portable applets in some form less than source code is an additional advantage to developers who wish to protect their intellectual property. Looking at someone else's script or source to see how they do something and just tweaking it a little or copying a piece of it to do the same thing in one's own program doesn't feel like stealing. But if one has to go to the effort of reverse engineering byte or binary code, it becomes more obvious that this code is someone else's intellectual property. For the vast majority of honest people on the Web, this subtle reminder may be enough. For some of the minority, the effort involved in reverse engineering may serve as a sufficient deterrent.

Safety. Viruses have proven that executing binary code acquired from an untrusted, or even moderately trusted, source is dangerous. Code that is downloaded or uploaded from random sites on the web should not be allowed to damage the user's local environment. Downloading binary code compiled from conventional languages is clearly unsafe, due to the power of the languages. Even if such languages were constrained to some ostensibly safe subset, there is no way to verify that only the safe subset was used or that the compiler used was trustworthy (after all, it is under someone else's control).

HTML proved that downloading source code in a safe language and executing it with a trusted interpreter was safe. You can't infect a client with a virus by fetching and displaying an HTML document (although you certainly can fetch a file with a virus in it, which could then be activated by executing the file, something which is not supported directly by HTML, although some browsers allow it). HTML is not sufficiently powerful. A middle ground is being sought in which the downloaded program is less limited in its capabilities than HTML and more limited than a conventional language. Even though HTML has limited power, the general idea behind HTML, that of a somewhat limited language interpreted by a trusted client-side interpreter, has been widely adopted with more powerful languages and interpreters.

**LAB
12.3**

Some languages achieve relative safety by executing byte-code compiled programs in a relatively safe runtime environment (a virtual machine). Yet other languages are fully interpreted on the client by an interpreter provided by the language developer. In either case relative safety can be achieved because the interpreter or virtual machine can make safety checks that are impossible to make statically at compile-time. Note that safety can only be provided by the interpreter or virtual machine, not by the language or the language's compiler.

Building a secure virtual machine is a non-trivial task. Not many virtual machines are needed since a single virtual machine can be the target of many languages.

This is not to say that lack of safety or platform-independence disqualify a language for a role in Web application development, but for dynamic applications likely to be downloaded from untrusted sources with current browsers and executed locally on mainstream platforms, a safe and platform independent executable is highly desirable. At the other extreme, the interpreters and runtimes that execute such programs are likely to be developed using unsafe languages and platform dependent executables will be distributed by their developers. For programs intended for execution on servers, there is some value to safety and platform independence, but not to the same degree as on clients.

Conclusions. HTML is proving insufficient by itself to develop the myriad Web-based applications envisioned. As extended by server and client programs, the task is feasible, yet awkward and sub-optimal in terms of performance and safety. The ability to easily develop sophisticated Web-based applications optimally segmented between client and server in the context of the heterogeneous and dynamic environment of the Web while not compromising safety, performance, nor intellectual property, is the goal of current efforts. The first significant result of those efforts is Java, a C++-derived language with capabilities specialized for Web-based application development. Java is compiled by the developer to a platform-independent byte code format, with byte codes downloadable via HTML browsers to the client, and interpreted by a virtual machine which can guarantee its safety. Sun is working to improve the safety, performance, comprehensiveness, and ubiquity of Java, and the industry appears to be accepting their approach. Others, especially other language developers, vendors and users, are taking similar approaches to developing Web-based applications in their languages, by supporting safe client-side execution in some manner, including targeting the Java Virtual Machine.

While Java certainly has the edge at the moment, a belief which was reinforced by the 5000+ attendance figure at the JavaOne conference in May 1996, we believe there is room for more than one winner, and that an end result somewhat broader than just Java would be in the best interest of developers and users alike.

Safety is the biggest issue. The safety of a program is a function of the safety of the environment in which it executes, which is just another program. At some level, the user must acquire a potentially unsafe program from a trusted source. At present, we acquire Netscape, Java, and Windows from trusted (relatively) sources. Because there must be a trusted environment in which to execute safe, platform-independent programs and because users are only likely to trust a limited number of big name sources for that trusted environment, there has been speculation that diversity, including diversity in Web programming language choices, would be reduced. While this could become true, it now appears unlikely because language developers are proving that they can retarget their programming language to someone else's execution environment. A more reasonable view of the future is a full diversity of programming languages supported by a few trusted execution engines. At present, most efforts are targeting Java's Virtual Machine(VM), mainly because it is widely distributed with Netscape and is being licensed by other browser vendors. It's possible that the Java VM ends up being the *one* trusted execution environment, but it will probably be one of several general purpose execution environments, that together with many special purpose environments, will be distributed by trusted sources. An ideal outcome might be industry-wide standardization on a trusted virtual machine specification and validation of implementations by an industry group such as X/Open. Regardless of how it occurs, we do not think diversity of programming language alternatives will be reduced in the long term. However, it is likely that we will see some narrowing of our choices in the short term as language developers adapt their existing offerings to this new area and develop new ones.

The rest of this document surveys languages and interfaces being used for Web programming, attempting to provide a snapshot view of the direction that language is going to meet the needs of Web programmers, and its status.

Languages and Interfaces

The languages and interfaces surveyed below represent various attempts to create the "ideal" Web programming language, usually by extending and restricting existing languages. Web programming languages have a variety of ancestors: scripting languages, shell languages, mark-up languages and conventional programming languages. The resultant Web programming languages show their ancestry in their syntax, computational and data model, and implementation style (subject to the design constraints discussed in the previous section), and as a result, there are a fair number of distinct approaches taken. However, it is instructive to note that the original language categories tend to blur as development progresses.

The surveyed languages are listed in alphabetical order. If you intend to read the entire survey section, you should first read about Java, Tcl, Python, and Perl, as many of the other languages are compared to them.

Not all relevant languages are discussed. Some entries consist only of a link. They are languages we've seen mentioned as applicable to web programming in some way, but haven't investigated further. We hope to do so in the future.

Ada95

Ada95 is the latest version of the Ada programming language, which now supports object-oriented programming. Ada is used widely in government and industry

AppleScript

AppleScript is Apple's object-oriented English-like scripting language and development environment for the Macintosh. It is bundled with

MacOS, and is used widely for all variety of scripting tasks on the Mac. Recently, it has been applied to web programming tasks. Web-Runner enables the execution of AppleScript scripts embedded in HTML files to be executed on a client running Netscape. The most widely used HTTP servers for the Macintosh, MacHTTP, a shareware product, and WebStar, its commercial sibling, both use AppleScript for recording and CGI scripting.

BEF

BEF is an object-oriented PASCAL-like scripting language for describing behavior in VRML.

CCI (Common Client Interface)

NCSA Mosaic CCI (Common Client Interface) is an interface specification (protocol & API) that enables client-side applications to communicate with NCSA Mosaic, the original Web browser, to control Mosaic or to obtain information off the Web via Mosaic. Note that this is not for invoking client-side applications (applets) from Mosaic, but for controlling Mosaic from the application. Invocation of client-side applications from a browser is currently specific to the browser, but most support NCSA helpers. Once the application is running, it can communicate with the browser with CCI. CCI is not the only interface currently defined for this purpose, but it seems to be meeting with some acceptance, as Tcl and Perl now support it.

CGI (Common Gateway Interface)

A Web daemon *executes* a CGI program on the server and returns the results to the client (e.g. a query against a database server), rather than simply returning a copy of the referenced file, as it does with an HTML reference. Parameters are passed from the server to the CGI program as environment variables. The program is sometimes written in C, C++, or some other compiled programming language, but more often it is written in a scripting language (e.g. Perl, Tcl, sh). To prevent damage to the server, CGI programs generally are stored in a protected directory under the exclusive control of the webmaster.

CMM

Cmm, now renamed ScriptEase: WebServer Edition, is a streamlined version of the C computer programming language. C and Cmm differ in one major area: memory management. With Cmm all memory management is handled automatically, so there is no need to create buffers, declare variables, or cast data types.

With this major exception, Cmm and C are virtually identical. Cmm supports all of the standard C functions and operators (including structures and arrays), and they are used in the same way as in C. For use with CGI programming, Cmm provides specialized functions to easily get data from forms and to create HTML pages on the fly.

Dylan

Dylan is a dynamic object-oriented programming language with a pascal-ish syntax, and a lisp-ish semantics. It was designed at Apple's Cambridge lab in cooperation with Carnegie-Mellon University and Harlequin, Inc., and reviewed by its potential user community, mostly former Common Lisp programmers disenchanted with C++. The goal of the designers was to create a language with syntax, performance, and executable footprint acceptable to mainstream programmers (i.e. C/C++), but with many of the characteristics that programmers value in Lisp (e.g. evolutionary development, optional type declarations, runtime safety, automatic storage management, and ease of maintenance). In late 1995, Apple released its implementation for the Macintosh as an unsupported $40 "Technology Release", and then, for the most part, shut down the Dylan project, although an effort to port Dylan to MacOS on the Power PC appears to have survived. CMU has developed a byte-code compiled version of Dylan called Mindy that runs on several Unix platforms and on Windows NT, and it continues development of a native Unix compiler. Harlequin plans the release of its native compiler and development environment for Windows NT and Windows 95 in mid-1996. See for a comparison of Common Lisp, Dylan, C++, and Java. Scott Fahlman states that Dylan is better suited to complex programming tasks than Java, and "can also be a good language for building safe, Web-mobile code", although I have not seen any effort to apply Dylan to the latter task.

Guile

Guile is GNU's *extension language library*. It includes a virtual machine, a run-time system, and front ends for multiple languages (e.g. Scheme, Ctax (scheme with C syntax, Emacs Lisp (future)). Guile interacts at several levels with Tcl/Tk. The VM can call Tcl programs, and, therefore, the front end languages can call Tcl programs. The Tk library is also accessible in this way. Tcl programs can call Guile programs written in any of the extension languages, like Scheme. The Guile Virtual Machine is similar to Java's. A byte-code interpreter is being developed. Guile is implemented in a mix of Scheme and C, and C and Scheme libraries are available to programmers using the extension langauges. TkWWW, GNU's Web Browser, written in Tcl, is being adapted to work with Guile.

HyperTalk

HyperTalk is the English-like scripting language for Apple's HyperCard. It's described by its fans as similar to AppleScript, but simpler and more forgiving. Given the large number of HyperTalk-literate programmers in the Mac world, HyperTalk might very well be preferred by many over AppleScript and UserTalk for many web scripting tasks on the Mac.

Icon

Icon is a full-featured programming language developed at the University of Arizona with a C-ish syntax and a SNOBOL heritage, making it particularly suitable for string processing, and, therefore, similar in this way to other languages being used for Internet programming. I've seen Icon mentioned in this context, but haven't come across any active efforts towards that end.

Java

Java is the leading contender for a full feature programming language targetted at Internet applications. Its advantages are: familiarity (derived from C++), platform independence (will run on any platform which implements the Java Virtual Machine), performance (byte-code compiled faster than fully interpreted), and safety (downloaded applets are checked for integrity, and only interpreted by trusted Virtual Machine). Java is being aggressively distributed and promoted by Sun Microsystems, which developed it, and, evidently, sees it as a way to loosen Microsoft's and Intel's grip on the computer platform. Netscape, the leading web browser, now includes the Java VM, and Java applets are appearing on Web sites everywhere. Even Microsoft, which is promoting Visual Basic Script for this purpose, has licensed Java from Sun and will be supporting it in its browsers. The list of Java licensees is long, and includes other major players, like DEC and IBM. Sun is distributing a Java developers kit free of charge as of this writing, in the interest of promoting Java's widespread use. It recently announced the development of microprocessors optimized for Java for different markets (from cellular phones to high performance 3D "Network Appliances.") If their strategy is successful, the application platform is raised, and Java displaces Windows or other OS's as the target platform of application developers, then the whole ballgame changes, and the impact is potentially across the entire computer industry, not just the Internet. The ability to deliver a platform-independent application, or, more correctly, an OS-independent application, is of great appeal to developers, who spend a large portion of their resources developing and maintaining versions of their products for the different hardware/ software platform combinations. With Java, one set of sources, and, even more important, one byte compiled executable, can be delivered for all hw/sw platforms. While interpretation of byte-compiled program is slower than execution of a native executable, the claim is made that, once interpreted, the resulting executable is of comparable performance, which means Java apps could be interpreted once and the result cached locally, and thereafter executed optimally. This is great news for Unix, OS/2, and Macintosh vendors and users, who often suffer from limited or delayed availability of software and high prices due to limited demand, and, likewise, for non-Intel chip and computer vendors. It's potentially disastrous news for Microsoft and Intel, who, arguably, often sell their products solely on the basis of their market position, rather than their technical merit. Hopefully, the result will be a more level playing field for vendors and more choice for consumers, and not just the replacement of Microsoft and Intel with Sun and Netscape.

That said, not everyone agrees that Java is the answer. The most common complaint is that Java is not simple; it's basically a slimmed down, cleaned up C++, with a big GUI library. C++ programming is not described by most as "simple", and Java programming is not much simpler, especially when compared to HTML, or some other languages put forward as its competition. Java is the market leader at the moment, so it is the obvious target.

HORB is a freeware implementation of a superset of Java.

Jylu adds support for Java clients and servers to Xerox's ILU, a sourceware ORB that supports interoperability between programs written in Python, Common Lisp, C, C++, and Modula-3.

JavaScript

JavaScript (nee LiveScript) is Netscape's scripting language for integrating HTML, Netscape plug-ins, and Java applets. It is based on Java, and is mostly syntactically compatible, but differs from Java in that it is interpreted, rather than compiled, only supports certain built-in objects and user-defined functions, rather than full support for user-defined classes with inheritance and methods, is integrated with HTML, rather than invoked from HTML files, weakly typed, and dynamically bound. JavaScript is meant to extend HTML to be more of a full programming language, but retaining HTML's ease of use. The principal criticism of Java programming is that it is *much* more complex than HTML programming, more like C++ programming, and therefore is not as accessible to users as HTML. This is an issue that JavaScript attempts to address.

KQML (Knowledge Query and Manipulation Language)

KQML is a language for describing the exchange of information among agents. Agents are one of the paradigms for how knowledge is accumulated and processed in a distributed heterogeneous environment like the World Wide Web. Telescript uses the agent paradigm. Standards for the interoperability of such agents are crucial to their use on the web, and KQML and its siblings provide such a standard.

Linda

Linda is an extension language for extensible Web browser architecture.

Lingo

Lingo is the object-based scripting language for Macromedia's multimedia authoring system created by John Thompson. It is often compared to ScriptX, Telescript, Java, Tcl, and HyperTalk, resembles the latter most, but it is more special purpose than any of those. It is specific to Director, which is used extensively for authoring CD-ROM titles, and is not available separately, which limits its applicability to other purposes. With the release of ShockWave, a free Netscape plug-in, software developed with Director can be displayed in Netscape, and soon other browsers.

Lisp

Lisp is a lisp processing language created for artificial intelligence research by John McCarthy at MIT in the late fifties.

Common Lisp is the dialect of Lisp with the most widespread current use, especially for large complex systems (esp. artificial intelligence) in industry, government, and academia. It was designed in the early eighties with some DARPA sponsorship by representatives of the several lisp dialects in use at that time as a way to converge on a common dialect. There is some use of Common Lisp for Web-based server applications. CWEST is a tool to convert CLIM GUIs to HTML and GIFs for display with a client's browser. CL-HTTP is an HTTP server implemented in Common Lisp and targeting the intersection of the interactive hypermedia and artificial intelligence research domains. Harlequin, the vendor of a commercial Common Lisp, offers WebMaker, which enables conversion of Framemaker documents to HTML.

Scheme is a statically scoped dialect of Lisp in widespread use, primarily in academia for research and educational purposes. Scheme 48 is an implementation of Scheme that compiles to a byte-code representation that is then executable by a Virtual Machine, much like Java does. The Scheme Underground is an MIT project aimed at developing a substantial body of Scheme48 software, including software appropriate to the Internet (e.g. TeX->HTML, Web agents, tk).

Emacs-Lisp (Elisp for short) is the dialect of Lisp used to implement and extend the Emacs text editor, which was developed at MIT in the sixties. It is similar to Common Lisp, but smaller and free, and is in very large distribution, as it comes with Emacs. A browser, GNU-scape Navigator, has been implemented in, and is extensible with, Elisp. Due to its widespread use as a scripting language, its small size, and the long-term Internet-awareness of its large user base, I would have expected to see some effort to apply Elisp to client-side applet execution, but I see no evidence of such an effort.

WINTERP is a GUI development environment comparable to Tcl/Tk and Python, but based on XLISP-PLUS, a small object-oriented lisp implementation, and including interfaces to the X Windows and Motif libraries. WINTERP runs on a variety of Unix platforms (XLISP runs on a variety of platforms), but has not been ported elsewhere. While WINTERP seems as suitable for adaptation to Internet programming as Tcl/Tk and Python, I see no effort to move it in that direction.

LAB 12.3

Perl

Perl is described as a compiled scripting language. It combines elements of C with some Unix scripting and text manipulation languages (e.g. sh, awk, sed) into a more complete language that subsumes the functionality of all into one consistent whole, and is compilable, and, therefore faster than its forebears. Perl's advocates tout its ease of use when comparing it to Java, especially. One of the motivations in developing Perl was to provide an alternative to C for tasks that were a little too hairy for an existing Unix tool, or where performance was an issue. C was seen as unnecessarily low level, and C development too time consuming. Perl tries to delay the need to program at a lower level. Its been very successful, especially among system administrators. Since CGI scripts are often built by systems folks, Perl is widely used for this, too.

The major difference pointed out between perl and tcl is that perl is somewhat faster because it is partially compiled and optimized, which dramatically reduces the parsing and reparsing required in tcl. There is also a heavy bias in tcl, and in other shell languages, towards string manipulation, which gets in the way when using tcl for programming types other than strings. On the other hand, tcl is simpler, and more useful as a meta-language, in developing special purpose languages, as it does with tk.

Perl's roots in the world of Unix system administration (e.g. C, awk, sed, sh), and its much larger user base, are the primary differentiators between Perl and Python.

Perl advocates eschew Java's greater complexity, and incredible hype. On no subject do emotions run hotter. Perl predates Java, better suits internet programming than Java, they say. A common comment is that Perl has proven to be a good language for this purpose, but there are other good languages. There are some reasons to believe Java might also be good, although there is counter evidence also, but, overall, there is no evidence that Java should be the one and only client extension language for the Internet, but it is being promoted as such by Sun and Netscape, and that infuriates users of other languages.

Perl, as a programming language, doesn't offer the graphics and security desired for Internet programming. Not to worry; those features are now available. Perl/TK extends Perl with access to the Tk GUI library (from tcl/tk). Penguin is a Perl module that enables perl code to be sent encrypted and digitally signed to a remote machine over the Internet, and executes such code in a secure, limited environment. Pgpsafeperl and LPSP (limited pgpsafeperl) are, I believe, names for Penguin precursors. The two together are equivalent (to some, superior) to Java. Perl CCI enables NCSA Mosaic CCI programs to be written in Perl. Safecgiperl executes CGI programs written in Perl in a safe environment on a WWW server.

Phantom

Phantom is an interpreted language targeting large-scale, interactive, distributed applications such as distributed conferencing systems, multi-layer games, and collaborative work tools. Phantom combines the distributed lexical scoping semantics of Obliq with a safe, extended subset of Modula-3. Objects, static-typing, threads, exceptions, garbage collection, and an interface to the Tk GUI toolkit, are included.

Python

Python is an interpreted, object-oriented language developed as a full-featured, but easy to use, scripting language, by Guido van Rossum at CWI in the Netherlands. Initially developed in a Unix environment, Python is now available on PCs and Macs, and applications are portable across platforms. Python has developed a substantial, although still modest, following, as a scripting language, an application development language, and an embedded extension language. Python's design was most influenced by ABC, a little known language also developed at CWI. Python's syntax evokes C and C++, but doesn't stick too closely to those languages. Python fans tout its clear, intuitive syntax in comparison to C, C++, Java, Perl, shell languages, and most other interpreted languages, the completeness of its type system and its suitability for significant application development in comparison to Tcl , and its extensibility with Python and C/C++ libraries. Like Java, Perl and Tcl, Python offers a portable GUI library, several really. Perl advocates complain about the lack of regular expression matching and output formatting natively in Python. Perl is a little more of a sysadmin's shell language than Python, and Tcl is a little simpler and less capable. Python is more of a regular programming language, but simpler and easier to program than Java. But, all are suited to Internet programming. Safe-Python is a design for changes to add safety to Python. Grail is a web browser which supports the download and execution of Python applets in a safe Restircted Execution Mode. Grail uses the Tk GUI library.

REXX

REXX is IBM's dynamic scripting and extension language, developed by Mike Cowlishaw at IBM's UK Labs in 1979. It is descended from EXEC, the command language for IBM's CMS operating system, and influenced by PL/I. REXX is used extensively on IBM platforms, especially OS/2, and is now available for other platforms (e.g. DOS, Windows, UNIX). REXX is like Tcl in that it is simple and the string is its only data type. REXX is easily interpretable, and many is often implemented only as an interpreter, although compilers are available. Object REXX extends REXX with object-oriented semantics, by adding objects, classes, and methods to REXX's strings and functions. It also adds a number of predefined classes. Object REXX programs can interact with Smalltalk, C, or C++, programs via SOM (or DSOM, IBM's OMG CORBA-compatible extension to SOM, for distributed interaction). IBM is also developing a VisualAge-based GUI builder and visual application development environment for Object REXX. Object REXX is being used by NIIIP, a US-government sponsored consortium aimed at facilitating electronic commerce on the Internet. NetRexx is REXX's response to Java, a REXX to Java translator that permits REXX programs to be delivered as Java bytecodes, and executed on client platforms with the Java Virtual Machine, combining the ease and efficiency of REXX programming with the performance and wide availability of the Java VM.

ScriptX

ScriptX, a multimedia object-oriented programming language, was the principal technology produced by Kaleida Labs, a joint venture of IBM and Apple started along with Taligent and PowerPC. Kaleida Labs was shut down late in 1995, with ScriptX considered two years behind schedule and having lost a significant portion of its potential market to MacroMedia's Lingo. Release 1.5 of ScriptX and the associated Media Player (required to view ScriptX scripts) was announced in January, as control was passed to Apple.

ScriptX proponents tout its platform independent persistent object store, and rich multimedia class library. One use of the former is as a local cache for applets retrieved over the Internet.

SDI (Software Development Interface)

Spyglass SDI (Software Development Interface) is the main competitor to NCSA Mosaic CCI (Common Client Interface). The expectation is that SDI and CCI will eventually converge into a common specification. In addition to what CCI offers, SDI also provides a protocol for initiating messages from the browser to the client application. This protocol causes the application to be informed when the certain events occur on the browser or actually diverts handling of those events to the application. This addition makes SDI an appropriate protocol for invoking a new client application from a browser. The Netscape Navigator Web browser supports SDI under Windows and MacOS.

sh, csh, ksh, bash, tcsh, rc, zsh (UNIX shell languages)

In Unix-speak, a shell is the user's command-level interface to the operating system. The Bourne shell (i.e. sh) was the initial Unix shell, and still is the most widely used, but, over the years, other shells were developed, differing primarily in the syntax and semantics of the command languages they implemented. Other Unix shell languages are csh (C shell), ksh (Korn shell), bash (Bourne again shell), tcsh (Tenex C shell), rc, and zsh (Z shell). I won't go into the differences here. My point here is that these shells are essentially interpreters for scripting languages, and are commonly used on Unix platforms for a variety of programming tasks, especially by system administrators, including Web site maintenance chores like CGI scripting. Newer languages used in this context, like Perl and Tcl, were heavily influenced by the shell language forebears, and were generally developed to deal with the ever increasing complexity of scripting tasks, and the desire to apply such high-level languages to somewhat different tasks. Perl is a case of the former, Tcl a case of the latter, with the new task being quick development of GUI interfaces.

Smalltalk

Smalltalk is a dynamic, object-oriented programming language with an integrated GUI development environment and execution environment. It has a considerable following. It was developed by Alan Kay and others at Xerox PARC in the early seventies. Smalltalk is the central language of the object-oriented programming community. The fully integrated nature of Smalltalk has been both a strength and a weakness. It provides a very consistent conceptual model and look and feel across all components of the system, but this also serves to accentuate the disconnect between it and more conventional languages. This has also been observed of Lisp and APL. It has kept the Smalltalk world somewhat isolated from the rest of the application development world, although the rise of the object-oriented analysis and design, the success of C++, and the adoption of the object-oriented model as a standard for interoperability in many domains has brought Smalltalk into the mainstream in the last several years. Smalltalk's dynamic nature, and extensive GUI orientation, make it a natural for Internet programming, but the Smalltalk community has been slow to capitalize on this.

ParcPlace-Digitalk recently introduced VisualWave, which facilitates the use of Smalltalk in Web-based applications, by generating the CGI between the HTTP server and a Smalltalk application, and by generating the HTML necessary to provide a GUI for the application in conjunction with a Web browser. VisualWave does not appear to include the ability to safely deliver and execute Smalltalk applets on the client platform, although the source is evidently portable, and connectivity with OLE, CORBA and Java is planned. The former is likely to result from their recent licensing of HP's Distributed Smalltalk, which adds CORBA compatibility to ParcPlace's Smalltalk. Whether the latter means the generation of Java byte code applets from Smalltalk is not known.

IBM has announced WWW Parts for Visual Age for Smalltalk. The latter combines a visual application builder with IBM Smalltalk and

SOM (and DSOM, IBM's OMG CORBA-compatible extension to SOM), to enable applications built graphically in Smalltalk to use components separately developed in other language. WWW Parts seems comparable to ParcPlace's VisualWave, described above.

If GNU Smalltalk is going to be an extension language for Guile, I haven't heard about it.

Tcl

Tcl (tool command language) is a widely used scripting language generally used in conjunction with the Tk GUI library for building quick and easy X windows GUIs on Unix platforms, but also valued for the ease by which C libraries can be imported and referenced from Tcl. Tcl/Tk was developed by John Ousterhout while at UC Berkeley. Development continues at Sun Labs under his leadership. It's interesting to see this going on at Sun, also Java's home. Java is probably Tcl's principle competitor. John Ousterhout addresses this in his article, "The Relationship Between Tcl/Tk and Java." His point is that it's true that both languages are appropriate to Internet programming, but they are different, have different strengths, and are likely to complement each other. Tcl is higher level, quicker to program, and slower to execute; Java is lower level, harder to program, quicker to execute. Tcl is mainly used to tie together other programs, generally written in C or C++. John expects Java to replace C++ in this role for Internet applications. This role puts Tcl in competition with Javascript.

A couple of years ago, Tcl was receiving the kind of attention that Java is receiving today, lots of it, with some of it overhyping Tcl's benefits, and some of it defensively attacking Tcl's weaknesses—the downside of success.

ftp://ftp.perl.com/pub/perl/versus/tcl-discussion and ftp://ftp.perl.com/pub/perl/versus/tcl-complaints compare Tcl to Perl. In the interest of hugely oversimplifying the arguments, let me summarize by saying that Tcl critics think Tcl is incomplete, inelegant, and inefficient. Its proponents say it is quick and easy to program for what it was intended.

There's quite a bit of activity at Sun, and elsewhere, that extends Tcl/Tk towards being more appropriate for Internet programming. Ports are underway (some are already available) to MS Windows et al and MacIntosh, so that scripts will run on any platform. A Tcl/Tk GUI builder and an on-the-fly Tcl compiler are being developed. Safe-Tcl adds security to Tcl. Sun is integrating Safe-Tcl into their release. ccitcl integrates Tcl/Tk, Safe-Tcl, and NCSA Mosaic CCI into a solution for client-side scripting for the WWW. Expect extends Tcl for interacting with other interactive programs or users. TclDii provides a Tcl interface to the OMG CORBA Dynamic Invocation Interface (i.e. Iona's Orbix), enabling Tcl scripts to interact with CORBA services.

Telescript

Telescript is General Magic's interpreted, object-oriented language with for remote programming. It uses an active agents paradigm. Agent programs are sent to places where they execute, possibly in conjunction with other agents. Agents can move themselves to new places to execute, taking their state with them. Places are subprocesses associated with a Telescript Engine, which is a server program that may be integrated with an HTTP server (with CGI) to produce what they describe as an active Web server. This is similar architecturally to ParcPlace's VisualWave and IBM's WWWParts, both for Smalltalk. Agents are mobile in that their site of computation can move from one place to another, but they can only execute in the context of a Telescript engine, so agent programs should not be considered client programs, as Telescript provides no runtime support on the www client side to execute agents. This separates them from Java applets, for instance, which move computation from web servers to clients. Telescript moves computation in a different direction, from one web server to other web servers. The Telescript language itself is similar to C++, but is specialized to support the agent paradigm with built-in support for moving agents and interacting with other agents, and supports advanced memory management, including the persistence of all objects. Like Java, Telescript is safe and platform-independent.

See http://www.sunlabs.com/people/john.ousterhout/agent.ppt for a comparison of Tcl, Telescript, Visual Basic, and Java by John Ousterhout, Tcl's creator.

http://www.genmagic.com/About/Releases/prre1960129.html explains the difference between Telescript and Java.

Frontier is another popular script development environment for the Macintosh, which comes with its own scripting language, UserTalk. It was developed by Dave Winer of UserLand Software. Frontier is used to develop scripts in UserTalk, or AppleScript, or any other scripting language conforming to Apple's Open Scripting Architecture (OSA). For the same reason, UserTalk scripts can be developed with AppleScript tools, and CGI scripts, and other web-related scripting applications, can be written in UserTalk, and/or developed in Frontier. For instance, CGI scripts for WebStar can be developed in UserTalk with Frontier.

VBScript (Visual Basic Script)

VBScript is Microsoft's planned candidate for an Internet scripting language. It is expected in mid-1996. It is a subset of Visual Basic,

**LAB
12.3**

Microsoft's popular visual programming language, with no GUI building capability, with unsafe operations removed, and with access to other applications via OLE. VBScript source code is embedded in HTML, and downloaded to the client in the HTML file, where it is compiled and executed in association with its runtime libraries. Microsoft envisions an OLE Scripting Manager on the client-side with which browsers interact with a specified interface. The Scripting Manager would manage compilation and invocation of downloaded scripts in Visual Basic Script or any other scripting language. Microsoft also intends to support Visual Basic and Java in this way. The idea is to make multiple language runtimes pluggable into browsers. Microsoft intends to elicit the cooperation of various consortia and vendors in defining and standardizing this interface. Microsoft intends to support VBScript on its various Windows platforms and on the Macintosh and will license the technology to UNIX vendors.

VRML (Virtual Reality Modeling Language)

VRML is a specialized language for describing 3D worlds and movement through them. VRML is the standard language in describing such scenes in the context of the Internet and the World Wide Web. As more and more sites include 3D simulations, VRML will become more omnipresent. VRML, like HTML, is downloaded from a server and executed using an interpreter on the client, just as a Java applet might be downloaded and executed. Netscape now supports such an interpreter, and there are many others.

WebScript

WebScript is the object-oriented scripting language for NeXT Software's development environment for Web-based applications. WebScript is an interpreted subset of Objective-C, in much the same way that JavaScript is a subset of C++. WebScript, however, is used in WebObjects primarily for Web server scripting, where CGI and Perl might be more commonly used, rather than for client-side applets. WebObjects is expected to support Java and JavaScript on the client side, and JavaScript on the server side, in addition to WebScript, which may relegate WebScript to the scripting language of choice only for Objective-C users.

There was also another WebScript, from WebLogic, Inc., which has since been renamed htmlKona. It is a Java package for generating HTML pages.

As a project manager, you do not need to know how to code an SQL database using Active Server Pages and VB Script. However, it's important to know the limitations of using these programming tools to accomplish this task. By introducing you to these programming tools and descriptions, it is hoped that you will be able to understand which tools offer the best functionality for the task at hand.

LAB 12.3 EXERCISES

12.3.1   OVERSEE CODING

a) Research and write descriptions for three relatively new programming tools. What are their best applications?

_____

_____

_____

_____

_____

_____

_____

_____

_____

_____

_____

_____

_____

_____

_____

_____

_____

_____

_____

_____

_____

_____

_____

_____

_____

b) A subcontractor fails to produce the functionality that has been contracted. What is your fall-back plan?

_____

_____

_____

_____

_____

_____

_____

_____

_____

c) Your company is dealing with a new programming language. There is a significant learning curve and the project is falling behind schedule and beyond budget. What are your options?

LAB
12.3

_____

_____

_____

_____

_____

_____

_____

_____

_____

_____

_____

_____

_____

12.3.2   OVERSEE TESTING

a) How would you verify that the Web site has been adequately reviewed for quality control purposes?

_____

_____

_____

_____

_____

b) Who would you have testing the Web site? What would their objectives be?

_____

_____

_____

_____

_____

_____

_____

_____

_____

_____

_____

_____

_____

_____

_____

_____

_____

LAB 12.3 EXERCISE ANSWERS

This section gives you some suggested answers to the questions in Lab 12.3 with discussion related to those answers. Please post any alternative answers to these questions at the companion Web site for this book, located at http://www.phptr.com/phptrinteractive.

12.3.1 ANSWERS

a) Research and write descriptions for three relatively new programming tools. What are their best applications?

Answer:

Macromedia Director 7

Used to build applications that enable real-time animation with graphics, sound, text, and video. Essentially, Director creates Shockwave multimedia content. Director supports Java, HTTPS, XML, and more. {Private} The Director 7 Shockwave Internet Studio specializes in creating multimedia productions, including interactive Web content (using Shockwave Player or Java), business presentations, interactive advertising, and CD-ROM or DVD-ROM titles and games.

In comparison, Flash produces vector graphics and animation, including navigation interfaces, technical illustrations, and long-form animations. Flash files can play back using the Flash Player, Java, Director projectors, or Shockwave Player.

XML

Also known as eXtensible Markup Language, XML is a new specification being developed by the W3C. XML enables developers to create customized tags to provide more functionality than HTML. XML programs are not yet supported by current Web browsers. However, Microsoft has committed to supporting XML in Internet Explorer sometime in the future.

XML's usefulness depends solely on its ability to be deployed cross-platform. Once Internet Explorer supports XML, it will become a player. In my opinion, its only use right now is on intranets, where XML-enabled browsers can be loaded onto company machines.

Active Server Pages

ASP is the scripting language supported on the NT platform. It allows the developer to embed functionality similar to that of Perl—providing the user with an interactive experience. The main difference between Perl and ASP is that Perl must be installed in the cgi-bin on the server side. However, ASP can be embedded right into the HTML code.

ASP can be used to access databases, set up in SQL Server or Oracle, and provide the user with searching capabilities and other personalized interactive sessions.

b) A subcontractor fails to produce the functionality that has been contracted. What is your fall-back plan?

Answer: First, you have to assess whether the subcontractor has generated substantial performance. What are the reasons why the subcontractor has failed to produce? Are they on the client side? Have they completed 70% of the requirements and were unable to finish because of any unreasonable expectations?

If the problem truly resides on the subcontractor side, then you, as the project manager, have the ability to cite the project specification and programming plan and ask the subcontractor to accept a reduction in fee, based on the amount of programming modules actually completed. If the subcontractor is leaving modules only half completed, then it's difficult to determine if the programming is even functional. Therefore, payment really needs to be made for functioning modules.

Also, it is always good to have several programming shops as outsourcing possibilities. Therefore, if a firm just cannot complete that ASP script, the project manager should be able to call on another ASP firm to fill in.

This is where a project manager needs to be fair. If the blame could possibly be laid at the contracting firm's feet or the client, the problem is really out of the subcontractor's control. If the client's requirements keep changing, it is up to the project manager to manage the client, **not** to expect the subcontractor to bear the burden of the client's changes, when most likely the sub has flat bid the project. This is how a project manager can easily alienate good firms and sharp programmers.

c) Your company is dealing with a new programming language. There is a significant learning curve and the project is falling behind schedule and beyond budget. What are your options?

*Answer: First, I feel that the client should never have to bear the burden of a learning curve. While the Web firm may feel that a particular project may be a good opportunity to get its feet wet with a new level of functionality, the extra costs associated with this should not be passed on to the client. This is true, unless the client is looking for something extremely new and innovative, which would take **any** firm some research and development to complete. This is the only circumstance in which I feel it's ethical to pass these costs along.*

Too many times I've heard of people just completing their first HTML class taking on a freelance Web project. If the new developer charges time and materials, unless it's about $5 an hour, the client is probably going to be paying too much. When the client figures this out, the freelancer's reputation is damaged.

How do you plan for this? Figure out how much a more experienced firm would charge to do this kind of work and then flat bid it. Any type of project that has a learning curve associated with it should not be undertaken for its profitability. The object usually is to cover the firm's costs. Rather, the project becomes a portfolio piece. The firm has gained experience and can bid other work based on the credibility this project has brought.

If all is going down the tubes fast, it's best to subcontract the more difficult functionality out to a more experienced firm. Hopefully, the project manager will have identified several "bail-out" options before contracting on the project and thus can contact another firm immediately to act as a back-up programming team.

12.3.2 ANSWERS

a) How would you verify that the Web site has been adequately reviewed for quality control purposes?

Answer: Interview the content editor. Has the site been proofread? The testing team should be able to produce screen shots of successful programming outcomes, as defined in the test plan.

b) Who would you have testing the Web site? What would their objectives be?

Answer: I would prefer not to use people who had been involved in any way on the project. Rather, I would prefer that a test team enter the Web site, figure out how it is supposed to work, try all possibilities, and try to break it using input that the Web site would not expect. I would also have a test plan that I would later want them to follow to the letter.

The testing team's objectives are to identify any and all unexpected responses by making the Web site jump through hoops.

LAB 12.3 SELF-REVIEW QUESTIONS

In order to test your progress, you should be able to answer the following questions:

1) (True/False) The following is beyond the subcontractor's control.
   a) _____ Changing programming requirements necessitate changes in completed programming code.
   b) _____ Illness rocks the subcontractor's firm, causing programming to fall behind because of employee absences.

2) (True/False) Which individuals would be a good addition to a Web site testing team?
   a) _____ Project manager
   b) _____ Programmer
   c) _____ Graphic designer
   d) _____ Editor

C H A P T E R   1 2

TEST YOUR THINKING

The projects in this section use the skills you've acquired in this chapter. The answers to these projects are available to instructors only through a Prentice Hall sales representative and are intended to be used in classroom discussion and assessment.

1)   Identify additional tools a project manager can use to keep the technical development of a Web site on track. Include software, Web-based tools, and/or written tracking mechanisms.

2)   If a major programming malfunction is detected during the testing process that requires reanalyzing programming functionality, how can the Web firm address the malfunction while cutting its losses?

CHAPTER 13

LAUNCH/ POSTLAUNCH ACTIVITIES

"Build it and they will come."

From the movie *Field of Dreams*

CHAPTER OBJECTIVES

In this chapter, you will learn about

Sometimes the implementation date sneaks up on the development team, and it is easy to skip some of the steps that are discussed in this chapter. How implementation is handled can better educate the client, not only regarding the use of the Web site but also how to market it. It also can build the client's confidence in the Web site because (1) it works and (2) the client knows how to make it work. There are no surprises.

In this chapter, Charles J. Bleau, the project manager behind Disabilitynews.net, contributes his ideas regarding plans for marketing a Web site (Lab 13.1). Charlie's material is meant to compliment the materials that my coauthor, Donald Emerick, has presented in Part I.

573

L A B   1 3 . 1

WEB MARKETING STRATEGY: LET'S PROMOTE THAT NEW WEB SITE!

LAB OBJECTIVES

After this Lab, you will be able to

- Define Marketing Communications Objectives and a Promotional Mix
- Promote a Web Site with an Existing Promotional Mix
- Identify Marketing and Promotional Opportunities on the Web

---

The actual technical and creative development of a Web site, and getting a working site up and running, is not the final part in Web project development. Somehow, visitors need to be attracted to the site—hence marketing communications also known as promotional strategy. The owners of a site for a small mom and pop retail store may not require 20,000 or even 100 visitors a month. However, if the new Web site is part of a new business process or is an e-company (i.e., an electronic commerce storefront like amazon.com), then developing a cohesive marketing communications plan is vital to promote the site after it has been launched.

A large Web site may spend thousands of dollars in media advertising monthly to promote itself to its target audience. On the other hand, a small Web site for a local florist may spend only $25 putting its Web address on its business cards.

Web marketing can be expensive in some cases, but there are also no-cost or low-cost strategies to make your site visible by both utilizing offline and online media vehicles.

MARKETING COMMUNICATIONS

Marketing communications or promotional strategy is part of the four P's of Marketing. Here's a refresher:

> Product—What is your product/service? Who are your customers? How will you position your product/service so it will appeal to your customers?

> Place—How will you distribute your product/service to your customers?

> Price—How much will your product cost?

> Promotion—What media vehicles (newspapers, magazines, direct mail, telemarketing, TV, radio, online/Web, etc.) will you utilize to promote your product/service to your customers (i.e., target audience)?

The **four P's**, including the marketing communications objectives for the product/service, are defined extensively as part of a marketing plan. The marketing plan will take into consideration all the business goals of the company and develop specific marketing objectives to achieve these overall goals. For the Web project, the project specification will function similarly to a business plan—including all the marketing objectives and communications objectives of the Web site.

MARKETING COMMUNICATIONS OBJECTIVES AND THE PROMOTIONAL MIX

To implement marketing communications objectives, a promotional mix or combination of media to reach the target audience needs to be designed. The promotional mix assumes the following:

> You know who your customer is—you've done research or know from past experience who they are (how old, how much money they make, where they live, male/female, etc.).

You understand the advantages of various media and media vehicles (or have an advertising agency you can consult with about it) and how they relate to your target audience.

With this in mind, a combination of various media and related media vehicles to reach the target audience needs to be identified. Examples of media and media vehicles utilized in the promotional mix include the following:

Media	Media Vehicle
Advertising	TV, radio, newspapers, magazines, outdoor, infomercials
Direct marketing	Mailings, telemarketing
Public relations	Press releases, publicity, trade shows, special events
Interactive/Web	Web sites, online banners, targeted e-mailing (spam)

Each media vehicle has relative advantages and disadvantages in reaching a specific target audience or customer group—a multitude of resources and studies are available, including Neilsen. There are also different media costs, production costs, and a variety of considerations for each of them. A good marketer or advertising agency can develop a promotional mix that will include all these factors, ultimately taking into consideration both the effectiveness of reaching a specific target audience and the overall budget.

PROMOTING A WEB SITE WITH AN EXISTING PROMOTIONAL MIX

Once a new Web site is ready to be launched, the marketing machine should already be rolling. Whether the Web site is a new service for customers, version 2.0 of an existing site, or a completely new e-business, the existing promotional mix for your company should be utilized as the backbone of all marketing communications—why spend more money if you don't have to? Additional marketing resources may be needed to help push customers onto the site if it's a new e-business; however, the small to medium-sized business may only need to promote the new Web site through existing advertising and promotional campaigns.

There are some small adjustments that can be made with little or no cost to promote the new Web site:

Put the Web address (URL) on business cards, letterhead, yellow page ads, and any other advertising the business conducts on a regular basis.

Display signage at point-of-sale promoting the new Web site.

Send a mailing to all existing customers promoting the new Web site and the services provided online.

Send a press release to local/region newspapers promoting the site. If it's an e-business, regional and national trade magazines can be utilized.

If the business regularly attends trade shows, promote the new Web site there.

If it is a medium to large business, integrate the Web address with existing advertising campaigns.

These are just a few of the traditional marketing tools that can be utilized to promote the new Web site without spending an armful.

MARKETING AND PROMOTIONAL OPPORTUNITIES ON THE WEB

So far, the focus of this discussion has been on understanding the promotional mix and how traditional media can be utilized as a means to promote a new Web site. As you may already know, the explosion of the World Wide Web has brought about an explosion of e-businesses, including our friends in the advertising industry.

Marketing and promotional opportunities on the Web are still evolving. Many people from the advertising and direct marketing communities have been trying to cookie cut the online advertising and marketing of Web sites into existing philosophies with little or no success. The World Wide Web is often equated with the Wild, Wild West, with few laws and all the control given to the consumer instead of the advertiser—something advertising agencies are not used to. The Web gives users the freedom to click away and avoid the advertising clutter they've been subjected to with other media, like TV and Radio.

As discussed in Part I of this book, successful Web developers need to be aware of the creative presentation of their web sites—give customers the opportunity to engage in an interactive experience that may encourage them to stick around and perhaps buy something. All the banner ads and targeted e-mails in the world won't keep customers on a boring, uninteresting site.

So, assuming that a new Web site is interactive and an enjoyable experience for the user, various forms of online marketing and promotional tools may be employed to further drive traffic to the site:

1. *Search Engines:* The first marketing tactic involves registering with the major search engines and Web directories: Yahoo!, Lycos, Alta-Vista, Webcrawler, Metacrawler, Excite, Hot Bot, Info Seek, and America Online Netfind. Registering is easy and free, and with the proper integration of some keywords in the <meta> tags of the home page can be a very successful way of promoting the new Web site online.

2. *Cross-marketing:* Swap links and banner ads with suppliers and other constituents the new Web site does business with. Cross-marketing can be an effective means of driving traffic to the sites of both parties involved. This approach is very effective with nonprofits and small to medium-sized businesses—it gets a little dicey if the competition shares the same suppliers, so be aware.

3. *Targeted e-mails:* Send targeted e-mails promoting the new Web site to existing customers or people who have visited the site in the past. Several sites have employed automatic e-mails and news services to people who have visited a site and subscribed to it. This approach can be very effective in keeping past customers and potential customers informed of any promotions and company news.

    "Spamming"—or mass e-mailing—is not a recommended approach for online marketing. Internet service providers (ISPs) as well as e-mail recipients are turned off by such activities. Most ISPs have employed systems to filter spamming and punish the spammers (i.e., the company that sent them). So try to avoid mass e-mailing.

4. *Banner advertising:* Unless the new Web site has a decent sized marketing budget, online banner advertising may be an expensive option. The cost of banner advertising is based upon cost per thousand impressions, or CPM. For example, for every 1000 viewings of a banner ad, a cost will be applied to the advertiser. Web sites that employ banner advertising base their CPM rate on number of visitors per page and how much business the site generates. Sites can also track the number of hits an advertiser's banner receives to measure its effectiveness and adjust future advertising prices.

LAB 13.1 EXERCISES

13.1.1 DEFINE MARKETING COMMUNICATIONS OBJECTIVES AND A PROMOTIONAL MIX

a) You are the president of a newly formed e-company selling books and music CDs online. If your Marketing Department has identified young college students as your business's primary target audience, what are some common media tactics (e.g., advertising, PR, direct marketing) currently employed to appeal to this target audience? Based on your experience, list some promotions and marketing ideas used to reach college students.

_____

_____

_____

_____

_____

_____

_____

_____

_____

_____

_____

_____

_____

_____

b) Develop a promotional mix for your new e-business. Think about the different media you will employ to promote your Web site at launch to reach your target audience and in what sequence (if applicable). For purposes of this exercise, your budget has no limitations.

_____

_____

_____

_____

_____

_____

_____

_____

_____

_____

_____

_____

_____

_____

c) What marketing strategies could you employ to keep the target audience coming back to your site? List your ideas.

_____

_____

_____

_____

_____

_____

_____

_____

_____

_____

_____

_____

_____

_____

_____

_____

13.1.2   PROMOTE A WEB SITE WITH AN EXISTING PROMOTIONAL MIX

a) You are the Marketing Director of a large clothing catalog retailer preparing to launch a new online e-commerce Web site. Currently, your company markets itself through the following ways: 1) a monthly catalog mailing to customers, and 2) A large advertising campaign in sports-related magazines. What are some strategies to get your customers to buy online using these existing media vehicles? Be creative.

What are some ways you can measure the success of your efforts?

_____

_____

_____

_____

_____

_____

13.1.3 *INDENTIFY MARKETING AND PROMOTIONAL OPPORTUNITIES ON THE WEB*

a) Using the catalog company example, the company now wants to drive new customers to the Web site with online marketing. Where and how would you promote your Web site to increase traffic and sales utilizing online marketing?

_____

_____

_____

_____

_____

_____

_____

_____

_____

_____

_____

_____

_____

_____

_____

b) Search on the Web for a clothing catalog retailer—how have they promoted their site online?

_____

_____

_____

_____

_____

_____

_____

_____

_____

c) What are some ways you can measure the effectiveness of your online marketing efforts?

_____

_____

_____

_____

_____

_____

_____

_____

_____

_____

LAB 13.1 EXERCISE ANSWERS

13.1.1 ANSWERS

a) You are the president of a newly formed e-company selling books and music CDs online. If your Marketing Department has identified young college students as your business's primary target audience, what are some common media tactics (e.g., advertising, PR, Direct Marketing) currently employed to appeal to this target audience? Based on your experience, list some promotions and marketing ideas used to reach college students.

Answer: As you may or may not know, the college population is a very diverse group of individuals. Traditionally, college students were considered to be very "brand loyal" purchasers of products and services (an example is the longevity in the popularity of Levi's jeans). Currently, these rules have changed and advertisers have been finding that brand loyalty is not the driving force—college students are more interested in products and services that deliver them more value for their money and quality. Levi's jeans have lost their appeal with Gen Xers to lesser known brands such as Arizona Jeans. Additionally, there are so many college students from other countries attending colleges in the United States that culture and other factors unique to a particular country come into play. So international marketing is an important consideration too.

A marketer needs to consider all the demographics and psychographics (common personality traits and habits of a consumer group) of potential target audiences of the product/service. From here, a marketing communications/promotional plan needs to be tailored to take into consideration the characteristics and buying habits of the target audience with the most market potential. So developing a Web site selling CDs to an eclectic market such as college students needs lots of research to identify the most effective means of marketing communications to reach this audience. Maybe posting flyers or sponsoring music concerts at various colleges across the country is more effective than doing a national television advertising campaign promoting the Web site.

Remember, there are no right answers when it comes to marketing a product or service, only different means of reaching the desired outcome. Obviously, some methods have been proven better than others—but even history is not a secure litmus test for changing consumer buying habits!

So to answer the question, advertising in college newspapers, on-campus concerts, a promotions table in the college Student Union, flyers, and mailings to students are all effective ways that companies have employed to reach college students. Which method that is used depends on solid research (no dart throwing!) and a good product (in this case, an interesting and interactive online experience).

b) Develop a promotional mix for your new e-business. Think about the different media you will employ to promote your Web site at launch to reach your target audience and in what sequence (if applicable). For purposes of this exercise, your budget has no limitations.

Answer: Let's say we received surveys from college students and did some focus groups and have nailed down a comprehensive marketing plan. Our research findings show that our primary target audience consists of college students who come from middle-class, working families and typically live in on-campus housing. They also are typically male (65% male, 35% female) and their music tastes are diverse: They prefer jazz and alternative rock.

So we gave our research findings to our advertising agency and they came up with a promotional mix (a.k.a. media plan in advertising language). The major push to generate interest in our new Web site is going to be special promotions, including coupons and giveways to frequent shoppers.

Here's our promotional mix:

Media	Media Vehicle
Advertising	A series of ads in college newspapers at major colleges across the country with cut-out coupon offering a "buy 1 CD get one free" promotion.
	Ads in the arts and entertainment section of large regional/metropolitan newspapers offering the same coupon promotion as above.
	Radio advertising on jazz and alternative radio stations in media markets of our major colleges. Also, look into advertising on local college stations.
Direct Marketing	Include the "buy 1 CD get one free" coupon in coupon packet distributed nationally by coupon mailing company.
Public Relations	Recruit college students at major colleges to man a promotional booth in the student unions of their college. Again, utilize the "buy 1 CD get one free" couponing program.
Interactive/Web	Selective banner advertising on jazz and alternative radio station Web sites in the major media markets of our major colleges.

Don't worry, there are no right answers to this scenario. Your promotional mix may look very different from the one just presented.

c) What marketing strategies could you employ to keep the target audience coming back to your site? List your ideas.

Answer: Since we mentioned earlier that typically college students are not the most brand loyal group of consumers, using couponing as a means of encouraging purchase is a viable option. The downside of using a coupon strategy is that it has historically discouraged brand loyalty—it encourages price sensitivity and an increased reliance on the future use of coupons by you, the advertiser, and your competition. But in our case, since we are launching a new Web site and are trying to generate visitation and hopefully purchase, a promotional mix dependent on couponing is a great way of encouraging that first visit. To encourage future visits to our site, we should follow the lead of a large-scale e-business retailer such as Amazon.com. They sell music CDs and offer price discounts on their products—so we could follow suit. Additionally, we could provide an outlet for our target audience to sample music online—the technology is available, and many music sites are already doing it.

Our overall goal is to use price sensitivity or "value" through the use of a coupon strategy to draw visitors and give them an interactive and enjoyable experience so they come back in the future.

13.1.2 ANSWERS

a) You are the Marketing Director of a large clothing catalog retailer preparing to launch a new online e-commerce Web site. Currently, your company markets itself through the following ways: (1) a monthly catalog mailing to customers, and (2) a large advertising campaign in sports-related magazines. What are some strategies to get your customers to buy online using these existing media vehicles? Be creative.

Answer: Of course, the first thing you need to do is put your Web address (URL) on all your marketing materials and advertising. Easy enough. If the goal is to have customers buy online, there are benefits for both you the catalog retailer and your customers as opposed to the traditional mail order way of doing things.

The benefits for you the retailer doing business online include

> *Cost savings.* No need to have that huge staff of intermediary customer service representatives; all the ordering and payment processing is done online.

> *Flexibility in selling products and merchandising.* Once that catalog is printed, you can't change it without incurring a huge cost. With an online catalog you can update products anytime. If there's excess inventory for a particular product, put it on sale right away.

> *Faster fulfillment.* Selling online will provide the business with a more streamlined system for fulfilling orders and minimizing data entry errors. This equals additional savings for your company and happy customers.

The benefits for your online customer include

> *A customizable shopping experience.* Today's Web technology can provide your customers with a customized shopping experience based on their past shopping habits and interests.

> *Interactivity.* Instead of talking to a customer service rep or mailing in a complicated order form, your customers can enjoy an interactive experience where they browse for clothing online and can see something in every color and drop the items they want to buy in their "shopping basket."

> *Quick order processing.* No more mailing in order forms and depending on the U.S. Postal Service. If it's two days before your brother's birthday, chances are you can get your gift in time without worrying about the queues in the fulfillment and mailing processes.

The aforementioned customer benefits need to be included in all your marketing materials and advertising. These are the reasons why your customers should buy online and the reasons why your online shopping experience is more convenient.

13.1.3 ANSWERS

a) Using the catalog company example, the company now wants to drive new customers to the Web site with online marketing. Where and how would you promote your Web site to increase traffic and sales utilizing online marketing?

Answer: Chances are if your catalog company is big, you have pretty high brand awareness. So assuming this scenario, you can do online banners on sports-related Web sites (i.e., the online versions of the magazines you already advertise with) and on the major search engine sites. As with our online music store example, you could do some price-related promotions and discounts to draw new customers. The real key is not just to draw people to your site but also to make your site appealing to customers so they'll come back again. Hopefully, this issue got addressed in the creative phase of the Web development project (see Chapter 12).

b) Search on the Web for a clothing catalog retailer—how have they promoted their site online?

Answer: L.L. Bean is a very good example. They are so well known that they derive much of their e-business from existing customers who receive their catalog. L.L. Bean is a major national and international advertiser—all their marketing and advertising includes their Web address. Additionally, the site has employed all the necessary tactics to make a customizable, interactive online experience. The creative presentation of the site is what makes it so successful. Check it out at www.llbean.com.

c) What are some ways you can measure the effectiveness of your online marketing efforts?

Answer: Some very comprehensive Web tracking software is now available. Microsoft Site Server Commerce Edition includes a comprehensive tracking component that can break down a wide variety of attributes and information relating to who is visiting your site, which Web site they came from, and how many hits your site receives at a certain hour of the day.

Besides tracking software and "hits," you can analyze how well your new e-business is doing in generating sales. You can compare your online sales figures to how much business you do offline, through your regular catalog mailers and phone sales. Obviously, if you do a significant amount of sales online without drawing away business from your regular catalog mailer and phone business, you know your advertising campaign is working—new customers are becoming aware of your Web site. If your catalog mailer and phone business takes a slight dip in sales, you know your existing customers are now buying online. Most likely your sales figures would be in the middle of these two extremes. A good way of getting solid feedback is having a simple question on your online order processing form, such as "Where did you hear about us?"

LAB 13.1 SELF-REVIEW QUESTIONS

In order to test your progress, you should be able to answer the following questions:

1) (True/False) One of the "4P's" is:
   a) _____ Planning
   b) _____ Procurement
   c) _____ Place

2) (True/False) Suggested methods of internet marketing include:
   a) _____ Targeted e-mailing
   b) _____ Banner advertising
   c) _____ Search engine placement

L A B   1 3 . 2

DOCUMENTATION/ TRAINING

LAB OBJECTIVES

After this Lab, you will be able to

*   Supply Site Administration Documentation
*   Perform Training
*   Develop Maintenance Agreement

I have heard it said that when a person is leaving a job, he or she tends to be remembered more by the last two weeks at a position than the entire time employed. If an employee has a chip on his or her shoulder or sleep walks through the last two weeks of a job, often that is how the individual is remembered.

How your firm wraps up a project has a lot to do with how the client will view your firm. If the project team is in a hurry and skims over the appropriate steps to end a project nicely, the client can feel resentment. Sure, the project was finished on time. The graphics may have been done perfectly, and the database functionality top notch. However, if the client does not fully understand how to administer the site, it's doubtful that the site can live up to its potential. It's also doubtful that when the client is ready to do an upgrade or maintenance he or she will feel comfortable contacting your Web firm again.

Taking the time to educate the client about how the site works, what requires maintenance by the Web firm, and what kinds of things can be handled on the client side puts the realization of the Web site's potential directly into the client's hands.

If the Web site is database enabled, the client will need training in order to understand how to add, modify, delete, and search for records. Maybe there are password-protected areas that the client needs to be shown how to access.

If the client is planning on updating static pages on the Web with Front Page, some instruction will need to be given regarding connecting to the site. Depending on the level of Front Page ability, the firm may want to offer training hours on how to use Front Page, allowing the client to use his or her own site as a model. The firm should be careful to compensate itself for this type of training. There's a big difference between showing the client how to connect to his or her Web site and showing the client how to use Front Page.

Should the client wish to outsource management of the Web site, it makes sense for the firm to offer a maintenance agreement to the client. There are several models available for an agreement of this sort. Your firm may wish to evaluate several models and decide which one makes sense.

Making a formal plan for updating the site keeps the material fresh, allows the Web firm to schedule the work, and can cut the client a better deal on maintenance. A firm can offer discounted services for the guaranteed work from the client.

Often you go to a Web site and feel like you're looking at an old issue of a magazine. The material is obviously old, and thus it lacks credibility—similar to how one might read a dated article and wonder if the information was still valid.

Let's investigate some techniques through which to make your firm's last impression with a client a very excellent one.

LAB 13.2 EXERCISES

13.2.1 SUPPLY SITE ADMINISTRATION DOCUMENTATION

a) How would you define site administration?

_____

_____

_____

_____

LAB
13.2

b) What sort of information should be included in site administration documentation?

_____

_____

_____

_____

_____

_____

_____

_____

_____

_____

_____

_____

_____

_____

_____

_____

_____

_____

_____

_____

13.2.2 PROVIDE TRAINING

a) What kinds of issues might a Web firm run into when trying to provide training to a client?

_____

_____

_____

_____

_____

_____

_____

_____

_____

_____

_____

_____

_____

_____

_____

_____

_____

_____

b) How could the problems discussed in 13.2.2a be avoided?

_____

_____

_____

_____

13.2.3 DEVELOP A MAINTENANCE AGREEMENT

a) How can a maintenance agreement benefit both the client and the Web firm?

_____

_____

_____

_____

_____

_____

_____

_____

_____

_____

_____

_____

_____

_____

b) Devise two plans through which a Web firm could offer regular maintenance.

LAB 13.2 EXERCISE ANSWERS

This section gives you some suggested answers to the questions in Lab 13.2 with discussion related to those answers. Please post any alternative answers to these questions at the companion Web site for this book, located at http://www.phptr.com/phptrinteractive.

**LAB
13.2**

13.2.1 ANSWERS

a) How would you define site administration?

Answer: Site administration involves the maintenance of an existing Web site and understanding the hosting and updating requirements that are necessary for its continued success. It also encompasses the follow-through of Web marketing initiatives, such as link exchanges and banner advertising.

b) What sort of information should be included in site administration documentation?

Answer: The following information is key to site administration:

- *Hosting requirements (operating system, middleware, support for programming languages used to develop the site)*
- *Step-by-step training materials that walk the site administrator through updating the database or online store through an administrative back room*
- *Requirements for performing updates to static Web pages, based on a maintenance plan discussed prior to launch between the client and the Web firm*
- *Contact information for the Web firm, additional vendors, and the hosting company*
- *A troubleshooting section that specifies who to call if certain problems arise*

13.2.2 ANSWERS

a) What kinds of issues might a Web firm run into when trying to provide training to a client?

Answer: The Web firm must really assess the computer skills of the client before setting up a maintenance and/or training agreement. If the client does not have computer-savvy people on staff, the Web firm may have to offer training on much more than just how to handle the Web application. Therefore, an estimated two hours of training can run into twenty. This is a burden that most Web firms cannot afford to absorb. If the firm runs into this situation, it's best to write a new maintenance contract that allows the Web firm to handle all of the maintenance.

Client frustration is also a factor when doing training. Sometimes clients have anxiety when dealing with new computer applications. Try to use your most patient and mature people on staff to handle client training sessions.

b) How could the problems discussed in 13.2.2a be avoided?

Answer: Try to assess up front what type of client you have and their capabilities. If the client is extremely computer literate and is not afraid of learning new things, it is probably a good bet that training can be successful. You can also get a feel for this during the Web build based on how open the client is to being educated about the process of building his or her Web site. If, after the Web site build, you feel that you will be showing the client where the "on" button is on the computer, you can best serve the client by setting up an agreement through which the client can outsource the maintenance to your firm.

13.2.3 ANSWERS

a) How can a maintenance agreement benefit both the client and the Web firm?

Answer: The client is assured of keeping the Web site updated and is usually offered discounted pricing, when signing a maintenance contract, versus calling the Web firm when an update is absolutely necessary. The client is also guaranteed a place in the production schedule, because the Web firm can schedule the work.

A maintenance agreement benefits the Web firm in that it can schedule the update, and it can rely on the regular cash flow.

b) Devise two plans through which a Web firm could offer regular maintenance.

Answer: There are several different ways to offer regular maintenance. One option may be to sign an annual contract with a client firm that guarantees a defined number of updates on a weekly, monthly, or quarterly basis. Another option involves collecting a monthly maintenance fee, and it is up to the client to provide update material. Some clients may send more than the firm expects and others may not send anything at all. Thus, the cash flow for the work tends to even out.

LAB 13.2 SELF-REVIEW QUESTIONS

LAB 13.2

In order to test your progress, you should be able to answer the following questions:

1) (True/False) Good site administration documentation should
   a) _____ Advise a client on how to use Front Page.
   b) _____ Explain FTP (file transfer protocol) in depth.
   c) _____ Offer alternative hosting options, should the client become dissatisfied with the current hosting company.

2) (True/False) A maintenance agreement should cover
   a) _____ HTML updates
   b) _____ Graphic design updates
   c) _____ Programming functionality upgrades

L A B   1 3 . 3

INTERNAL AUDIT

LAB OBJECTIVES

After this Lab, you will be able to

- Assess Team Performance
- Evaluate Client Questionnaires
- Make Phase II Recommendations

Once the project is finished and delivered, it's easy to look forward to the next exciting project in the pipeline. After all, by the time a project reaches launch, everyone on the project team has hopefully given it their all and is looking forward to taking on something new. A project team can be ready to move on. However, unless it looks backward, the team does not grow.

Identifying the steps that went well and the steps that did not go as smoothly is important. Has someone on the team been dealing with a subcontractor who did not deliver as agreed? Unless this is talked about with the project team, a decision may be made to hire that subcontractor. Could better communication between the project manager and the creative team have circumvented several composite stages? It's time to brainstorm how that process can be streamlined. Maybe it's time to bring several members of the creative team along on project meetings. How does everyone see the Web site evolving? Creative team members may see a Shockwave application. The technical team may see e-commerce. Making these suggestions to the client can help define the direction he or she will eventually go with the site and secure new business for the Web firm.

The team may want to send a questionnaire to the client asking how he or she felt the process went. A report card helps anyone to improve their performance.

Conducting an internal audit of the project does not mean that the team should walk away feeling badly about the negative points of the project process. Rather, the tone of these internal audits should be very positive. Maybe the audit should be conducted during a company-sponsored lunch at which the team does not take on other business. Successful completion of the project should be cause for celebration, not anxiety.

A positive approach to this internal audit is good for project team morale. Rather than singling out nonperformers, the project manager can make a point of singling out performers. This can spur others to wish to be recognized next time. The project manager can show specific pieces of the Web site that were outstanding and design quality or functionality to be emulated next time.

Call it a dead dog party, Monday morning quarterbacking, or a company field trip to the local laser tag establishment, an internal audit done well can help to identify aggravating stumbling blocks, throw a spotlight on most valuable players, and enhance the client relationship.

Let's see how you would conduct this process.

LAB 13.3 EXERCISES

13.3.1 ASSESS TEAM PERFORMANCE

a) What is the best setting in which to conduct a postproject meeting?

_____

_____

_____

_____

_____

_____

_____

_____

_____

_____

_____

_____

_____

_____

_____

_____

_____

_____

_____

_____

_____

_____

_____

_____

b) Develop a sample agenda for a postproject meeting.

_____

_____

_____

_____

**LAB
13.3**

_____

_____

_____

_____

_____

_____

_____

_____

_____

_____

_____

_____

_____

_____

_____

_____

_____

_____

13.3.2   EVALUATE CLIENT QUESTIONNAIRES

a) What sort of questions would you ask a client on a postproject questionnaire?

_____

_____

_____

b) How much emphasis should the project team place on this sort of feedback?

_____

_____

_____

_____

_____

_____

_____

_____

_____

_____

_____

_____

_____

_____

_____

_____

_____

_____

_____

_____

_____

_____

13.3.3　MAKE PHASE II RECOMMENDATIONS

a) How would a project team best identify any Phase II recommendations for the client?

_____

_____

_____

_____

_____

_____

_____

_____

_____

_____

_____

_____

_____

_____

_____

_____

_____

_____

_____

_____

_____

_____

b) How should these recommendations be best presented to the client?

_____

_____

_____

_____

_____

_____

_____

_____

_____

_____

_____

_____

_____

_____

_____

_____

LAB 13.3 EXERCISE ANSWERS

This section gives you some suggested answers to the questions in Lab 13.3 with discussion related to those answers. Please post any alternative answers to these questions at the companion Web site for this book, located at http://www.phptr.com/phptrinteractive.

13.3.1 ANSWERS

a) What is the best setting in which to conduct a postproject meeting?

Answer: Hopefully, you have mature, talented people on your project team who truly care about the quality of the work they produce. However, this is not always the case. Some team members may feel insecure about their contributions to the team. Or some members may bog down under the weight of their own attitude. Unfortunately, this is not a perfect world.

Thus, when planning a postproject meeting, the setting should be informal and relaxed, perhaps an impetus to allow those people who don't usually have a lot to say in project meetings the atmosphere in which to contribute their ideas. Some uncomfortable topics may be identified at this meeting. Perhaps the amount of time Bill took off as a result of his girlfriend being in town hindered the creative process. While these issues don't have to be exposed specifically for all to scrutinize, they can be identified in a more generalized fashion so that the person involved gets the point. A relaxed atmosphere, preferably away from the office, can do a lot to facilitate open communication.

a) Develop a sample agenda for a postproject meeting.

Answer:

I.   Introductions

II.   Scope of Work

III.   Review of Final Product

IV.   Feedback from Client Questionnaires

BREAK FOR LASERTAG, FOOD, BASEBALL, WHAT HAVE YOU

V.   Project Stumbling Blocks

VI.   Project Successes

VII.   Experience We Bring from This Project to the Next

VIII. Recognition of Individuals for Outstanding Performance

IX.   Close

BREAK FOR MORE LASERTAG, FOOD, BASEBALL, WHAT HAVE YOU

13.3.2 ANSWERS

a) What sort of questions would you ask a client on a postproject questionnaire?

Answer: A very short questionnaire could resemble the following. However, you might like to find out more specifics.

Rate from 0 to 10 (10 being excellent) your satisfaction level with the following project areas:

- *Responsiveness of the project manager*
- *How closely the final product resembled expectations*
- *Adherence to project schedule*
- *Graphic design of Web site*
- *Functional design of Web site*
- *How your company's Web site compares against competition*

b) How much emphasis should the project team place on this sort of feedback?

Answer: Client dispositions vary. Some clients are very reasonable to walk through a Web site build. Others can be extremely difficult. Based on the attitude of the client during the Web site build, a project team can probably judge how much importance the client questionnaire will have to them. I'll be honest: I have had a few clients that I would not bother sending a client questionnaire to. The client's behavior during the Web build made things difficult. Rather, I would want to discuss with my project team how we might have made things easier for this difficult client to understand. Or I would want to discuss whether we should have taken on the project at all.

With a reasonable client who has been participatory in all phases, I would place a great deal of emphasis on the client questionnaire. This client will tell you where you can improve, and the project team members can find out more about the client, so that they can better service his or her needs in the future.

13.3.3 ANSWERS

a) How would a project team best identify any Phase II recommendations for the client?

Answer: As the project is progressing, various technical and creative team members will have ideas for the Web site, and while they may not be covered under the budget or schedule guidelines for the present phase, these enhancements could be accommodated in a Phase II implementation. Ideas for Phase II should be brought to and documented by the project manager.

During the internal audit, the last step may be to come up with Phase II recommendations for the client. Once everyone has had a little distance from the project, but not too much, it is a good time to look at it with a fresh perspective and perhaps brainstorm its next incarnation.

b) How should these recommendations be best presented to the client?

Answer: Often these recommendations generate organically during project status meetings with the client. However, the project manager should schedule a wrap-up meeting where site administration and any Phase Ii recommendations can be discussed in depth. Presenting the client with examples of working prototypes for these sort of enhancements is always helpful.

LAB 13.3

LAB 13.3 SELF-REVIEW QUESTIONS

In order to test your progress, you should be able to answer the following questions:

1) (True/False) An internal audit should identify
   a) _____ Nonperformers
   b) _____ Functionality that the firm is particularly proud of
   c) _____ Phase II recommendations

2) (True/False) Using postproject client questionnaires can help the Web firm to identify
   a) _____ Nonperformers
   b) _____ Snags in team communication
   c) _____ Which project team members deserve raises

CHAPTER 13

TEST YOUR THINKING

The projects in this section use the skills you've acquired in this chapter. The answers to these projects are available to instructors only through a Prentice Hall sales representative and are intended to be used in classroom discussion and assessment.

1) What kinds of problems among the project team might the project manager run into by conducting an internal audit? How can they be avoided?

2) How would you approach a client who is certain that a Phase II recommendation should have been included in Phase I?

C H A P T E R 1 4

WEB FIRM START-UPS

"During the gold rush, who made more money? The miners? Or Levi Strauss?"

—Kim Round

CHAPTER OBJECTIVES

In this chapter, you will learn about

Those people who have spent a significant amount of their lives working for someone else may find the prospect of owning and operating their own business both terrifying and thrilling at the same time. Having done it, I can easily say that the feeling doesn't necessarily go away, although I do get to sleep more than I used to.

The Web is opening up all sorts of entrepreneurial opportunities for people who may not have ever considered themselves potential entrepreneurs. Like many of my contemporaries, I planned on settling in with a nice corporate engineering job and seeing it through. However, when two babies came into my husband's and my life, I wanted to spend some time at home with them. I dreamed of a career that would allow me to adopt the parenting style that I was comfortable with while challenging my intellect. In a sense, it started out as a way to bring in a modest second income while giving me the time to tote my boys to softball practice. Now, I could work twenty-four hours a day, and I'm always grateful to have these opportunities, although I can't explore them all. Many of you have individual reasons for wanting to explore this territory. Maybe you're unhappy in your present job. Maybe you've always dreamed of running your own business. Perhaps you've fallen in love with creating Web sites, and you see an excellent business opportunity.

My Web company started with an online class through the University of Massachusetts at Dartmouth. My class project was a four-page Web site that I built for my husband's hardware store. I never intended for it to go any further than that, but I began to dream about the name of the firm that I would have and the people I would like to work with. Soon, I had some very nice people who were interested in sharing this dream with me, but we had no idea about how to get the word out. All of us had worked for other companies, and we had no idea how to market ourselves and get work. Plus, straight HTML does not make a Web firm. I needed to find one or two talented graphic artists and come up to speed very quickly on some hardcore interactive programming. There was a nice period in which I could expand my knowledge by taking yet more courses in Web development while I picked up a job or two. Had I planned it that way, I would have thought it was a conservative and prudent approach. However, the truth was that I couldn't wait until I had some serious business coming through the door. If that did not happen, I felt like my whole endeavor and all the hard work would be for naught, and I was anxious to make the dream fly.

Of course, impatience is always an enemy. For someone who is growing a Web firm organically, it can be frustrating to wait for calls to come in. After all, the day you turn on a business line doesn't mean there is an automatic listing in the yellow pages. And even so, the business of Web site design is very similar to that of carpentry or even dentistry. Most potential clients would prefer to be referred to someone who is good. Web development is truly a "Don't tell me . . . show me" type of business. If a new firm doesn't have many Web sites to show, it can be difficult to gain credibility.

I vividly remember agonizing over every new tool that I bought. After all, if the Web biz didn't take, what was the point of having so many books and software programs? However, as the old adage goes, "You have to spend money to make money." Unfortunately, there wasn't a whole lot of money to spend. Surf's Up literally started from nothing. In the winter of 1995, I spent $200 to pull apart an old 486 computer and add a sound card, video card, and modem. You could say Surf's Up was built organically from the microchip level.

Another hurdle many new Web freelancers or firms face is that while they may be excellent technicians, they may not have been trained to do technical sales. Most of us hate going for job interviews, let alone having to sell ourselves every day. This was one of the biggest nerve-wracking activities for me. As I would get ready to go into a potential client's office, my palms would sweat and my mind would be more focused on how to get the job than truly evaluating the project at hand. During this period, I was asked to get up and give a ten-minute presentation about my company. Not having done this before, I don't think I was a very engaging speaker.

However, after representing myself for six months or so, I began to relax. Now I rarely think about whether I'll want the job and not get it. Rather, when I go to see a new potential client, I'm in screening mode. I want to evaluate the project, the client, and what my firm can bring to the table. This isn't because I need the work any less than I did back then. I probably need it more. I have overhead now. Rather, this attitude is just a result of building up a little self-confidence and knowing that it's much better to walk away from a job that isn't a good fit than to struggle through it and lose money. If the potential client would rather have someone else do the job, I know that it rarely has anything to do with me. The other firm may have an incentive that the client feels more comfortable with. The project must be a good fit for both sides.

What I do try to do is limit my exposure to taking too many meetings, which may not pan out. Before I take the time to meet with a client, I want to know that the client wants a Web site now, not six months from now, so there's urgency. I want to hear that there's been some research and preparation done ahead of time, so I know there's some commitment. And I want to know if the client is aware of what Web development can cost. Any other scenario makes for a waste of time and energy.

Like other people in creative occupations, Web developers have to watch the expectation on the part of a client that work can be done on "spec." So often I ran into clients who showed me a Web site that some well-meaning Web developer had begun for free, to give the client a view of how the Web might increase their business, only to have them ask me for a bid. The free work was not respected. It never is. Many potential clients who aren't serious about paying a professional firm to do a good job on a Web site are very quick to ask for "spec" work. The only thing a Web developer has to sell is his or her time. Don't give it away for free. You might as well throw money into the street, no matter how much a potential client assures you that they just need to see "something" before committing. Web developers can point clients to other sites that they have built, if the business owner needs assurance of their skills. If you need to build a few free sites to broaden a portfolio, build them for nonprofit or charitable organizations that might not be able to afford a Web site ordinarily. Your work will be appreciated, and it will do some good.

LAB 14.1

EVALUATING FINANCING

LAB OBJECTIVES

After this Lab, you will be able to

- Analyze Current Resources
- Determine Need for Outside Investors

You don't necessarily have to build your business purely organically. There are many options available for people who are willing to define what they want to accomplish and put it into a business plan. However, you have to determine what your prospective Web firm might have to offer, which makes it worthwhile for other people to be interested in it. Is it the talented people who would contribute to projects? Is it your innovative approach to the Web? Is it an ability to make a Web-based product that can be resold?

Venture capital and bank loans can pave the way so that a Web firm can effectively market itself, giving the firm the exposure to build up a nice portfolio and hire talented individuals. However, a bank loan generates risk. Venture capital implies a partial or total loss of ownership interest. Some term venture capital as "vulture capital." Unfortunately, most people cannot enter into a viable Web business, which is going to generate an acceptable level of revenue right away, unless there is some outside funding.

So you don't want to mortgage your house or beg for OPM (other people's money). A nice way to begin is to start building Web sites part time. At Surf's Up, we've used many contractors who are only available at night or on weekends. This gives us the flexibility to use highly talented individuals on a project-by-project basis without having to carry these individuals during slow periods. For the subcontractor, hooking up with another Web firm in this fashion is not a bad idea. It's a great way to ease into the business and put away a little seed money without assuming a great deal of risk. While helping out at a large Web firm in Boston this summer, I was surprised at how many of the team members freelanced. They spent their days working on projects for the firm and then went home to their own lucrative projects. These people have the security of a regular paycheck while having the opportunity to run and bid their own Web projects. It's a very exciting time for skilled Web professionals. There's plenty of work if you know where to look for it.

LAB 14.1 EXERCISES

14.1.1 ANALYZE CURRENT RESOURCES

a) Who do you know who has excellent Web skills? In what areas (graphics, programming, editing, etc.) do these people have their strengths?

_____

_____

_____

_____

_____

_____

_____

_____

_____

_____

_____

_____

_____

_____

_____

_____

_____

_____

_____

_____

_____

_____

_____

_____

_____

_____

b) What kinds of attachments might you have to the business community? Do you belong to the chamber of commerce or any other networking group? Would you be willing to join?

_____

_____

_____

_____

_____

_____

_____

_____

_____

_____

_____

_____

_____

_____

_____

_____

_____

_____

_____

_____

c) What are your best skills? Are you a good manager? Are you a strong programmer?

_____

_____

_____

_____

_____

_____

_____

_____

_____

_____

_____

_____

_____

_____

_____

_____

_____

_____

_____

_____

_____

_____

_____

14.1.2   DETERMINE NEED FOR OUTSIDE INVESTORS

a) Research venture capital. Would this be a viable option for your firm?

_____

_____

_____

_____

_____

_____

_____

_____

_____

_____

_____

_____

_____

_____

_____

_____

_____

_____

_____

_____

_____

_____

_____

_____

b) Research commercial loans through a bank. How could a bank loan benefit your business plan?

_____

_____

_____

LAB 14.1 EXERCISE ANSWERS

This section gives you some suggested answers to the questions in Lab 14.1 with discussion related to those answers. Please post any alternative answers to these questions at the companion Web site for this book, located at http://www.phptr.com/phptrinteractive.

14.1.1 ANSWERS

a) Who do you know who has excellent Web skills? In what areas (graphics, programming, editing, etc.) do these people have their strengths?

Answer: As more people become interested in Web-based careers, there are more individuals available who are well trained to take on a project team role. I am very lucky in that I am exposed to some wonderfully talented people through the classes that I teach. Some of my former students have become indispensable team members. However, not everyone teaches in a Webmaster certification program and has the chance to evaluate an individual's skills first hand before getting involved on a project with him or her.

There are several crucial points when hiring team members. First rule, be aware of what your best skills are and hire people who complement you.

Rule 2: Hire up. Don't be afraid to hire people who you feel are more skilled than yourself. They can only enhance the product. As long as they don't have an attitude and you can feel pleased to have them on your team, instead of feeling insecure, it's a wonderful opportunity to learn, create, and surpass expectations.

In forming your own project team, think about your neighbors, friends, and co-workers. Who has skills that would complement yours? Who has a good team player attitude? Who has the knowledge to bring a project to a higher level? Who respects your time and wallet? When starting out, don't plan on mentoring. Get good competent people initially. If you want to teach less skilled Web professionals, get paid to do it. Don't do it on your own dollar. After you've made your first million, you can consider taking on people in need of grooming.

b) What kinds of attachments might you have to the business community? Do you belong to the chamber of commerce or any other networking group? Would you be willing to join?

Answer: How can you generate business organically? The most inexpensive way to generate business is through word of mouth. It's true that sometimes people are more comfortable doing business in new media with someone they know and have confidence in.

One doesn't necessarily want to become like a new life insurance salesperson. Often, these people are advised to make a list of every person they know, including family members, and call them, asking if they need life insurance. However, it might be good to analyze whether you know anyone who has a business that could benefit from a Web presence.

c)   What are your best skills? Are you a good manager? Are you a strong pro-grammer?

Answer: My strong points are that I am a good hardcore programmer, I understand project flow, and I interact well with clients. A highly valued member of my project team is an excellent conceptualist. Having had a background in advertising and marketing, Charlie can key in on the message the client is trying to send and come up with innovative ways to get it across via Web-based media. We always tease each other that when we're listening to a client, I'm thinking, "How does it work?" and Charlie's thinking, "What should it say?" This way, we balance each other well. We also have another team member who is a terrifically talented graphic artist. He can work from Charlie's concepts to create a beautiful user interface. Powell's sense of style comes from a natural feel for artwork. His talent isn't learned but rather a natural one. Without my team members, I am just a good coder, project manager, and client account manager. When selecting team members, I keep this in mind and hire people who can take up the slack.

14.1.2 ANSWERS

a)   Research venture capital. Would this be a viable option for your firm?

Answer: When I first heard someone refer to venture capital (VC), I initially thought he was talking about the Vietnam War. Now, people drop this term around Web firms as freely as they talk about HTML. VC, a.k.a. "vulture capital" or venture capital, used wisely can jump-start a business, benefiting both investors and the company founders.

There's a lot of money to be had for Internet start-ups. Unfortunately, there are a lot of inexperienced people unwittingly mortgaging their future with an ill-conceived business plan. If the company is already generating revenues, this is valid consideration. However, accepting venture capital before the first dime has been turned is risky at best. Think carefully before giving away a piece of your business. If you want to go into business for yourself to allow for greater flexibility to exercise your vision, you may be just trading one boss for another should your business plan fail.

Another option is angel capital. Usually, the ownership of the business is not diluted to the same extent as venture capital, mostly because there is less money involved. However, $30,000 to $50,000 can go a long way to initiate a good marketing effort while avoiding some hefty bank interest rates or an intensive loan application procedure.

b) Research commercial loans through a bank. How could a bank loan benefit your business plan?

Answer: If you have good personal credit, you might consider going to a bank for $30,000 to $50,000 to initially market your Web firm. Radio and print advertising can be expensive. Also, some clients have a greater comfort level if they can come into an office atmosphere as opposed to someone's home office. My firm has been operated as a home office for three years, and we've saved a great deal of money this way. However, we have run into problems time to time with clients who dropped by the house and felt since we were carrying such low overhead, our time wasn't worth as much. Most of these folks are not educated as to how much a Web developer's time costs. They jump to conclusions. Sometimes clients feel that a business run out of a home office is not serious. There are also some inherent risks involved in opening one's home to the public, be it clients or employees. A bank loan can generate a little seed money to get a business into office space, market the firm to get money flowing through the door, and hire competent professionals.

LAB 14.1 SELF-REVIEW QUESTIONS

In order to test your progress, you should be able to answer the following questions:

1) (True/False) Angel capital can be more preferable to a bank loan in that
   a) _____ Ownership interest in the Web firm is not diluted.
   b) _____ If you have poor or nonexistent personal credit, it is a viable cash resource.

2) (True/False) If I were a strong graphic designer, I would want to hire
   a) _____ A good multimedia professional
   b) _____ An ASP and/or VB Script programmer
   c) _____ An administrative assistant

L A B   1 4 . 2

MARKETING

LAB OBJECTIVES

After this Lab, you will be able to

- Utilize Networking Opportunities
- Develop Strategic Partnerships
- Analyze Advertising Options

How will we get the work? That's what most Web firm start-ups ask themselves. You can have all the talent in the world available to build Web sites, but without opportunities to bid projects, there is no way to win them and knock client's socks off. After all, most Web firms worth their salt could build an attractive Web site for the White House, but who actually gets the opportunity to do so? It's all about contacts.

After a while, when there is enough work out there, the phone will ring because of word of mouth referrals. However, until that occurs, a Web firm will need to make the effort to network with other business professionals in order to attract work and build strategic partnerships. Advertising, while I do not believe it is the best option, is still a consideration. You want to build relationships that lead to not only one or two projects but a steady stream of projects. If you can establish an easy working relationship with a complementary business entity, where you can bring something to the table for this company as well, and treat this relationship like gold, this relationship becomes invaluable for everyone involved.

Nothing annoys me more than when another business entity calls me and basically announces that they are on the scene and I will definitely want to use them because of how great they are. They are offering me nothing to do business with them. Rather, they want me to send all of my hosting and/or equipment leads their way but aren't willing to work in a mutually supportive fashion. I'm very proud of the supportive relationships I have built up over the last few years with other businesspeople. I'm excited to hear of their successes, and we encourage each other. When I hear of someone who needs a good florist or bricklayer, I know businesses I'll recommend. That doesn't mean I'll recommend any business that isn't wonderful, because I will not make such a referral and steer someone wrong. Such an action devalues my integrity. However, with those businesses that provide excellent products and services, I am happy to be supportive if I see a sales lead for them. In fact, I will look for leads for others when I'm in a meeting with a client who seems to be a good person to do business with. This is how businesses get ahead. However, many Web firms start up considering whether they should bring on a Flash programmer before they take the time to build relationships in the business community. Much of my work comes from word of mouth referrals through other business owners. If I keep them in mind, they will be sure to speak up if they hear that someone needs a Web site.

Therefore, I see the business referrals that I can generate as marketing opportunities for my own business. This doesn't mean that I keep score. No one can do that. Sales challenges are different for every industry. However, if I am going to be sending clients to a hosting company, I prefer that they know who I am and that I am generating business for them, so that the next time someone asks them about a Web developer, they will remember me.

Even though the firm must always be on the lookout for new clients, a Web development company should act as a cheerleader for existing clients. It's a tremendous opportunity to get to know other industries and industry leaders and aid these businesses in growing. If a client feels that you are on their side and are truly wishing the best for them, this goes a long way not only to facilitate the project but to generate word of mouth referrals. The client wants to see your firm be successful too, not only because he or she senses your sincere wish to help grow his or her business but because the client wants you to be around in the future to continue to do so. So it's always helpful to choose clients whom you respect and can easily get behind.

Of course, Web development could be considered an advertising medium, among other things. A Web developer has the unique knowledge of understanding how to market businesses over the Web and can apply those techniques to his or her own firm. Some Web firms do radio and print advertising. However, one must have the portfolio to show prospective clients online, before most people will initiate a contract. A good marketing representative, whether it is you or your partner, who has excellent communications skills can engender trust among potential clients and work to build that portfolio.

We've discussed before the pitfalls of telling a client that you are able to leap tall buildings at a single bound in order to get the contract. We know this is a recipe for disaster. Most good clients respect someone who can say "I don't know" or "I'll have to check into that" or "I'm sorry, but that's beyond what I can do." It's important to be open and honest. No matter how much you're burning to do this potential client's Web site, if you're not absolutely sure that you can meet and surpass the requirements, don't waste their time. This is where a decent sales representative, who also has good technical skills, can be a key player on the team. In networking meetings, this person will not hang the moon on their Web company as being all things. Very few Web firms are all things. Some firms' strengths lie in their innovative designs. Others are very strong in cutting-edge programming. Yet another firm might specialize in multimedia presentations. A sales representative who can screen projects that are unsuitable for the Web firm because they don't lend themselves well to the firm's current resources is golden. This type of person breeds trust for your firm in the business community.

No matter what, despite all of your good intentions, a difficult client who isn't paying attention or refuses to allow you to educate them about the process of building a Web site will love to accuse you of boasting that you could provide certain services and have fallen short. However, this is usually not the firm's fault, nor should the sales representative beat himself or herself up about this situation. Most of this problem lies on the client side, and the firm must employ good project management procedures to document client requirements and how they were responded to.

Let's examine what kinds of opportunities might be available to help you to build and keep the right type of clientele for your Web firm.

LAB 14.2 EXERCISES

14.2.1 UTILIZE NETWORKING OPPORTUNITIES

a) How would you define a networking opportunity? What elements make for a good one?

_____

_____

_____

b) Can you identify three groups through which you may be able to drive traffic to your business?

_____

_____

14.2.2   DEVELOP STRATEGIC PARTNERSHIPS

a) What is a strategic partnership?

_____

_____

_____

_____

_____

_____

_____

_____

_____

_____

_____

_____

_____

_____

_____

_____

_____

_____

_____

b) Identify several types of businesses through which your firm might develop a beneficial strategic partnership.

14.2.3 ANALYZE ADVERTISING OPTIONS

a) Who is your target audience?

b) What kinds of advertising options might reach that target audience?

_____

_____

_____

_____

_____

LAB 14.2 EXERCISE ANSWERS

This section gives you some suggested answers to the questions in Lab 14.2 with discussion related to those answers. Please post any alternative answers to these questions at the companion Web site for this book, located at http://www.phptr.com/phptrinteractive.

14.2.1 ANSWERS

a) How would you define a networking opportunity? What elements make for a good one?

Answer: First, you need to analyze the type of people that you are marketing to. If you want to build educational Web sites for use by people in schools or colleges, then you will want to attend networking meetings where those kinds of people may be present.

If you want to build commercial Web sites, then it's best to attend functions where viable corporate entities might be present.

A networking opportunity is any event where your target audience might be present and open to discussing business. If you know that your child's best friend's father owns a computer store that does not yet have a Web site, it may not be a good idea to make a pitch at softball practice. Usually, this only generates resentment. However, you might casually ask this individual about how the store is going. Out of politeness, your child's best friend's father might ask you what you do. If you mention casually that you own a Web firm that specializes in online stores, this person will make the obvious connection and may ask you more about it on his own. If he's interested, he will ask more about your services. After all, most business owners are always looking for opportunities to increase their exposure. If he isn't interested, then you haven't stuck your foot in your mouth.

However, the more traditional networking opportunities usually involve a more formal setting. The people that are there are present for the specific reason of networking their businesses. They are also expecting to learn more about the other businesses that are there as well.

Elements that make for good networking opportunities include the presence of complementary but not competitive businesses. Also, the presence of businesses that would lend themselves well to a Web presence is desirable. Preferably this meeting allows for a free exchange between attendees as opposed to being focused completely on a speaker. If too many people are speaking, there is little chance to meet and greet. The crowd can mostly disperse after the speakers finish. This isn't a networking opportunity but rather an informational meeting.

Also, I wouldn't bother to show up at a mixer where ten other Web development firms are attending, with the idea of generating business, unless I felt that the product or service that I could offer was unusual and one that might be used by the other Web firms. I would rather attend a mixer with other Web developers in order to discuss business issues that are common to all and view this occasion as more of an educational conduit.

b) Can you identify three groups through which you may be able to drive traffic to your business?

Answer: Entrepreneurial groups are always good to belong to. The people that belong to the group have to have the ability to be the marketing decision maker or directly influence the marketing decision maker. In other words, the local Mary Kay representative is not going to be able to get you the contract for the Mary Kay Web site. However, she can be a wonderful source for ordering your employee gifts and give you wonderful attention.

Groups like the local chamber of commerce, Business Network International, or the Rotary Club are all good places to network your business. However, you have to be willing to help other business owners. Networking is Net-WORKING. If you aren't willing to help other business owners, and you only have time to be out for yourself, then other people will recognize this very quickly. They will shoot their business to someone who is willing to work with them in a reciprocal fashion.

Web site development, from the outside, doesn't necessarily have weights and measure attached to it. Hosting companies and other technically oriented entities might be able to appreciate how your firm is better than another, but people in other industries might not understand this. To them, a Web developer is a Web developer. A helpful attitude goes a long way.

14.2.2 ANSWERS

a) What is a strategic partnership?

Answer: A strategic partnership is a loose agreement, usually not in writing, between two businesses that provide services that are complementary. A wedding photographer might be able to develop a strategic partnership with a caterer; the same is true of Web developers. If the photographer feels comfortable referring the caterer and vice versa, they can refer each other almost exclusively. After all, both business owners probably get asked all the time about who else might know who might provide other kinds of wedding services.

Last summer we brought a boat into one of the ports on Lake Winnipesaukee in New Hampshire. One of the first places we ran into was the drug store, which was located conveniently for people coming off their boats to pick up sunblock, aspirin, hats, or sunglasses. While we were there, the people were extremely friendly, and we were hungry. We asked them where we could find a good place to eat, and they referred us down the street to a super diner. This is a type of a strategic partnership, because I'm sure if I had asked a waitress where the best place to get a set of sunglasses might be, she would have told me to go to the drug store. They all know each other and drive traffic to each other's establishments. However, I'm sure that neither of these business owners would let the other one down by ever providing poor service. A strategic partnership can't work if one of the entities provides marginal service. It will generate resentment.

The best kinds of strategic partnerships usually are generated when people begin to refer each other on the quality of the other's work and then discover that they are mutually sending each other referrals. Sometimes it can work into something more formal. I wouldn't like to tie another business owner's hands and ask for exclusivity either. This limits their playing field and mine. However, if I know that I'm getting a majority of their referrals, and I am sending the other company a majority of mine, I feel that this type of arrangement works well.

b) Identify several types of businesses through which your firm might develop a beneficial strategic partnership.

Answer: Local Web hosting and advertising companies are great to develop strategic partnerships with. I wouldn't necessarily spend very much time lobbying for a nationwide hosting company to shoot me its Web site design referrals. This is a big entity. I probably would never find a contact there that I could build a relationship with. It probably just isn't going to happen unless I really know someone. And anyone worth their salt at the big nationwide hosting company will probably analyze what I can do for them. Am I generating enough business to send to them as well? Probably not.

However, a Web development firm can hopefully shoot enough business to a local Internet service provider to make a little difference in its bottom line. If the hosting company provides good service, this complements the Web firm's ability to implement good work. After all, most Web sites, unless a company has a T1 hooked up to Web-ready servers, need an ISP, even if it's just being co-located on the client's own machine.

Local advertising firms are great to hook up with as well. Many people are excited about Web sites and at the time when they are considering either an interactive campaign or a print version, the potential client may find that he or she needs to do both. A lot of advertising firms do tend to subcontract Web sites, as maintaining a Web de-

velopment team is expensive, and it is probably more cost-effective to subcontract work on a project-by-project basis. This type of relationship allows for a foundation of providing reciprocal referrals and strengthens both entities.

A good strategic partnership doesn't limit a firm in any way. Rather, the partnership provides another service, almost like it was under the same roof, but without taking on the expense. Besides, I'm a good Web developer. I'm not a server administrator or someone who knows print advertising, although I'm constantly asked about both. Similar to how the plumber can defer to the electrician, it's best for me to defer to good people who have specialized in these other areas. In turn, these people send me clients who would like me to develop a rocking Web site, and they don't try to take this function on themselves.

14.2.3 ANSWERS

a) Who is your target audience?

Answer: Most Web firms like to build either a deep portfolio in one particular industry or a broad portfolio demonstrating how they have the ability to adapt many types of businesses to the Web.

Your target audience is definitely other businesses. If you're building a deep portfolio specializing in a certain area, like real estate companies, then your target audience is the owners or marketing directors of real estate companies. If you're building a broad portfolio, your target market should be businesses, which could benefit from a Web presence.

b) What kinds of advertising options might reach that target audience?

Answer: Anything that is a prominent business-to-business publication would be a good source of advertising. I wouldn't advertise in anything that is more consumer driven with the local hardware stores or photography studios. My target market may well be the hardware store and photography studio, but not their customers. Given that my firm is located outside the city in the suburbs, if I wanted to step up business, I might consider an ad in the Boston yellow pages rather than the yellow pages in my area. I would reach more commercial businesses that way. Also, a Web firm might consider contributing tech articles to business-oriented technical publications. This is a great form of frequent free advertising, and your company's name on a byline can generate name recognition.

LAB 14.2 SELF-REVIEW QUESTIONS

In order to test your progress, you should be able to answer the following questions:

1) (True/False) The following sounds like a good networking opportunity:
- **a)** _____ A speaker series on small business at the local library
- **b)** _____ Lunch with the owner of an Internet service provider
- **c)** _____ A chamber of commerce trade show

2) (True/False) The following would be good advertising for a Web development company:
- **a)** _____ The classified section of the local newspaper
- **b)** _____ Little League jerseys
- **c)** _____ A church bulletin

L A B   1 4 . 3

WORK FLOW

LAB OBJECTIVES

After this Lab, you will be able to

- Keep Business Coming In
- Determine Personnel Requirements

Sometimes I feel like an errant girlfriend, interested in dating but afraid of deeper commitment. Since I'm an old, long-time married lady, I'm not really referring to romantic attachments. Rather, from a business standpoint, I understand that firms can experience highs and lows in the number of project contracts they undertake. I never want to take a project that I'm uncomfortable with because I have a lot of overhead to support. Unfortunately, employees contribute to overhead. I need competent people available when I need them, but don't want to carry them when I don't have enough work to support everyone comfortably. Thus, this generates my "dating versus deeper commitment" dilemma. I'm always afraid that people will tie themselves to me exclusively and then project work will dry up and I'll have to let them go.

How do you keep work coming through the door so that talented people will be interested in working with you on a regular basis? How do you make sure that you have people available to do the work when it comes in without hamstringing yourself when there isn't enough?

This is where strategic partnering can extend to getting work done. Surf's Up has been able to expand its ability to take on many kinds of projects because we use highly conscientious and competent subcontractors. Because of this, we can easily take on multimedia, NT, and UNIX projects seamlessly. My subcontractors and I have all worked together on projects before, so it feels like we are long time co-workers. However, we all understand that we work together when there's work, and when projects can be handled in house, that's understandable, and it leaves these peope free to pursue other projects. If my NT contractor has a UNIX project, I jump in and help him. If I have an NT customization situation, he jumps in and helps me. We shoot each other RFQs (requests for quotes) as they come in and draft bids together, so that neither party gets stuck with a big bill that eats away at project profits. It becomes a virtual organization. However, if there are people that you can trust implicitly along the way, it broadens the scope of the projects you can bid on.

Through strategic partnering and supplying excellent customer service to existing clients, a Web firm can expand the number of projects it's available to bid and is a firm that the clientele will approach again for upgrades and maintenance of their existing Web sites. If I've had a client who was extremely difficult to get through the Web build, I would rather that my firm isn't approached for maintenance. Most likely, it will be unprofitable. However, I'll bend over backward to keep our other clients. I want them to know what we're up to, and if we did their Web site a year ago, there are additional things we can do for their Web site. I'm hoping the client will want my firm to do an upgrade, that they had a good experience with us the first time and will want to work together on an ongoing basis. So you must not consider a project a one-time association. A good Web firm should be in business to earn the client's business for the long term. This generates repeat business and business by referral.

If the Web firm is attracting a lot of business, it's important to keep a list of talented and reliable people to call on for help. Sometimes it takes a few stubbed toes to select good subcontractors. When I first started out, I remember arranging a meeting with an ISP and going on about a graphic designer that I had available. I had seen some of his print work and a little Web work, and I was impressed with what I saw. I was told that he had done Web sites, and I trusted that there would be many to show a prospective client. So I really went on faith. When the ISP asked to see his work, I passed along the request only to find out that when it came down to it, we had nothing to show. This was an extremely talented graphic artist, but how could I get prospective clients to buy into this situation without work that was easily accessible to show them? By this point, I had blown my credibility with the ISP, and I had wasted their time. It took me a little while to understand where and how to use subcontractors. You should have several people in each discipline to call upon and always ask for a broad portfolio. A prospective client will ask for one. Unfortunately, you can't do projects with people because you think they are wonderful individuals and like them. It's not like the garage rock bands that we formed when we were kids—"Well, we need a drummer, so my best friend Jimmy can figure it out—we gotta fit him in." Even if an individual is extremely talented, you have to see that he or she also has the ability to take on a project and deliver it on time successfully.

Once a subcontractor slips a deadline with me, that's the end. I'm not talking about unforeseen circumstances, server glitches, or blowing a few days past the deadline ending the relationship. But if I'm a week or two past a delivery date with a client for no good reason, I'm going to reevaluate whether I will use the subcontractor again. So, over time, you can build up a trusting relationship based on performance.

In the following exercises, you can evaluate how you might handle the various issues involved with keeping a good level of work flowing through a firm and allowing for the ebb and flow of personnel requirements.

**LAB
14.3**

LAB 14.3 EXERCISES

14.3.1 KEEP BUSINESS COMING IN

a) How would you generate business among your existing clientele?

_____

_____

_____

_____

_____

_____

_____

_____

_____

_____

_____

_____

_____

_____

_____

_____

_____

_____

_____

_____

_____

_____

_____

_____

_____

b) How much effort should you, the owner of the Web firm, spend on generating new business as opposed to working on existing projects?

_____

_____

_____

_____

_____

_____

_____

_____

_____

_____

_____

_____

_____

_____

_____

_____

_____

_____

_____

_____

_____

_____

_____

_____

_____

14.3.2   DETERMINE PERSONNEL REQUIREMENTS

a) What kinds of questions might you ask a prospective subcontractor?

_____

_____

_____

b) When should you bring on employees?

_____

_____

_____

_____

_____

_____

_____

_____

_____

_____

_____

_____

_____

_____

_____

_____

_____

_____

_____

_____

_____

_____

LAB
14.3

LAB 14.3 EXERCISE ANSWERS

This section gives you some suggested answers to the questions in Lab 14.3 with discussion related to those answers. Please post any alternative answers to these questions at the companion Web site for this book, located at http://www.phptr.com/phptrinteractive.

14.3.1 ANSWERS

a) How would you generate business among your existing clientele?

Answer: There are several ways to generate business by annuity. A monthly newsletter, either through e-mail or print, sent out to your client base can keep your firm in mind the next time they initiate a Web project. Such a newsletter can be informational for the client and perhaps give the client ideas regarding upgrades and maintenance. The Web is changing all the time. A newsletter keeps your clientele educated, aware of how to keep their Web site successful, and able to determine when it's time to upgrade their site.

Another very helpful way to generate business is to print out client Web sites every month or quarter and send the printout to the client with blank pages attached to each printed Web page, requesting that the client review the Web site and make any changes on the pages provided.

Some Web firms offer their clients maintenance agreements. The client pays so much for the year, and that covers monthly HTML maintenance.

b) How much effort should you, the owner of the Web firm, spend on generating new business as opposed to working on existing projects?

Answer: At first, it seems like generating new business is all the Web firm owner does. After all, in the beginning, it's time to build a clientele.

However, once the Web firm is up and chugging, the search for new business does not cease. Most owners probably spend 20% of their time generating new business for the Web firm. Whether it's evaluating whether to bid a project, following up project bids, or developing strategic partnerships, this is a very important part of the Web firm owner's function.

Sometimes if we're going through a very hectic period and have long-term contracts, I will back off on the new business initiative—just because I know that we might need to build in some time for vacations after projects are finished. However, I always give a certain amount of time to it every week. You can do very well on a contract, but if the next job isn't in the offing because the firm is so busy doing the contract, then that contract is not so lucrative. The Web firm owner cannot become 100% committed to the present production cycle. There's got to be some room for lining up the next contract.

14.3.2 ANSWERS

a) What kinds of questions might you ask a prospective subcontractor?

Answer: I would ask the following questions of a prospective subcontractor:

- *Could you supply a list of Web sites that you have worked on?*
- *Could you describe your previous work experience?*
- *What are your best skills?*
- *Do you have references?*
- *Will you have any trouble making the deadline?*
- *Can you work with the payment schedule that the firm has outlined?*
- *If you do not make the deadline and there is not a good reason for not making the deadline, do you understand that there will be a penalty?*
- *Where and how can we contact you?*
- *When will the work be performed?*

b) When should you bring on employees?

Answer: I would not bring on employees until the firm has a well-established name with a steady income. Unless the firm has received venture capital and has a big budget to work with, you have to be extremely judicious about the people brought on board as employees, unless you're pretty heartless and don't mind giving people pink slips after the project is over.

Don't hire people whom you can see only using on certain projects. You should have a pretty good idea of the type of skill set that is constantly in demand for every project and subcontract the rest. It's best to hire people when you know the need to hire someone for a particular function is long and well overdue. It's easy for the scope of the projects to drive the personnel requirements. However, if the need for a particular type of person is consistent through a slew of projects, you can feel pretty comfortable that this person will have a role in anything that the firm is doing and is necessary.

Of course, being the noncommittal type, I still like to subcontract work and keep a small internal staff.

LAB 14.3 SELF-REVIEW QUESTIONS

In order to test your progress, you should be able to answer the following questions:

1) (True/False) The following methods are probably good ways to generate business:
   a) _____ Sending e-mails to people who you think have poor looking Web sites, offering your services to improve them
   b) _____ Telemarketing
   c) _____ Offering a Web workshop for small business owners

2) (True/False) Web firms regularly use the following types of employees:
   a) _____ Project managers
   b) _____ Administrative assistants
   c) _____ Flash programmers

L A B   1 4 . 4

REPUTATION

**LAB
14.4**

> ## LAB OBJECTIVES
>
> After this Lab, you will be able to
>
> * Charge Clients Fairly
> * Underpromise and Overdeliver
> * Understand the Value of Reputation

Some Web firms love to go for an eclectic image. They may wish to have a reputation for innovative design. This office may operate in a laid-back way that allows people the freedom to dress and behave in a way that fosters creativity and allows for individuality. Other firms, which are in a ferocious search for venture capital, may want to present a more buttoned-down image and a strong entrepreneurial focus. Which type of reputation do you want your Web firm to have?

Of course, so much depends on who you are and what your goals may be. However, never confuse image with reputation. Image is superficial. Reputation is set in stone and is based upon performance. Let your image feed into the reputation you wish to create. However, do not let image drive your reputation.

Reputation is about quality of work, fairness, and doing the things that you say you are going to do when you say that you are going to do them. I knew of a firm that was in a big search for venture capital. Eventually, they got it. However, in the beginning, their focus on customer service was lacking. They were not concerned with their reputation among their existing clientele. Once that focus changed and the firm was concerned with providing a service that simplified the process for their clients, they did receive venture capital. So, by taking care of business correctly, the firm eventually got what it wanted.

Everyone is in business to make money—hopefully, lots of it! However, as in any business, your own personal set of ethics will drive how you make your money. It's often best to walk away without a dime, maybe even owing one, than to allow the reputation of the firm to be tarnished. I'm not advocating letting people walk all over you, because, unfortunately, as your business grows, you will be dealing with all kinds of people and some may surprise you, despite your screening efforts. However, I would never want someone who is mostly reasonable to walk away from my firm feeling that we were unfair to him or her. You can make a mistake programmatically, but hopefully not too many. Maybe the graphics don't necessarily meet the client's liking. However, all of these things can be fixed. If you are unfair to a client, in pursuit of padding your own wallet, it's obvious, and these kinds of transgressions aren't forgiven in the business community. They ruin strategic partnerships and no one feels comfortable referring business to you.

LAB
14.4

LAB 14.4 EXERCISES

14.4.1 CHARGE CLIENTS FAIRLY

a) How would you develop a price list that is fair to your firm and your clientele?

_____

_____

_____

_____

_____

_____

_____

_____

_____

_____

_____

b) If a client is unhappy with the quality of your work, what kinds of questions should you ask yourself? How would the answers impact on price?

_____

_____

_____

_____

_____

_____

_____

_____

_____

_____

_____

_____

_____

_____

_____

_____

_____

_____

14.4.2 UNDERPROMISE AND OVERDELIVER

a) What do you think the statement "Underpromise and overdeliver" means?

_____

_____

_____

b) Describe ways that you "underpromise and overdeliver" when building a Web site.

_____

_____

_____

_____

_____

_____

_____

_____

_____

_____

_____

_____

_____

_____

_____

_____

_____

_____

_____

_____

_____

_____

LAB
14.4

14.4.3 UNDERSTAND THE VALUE OF FIRM REPUTATION

a) What kinds of positive outcomes can occur from having a good reputation for your Web firm?

_____

_____

_____

_____

_____

_____

_____

_____

_____

_____

_____

_____

_____

_____

_____

_____

_____

_____

_____

_____

**LAB
14.4**

b) What kinds of actions might contribute to a good reputation for the Web firm?

_____

_____

_____

_____

LAB 14.4 EXERCISE ANSWERS

This section gives you some suggested answers to the questions in Lab 14.4 with discussion related to those answers. Please post any alternative answers to these questions at the companion Web site for this book, located at http://www.phptr.com/phptrinteractive.

14.4.1 ANSWERS

a) How would you develop a price list that is fair to your firm and your clientele?

Answer: You may consider calling a noncompetitive Web firm, maybe one in another city, and inquiring about procuring consulting services. Present them with several models for Web sites that you might expect to bid on and ask how they would handle the bid. Often we get vague requests for quotes that come through our Web site. We can usually tell that they are most likely bogus because there isn't any contact information attached to them besides an e-mail address. When we write back and ask the person to tell us more about the project, we never get a response. Most likely, these inquiries are from other developers who are trying to figure out how to price a Web project. We caught on and don't respond with anything more than a request for further information. However, if you called and set up a phone consult with a Web firm, you might be pleasantly surprised by the response you get by being up front.

Another option is to talk with a local ISP. They usually hear through the grapevine what is being charged for sites that reside on their servers. A talk with someone at the ISP is a discreet way to find out how much you should be charging. Prices differ by region, quality of graphics, firm track record, and complexity of programming.

You might also consider researching prices that are given on the Web. Many firms do not post pricing online, but some do. Pricing can vary greatly depending on the amount of overhead and the staff a firm might have. What's the difference between a $3000 graphic job and a $13,000 job? Usually the difference lies in the ability to give a lot of composites in a short amount of time or to take a team approach to the creative direction.

Do not steal space in a busy person's brain by pretending to have a Web site you need to have a price on. When you become busy, you won't like it either. However, if someone calls you and asks politely if they can take you to lunch or hire you for an hour of consulting time, your response may be very helpful.

b) If a client is unhappy with the quality of your work, what kinds of questions should you ask yourself? How would the answers impact on price?

Answer: Sometimes it may seem like the client is being unreasonable. However, before you make that determination, you need to take a hard look at your actions during the execution of the contract. If you can see any area in which your client may have a point, it's important not to allow your emotions to get in the way and try to understand and accommodate your client. If that means cutting the client a break on price because you feel that somewhere along the way they could have been let down, then so be it.

Once in a while, a client will attempt to grind the price down by complaining. This is a much different scenario. If you have performed well, there's no reason why you should bend to this kind of pressure. Rather, in the event of a situation where you can assign some fault to your project team, it makes sense to make amends by either adding some extra value to the Web site or by cutting a little off the final payment. This can go a long way toward securing the client's long-term business and regard.

14.4.2 ANSWERS

a) What do you think the statement "underpromise and overdeliver" means?

Answer: Those of us who grew up with Star Trek *witnessed how Scotty would underpromise and overdeliver when responding to his captain's requests. He never shaved any time off of what he thought was realistically necessary to complete a task to try to pacify his superior momentarily. In fact, in* Star Trek: The Next Generation *he admitted to heavily padding time estimates. I'm not suggesting that anyone pad time estimates, but giving yourself a little leeway doesn't hurt. Nothing angers a client like having a certain expectation, being assured by the developer that the firm could meet that expectation, and finding that the firm has missed the target.*

b) Describe ways that you "underpromise and overdeliver" when building a Web site.

Answer: Previously, we spoke about not skimping on time estimates as a way to underpromise and overdeliver, but throwing in an extra effort to further simplify a user interface can accomplish the same thing. Adding some extra graphics or spending some extra time consulting with a client about an Internet-related, as opposed to project-related, concern is also helpful. I've had several clients whom I've walked through solving computer problems after giving project updates. It's part of underpromising and overdelivering.

The worst thing that you can do is to tell a client that your firm can leap tall buildings at single bound but fall far short. If you're not sure you can meet an expectation, do not promise it. If you find that you can in fact do it, do it and pleasantly surprise your client.

14.4.3 ANSWERS

a) What kinds of positive outcomes can occur from having a good reputation for your Web firm?

Answer: If your firm has a good reputation, you will

- *Bid bigger projects.*
- *Charge the going rate for development services.*
- *Attract more business.*
- *Have more credibility with clients should there be a disagreement about a technical or creative direction.*

b) What kinds of actions might contribute to a good reputation for the Web firm?

Answer:

- *Charge fairly.*
- *Deliver projects on time.*
- *Underpromise and overdeliver.*
- *Deliver project according to specification.*
- *Provide excellent customer service.*
- *Truly care about the client's experience building the site and make efforts to simplify it.*

**LAB
14.4**

LAB 14.4 SELF-REVIEW QUESTIONS

In order to test your progress, you should be able to answer the following questions.

1) (True/False) The client is unhappy that his finished site does not exhibit multimedia capabilities, which were not previously discussed.
a) _____ The firm should consider refunding money.
b) _____ The firm should consider offering an upgrade gratis.
c) _____ The firm should offer an upgrade at a discounted price.

2) (Yes/No) Is the customer always right?

C H A P T E R   1 4

TEST YOUR THINKING

The projects in this section use the skills you've acquired in this chapter. The answers to these projects are available to instructors only through a Prentice Hall sales representative and are intended to be used in classroom discussion and assessment.

1) If you were going to start your own Web firm, what type of financing would you pursue and why?

2) Based on this financing, how would you market your firm?

3) Should you concern yourself with the firm becoming so busy with projects that you will have to turn others down?

4) Name two other ways that have not been discussed in which your firm could cement a good reputation in the business community.

A P P E N D I X

ANSWERS
TO SELF-REVIEW
QUESTIONS

CHAPTER 1
Lab 1.1 ■ Self-Review Answers

Question	Answer	Comments
1	d	Good pricing is a basic marketing principle that also enhances relationships. Personalized interactions, customized ordering, and personal suggestions drive relationship marketing.
2	c	Although this depends on your situation and your audience, electronic mail is the easiest, cheapest, and most efficient communication method going.
3	False	Though the technology is evolving, some type of networked computer communication is fast becoming the primary business communications model.

Lab 1.2 ■ Self-Review Answers

Question	Answer	Comments
1	e	The Web provides a multitude of technologies for direct customized communication between customers and marketers.
2	a,b,c	Branding and sales calls are traditional marketing methods that are more expensive than relationship marketing techniques.
3	a	This is now also your responsibility to your audience.

CHAPTER 2
Lab 2.1 ■ Self-Review Answers

Question	Answer	Comments
1	a,d	So many options and a business need to measure success are the two most compelling reasons to plan first.
2	Who What Where When Why How	The basis of concise and effective communication was stolen directly from Journalism 101.
3	False	Real planning is rarely considered in the rush to the Web.

Lab 2.2 ■ Self-Review Answers

Question	Answer	Comments
1	c	Who defines the audience. The communications target.
2	b	The audience defines the presentation development. The presentation must be targeted at the audience.
3	b	While free stuff may attract one audience, targeted content will attract the appropriate one.

Lab 2.3 ■ Self-Review Answers

Question	Answer	Comments
1	c	Without interaction, a Web site is a repurposed brochure.
2	False	We can (hopefully) skip the early levels and begin meaningful communication quickly.
3	a,b,c	All are examples of business transformation through Internet communication. I wouldn't become a travel agent right now.

CHAPTER 3
Lab 3.1 ■ Self-Review Answers

Question	Answer	Comments
1	a	Searching the classifieds is a means to get the end.
2	c	In this world money talks loudest.
3	True	Use by a targeted audience is the reason you got onto the Web in the first place.
4	d	Tactic should be employed to complete a strategy that fulfills wants, needs, and desires by providing useful information and transactions.

Lab 3.2 ■ Self-Review Answers

Question	Answer	Comments
1	d	A newspaper, magazine, or Web site banner as may be seen by thousands of people, making it the least expensive cost per contact.
2	d	Seen does not mean read or responded to, so although space advertising is inexpensive, it is not very valuable for relationship marketing.
3	b	Since Internet communication can deliver customized interactions, it provides high value. Although initial development incurs expense, the cost is still low for each contact once in use by the audience.
4	False	Unlike most other communication methods, as Internet communication increases variable costs do not. Major usage requires technology investments, but these can be seen as additional fixed costs.
5	True	This is very good news.
6	True	This is even better news as Internet communication can replace more expensive traditional methods (e-mail is free versus mail requires postage). And the value of Internet communication can be greater (e-mail is immediate versus mail takes time).

Lab 3.3 ■ Self-Review Answers

Question	Answer	Comments
1	b	A plan usually involves moving forward. To do so we must first assess where we are starting from.
2	c	These levels are somewhat arbitrary but useful when assigning qualitative value for comparison purposes.
3	c	Though Internet communication requires technology people for execution, communication is the purpose. And appropriate communication requires communications professionals to call the shots.
4	e	Any information exchange can be automated using Internet communication over public and private networks.

Lab 3.4 ■ Self-Review Answers

Question	Answer	Comments
1	b	Though it may not seem so sometimes, the IS department is inside your organization.
2	True	Many times, channel participants are a company's biggest or only customers.
3	c	After deciding who we are in communication with, we need to decide what the communication needs are.
4	True	External parties have wants, needs, and desires and our job as Web communicators is to fulfill them.

5	e	Merrimack College has a partnership with WOW. A relationship with many vendors. A credit card transaction system. And a distributor for its education product.
6	d	All three are possible vendors for an Internet communication system that completes transactions over the Web and ships product directly to customers. Many vendors have been already been supplying these services to direct and catalog marketers.

CHAPTER 4
Lab 4.1 ■ Self-Review Answers

Question	Answer	Comments
1	d	A good way to build visual presentations involves creating explanations of visual activity or models of them.
2	False	Direction should be given from the driver's perspective. Ever tried it the other way?
3	c	If the home page is the big identifiable road, the first step to to the communications goal involves getting off at an exit.
4	b	In this road analogy, the goal is the destination.
5	e	Again, building model interactions is a great tool.
6	d	Fulfillment of wants, needs, and desires is much more important than any fluffy or dramatic presentation.

Lab 4.2 ■ Self-Review Answers

Question	Answer	Comments
1	b	Assess current activity first.
2	False	It is always included in every discussion.
3	d	Who, what, and how are always important.
4	a, c	Goals should already be known. But if they are not known, then answering d is OK as well.
5	e	Transforming communication to cut costs and increase relationships is the name of the game.

Lab 4.3 ■ Self-Review Answers

Question	Answer	Comments
1	b	The who, what, where, when, why, and how always get answered first. Then deal with appearances and technology.
2	d	Again, plan before you build.
3	c	Determining communication goals may be a surprising experience.
4	e	Since these will be the basis for actual page development, they need to include content, links, and back-end support.
5	True	Aides help the audience reach goals quickly.

CHAPTER 5
Lab 5.1 ■ Self-Review Answers

Question	Answer	Comments
1	d	The big idea is used for all creative development.
2	a,d	Looks involve visuals, which affect people emotionally.
3	False	Branding is about building recognition. That recognition supposedly indirectly inspires sales.
4	True	See above.
5	c	It's all about engagement of an audience.

Lab 5.2 ■ Self-Review Answers

Question	Answer	Comments
1	b,d	Headlines are text. Sound files are multimedia, which is important but not widely utilized. Logos can be considered visuals.
2	c	Both should be included for accessibility and ease of use.
3	False	Color is a big part of emotional response.
4	True	Text is very effective for some big ideas.
5	a	Again, it's all about the audience. That's why planning is crucial.

Lab 5.3 ■ Self-Review Answers

Question	Answer	Comments
1	d	Why should the audience care?
2	c	Answer the "what's in it for me" question on behalf of the audience.
3	True	
4	False	It's everything.
5	False	Except in certain situations where they want or have to, people don't read. They just look.
6	e	Any material can be repurposed as long as it is appropriate.

Lab 5.4 ■ Self-Review Answers

Question	Answer	Comments
1	d	Basically they all mean the same thing, a fulfilled audience.
2	e	Many exist.
3	True	Beauty is only skin deep.
4	a	At least until the next buzz word. What's after engagement, marriage?

CHAPTER 6
Lab 6.1 ■ Self-Review Answers

Question	Answer	Comments
1	d	
2	b	If you care to play, a top ten result is victory.
3	c	Engines catalog the Web on their own. Directories rely on submissions.
4	e	At this time banner ads are basically space ads that provide an immediate response vehicle using click-through.

Lab 6.2 ■ Self-Review Answers

Question	Answer	Comments
1	d	A lot of information about software clients, hardware monitors, and the activity generated by promotional efforts can be gleaned from boring log files.
2	d	Link history is even more valuable for deciding linking strategies.
3	False	They identify a client computer but not a user. But if that user identifies herself, then the connection can be recorded for customization.
4	c	Reviewing direct communication with people is the best measurement of success.

CHAPTER 7
Lab 7.1 ■ Self-Review Answers

Question	Answer	Comments
1	b,c	A good contract documents the requirements, responsibilities, and price of the project, which, hopefully, means that the parties have discussed and agreed on many key aspects of their working relationship and the end product. This process and the resulting document (the contract) should be useful if disagreements arise during the course of the development effort (and afterward). A verbal agreement is extremely difficult, if not impossible, for a court to enforce.
2	a	If you find a mistake in your proposal or offer before it has been accepted, withdraw it immediately! Indicate that you will resubmit. Technically, once an offer has been accepted, you (or the other parties) are obligated to perform. If you find a mistake in a proposal submitted to you, you may accept it and hold the parties to perform. However, that may become a "win-lose" scenario, which can quickly evolve into a "lose-lose" for all involved. It is usually better to negotiate out of those situations—if the other side has requested a favor (by correcting a mistake in their proposal or offer), you can request a reciprocal favor from them since they have, in effect, reopened the negotiation.

3   c   The contract should specify the terms under which it may be cancelled. If any party cancels outside of (or without) such terms, they may rightfully be subject to suit by the other parties.

Lab 7.2 ■ Self-Review Answers

Question	Answer	Comments
1	False	It is not illegal to link to another Web site without their permission. It may be bad netiquette, depending on the situation, but it is not illegal. Just be sure that you comply with any terms given on the "linkee" Web site, if there are any terms. And do not make it appear that the contents of another Web site are actually the contents of *your* Web site (as in a "frame"). Use your common sense—if you would object if the positions were reversed, expect them to feel the same way.
2	e	Unless it is otherwise specified in an employee's employment contract, the employer usually owns the copyright to anything produced by the employee in the course of doing the job the employer pays them to do. This is called "work for hire" or "work product."
3	True	If you own a trademark, you must protect it to keep it valid. Unprotected trademarks lose their effectiveness when other users dilute their original meaning and value.
4	False	The Coca-Cola trademark is one of the most recognizable trademarks in the world and, like any other trademark, should not be used on a Web site without the permission of the trademark owner. There are *many* other ways to add color to your Web site—a court would believe that you were trying to leverage someone else's trademark, not just add color. Coca-Cola would probably recover some damages from you for the damage done to their trademark.
5	a,c	Borrowing content without permission is very risky unless you *know* that something is in the public domain. Copyright owners have a right to recover damages from you for use without permission.
6	False	Just as you cannot use someone's trademark on the visible part of your Web site without permission, so are you also barred from using that trademark on the "invisible" part of your Web site, like a meta tag. Inappropriate use is inappropriate use. Expect a lawsuit when you are discovered.

CHAPTER 8
Lab 8.1 ■ Self-Review Answers

Question	Answer	Comments
1	a,b,d	Don't depend on the client to set the schedule of payment. The firm must determine this and insist that the client adhere to the agreement.

2   a,b,c,d   A good Web firm should concern itself with all of these is-
                     sues, including saving the client money.

Lab 8.3 ■ Self-Review Answers

Question	Answer	Comments
1	a,b,d	The technical team is going to concern itself with using cross-platform solutions, which do not cause browser loading problems. Animations, Java Script rollovers, and multimedia embedded objects would need support from the technical team.
2	a,e	Creative can put the marketing team a step ahead by identifying key points that are important to the client.

Lab 8.4 ■ Self-Review Answers

Question	Answer	Comments
1	b	While coordinating skills comes a very close second, a project manager who does not have excellent negotiating skills will undermine a project every time.
2	e	The project manager plays a major role in every phase.

CHAPTER 9
Lab 9.1 ■ Self-Review Answers

Question	Answer	Comments
1	True	One process does not necessarily complement the other.
2	False	Understanding the process involved can help the project manager to educate the client regarding realistic expectations.

Lab 9.2 ■ Self-Review Answers

Question	Answer	Comments
1	False	The project manager should only involve himself or herself in conflicts that inhibit the creation of the Web site. Not all conflicts between team members cause this sort of problem.
2	False	Team member conflicts do not always slow down production. However, these conflicts have a great potential to do so.

CHAPTER 10
Lab 10.1 ■ Self-Review Answers

Question	Answer	Comments
1	b	A defined scope of work provides a measure for success. A Web firm cannot be successful without a defined scope of work.

2	c	Negotiating is key here. Yes, the project manager provides Internet consulting, but the deal cannot be made effectively without excellent communication/negotiation skills.

Lab 10.2 ■ Self-Review Answers

Question	Answer	Comments
1	a	An online banking site will most likely generate the most financial transactions. There is also liability in that customer information must be kept secure.
2	b	Payment schedule is generally included in the work order. The other points can be defined in the project specification.

Lab 10.3 ■ Self-Review Answers

Question	Answer	Comments
1	a,b	Payment schedule is generally defined in the work order.
2	b,c	New Web developers tend to assess the time spent to code the site and develop the graphics. However, they begin to realize after the first few projects that a significant amount of time can be spent interacting with the client, and this needs to be covered in the bid.

CHAPTER 11
Lab 11.1 ■ Self-Review Answers

Question	Answer	Comments
1	a	Anyone who has ever gotten married understands how someone else's taste does not always echo one's own.
2	a,b	Document! Document! Document!

Lab 11.2 ■ Self-Review Answers

Question	Answer	Comments
1	a,b,c	A good creative spec should address all of these issues.
2	c	Use the medium that best conveys the most sensory information to the client. If you are upset with the client, let someone else speak with him or her directly, and then deal with the client when you are more relaxed. Never send e-mail when you are upset.
3	none	None of these tools provide a cross-platform solution.

Lab 11.3 ■ Self-Review Answers

Question	Answer	Comments
1	b,c	Credibility is key!
2	b,c	Some Web firms do offer writing services. However, this needs to be covered in the project bid. I prefer to stay away from taking on the responsibility of functions with which the client can take issue. The success of a graphic design or written initiative is harder to gauge because it depends solely upon the client's taste.

Chapter 12
Lab 12.1 ■ Self-Review Answers

Question	Answer	Comments
1	a,b,c	These are all crucial factors.
2	a,b,c	These are all important points as well.

Lab 12.2 ■ Self-Review Answers

Question	Answer	Comments
1	a	This will not mean anything to the client, whereas the version of Perl stipulates which servers the Web site can be hosted on.
2	a	Both the project specification and the programming specification should reference the choice. However, the client would have signed off on the project specification.

Lab 12.3 ■ Self-Review Answers

Question	Answer	Comments
1	a	Human resources, even in the face of illness, is still the contractor's issue.
2	d	Use people to test the site who have had the least exposure to plans for its projected functionality.

Chapter 13
Lab 13.1 ■ Self-Review Answers

Question	Answer	Comments
1	c	Place, the way a product is distributed.
2	b,c	Targeted e-mailing is a consumer turn off.

Lab 13.2 ■ Self-Review Answers

Question	Answer	Comments
1	c	Site administration documentation should be written specifically for the Web site. However, it should not undertake the burden of explaining other software programs.
2	a	Graphic design and hardcore programming can be extremely expensive. These should be covered as upgrades.

CHAPTER 14
Lab 14.1 ■ Self-Review Answers

Question	Answer	Comments
1	a,b	
2	b	Hire highly skilled people whose talents complement yours.

Lab 14.2 ■ Self-Review Answers

Question	Answer	Comments
1	b	A strategic partnership with an Internet service provider or an advertising firm can drive more business to your firm than just about anyone else.
2	none	Advertise in business-to-business publications.

Lab 14.3 ■ Self-Review Answers

Question	Answer	Comments
1	c	It's helpful, positive, and you have an interested audience.
2	a,b	If yours is a small firm, subcontract tasks that are not used regularly.

Lab 14.4 ■ Self-Review Answers

Question	Answer	Comments
1	c	If your firm is interested in a continued relationship with the client.
2	No	One would like to think so and operate under that assumption. However, one can also kiss a Web business goodbye after just a few projects by not covering the firm with documentation, which can prove the firm's position.

INDEX

675